FEMINIST KNOWLEDGE

FEMINIST KNOWLEDGE

CRITIQUE AND CONSTRUCT

edited by
Sneja Gunew

London and New York

First published 1990
by Routledge
11 New Fetter Lane, London EC4P 4EE

Simultaneously published in the USA and Canada
by Routledge
a division of Routledge, Chapman and Hall, Inc.
29 West 35th Street, New York, NY 10001

Reprinted 1992

Typeset in 10/12pt Times by
Hope Services Ltd.
Printed in England by Clays Ltd, St Ives plc

British Library Cataloguing in Publication Data
Feminist Knowledge: critique and construct.
1. Feminism
I. Gunew, Sneja
305.4′2

Library of Congress Cataloging in Publication Data
Feminist knowledge: critique and construct/edited by Sneja
Gunew.
p. cm.
Includes bibliographical references.
1. Feminism – Philosophy. 2 Feminist criticism.
I. Gunew, Sneja Marina
HQ1154.F44565 1990
305.42′01–dc20 89–10960

ISBN 0 415 01227 9 (pbk.)

CONTENTS

INTRODUCTION
Sneja Gunew 1

Part I Feminist knowledge

1 FEMINIST KNOWLEDGE: CRITIQUE AND CONSTRUCT
Sneja Gunew 13

2 FEMINIST KNOWLEDGE, WOMEN'S LIBERATION, AND WOMEN'S STUDIES
Susan Sheridan 36

Part II Contemporary theories of power and subjectivity

3 CONTEMPORARY THEORIES OF POWER AND SUBJECTIVITY
Elizabeth Grosz 59

4 FEMINISM, SUBJECTIVITY, AND SEXUAL DIFFERENCE
Philipa Rothfield 121

Part III Discourses of definition

5 PHILOSOPHY
Elizabeth Grosz 147

6 PSYCHOANALYSIS AND FEMINISM
Hazel Rowley and Elizabeth Grosz 175

7 THE DEFINITION OF MALE AND FEMALE: BIOLOGICAL REDUCTIONISM AND THE SANCTIONS OF NORMALITY
Gisela T. Kaplan and Lesley J. Rogers 205

8 RELIGION
Marie Tulip 229

Part IV Feminist interventions

9 RADICAL FEMINISM: CRITIQUE AND CONSTRUCT
Robyn Rowland and Renate D. Klein 271

10 SOCIALIST FEMINISMS
Louise C. Johnson 304

11 CONCLUSION: A NOTE ON ESSENTIALISM AND DIFFERENCE
Elizabeth Grosz 332

Notes on contributors 345

Index 349

INTRODUCTION

Sneja Gunew

As this book was being prepared an article in the Australian press diagnosed another fracturing of the Greenham Common enterprise,[1] this time perceived as being due to racist divisions within the group itself. Meanwhile, Australians were weeks away from the dreaded crossover into 1988 heralding a year in which the country would be swamped by celebrations of 200 years of white settlement. Australian feminists, together with other groups concerned with bringing about social change, have long been discussing tactics for undermining any versions of complacent postcolonialism. One positive outcome of the Bicentenary is the fact that there is a general heightening of awareness that Australian history is based on attempted genocide and that Australian national identity is predicated on a range of exclusions.

On the theme of exclusions, we have also long been frustrated by the map of international feminism which traces a line between Britain, America, and France but rarely includes other groups. As Australian feminists we are excellently placed to be a clearing house for those mainstream feminisms and have towards them a degree of eclecticism which allows us to adapt what we need and to be more generally critical towards the rest. We are emphatically not, for example, caught up in the same sectarian splits (though we do have our own schisms). Thus a measure of the difference we are able to offer is graphically displayed in the very fact that both Radical and Socialist Feminists have agreed to contribute to this book alongside accounts which come from poststructuralist feminists. In a situation where there are so few of us we cannot afford to be too intransigent and exclusive about our positions and interactions.

Having said this, and to temper its piety, we are also conscious that the absence of accounts from Aboriginal women signifies glaringly our own lack. The negotiations are continuing and their outcome will redefine the priorities of all Australian feminism. Meanwhile we offer from a spectrum of positions our own contributions to feminist knowledge.

In chapter 1, 'Feminist knowledge: critique and construct', Sneja Gunew analyses the distinctions between knowing (as a process), knowledge (emanating from an institutional base), and theory (truth claims). How are these concepts traditionally constituted and legitimized and to what extent are they dependent on a notion of the unified subject? The assumptions in this introductory chapter will be that the production of meaning is inevitably mediated both by languages (a variety of sign systems) and by social practices ('experience') which construct: how we know, what we know, and who 'we' think 'we' are while doing this. The chapter also addresses the issue of who decides what is legitimate knowledge (drawing on the work of Foucault) and to what extent knowledge and power are intertwined. The further question of how truth and knowledge relate to the knowing subject will be examined in relation to the concept of 'discourse'. The chapter then analyses the extent to which feminist knowledge, operating as critique, has revised all these questions by inserting gender (the social construction of sexual difference) as a problematic element. Subsequently it delineates the new spaces which feminist theory, operating as construct, has created in order to provide positions from which the critiques may operate. Finally, it examines the extent to which feminist knowledge needs to be alert to what is legitimated under its own banners and what, importantly, becomes excluded in the process. In the 1980s feminist knowledge has become increasingly diversified as a result of critiques emanating from so-called marginal women's groups (black, Third World, lesbian).

In chapter 2, 'Feminist knowledge, women's liberation, and women's studies', Susan Sheridan provides a discussion of the institutional and practical conditions of existence of feminist knowledge, and therefore of its relationship to both the women's movement generally and to the academic discipline of women's studies. It explores some of the tensions in women's studies between the demands of women's education, academic research, and cultural politics.

The first section sketches the social and economic preconditions that have enabled feminist interventions in higher education. It argues that women's studies should be seen as one of several modes in which women are currently taking control of their own education and expanding their capacity to intervene in social and cultural processes. It looks at four kinds of feminist knowledge produced by the women's movement outside of the academy; these are conceptualized as 'subjugated knowledges', in Foucault's sense of local, popular knowledges and neglected works of learning. They include: processes of group learning and decision-making, activism as knowledge, feminist theories of women's oppression, and women-centred cultural production (the attempt to articulate women's experience, past and present). The strengths and limitations of each are considered.

The second section, 'Politics in the academy', asks what happens when these 'subjugated knowledges' are brought into the mainstream, in women's studies courses and research in the academy. It considers broad differences between the kinds of women's studies projects that have emerged in Australia, Britain, and the US, and major changes of emphasis since the early 1970s. It questions the role of women's studies in relation to the women's movement: as the 'intellectual arm of women's liberation'? as a recruiting ground for feminism? as a revolutionary challenge to the academy? or as 'academic feminism', comfortable in and confined to the institutions of higher education? In the final section, on feminist scholarship, discussion covers current debates on the autonomy versus integration of women's studies, on multidisciplinary versus transdisciplinary learning, and on the relations between disciplinary critiques and the construction of feminist knowledge in the spaces between disciplines.

In chapter 3, 'Contemporary theories of power and subjectivity', Elizabeth Grosz addresses the question of what kinds of relations feminist theory should develop with the male theoretical mainstreams out of which it developed, and which it attempts to supersede. If feminist theory simply addresses itself to the misogyny and phallocentrism of mainstream knowledges, it remains at the level of an anti-sexist critique: it remains on the intellectual terrain of patriarchal theory, even if on the negative side. On the other hand, if feminist theory simply aims at being different or other to these male mainstreams, it risks posing utopian solutions which leave the ongoing dominance of male intellectual norms intact. It must engage in the negative, critical, or reactive strategy of anti-sexism at the same time as being committed to developing new, alternative paradigms and models, methods and norms for knowledge.

An examination of the contributions of four major contemporary male theorists of subjectivity and power – Althusser, Lacan, Foucault, and Derrida – will be used to outline and illustrate the ways in which feminist theory has utilized their work by developing *internal* critiques – critiques developed from within one or other framework – in order to use that framework to go beyond itself, and ultimately, to provide tools and resources for the development of theory more accommodating to feminist values and commitments. The complex relations between the works of these four theorists, whose collective works have been crucial to the form contemporary French philosophy takes today, will be analysed.

If Althusser developed an account of ideology as a system of power which utilizes various representational systems to constitute subjects as concrete social agents, then Foucault's, and in very different ways Lacan's, work can be seen as alternatives to and critiques of Althusser. Lacan's account of the genesis of the ego and the development of the subject as a speaking, symbolic being provides many of the key elements of Althusser's account. Yet they also exceed Althusser's use of them, and threaten to pose major problems for the latter's understanding of ideology. Foucault can also be seen to depart from an Althusserian framework by refusing the framework of ideology and representation and the notion of the psychoanalytic subject. Instead, Foucault is more interested in understanding power according to its multiple connections, with knowledges on the one hand, and bodies on the other. In place of ideologies (i.e. false belief systems) and subjects (physical beings) Foucault positions knowledges and bodies as the 'surfaces' on which power functions. Jacques Derrida's strategy of deconstructive reading, and Foucault's understanding of power as it is invested in discourses, shows the fundamental violence and coercion at work in the production of knowledges and shared theoretical presuppositions.

Finally, this chapter outlines the ways in which, despite the problems (feminist and otherwise) each faces, they have been enormously powerful in the introduction of feminist knowledges. They have been used both as tools or weapons of combat against a more metaphysical and tradition-bound system of knowledges than they are themselves; and they have provided intellectual 'raw materials' that are the starting points of autonomous or woman-defined self-representations and representations of the world.

In chapter 4, 'Feminism, subjectivity, and sexual difference', Philipa Rothfield introduces the notion of subjectivity where it is seen as a product of the rise of modernity and modern social thought. Subjectivity begins with the growth of humanism which is an historical product of the Enlightenment. Yet humanism has come to be critically reviewed, especially in the context of recent French thought. When we then look at feminist theory, which generally questions the latent male character of the 'human' subject, what is to be said of the anti-humanist critique? Many fields incorporate a discussion, implicit or explicit, of subjectivity. At its most general level, feminist theory looks at the relationship between gender and subjectivity. A brief discussion of humanism and anti-humanism follows, along with the relevance of such work for feminist theory.

'The women's liberation movement: opening gambits' looks at the relation between some central elements of the women's liberation movement and the theory of subjectivity. Those elements discussed include the personal as political, the public/private distinction, consciousness-raising, and the sex/gender distinction.

'Beyond humanism: theoretical directions' discusses humanism and its critique, anti-humanism. The notion of a universal voice of/for women is discussed, along with some other possibilities which arise from a political consideration of postmodernism. Some postmodern women artists, such as Barbara Kruger and Mary Kelly, are considered. The usefulness of Althusser's work for feminist theory is discussed, especially its focus on ideology, social practice, and the subject as inscribed in various cultural forms.

'The mindful body/the embodied mind: beyond dualism' looks at the importance of reconceptualizing the body's participation in our view of subjectivity. In particular, the place of women's bodies in our culture calls for feminist theorization on this question. A brief discussion of the role/contribution of movement therapy and performance art in an understanding of the body follows. The last section, 'Final words', briefly discusses the separation of sexual activity from other aspects of everyday life and the need to reassess this.

In chapter 5, 'Philosophy', Elizabeth Grosz elaborates the distinctive ways in which philosophy as an academic discipline participates in the oppression of women; and an analysis of the ways in which women philosophers have attempted to address the implicit misogyny underlying their discipline. Philosophy is, of course, not unique in its participation in patriarchal power structures, but because of its self-image as a rigorous, 'objective', or 'truthful' branch of the humanities, it has a higher profile than most other disciplines in defining and providing critical reflection on the methods and assumptions of all knowledges.

The particular, sexually discriminatory effects of western philosophy are divided into three distinct but related forms of oppression: first, philosophy can be seen as a form of *sexism*, that is, as a body of knowledge that, when it includes women at all, does so in a manner that ensures women are disadvantaged when compared to men. Philosophical sexism consists in the pronouncements (male) philosophers make about women, femininity, or relations between the sexes. However, sexism is only symptomatic of a broader, more insidious and underlying system of oppression that could be described as patriarchal. Here it is not simply men and women that are the objects of analysis, but rather qualities that are indirectly or directly coded as masculine or feminine. Here the scope of feminist intervention broadens, for central intellectual categories and concepts – truth, reasons, virtue, social and political life, etc. – are implicated in the sexual division. And third, philosophy can be seen to participate in phallocentrism, a more particularized and specifically discursive form of oppression whereby norms, criteria, and values based on the masculine are taken to be universal and thus inclusive or representative of the feminine.

The recognition of these three forms of patriarchal oppression has prompted a number of diverse feminist responses, which can also be divided into three categories: egalitarian or liberal feminists, who attempt to eliminate sexism but leave the broader (patriarchal) structures of philosophical knowledge intact; conservative feminists, who, in recognition of the accusation of participating in patriarchal forms of oppression, have defended philosophy at the expense of feminism – here feminist theory is either criticized from a philosophical point of view, or philosophy is justified as a form of latent or proto-feminism; and third, the 'radical feminists', who attempt to challenge philosophy's phallocentrism, and to question the underlying ontological, epistemological, and methodological norms by which it functions. This third category of feminists are also committed to developing new philosophical models and methods, instead of, as with egalitarian feminists, attempting to alter only the 'contents' of knowledges.

The final part of this section is a speculative discussion of what a *feminist philosophy*, a philosophy compatible with rather than hostile to feminism, may be like.

In chapter 6, 'Psychoanalysis and feminism', Hazel Rowley and Elizabeth Grosz analyse the encounter between psychoanalysis and feminism. In it the central tenets of psychoanalysis are discussed: the role of the Oedipus complex and castration complex in the formation of the unconscious and sexual identity. The chapter examines Freud's various essays on female sexuality, as well as other diverging views on the subject from Horney, Klein, and Jones, in order to consider which aspects are intrinsic to psychoanalytic theory and which aspects reflect prevailing cultural assumptions. With this in mind, we look at hostile feminist reactions to Freud's work from de Beauvoir, Friedan, Firestone, Millett, etc., in the light of Mitchell's more sympathetic feminist intervention in 1974, with her book *Psychoanalysis and Feminism*. In this she emphasized that Freud's work is invaluable to feminists in their attempt to understand the construction of gender. *Psychoanalysis and Feminism* introduced the work of Jacques Lacan to Anglo-Saxon feminists, acting as a bridge between French rereadings of Freud in the light of structural linguistics, and the more empirical readings of Freud by English-speaking feminists.

The second half of the chapter looks in some detail at Lacan's work and its relevance to feminism. It discusses the various ways in which his ideas have been taken up and challenged by French feminists, in particular, Irigaray, Kristeva, and Cixous. The concluding section reflects on possible directions and possible dangers associated with the contemporary feminist reappraisal of psychoanalysis.

In chapter 7, 'The definition of male and female: biological reductionism and the sanctions of normality', Gisela T. Kaplan and Lesley J. Rogers deal with constructs of maleness and femaleness and explore the way in which science, more specifically biology, has superimposed social beliefs and conventions on biological data. The chapter shows how certain constructs, masquerading as biological facts, have been used in oppressive arguments against women. Sociobiology, as a very recent example of such reductionist and manipulative use of biology, will be discussed.

The chapter critically assesses findings on biological differences and similarities of male and female. The male–female dichotomies, which stem from the morphology of genitalia, have been extrapolated to a host of biological functions, particularly to functions of the brain. Femaleness and maleness is said to be stamped on the brain by biological processes. How debatable such findings have been will be discussed in the light of recent scientific evidence showing that no major differences between female and male brains exist. The more controversial issues concerning the importance of hormones in the debate on femaleness and maleness are addressed as well.

Moreover, the chapter points out that biological norms are often based on myths, which, however, have far-reaching implications for women and even for sexual orientation. Models of human sexuality based on such constructs must, in their very formation, declare sexual variation as diseased or disordered. The sanctions of normality across the whole spectrum of human behaviour have too long been tied to assumptions about 'human nature' which are ultimately ideological and political in nature.

The chapter not only questions the validity of the traditional male–female dichotomy, but it also points to some of the implications and social manifestations of such a model. The latest biological theories and medical practices based on them are discussed. The diversity and malleability of human behaviour does not allow for constructs claiming that males and females fall into clearly distinguishable, discrete categories. Such rigidity of models, as the chapter shows, have been particularly detrimental to women. The male–female dichotomy, as the chapter argues, is a construct and a paradigm which must be exploded in order to make way for a new and more open way of thinking.

In chapter 8, 'Religion', Marie Tulip deals with ways in which feminists have engaged in intense dialogue with patriarchal religion in the Judaeo-Christian tradition, either as a way of transforming it, or to find a new language outside it.

The first part focuses on *Beyond God the Father*, where Mary Daly made a comprehensive and radical critique of the patriarchy, speaking 'on the boundary' of philosophy and theology and showing that 'the women's revolution is an ontological, spiritual revolution'. Daly demonstrates the patriarchy's destructive idolatry of God the Father, of a male Christ (Jesus was a feminist, but so what?), and of phallic morality, and calls for an Exodus into new ways of Be-ing, a new ethics of 'existential courage', a reclaiming of the right to name the self, the world, and God, 'participating in new creation'. In *Gyn/Ecology* the critique is more severe, the construct more abstract – a leap into a spiritual Otherworld of spinning and sparking.

In contrast to Daly, feminist theologians such as Rosemary Radford Ruether and Elisabeth Schüssler Fiorenza, and other groupings of women, work to transform the sexist structures of the Judaeo-Christian tradition while remaining based within it. Ruether sees sexual dualism (the 'Other') as the basis for the oppression of women and all other forms of domination. With a wide-ranging use of socio-economic and cultural history, Ruether uses a feminist critique to transform systematic theology and envisions a non-sexist Christianity, a new community of peace and justice, a 'livable world'. Fiorenza bases herself in the community of women and reconstructs early Christian history as a way of undermining the androcentric bias of the biblical text and restoring women's proper heritage. Both Ruether and Fiorenza are involved in the recent development of Women-church, as opposed to patriarchal church, and claim 'the church is in Exodus with us'. The energy and passion of other groups, from Quakers to Greenham women to the participants in *God's Fierce Whimsy*, emerge in feminist theology and praxis which is focused on immanence and arises from women's body selves and daily lived reality in the context of love and justice.

The third part explores women's spirituality as expressed in many women's lives and art and writing, and the attempt to find a way of organizing these areas of experience by using the ancient languages of Goddess religion and Witchcraft, or by finding new ways of expressing feminist spiritual reality.

In chapter 9, 'Radical feminism: critique and construct', Robyn Rowland and Renate D. Klein construct and critique Radical Feminism from the writings of Radical Feminist authors in Australia, Britain, America, and France.

Radical Feminism contends that the oppression of women is the first and primary oppression. It is a woman-centred interdependent theory and practice which is created from women's lived experience, making the personal political. It maintains that men oppress women through patriarchy, a system of structures, institutions, and ideology created by men in order to sustain and recreate male power and female subordination.

While recognizing and accepting differences between women, Radical Feminism holds the oppression of women to be universal, crossing race and culture boundaries, so that 'sisterhood' becomes an empowering concept. It does not neglect these differences but incorporates them as important in defining the nature of women's oppression as women.

Radical Feminism has focused on male power at significant sites for women. It has stressed women's control of our bodies as crucial to liberation, giving rise to analysis and action within the Women's Health Movement, in the naming and analysis of violence against women, and in an analysis of sexuality and the imposition of heterosexuality as an institution.

The institution of the family has been seen as tying women to compulsory heterosexuality, economic dependence and a patriarchal ideology of motherhood which is alienating and self-destroying.

Radical Feminism has also stressed the importance of creating and sustaining women's culture in its various forms, as a political act. And it stresses women's resistance to patriarchy currently and historically.

Radical Feminism is the only theory created from, by, and for women. Its protagonists link action and theory constantly in a passionate, angry, joyful, and empowering commitment to the economic, personal, political, and social liberation of women.

In chapter 10, 'Socialist feminisms', Louise Johnson characterizes Socialist Feminism as a set of interventions by feminists into socialist, and particularly into Marxist, theory, which aims to analyse and end the oppression of women in capitalist societies. The theoretical hegemony of Marx and Engels means that her analysis begins with their theories of capitalism and the family. How their ideas are later used by Socialist Feminists is illustrated by examining debates on women's place in production and social production, and in the attempts to theorize relations between Marxism, feminism, and patriarchy. Over the course of this discussion it is argued that Marxism set a problematic agenda for Socialist Feminists. For in the work of Marx and Engels gender was both a marginalized and a presumed category. Putting women into Marxism is therefore extremely difficult, if not impossible. As a result Socialist Feminists have had to move from *applying* Marxist concepts to women, to *redefining* those same concepts. The outcome, Johnson suggests, is a new materialist foundation for Socialist Feminism which owes much to feminist priorities and theorizations, a major debt to historical materialism, but little else to the whole theoretical edifice developed by Marx and Engels.

What constitutes this new materialist foundation for Socialist Feminism is sketched in the final section. Socialist Feminism itself has been subjected to scrutiny and revealed as primarily the creation of white, privileged women bound more to Marxism than feminism. It is from this realization that a new awareness that the world is being redifferentiated by capital, class, and sex that new Socialist Feminisms can be written.

In the Conclusion Elizabeth Grosz restates the rationale for this collection, namely that feminist theory is often caught in the contradiction of being both critique and construct, that is, of offering a critique of traditional knowledge which is controlled by patriarchal structures while at the same time existing within and being compromised by these same structures. Yet feminist theory must also be a new construct, must move beyond the reactive and oppositional position to create new forms of knowledge.

In her discussion of essentialism and difference Grosz distinguishes the former from adjacent terms such as biologism, naturalism, and universalism in order to clarify more precisely the cluster of concepts and different projects which are often subsumed under the heading 'essentialism'. Her distinction between egalitarian feminists and those who argue for difference defines the former as ultimately leaving intact patriarchal structures because of their inability to theorize women's sexual and reproductive capacities, precisely those specific elements which situate women's difference in the social and symbolic orders. In her focus on difference Grosz argues for a concept of pure difference rather than one based on binary opposition in which one term is always dominant. This would allow feminists to use essentialism (and its adjacent terms) as strategies for working against patriarchal structures rather than assuming that such terms have absolute or universal meanings.

In the companion to this volume *A Reader in Feminist Knowledge* the information covered in each of these chapters is developed further by being attached to a series of articles which each writer considered as exemplifying the debates in her specific terrain. Readers are directed to this volume as providing further tools for studying the contours of feminist knowledge.

Notes

1 D. Smith, 'Showdown at Greenham Common,' *Sunday Times*, 25 October, 1987, p. 27.

Part I
FEMINIST KNOWLEDGE

1

FEMINIST KNOWLEDGE: CRITIQUE AND CONSTRUCT

Sneja Gunew

What is the relationship between knowing, or, meaning production, knowledge, and theory? This chapter will analyse the kinds of legitimation conferred by institutionalized knowledge, in this case the specific machinery of formal education. What happens when what is termed mainstream academic knowledge becomes interrogated by certain kinds of theory: Marxism, psychoanalysis, poststructuralism, feminism? The chapter will also explore the ways in which knowledge has been linked to various kinds of quests for truth, or, science, in the sense of objective truth. The quest could perhaps be reformulated as being one for 'truth effects' rather than any absolute truth since the latter is difficult to discover and might be said to belong to the domain of rhetoric (persuasive speech) rather than to any kind of objective reality. Who or what decides how or when knowledge in the sense of 'truth' has been reached? Does gender come into this? Is it appropriate to ask whether in the history of western (and other) knowledge there have been any great women thinkers or theorists? Might this be more constructively reconceptualized?

The chapter will then move on to consider the relationships between knowledge and political change in the light of feminism. Do feminists have any use for a body of theory which has largely misrepresented and/or excluded women? We will look at some of the ways in which feminism, on this basis, has operated as a powerful critique of existing areas of institutionalized knowledge. But where does this critique come from? If women have for so long been misrepresented by male-defined theory then isn't it rather rash to assume that women themselves have not internalized these same definitions? Is it enough to take for granted that we know what 'woman' is? Can women safely presume that their own experience is sufficient validation for a feminist knowledge?

From here we will consider the paradoxical interaction of feminist theory and women's experience. A dialectic between the two is needed otherwise women will never go beyond the oppositional structures which have always constructed them (Lloyd 1984, p. 105; Gross 1986). Finally, the chapter will focus on the implications surrounding the appearance of feminist knowledge as a legitimate area of institutional knowledge. On this basis it too has marked out a territory which excludes, or declares illegitimate, some kinds of knowing. We will examine briefly some of the critiques of feminism which have emerged from lesbian, black, and Third World women.

WE ARE WHAT WE KNOW

All definitions are always to some extent arbitrary but, for the moment, knowing will be defined as any kind of meaning production, as the way in which we make sense of the world by learning various sets of conventions. These sets could also be described as systems in which particular terms have meaning only in relation to each other but no absolute meanings outside their own specific systems. Language itself is such a system but there are others as well: manners, dress, music, films, mathematics, etc. (Hawkes 1977; Barthes 1979). These systems help us share our awareness of the world; they represent interpretative grids through which we experience sensory data. At the same time they also operate, so to speak, in reverse by reflecting us back to ourselves. In other words, these sign systems help construct our sense of identity. Some theorists encountered in greater detail in chapter 3 suggest, for example, that it is quite appropriate to see human beings as networks of sign systems (semiology),[1] and that there is no essential and stable core, or self (Henriques *et al.* 1984). Each moment of interaction (conversation or other exchanges) to some extent constructs a relative self.

This brings us from knowing, a process, to the question of knowledge. Knowledge could be described in territorial terms: knowledge as it has been legitimated within certain institutions, notably (but not only) the education system. Knowledge here becomes authorized learning to which only some have access. Below is a famous fictional version of a woman's encounter with institutional knowledge.

> It was thus that I found myself walking with extreme rapidity across a grass plot. Instantly a man's figure rose to intercept me. Nor did I at first understand that the gesticulations of a curious-looking object, in a cut-away coat and evening shirt, were aimed at me. His face expressed horror and indignation. Instinct rather than reason came to my help; he was a Beadle; I was a woman. This was the turf; there was the path. Only the Fellows and Scholars are allowed here; the gravel is the place for me. Such thoughts were the work of a moment. As I regained the path the arms of the Beadle sank, his face assumed its usual repose, and though turf is better walking than gravel, no very great harm was done.
>
> (Woolf 1967, pp. 7–8)

Knowledge can easily be imagined in terms of an institutional ordering, but the emphasis does not usually fall on who is doing the ordering or on what is excluded in this process. Knowledge is not usually seen as being attached to specific people who 'master' it, process it, and then dole it out to those who succeed in gaining access to certain privileged territory: the school, the college, the university (to know in the dictionary sense of 'to acknowledge the claims or authority of': *Oxford English Dictionary*). What, on the face of it, has gender to do with institutions of knowledge?

The struggle by women to gain equal access to the academy is a bulky chapter in the history of feminism and is far from over (Rosenberg 1982; Thompson 1983). It was only slowly and grudgingly that the various doors in the academy of knowledge were, in principle, opened to women. In practice this did not mean that women were actually encouraged to go there (Spender 1982; 1983). Theories about women's inability to think at basic levels, much less the higher branches of so-called pure knowledge, abounded.[2] Thus one can safely say that the academy was largely operated by men who were in the privileged position of creating meaning in terms of its public discourses. Consider the following statement (written in 1792) of a frustrated scholar caught in her age's assumptions concerning the essential opposition between male and female knowledge:

> To render mankind more virtuous, and happier of course, both sexes must act from the same principle; but how can that be expected when only one is allowed to see the reasonableness of it? To render also the social compact truly equitable, and in order to spread those enlightening principles, which alone can ameliorate the fate of man, women must be allowed to found their virtue on knowledge, which is scarcely possible unless they be educated by the same pursuits as men. For they are now made so inferior by ignorance and low desires, as not to deserve to be ranked with them: or, by the serpentine wrigglings of cunning, they mount the tree of knowledge, and only acquire sufficient to lead men astray.
>
> (Wollstonecraft 1978, pp. 293–4)

Wollstonecraft (like de Beauvoir) believed that male knowledge constituted the preferred model.

So long and bitter has this struggle been that there are many women who prefer to acquire their knowledge outside the formal education machine, for example, by organizing their own research groups (Bunch and Pollack 1983, part II). In part this has been because the academy has made entry for women such a difficult or impossible process but, as well, it has been because the kinds of 'knowing' which were taught were not necessarily of interest to women; for example, they ignored the role of women themselves in the construction of various areas of knowledge. In the next chapter Susan Sheridan examines the history and politics of trying to introduce women's studies as a legitimate area of knowledge into the halls of learning. Consider also the following:

> What is an educational system, after all, if not a ritualisation of the word; if not a qualification of some fixing of roles for speakers; if not the constitution of a (diffuse) doctrinal group; if not a distribution and an appropriation of discourse, with all its learning and its powers?
>
> (Foucault 1972, p. 227)

Theory often functions as the attempt to turn knowledge into a truth or science, the latter not in the sense of the natural or physical sciences but as representing an attempt to produce methodical and objective theory (Williams 1979, pp. 232–5). Theory represents an attempt to move beyond the chaos and abstractions of individual experience to objective and universal truth: to transcend the particular. One could argue that it is an attempt to turn sensory data into a fixed order comparable (one could imagine) to the model of a supreme being who creates a complex but totally logical world. In some respects, then, theory, the most abstract version of knowledge, has traditionally represented the attempt to understand God.[3] Not surprisingly, therefore, we see the earliest forms of theory as being entwined with theology. Philosophy and religion have a long association. The earliest universities were, for example, staffed by theologians. Legitimate theory was inextricably bound up with legitimate beliefs. Most of us have heard echoes of the great heresy battles, and secular and sacred knowledge have often been difficult to disentangle.

Within these boundaries there have been constant tensions between empiricism (theory based on experience) and abstract or universal theory which may or may not draw on experience. Recently Genevieve Lloyd (1984) has charted such a pattern, which shows the history of 'reason' to be the history of a gendered metaphor. By examining the ways in which various key male philosophers have metaphorized reason and distinguished it from 'non-reason' Lloyd has revealed that women, or the female principle, has always occupied the place of 'non-reason'. This has prevailed from the Platonic spirit–matter division to the soul–body split of Christian philosophers which culminates in our own age in the concept of nature as necessarily controlled by culture.

The apparent unity of all knowledge was and still is an important impulse in western thought (Lyotard 1984, p. ix). At this level it is often dignified with the name of 'science' (Williams 1979, pp. 232–5) which came, increasingly, to be distinguished from 'art'. So-called pure theory became progressively interchangeable with the notion of 'science' so that the aim of all territories of knowledge was to reach a state in which the whole interpretive process itself (that someone decides what is a legitimate interpretation) was rendered invisible.

Michel Foucault describes the will to knowledge as being synonymous with a will to truth. In these terms the quest for theory translates into the quest for science or truth which in turn confers authority and legitimation. These languages of truth and science were carefully circumscribed and processed by the kinds of metaphorical underpinning charted by Lloyd (1984) and were also patrolled by institutions from which women were, until relatively recently, excluded. As were those of the wrong class, or race, or religion. Somehow this strategy was believed to guarantee objectivity in the recovery of the essential and universal human being so that what that concept exactly comprised might be a matter of complete consensus across time and space.

THE KNOWING SUBJECT

The concept of theory in the sense of truth has, in turn, served to construct a unified human subject, an intellect governed by reason, who was perceived, in a sense, as the microscopic embodiment of legitimate knowledge. Knowledge was legitimated in the appropriate institutions and was incorporated at another level as the knowing subject who was seen, in some respects, as constituting the origins of meaning. This unified subject was, for example, conceived of in the nineteenth century as the liberal bourgeois subject who was a descendant of the Enlightenment concept of the self as an autonomous rational being. In the twentieth century we encounter the transcendental subject of the phenomenologists (Husserl 1970) derived via the Kantian concept of the subject as the unifier of structures of pure reason. In other words, the unified subject was never the same (this would be a ridiculous oversimplification) but the emphasis generally was on a kind of coherence which in turn reinforced a certain claim to authority. For example, Lloyd (1984) examines another version of this subject (in terms of Existentialism via Phenomenology) in her description of Sartre and de Beauvoir's distinction between immanence, or immersion in life, and the need to transcend this (Lloyd 1984, pp. 93–102).

Although the unified subject probably never existed simply as a given (the unity was always seen as a struggle in which some aspect needed to be suppressed) it certainly was a general ideal. Though this unity has always been a qualified one, recent theorists have questioned this ideal in specific ways, as Philipa Rothfield discusses in Chapter 4. One could argue that the recent challenges began with Freud (the discovery of the unconscious) and with Marx (that such an ideal ignored class suppressions and history), together with structuralism, which emerged from linguistics and examined the world in relation to sign systems (semiology). Language was an obvious sign system and questions were raised concerning the relationships between languages and the so-called 'real' world to which they referred. What were the relationships between individual subjects and the production of meaning and to what extent was meaning communicated or shared?

> Meaning was not 'natural', a question of just looking and seeing, or something eternally settled; *the way you interpreted your world was a function of the languages you had at your disposal*, and there was evidently nothing immutable about these. *Meaning was not something which all men and women everywhere intuitively shared*, and then articulated in their various tongues and scripts: what meaning you were able to articulate depended on what script or speech you shared in the first place.
>
> (Eagleton 1983, p. 107; emphasis added)

The phrases in italic emphasize the role of language itself in the production of meaning, which in turn undermines the notion of the individual as any simple origin of meaning. In a sense, language itself constructs the individual, as the sender and receiver of meaning (language pre-dated the individual). Knowledge usually becomes accessible through language and language in turn manifests itself in various forms of discourse (Foucault 1972).

> 'Language' is speech or writing viewed 'objectively', as a chain of signs without a subject. '*Discourse*' means language grasped as utterance, as involving speaking and writing subjects and therefore also, at least potentially, readers or listeners.
>
> (Eagleton 1983, p. 115)

DISCOURSE

There is no simple definition of the term 'discourse' and it really does depend on who is doing the defining. Etymologically it means 'to run in different directions' (Sturrock 1979, p. 82). Linguists took up the concept in a very particular way,[4] and Benveniste,[5] for example, in the analysis of narratives, differentiated between *histoire* (the events of a story) and *discours* (the way it was told). Later critics quickly pointed out that the way a story was told couldn't really be distinguished from the story itself (Culler 1975; McCabe 1981).

Sociolinguists such as Roger Fowler emphasized the *context* in which a story is exchanged, and likened 'discourse' to point of view:

> Discourse is the property of language which mediates the interpersonal relationships which must be carried by any act of communication. In fiction, the linguistics of discourse applies most naturally to *point of view*, the author's rhetorical stance towards his narrator,

> towards his characters (and other elements of content), towards his assumed readers.
>
> (Fowler 1977, p. 52)

He also stressed that it is impossible to be neutral within language and that one's usage of it always signals one's membership of a social group. In addition there is the awareness in discourse of who is being addressed:

> Narrative discourse is created out of the interaction of the culture's conventions, the author's expressive deployment of these conventions as they are coded in language, and the reader's activity in releasing meaning from the text. The co-operative process is not *personal*, in that it does not depend on the private feelings of writer or reader, nor *impersonal*, in that human beings are vitally involved, but *intersubjective*, a communicative act calling upon shared values.
>
> (Fowler 1977, p. 81)

Thus literary discourse (in this instance) is not simply a matter of the individual idiosyncracies of an author. Furthermore, there is always an interaction with institutional dimensions as well as the interpersonal relations of author and reader. 'To treat literature as discourse is to see the text as mediating between language-users: not only in relationships of speech, but also of consciousness, ideology, role and class. The text ceases to be an object' (Fowler 1981, p. 80).

If the sociolinguists argued for returning the text to the world (social processes) certain philosophers, such as Michel Foucault, in a sense turned this world into texts by stressing the importance of language in mediating socio-political relations. How something is spoken about reveals a great deal about the operation of power relations. At the same time, Foucault decentred the notion of an individual point of view much more than, for example, Fowler does in the above quotations: 'We no longer ask, Foucault recommends, "What was the meaning or intention behind what was written or said there?" Rather, the question is simply, "Why these particular groupings of statements at that time and not others?"' (D'Amico 1982, p. 204). Foucault's theory of discourse is set out in an early essay 'The Discourse on Language' (Foucault 1972, pp. 215–37).[6] As the essay demonstrates, discourse serves desire and power and arguably other combinations, such as reason and folly, truth and falsity, at the same time that it covers over these relations. The prohibitions which regulate discourse determine who may speak and who may not and what conventions need to be employed. Foucault's later studies concentrate on what is left out of these discourses and what is covered over by them.

Despite its purported transparency, language is thus neither a neutral tool nor a transparent reflection of reality. Its component parts in fact shape the ways in which reality is perceived. Within literature, language is being crafted in even more particular ways and recent criticism attempts to disrupt the surface calm that has long reassured people that language is neutral and that its specific unities reflect unproblematically the supposed unities of the 'real' world. Instead, signification is revealed to be implicated in the construction of ideologies of all kinds. By focusing on the manner in which meaning is produced from texts (texts interact with both authors and readers as well as with other texts) feminist critics reveal the gender bias within the use of language. Nelly Furman, for example, suggests that we study not only women as writers but also women as readers according to a process she designates 'textual feminism': 'Textual feminism implies a recognition of the fact that we speak, read, and write from a gender-marked place within our social and cultural context' (Furman 1980, p. 54).

THE POLITICAL COSTS OF KNOWLEDGE

Concurrently with structuralism and its emphasis on sign systems, Marxists too had begun to interrogate those central tenets regarding the objectivity, universalism, and transcendental nature of theory and the institutions which purveyed it as legitimate knowledge. A further development of this criticism occurred in materialist feminism:

> There is no Science with a capital S. This is for me the inevitable corollary of a materialist position of any consequence. An analysis has value only from a class position, in so far as it serves this position. (This means of course that reactionary analyses are not 'wrong' in the absolute. They are correct from the point of view of the dominants.) If there is no Science, *there is also therefore no neutrality*. This means that once an analysis no longer serves a particular class position, it does not therefore become neutral, still less 'objective'. It deserts the first position, but, being unable to be outside class, it then serves another class position.
>
> (Delphy 1984, p. 150; emphasis added)

Recent Marxism questions the so-called neutrality of theory from the standpoint of class, economy, and history. Since theory was quite obviously subject to change it was clearly, therefore, seen to be a social construct which both emerged from specific groups and, as an inevitable corollary, served to maintain their privileges. Instead of being objective truth, theory could thus be seen as intimately bound up with the ruling elite. Initially this survey of the excluded was conducted from the standpoint of class, specifically the proletariat or working class who were most obviously excluded. But this was eventually seen as collapsing too many specific differences, one of which was gender.[7]

Marginalized groups (the working class, women, blacks) increasingly interrogated the conditions of knowledge production by means of which certain kinds of truth or science came to appear as 'legitimate' at the same time that certain specific groups were authorized to articulate these truths. It was no longer sufficient to ask why were there no working-class, or black, or female, scientists, philosophers, artists. The questions were increasingly reframed to take into account the production and consumption of knowledge and culture (Hall *et al*. 1980). Who had access to the resources and in what kinds of contexts? To put it another way, it was not a question of, why are there no great women artists/writers, rather, why in our production and consumption of art/literature, do we need to construct the idea of the 'great artist'? Why do we have to have hierarchies and genealogies of greatness? Whose interests does this serve? Who has access to the resources which facilitate cultural production? (Parker and Pollock, 1981). Similarly, the concept of objective theory and the transcendental subject just happens to serve and to perpetuate the interests of privileged males.

At least for the present, male-defined models of knowledge and ways of gaining access to knowledge prevail. However, they are not seen as being specifically male-oriented since they are still camouflaged as being universal and objective. Often in the past, the occasional women who tried to sneak into the academy did their best to show that they could be better transcendental subjects than the men: outside history, class, and gender. They learnt, or aspired to learn, to 'know' as men. The cost of such 'translations' for women entering the academy is pointed out by Adrienne Rich.

> But when a woman is admitted to higher education – particularly graduate school – it is often made to sound as if she enters a sexually neutral world of 'disinterested' and 'universal' perspectives. It is assumed that coeducation means the equal education, side by side, of women and men. Nothing could be further from the truth; and nothing could more effectively seal a woman's sense of her secondary value in a man-centered world than her experience as a 'privileged' woman in the university – if she knows how to interpret what she lives daily.
>
> (Rich 1979, p. 134)

Coincident with the rise of Marxism, black civil rights, and the anti-Vietnam-war movement, second-wave feminism was helped by these political groups to relativize the monolithic and universal representations of knowledge. The specific interests which lay behind all so-called objective pronouncements were laid bare. Thus 'the personal is political' of feminism became a powerful and enabling slogan. In terms of feminist theory, however, the central question was where did the 'personal' come from? As we have seen, the tendency in certain kinds of thinking was to suggest that the individual subject was in fact a rather problematic entity. If the individual was to some extent the product of discursive networks (for our purposes many of these networks are inimical to women) then what did 'personal' mean?

KNOWLEDGE AND POWER

> It is true, it seems to me, that power is 'always already there', that one is never 'outside', that there are no 'margins' in which those in rupture with the system may gambol. But this does not mean that it is necessary to admit an unavoidable form of domination or an absolute privilege of the law. That one can never be 'outside of power' does not mean that one is in every way trapped.
>
> (Foucault 1979, p. 55)

How do knowledge and power interrelate? Is it possible for those long excluded from traditional institutions of knowledge and from conceptualizing theory, ever to gain the power that comes with these forms of knowledge?

> For the State to function as it does, it is necessary that there be between the man and woman or the adult and child quite specific *relations of domination*, which have their own configuration and their relative autonomy.
>
> Generally speaking, I believe that power is not constructed on the basis of 'wills' (individual or collective), no more than it is derived from interests. Power constructs itself and functions on the basis of powers, of multitudes of questions and effects of power. It is this complex domain that one must study. This is not to say that power is independent, or that it could be deciphered outside of the economic process and the relations of production. . .
>
> The idea that the State is the source of accumulation point of power and can therefore account for all the apparatuses of power appears to me to be without great historical fecundity.
>
> (Foucault 1979, pp. 70–1)

Power, according to Foucault, is not conceived in any monolithic or centralized way and is not, in other words, simply a matter of 'us and them', or, of the state versus 'us', or even of men versus women. Power is reproduced in discursive networks at every point where someone who 'knows' is instructing someone who doesn't know. It gives an added dimension to the notion that the personal is political because it seems that power relations are sustained at every level and not only in the public domain. Indeed, it helps us to rethink that hoary division of the private and the public in which women are usually consigned to the former and men to the latter.

If power relations are reinforced whenever there is an exchange of knowledge, what is the role of the so-called intellectual or theorist in all this? Christine Delphy points out that the academy produces knowledge in the form of 'learned discourse' which often effectively prevents its use by those who are not privy to these conventions (Delphy 1984, p. 151).

For example, it is of limited usefulness to the women's movement to be told that their own specific struggles are subordinate to and contained in generalized images of the workers' struggle. This has led to the problem that women's own struggle becomes invisible in this context, as has often been documented (*Politics and Power*, 1981). What, for example, are the dangers of appropriation when the discourses of the marginal are mediated by other institutionally based discursive networks? Even when recorded in oral histories, for example, the so-called voices of immediate experience are mediated (edited, translated, corrected) by 'intellectuals'. So it is possible to read this desire to hear the marginal, to let it speak for itself, as nothing more than an alibi to excuse intellectual elitist practices. What remains important to the context of feminism, however, is the idea that power does not necessarily reside only and always in a centre. It is not simply a question of storming a series of male citadels and of occupying the controls. And, to extend this, it is not merely a question of women taking over from men: witness the rule of Margaret Thatcher (Coote and Campbell 1982). It may well be quite misleading to think of power as consisting of a centre and a periphery and may be more productive to think of power as a network which operates everywhere in contradictory ways and can therefore be strategically resisted anywhere.

FEMINISM AS CRITIQUE

It is clear that the feminist as sceptical reader or receiver of traditional knowledge is the basis for a *feminist critique* (Langland and Gove 1981; Spender 1981) but where the authority or *basis* for this scepticism comes from is not always clear.

Catherine Stimpson gives a lucid, if somewhat schematized, picture of the shape of feminism as a critique operating within the academy over the past two decades (Stimpson 1984). But the various stages of her threefold plan, deconstruction, reconstruction, construction, need not necessarily be seen as consecutive phases. Rather, they could be described as continuing to exist in a circular or spiral fashion: the deconstruction of error goes on, informed by various theoretical constructions. The nature of the relationship between feminism as critique and feminism as construct continues to be both a problem and an inspirational spur towards action. 'The trap', as the French psychoanalyst Julia Kristeva puts it, 'is that we will identify with the power principle that we think we are fighting' (Marks and de Courtivron 1980, p. 141). From what position of institutional knowledge and theory *not* permeated by patriarchy can feminists construct a new body of both knowledge and theory? How can one be both constructed by certain concepts, through discourses, and yet also be outside them?

One of the first ways that second-wave feminists went about finding a place from which to project their critique of existing knowledges was that of consciousness-raising (Eisenstein 1984). At the same time that consciousness-raising groups undermined the concepts of group hierarchy and traditional ideas concerning authority, they also gave women the authority to speak out from their own experiences. Here, for the first time, was the idea that women's collective experience could exist as a basis (initially of resistance) for the new area of feminist knowledge (Rich 1979, pp. 203–14). And from the beginning, implicit in Eisenstein's description, there existed the tension (varying in its degrees of constructiveness) between the commonality of women's experience and its diversity, based on race, class, religion, age, etc. In some respects, Nancy Hartsock addresses the positive aspects of this tension:

> Women who call themselves feminists disagree on many things. Many are not socialists at all. *One would be hard pressed to find a set of beliefs or principles, or even a list of demands, that could safely be applied to all feminists*. Still, when we look at the contemporary feminist movement in all its variety, we find that while many of the questions we addressed were not new, there is a methodology common among feminists that differs from the practice of most social movements, particularly from those in advanced capitalist countries. At bottom, feminism is a mode of analysis, a method of approaching life and politics, rather than a set of political conclusions about the oppression of women.
>
> The practice of small-group consciousness raising, with its stress on examining and understanding experience and on connecting personal experience to the structures that define our lives, is the clearest example of the method basic to feminism.
>
> (Hartsock 1981, pp. 35–6; emphasis added)

The problem with simply looking at one's own experience as a woman lies in the fact that it is based on a prior concept of the essential female which sounds very much like the one defined by men for centuries. Essentially, woman in this structure makes the human condition possible but is not human herself (O'Brien 1982). Some Radical Feminists tended to invert the values attached to this schema so that aspects which were devalued when defined from the male standpoint were now revalued and perceived as quintessentially human: to be human was to be female. The essence of the problem was that just to value women did not remove the old deterministic trap of defining them in terms of their reproductive biology. It was suspicious that all these metaphors of women produced by patriarchal discourses over the centuries (O'Faolain and Martines 1973) were *reappearing* in the writings of those who now perceived women as the utopian future. The assumption was that wom*en* themselves were untouched by the long tradition of these metaphorical constructions of wom*an*. In fact, one could argue, patriarchal paradigms were as much an influence on women as they were on men. To say that woman was 'good' instead of 'evil' did not hide the fact that woman was permanently and universally 'other' – it also rendered invisible another feminist strategy which was to show how gender itself was largely a matter of *social* rather than natural constructs (Lloyd 1984, p. 105).

Bearing in mind that the following is rather general and reductive, one could describe the first impulse of feminist knowledge as that of taking issue with the inadequate or negative images of what one might wish to term the 'material reality' of women. It did not really focus on the category (or 'sign') of 'woman' itself. So the notion that masculine and feminine were constructed only on the basis of their difference from each other and that they were not absolute self-contained categories of difference, was not a central aspect of this approach. Only later, in an attempt to challenge these paradigms, was the point reiterated that different cultures filled 'masculine' and 'feminine' with a huge variety of characteristics so that the two terms existed always and *only* in relation to each other (Mitchell 1976).

FEMINISM AS CONSTRUCT

Feminism as construct is an attempt to move feminist knowledge beyond the stage of being an oppositional critique of existing male-defined knowing, knowledge, and theory. The central paradox in this area is the question of where feminist knowledge should situate itself, from where does it derive an authority or legitimacy which is *not* constructed by the prevailing structures of knowledge? Theory constructed in and through discourses, knowledge patrolled by institutions, and knowing as a process imbued with centuries of constructions of the category 'woman' render this enterprise a difficult one. Finally, at the same time as it precariously constructs itself, feminist knowledge must also remain constantly alert to its own conditions of existence, and in particular, to its own conclusions.

The problem with theory

Because the language we use now enshrines certain patriarchal concepts (Miller and Swift 1976; McConnell-Ginet *et al.* 1980, part II; Martyna 1982; Poynton 1985; Baron 1986) it is targeted by many feminists as a major factor in the reproduction of patriarchy. Thus the prime agency for communication perpetuates a male bias. Because of the role of language in the production of theory and because of the many ways in which institutional knowledge is controlled by men, certain feminists felt that all theory was patriarchal and hence suspect.

> The underground language of people who have no power to define and determine themselves in the world develops its own density and precision. It enables them to sniff the wind, sense the atmosphere, defend themselves in a hostile terrain. But it restricts them by affirming their own dependence upon the words of the powerful. It reflects their inability to break out of the imposed reality through to a reality they can define and control for themselves. It keeps them locked against themselves.On the other hand the language of theory – removed language – only expresses a reality experienced by the oppressors. It speaks only for their world, from their point of view. Ultimately a revolutionary movement has to break the hold of the dominant group over theory, it has to structure its own connections. Language is part of the political and ideological power of the rulers.
>
> (Rowbotham 1977, pp. 32–3)

This suspicion of anything which labelled itself theory represented the furthest extreme of tension between theory and practice. There was a necessary scepticism concerning those who made it their business (intellectual or revolutionary) to speak on behalf of others, in this case a feminist intellectual elite. No theorists, not even feminist ones, are neutral, apolitical, ahistorical, or classless. Another point is that theorists cannot be condemned simply for using difficult language. The problem lies in deciding whether, indeed, new theories *require* a new language (Belsey 1980, p. 5) or whether difficult language signals that there is simply a type of obfuscation going on which assures the kind of class control by an intellectual elite that is referred to below:

> The analyses of our Marxist intelligentsia are astonishingly revolutionary. The only problem is that they are written in language which can only be understood by a ridiculously small proportion of the population. . . . Many intellectuals believe that it is Marxist analysis which establishes the reality of proletarian oppression, a belief which is both historically and logically absurd.
>
> (Delphy 1984, pp. 148–9)

On this basis one could argue (with respect to any area of theory) that any overarching explanation produces a sense of determinism and resultant passivity. For example, this is what many feminists accuse psychoanalysis of being and it is a claim often heard in the debate surrounding the concept of patriarchy.

> without any engagement on the political level, abstraction and analysis can easily reinforce passivity in the face of overwhelming structures of oppression, rather than providing the means of escaping

> the confusing and seemingly inexplicable nature of individual experience.
>
> (Hurstfield and Phillips 1983, p. 95)

As a result of certain tendencies to rely, in unproblematic ways, on common sense and the first-hand experience of women (which rested on the assumption that an essential core within women was born and not made) at the expense of theory, several important essays appeared which emphasized and analysed the imperative need for theory. Not that consciousness-raising was seen as being simply inadequate but the more that feminist activists set up health or rape crisis centres, and the more faminist scholars unearthed earlier waves of feminism (Ascher *et al.* 1984), the more they realized that new strategies had to be forged to escape permanently from the constructs which confirmed patriarchy.

It is clear that feminism will remain forever a discursive practice constructed by its opposition unless feminist theory attempts to conceptualize new paradigms. The dangers of remaining forever oppositional are (a) that feminism can always be subsumed in other dominant oppositional discourses such as Marxism or black power and (b) that the models or paradigms upon which theory is constructed will never change.

Theory from where?

> But where was an alternative consciousness of ourselves to come from?
>
> (Rowbotham 1977, p. 31)

Always, at some level, conscious of the fact that they have to work on the constructs of patriarchal theory from within this theory and its attendant institutional knowledge, feminist theorists none the less continue to attempt to construct new positions from which to speak and to employ new strategies for theory construction. As Gilles Deleuze points out, 'only those directly concerned can speak in a practical way on their own behalf' (Foucault 1977, p. 209). To rescue this from being a mere piety, it is crucial for feminist theorists to combine carefully their political practice (often framed by institutional politics) and their theoretical discourses. On the one hand there is Belsey's statement that 'Experience must be the most unreliable source of theoretical production that we could possibly have chosen' (Belsey 1982, p. 179) and on the other we have Teresa de Lauretis's careful delineation of what 'experience' might mean for feminist theorists.

> I should say from the outset that, by experience, I do not mean the mere registering of sensory data, or a purely mental (psychological) relation to objects and events, or the acquisition of skills and competences by accumulation or repeated exposure. I use the term

> not in the individualistic, idiosyncratic sense of something belonging to one and exclusively her own even though others might have 'similar' experiences; but rather in the general sense of a process by which, for all social beings, subjectivity is constructed. Through that process one places oneself or is placed in social reality, and so perceives and comprehends as subjective (referring to, even originating in, oneself) those relations – material, economic, and interpersonal – which are in fact social and, in a larger perspective, historical. The process is continuous, its achievement unending or daily renewed. For each person, therefore, subjectivity is an ongoing construction, not a fixed point of departure or arrival from which one then interacts with the world. On the contrary, it is the effect of that interaction – which I call experience; and thus it is produced not by external ideas, values, or material causes, but by one's personal, subjective, engagement in the practices, discourses, and institutions that lend significance (value, meaning, and affect) to the events of the world.
>
> (de Lauretis 1984, p. 159)

Maria Mies, for example, sets out a sevenfold scheme for conducting feminist research (Mies 1983). Another aspect of feminist strategy is that of marking all male productions as being specifically male instead of leaving the implication of universalism:

> We see one of the major political problems confronting feminism to be the need to force men to recognize themselves as men. . . . The women's movement takes its existence from the fact that however differently we are constituted in different practices and discourses, women are constantly and inescapably constructed as women. There is a discourse available to men which allows them to represent themselves as people, humanity, mankind. This discourse, by its very existence, excludes and marginalises women by making women the sex. Our aim is not just to validate the new meanings of women but to confront men with their maleness. This is not just about masculine behaviour, but about discursive practices. It is about making men take responsibility for being men.
>
> (Black and Coward 1981, p. 85)[8]

Feminist theorists can also borrow from and adapt other bodies of theory; the influence of Marxism has already been mentioned. From psychoanalysis there is the concept of what it means to enter the social realm as a gendered subject. When historically situated, psychoanalysis makes it possible to become explicit about the political implications of each stage of the process of becoming a human subject and above all makes it clear that there are no unified, transcendental subjects. Rather, what we have is the subject-in-process constantly being reproduced and repositioned through discursive networks (Henriques *et al.* 1984). From Marxism, feminist theorists learn to be attentive to the material practices within which these discourses are produced as well as their historical specificity. For example, while it seems that patriarchy has always existed everywhere, it has never been the same anywhere. What feminist theorists need to reiterate with wearisome regularity is the diversity and specificity of wom*en* rather than any notional wom*an*. And this includes the diversity amongst feminist theorists themselves who don't all speak from the same position.

The exclusions of feminist theory

It is no longer a revelation that feminists differ among themselves. Not only have there long been different orientations and theoretical emphases between Socialist and Radical Feminists but the most recent interrogations have come from various groups of black and Third World women, as well as from lesbian women. As Gayatri Spivak puts it:

> Feminist criticism can be a force in changing the discipline. To do so, however, it must recognize that it is complicitous with the institution within which it seeks its space. That slow labour might transform it from opposition to critique. . . .
>
> Thus, even as we feminist critics discover the troping error of the masculist truth-claim to universality or academic objectivity, we perform the lie of constituting a truth of global sisterhood where the mesmerizing model remains male and female sparring partners of generalizable or universalizable sexuality who are the chief protagonists in that European contest. In order to claim sexual difference where it makes a difference, global sisterhood must receive this articulation even if the sisters in question are Asian, African, Arab.
>
> (Spivak 1986, pp. 225–6)

Lesbian critiques

The article which drew many women's attention to this issue was Adrienne Rich's 'Compulsory heterosexuality and lesbian existence' (1980, pp. 631–60). Rich's argument is summarized in the first two paragraphs:

> The bias of compulsory heterosexuality, through which lesbian experience is perceived on a scale ranging from deviant to abhorrent, or simply rendered invisible, could be illustrated from many other texts than the two just preceding. The assumption made by Rossi, that women are 'innately sexually oriented' toward men, or by Lessing, that the lesbian choice is simply an acting-out of bitterness

> toward men, are by no means theirs alone; they are widely current in literature and in the social sciences.
>
> I am concerned here with two other matters as well: first, how and why women's choice of women as passionate comrades, life partners, co-workers, lovers, tribe, has been crushed, invalidated, forced into hiding and disguise; and second, the virtual or total neglect of lesbian existence in a wide range of writings, including feminist scholarship. Obviously there is a connection here. I believe that much feminist theory and criticism is stranded on this shoal.
>
> (p. 632)

After documenting the invisibility of lesbian experiences in works by many feminists, Rich goes on to argue that: 'Feminist research and theory that contributes to lesbian invisibility or marginality is actually working against the liberation and empowerment of woman as a group' (pp. 647–8). She suggests the term 'lesbian continuum' to describe all woman-identified experience, thus removing the traditional fixation on genital intercourse implied by the term 'lesbian'. The results of this reconceptualization would be, she believes, that women's studies would 'move beyond the limits of white and middle-class' limitations (p. 659).[9]

Another Rich essay represents an important milestone in the acknowledgement by the women's movement of its own racist blindspots (Rich 1979, pp. 275–310).

Critiques from women of colour

Rich's essay cautions that whereas academic white women are indeed capable of comprehending the *intellectual* theories of racism they find it more difficult to acknowledge and to identify the *material reality* of racism, not only in the lives of others but, more particularly, in the fabric of their own lives. Women, Rich maintains, have always been asked to identify with male models, including the submersion of their own specific oppression, as appears to have been the case in the black movement, at least until recently. While not wishing to advocate a game of 'hierarchies of oppression', Rich does emphasize that white feminists need to explore these issues, particularly in their most insidious form, that of 'colour blindness' in which the particularities of non-white women's experiences are not actively opposed so much as rendered completely invisible.

The critiques from so-called minority women issue from many directions. One such is provided by Moraga and Anzaldua

> As Third World women, we understand the importance, yet limitations of race ideology to describe our total experience. Cultural

> differences get subsumed when we speak of 'race' as an isolated issue: where does the Black Puerto Rican sister take out her alliance in this country, with the Black community or the Latin? And color alone cannot define her status in society – How do we compare the struggles of the middle class Black woman with those of the light-skinned Latina welfare mother? Further, how each of us perceived our ability to be radical against this oppressive state is largely affected by our economic privilege and our specific history of colonization in the US. Some of us were brought here centuries ago as slaves, others had our land of birthright taken away from us, some of us are the daughters and granddaughters of immigrants, others of us are still newly immigrated to the US.
>
> (Moraga and Anzaldua 1981, p. 105)

Hazel Carby cautions feminists that:

> The herstory of black women is interwoven with that of white women but this does not mean that they are the same story. Nor do we need white feminists to write our herstory for us, we can and are doing that for ourselves. However, when they write their herstory and call it the story of women but ignore our lives and deny their relation to us, that is the moment in which they are acting within the relations of racism and writing *history*.
>
> (Carby 1982, p. 223)[10]

Under the subheading of the exclusions of feminist theory, the absence of critiques by Aboriginal women in a study which emanates from Australia is a painful and glaring one. While Diane Bell's *Daughters of the Dreaming* (1983) has alerted many to some of the misconceptions regarding appraisals of women's roles in Aboriginal society, Aboriginal women's own statements are still difficult to locate: an excellent example, referring back to Deleuze's point, of people *not yet* being allowed to speak on their own behalf.[11]

Finally we might bear in mind the following:

> The real difficulty, but also the most exciting, original project of feminist theory remains precisely this – how to theorize that experience, which is at once social and personal, and how to construct the female subject from that political and intellectual rage.
>
> (de Lauretis 1984, p. 166)

Far from being disabling, the paradoxes of feminist knowing, knowledge and theory are creative contradictions which remind feminists both of their history of misrepresentations and of the possibilities for constructing liberating *re*-presentations.

NOTES

1 Semiology: 'The general (if tentative) science of signs: systems of signification, means by which human beings – individually or in groups – communicate or attempt to comunicate by signal: gestures, advertisements, language itself . . .' (*Fontana Dictionary of Modern Thought* 1977, pp. 566–7).

2 The bizarre pseudo-biological cases for such claims are discussed in ch. 7.

3 That God is usually seen as male and that the body is often seen as female and bestial is a theme discussed in chs 5 and 8.

4 See the extensive definition provided in *Semiotics and Language: An Analytical Dictionary* (Greimas and Courtes 1982).

5 Emile Benveniste, whose influential *Problems in General Linguistics* was published in France in 1966 and in England in the early 1970s.

6 For a summary you might like to consult D'Amico (1982, pp. 210–11).

7 The various arguments about whether feminism should subsume its struggles under class are discussed at greater length in chs 9 and 10.

8 In recent years there has been a proliferation of studies on masculinity conducted both by men themselves and by feminists. See Gunew (1987); Jardine and Smith (1987); and Theweleit (1987).

9 See a response to this paper by Ferguson *et al*. in Keohane *et al*. (1982, pp. 147–88); see also *Signs* (1984).

10 The following is by no means a complete list but it is a start and each article or book mentioned also contains guides to further reading: Bambara (1970); Eisenstein (1979, pp. 362–72); al Sadaawi (1979); Hooks (1981); Moraga and Anzaldua (1981); Carby (1982, pp. 212–75); Davis (1982); Gardiner *et al.* (1982, pp. 629–75); Hull *et al.* (1982); Parmar (1982, pp. 236–75); Palmer (1983, pp. 151–70); *Feminist Review* (1984); Lorde (1984); Morgan (1984); Smith (1985); Spivak (1987).

11 Readers are asked to consult the companion volume to this study, *A Reader in Feminist Knowledge*, for articles by Bell, Higgins, Hooks, and Trinh, who give further details as to the diversity of women's experience and their sometimes problematic relations with so-called mainstream feminism.

REFERENCES

Ascher, C., De Salvo, L., and Ruddick, S. (eds) (1984) *Between Women: Biographers, Novelists, Critics, Teachers and Artists Write About Their Work on Women*, Beacon Press, Boston.

Bambara, T. C. (ed.) (1970) *The Black Woman: An Anthology*, New American Library, New York.

Baron, D. (1986) *Grammar and Gender*, Yale University Press, New Haven, Conn.

Barthes, R. (1979) *Elements of Semiology*, Hill & Wang, New York.

Beauvoir, S. de (1974) *The Second Sex*, Random House, New York.

Bell, D. (1983) *Daughters of the Dreaming*, McPhee Gribble and Allen & Unwin, Sydney.

Belsey, C. (1980) *Critical Practice*, Methuen, London.

Belsey, C. (1982) 'Problems of literary theory: the problem of meaning', *New Literary History*, 14:1, pp. 175–82.

Black, M. and Coward, R. (1981) 'Linguistic, social and sexual relations: a review of Dale Spender's *Man-made Language*', *Screen Education*, 39, pp. 69–85.

Bunch, C. and Pollack, S. (eds) (1983) *Learning our Way: Essays in Feminist Education*, Crossing Press, New York.

Carby, H. V. (1982) 'White woman listen! Black feminism and the boundaries of sisterhood', in *The Empire Strikes Back*, Centre for Contemporary Cultural Studies, Hutchinson, London, pp. 212–35.
Coote, A. and Campbell, B. (1982) *Sweet Freedom: The Struggle for Women's Liberation*, Picador, London.
Culler, J. (1975) *Structuralist Poetics: Structuralism, Linguistics and the Study of Literature*, Routledge & Kegan Paul, London.
D'Amico, R. (1982) 'What is discourse?', *Humanities in Society*, 5:3/4, pp. 201–12.
Davis, A. (1982) *Women, Race and Class*, Women's Press, London.
Delphy, C. (1984) *Close to Home: A Materialist Analysis of Women's Oppression*, Hutchinson, London.
Douglas, M. (1975) *Implicit Meanings*, Routledge & Kegan Paul, London.
Eagleton, T. (1983) *Literary Theory: An Introduction*, Blackwell, Oxford.
Eisenstein, H. (1984) *Contemporary Feminist Thought*, Allen & Unwin, London and Sydney.
Eisenstein, Z. (ed.) (1979) *Capitalist Patriarchy and the Case for Socialist Feminism*, Monthly Review Press, New York.
Feminist Review (1984) 17, 'Many voices, one chant: black feminist perspectives'.
Fildes, S. (1983) 'The inevitability of theory', *Feminist Review*, 14, pp. 62–70.
Fisher, B. (1984) 'Guilt and shame in the women's movement: the radical ideal of action and its meaning for feminist intellectuals', *Feminist Studies*, 10:2, pp. 185–212.
Fontana Dictionary of Modern Thought (1977), Bullock and Stallbrass (eds), Fontana/Collins, London.
Foucault, M. (1972) 'The discourse on language', in *The Archaeology of Knowledge*, Harper & Row, New York, pp. 215–38.
Foucault, M. (1977) *Language, Counter-memory, Practice*, ed. D. F. Bouchard, Cornell University Press, Ithaca, N Y.
Foucault, M. (1979) Essays in *Michel Foucault: Power, Truth, Strategy*, ed. M. Morris and P. Patton, Feral Publications, Sydney.
Fowler, R. (1977) *Linguistics and the Novel*, Methuen, London.
Fowler, R. (1981) *Literature as Social Discourse*, Indiana University Press, Bloomington.
Furman, N. (1980) 'Textual feminism', in S. McConnell-Ginet, R. Barker, and N. Furman (eds) *Women and Language in Literature and Society*, Praeger, New York.
Gardiner, J. K., Bulkin, E., Patterson, R. G., and Kolodny, A. (1982) 'An interchange on feminist criticism, *Feminist Studies*, 8:3, pp. 629–75.
Greimas, A. J. and Courtes, J. (1982), *Semiotics and Language: An Analytical Dictionary*, Indiana University Press, Bloomington.
Gross, E. (1986) 'Conclusion: what is feminist theory?', in C. Pateman and E. Gross (eds) *Feminist Challenges: Social and Political Theory*, Allen & Unwin, Sydney, pp. 190–204.
Gunew, S. (1987) 'Male sexuality: feminist interpretations', *Australian Feminist Studies*, 5, pp. 71–84.
Hall, S., Hobson, D., Lowe, A., and Willis, P. (eds) (1980) *Culture, Media, Language*, Hutchinson, London.
Hartsock, N. (1979) 'Feminist theory and the development of revolutionary strategy', in Z. Eisenstein (ed.) *Capitalist Patriarchy and the Case for Socialist Feminism*, Monthly Review Press, New York, pp. 56–82.
Hartsock, N. (1981) 'Fundamental feminism: process and perspective', in C. Bunch *et al.* (eds) *Building Feminist Theory: Essays from Quest, A Feminist Quarterly*, Longman, New York and London.

Hawkes, T. (1977) *Structuralism and Semiotics*, Methuen, London.

Henriques, J., Hollway, W., Urwin, C., Venn, C., and Walkerdine, V. (eds) (1984) *Changing the Subject: Psychology, Social Regulation and Subjectivity*, Methuen, London.

Hooks, B. (1981) *Ain't I a Woman: Black Women and Feminism*, Pluto, London.

Hooks, B. (1986) 'Sisterhood: political solidarity between women', *Feminist Review*, 23, pp. 125–38.

Huggins, T. (1987) 'Black women and women's liberation', *Hecate*, XIII:I, pp. 77–82.

Hull, G. T. *et al.* (1982), *All the Women are White, all the Blacks are Men, but Some of Us are Brave: Black Women's Studies*, Feminist Press, New York.

Hurstfield, J. and Phillips, E. (1983) 'Teaching feminism – a contradiction in terms?', *Feminist Review*, 15, pp. 94–8.

Husserl, E. (1970) *Logical Investigations*, vol. 1, Routledge & Kegan Paul, London.

Jardine, A. and Smith, P. (eds) (1987) *Men in Feminism*, Methuen, New York.

Keohane, N. O., Rosalelo, M. Z., and Gelpi, B. C. (eds) (1982) *Feminist Theory: A Critique of Ideology*, Harvester Press, Sussex.

Langland, E. and Gove, W. (eds) (1981) *A Feminist Perspective in the Academy: The Difference it Makes*, University of Chicago Press, Chicago and London.

Lauretis, T. de (1984) *Alice Doesn't: Feminism, Semiotics, Cinema*, Macmillan, London.

Lloyd, G. (1984) *The Man of Reason*, Methuen, London.

Lorde, A. (1984) *Sister Outsider: Essays and Speeches*, Crossing Press, New York.

Lyotard, F. (1984) *The Postmodern Condition: A Report on Knowledge*, Manchester University Press, Manchester.

Marks, E. and Courtivron, I. de (eds) (1980) *New French Feminism*, University of Massachusetts Press, Amherst.

Martyna, W. (1982) 'Beyond the "he/man" approach: the case for non-sexist language', in M. Evans (ed.) *The Woman Question*, Fontana, Oxford.

McCabe, C. (1981) 'On discourse', in C. McCabe (ed.) *The Talking Cure*, Macmillan, London, pp. 188–217.

McConnell-Ginet, S., Barker, R., and Furman, H. (eds) (1980) *Women and Language in Literature and Society*, Praeger, New York.

Mies, M. (1983) 'Towards a methodology of feminist research', in G. Bowles and R. D. Klein (eds) *Theories of Women's Studies*, Routledge & Kegan Paul, London, pp. 117–39.

Miller, C. and Swift, K. (1976) *Words and Women: Language and the Sexes*, Penguin, Harmondsworth.

Mitchell, J. (1976) *Psychoanalysis and Feminism*, Penguin, Harmondsworth.

Moraga, C. and Anzaldua, G. (eds) (1981) *This Bridge Called My Back: Writings by Radical Women of Color*, Persephone Press, Massachusetts.

Morgan, R. (ed.) (1984) *Sisterhood is Global*, Anchor Press/Doubleday, New York.

O'Brien, M. (1982) 'Feminist theory and dialectical logic', in N. O. Keohane, M. Z. Rosalelo, and B. C. Gelpi (eds) *Feminist Theory: A Critique of Ideology*, Harvester Press, Sussex.

O'Faolain, J. and Martines, L. (eds) (1973) *Not in God's Image: Women in History*, Virago, London.

Palmer, P. M. (1983) 'White women/black women: the dualism of female identity and experience in the United States', *Feminist Studies*, 9:1, pp. 151–70.

Parker, R. and Pollock, G. (1981) *Old Mistresses: Women, Art and Ideology*, Routledge & Kegan Paul, London.

Parmar, P. (1982) 'Gender, race and class: Asian women in resistance', in *The Empire Strikes Back*, Centre for Contemporary Cultural Studies, Hutchinson, London, pp. 236–75.
Politics and Power (1981) 3, pp. 1–20.
Poynton, C. (1985) *Language and Gender: Making the Difference*, Deakin University Press, Victoria.
Rich, A. (1979) *On Lies, Secrets and Silence: Selected Prose 1966–1978*, W. W. Norton, New York.
Rich, A. (1980) 'Compulsory heterosexuality and lesbian existence', *Signs*, 5:4, pp. 631–60.
Rosenberg, R. (1982) *Beyond Separate Spheres: The Intellectual Roots of Modern Feminism*, Yale University Press, New Haven, Conn.
Rowbotham, S. (1977) *Woman's Consciousness, Man's World*, Penguin, Harmondsworth.
Sadaawi, N. al (1979) *The Hidden Face of Eve*, Zed Press, London.
Signs (1984) 9:4, 'The lesbian issue'.
Smith, B. (1985) 'Toward a black feminist criticism', in J. Newton and D. Rosenfelt (eds) *Feminist Criticism and Social Change*, Methuen, New York, pp. 3–18.
Spender, D. (ed.) (1981) *Men's Studies Modified*, Pergamon Press, Oxford and New York.
Spender, D. (ed.) (1982) *Invisible Women: The Schooling Scandal*, Writers and Readers Publishing Co-op, London.
Spender, D. (1983) *Women of Ideas and What Men Have Done to them*, Ark, London.
Spivak, G. C. (1986) 'Imperialism and sexual difference', *Oxford Literary Review*, 8:1–2, pp. 225–40.
Spivak, G. C. (1987) *In Other Worlds: Essays in Cultural Politics*, Methuen, London.
Stimpson, C. R. (1984) 'Women as knowers', in D. L. Fowlkes and C. S. McClure (eds) *Feminist Visions*, University of Alabama Press.
Sturrock, J. (1979) *Structuralism and Since*, Oxford University Press, Oxford.
Theweleit, K. (1987) *Male Fantasies*, Polity Press, Cambridge.
Thompson, J. (1983) *Learning Liberation: Women's Responses to Men's Education*, Croom Helm, London.
Trinh T. Min-ha (1987) 'Difference: a special third world women issue', *Feminist Review*, 25, pp. 5–22.
Williams, R. (1979) *Keywords: A Vocabulary of Culture and Society*, Fontana, Glasgow.
Wollstonecraft, M. (1978) *Vindication of the Rights of Women*, Penguin, Harmondsworth.
Woolf, V. (1967) *A Room of One's Own*, Penguin, Harmondsworth.

2

FEMINIST KNOWLEDGE, WOMEN'S LIBERATION, AND WOMEN'S STUDIES

Susan Sheridan

Women's studies[1] names a major strategy for change that has come out of the contemporary women's movement in the industrialized west.[2] It owes its origins and much of its impetus to the wider social and political movement of women's liberation, although in many respects it is now structurally (and, some would maintain, ideologically) distinct from that movement. It may be too separate now to function as 'the academic wing of the women's liberation movement', as one of its US initiators once put it (Gordon 1975, p. 565), but women's studies is nevertheless significantly shaped by its relationship to that movement and the feminist knowledge produced through its activities and debates. That knowledge is reflected on, added to, and sometimes transformed by women's studies in educational institutions. And these courses, research, and publications serve as a crucial site for the dissemination and production of feminist knowledge – indeed, this book began its existence as a women's studies course.

In pointing here at the outset to the interrelationship of women's studies and the wider women's movement, I want to suggest two things: first, the feminist knowledge with which we are concerned in this book is not coterminous with the feminist scholarship produced in the academy, although it includes that field; second, both the teaching and the scholarly projects of women's studies are shaped by and in turn have some impact on the movement. While the interests of women's studies practitioners are not identical with those of feminist activists in other institutions, and while neither group is answerable to the women's movement (which, fortunately, has never become institutionalized), they are all part of the same historical phenomenon.

It may be objected that in insisting on this historical link between women's studies and the wider movement, I am condemning the former to the status of a passing fashion associated especially with the 1970s. Two points may be made in reply to that objection. The first is that the movement has changed and diversified enormously since its beginnings in the late sixties but that its lines of continuity are real and demonstrable, and its tasks are still far from accomplished – it is no mere passing fashion. The second is that an acquaintance with the history of traditions of thought and educational practice will show that they always, like women's studies in the 1970s, emerge out of specifiable social and even political conditions and survive, if they do survive, by adapting to changes in those social and political conditions.

Having argued that women's studies is both a product and a producer of feminist knowledge, it is important to go on and consider the extent to which its purposes and ideas are shaped by its location within educational institutions. Women's studies teaching and scholarship must engage in debate with the institutions to which they are formally answerable, and this is most evident within the academy, from which most of the debates rehearsed in the second half of this article originate. Current debates around women's studies in the academy include whether its principal role should be the critique of existing disciplines and traditions of thought (the 'discourses of definition' which are considered in later chapters of this book), or the construction of a new interdisciplinary model of knowledge production; whether its energies should be directed towards transforming the general curriculum or establishing its own autonomous existence and concerns; whether women's studies is by definition in conflict with the present structures of educational institutions, especially their hierarchies of personnel, assessment procedures, and teaching/research priorities; how far its work can be relevant and useful to the women's movement; and finally, what its relationship should be to women's studies projects in other educational fields, especially adult and community education, where much unpaid or underpaid women's labour is expended in offering courses to the majority of women who are still educationally disadvantaged even in the affluent west.

WOMEN'S LIBERATION AND THE PRODUCTION OF FEMINIST KNOWLEDGE

From the very beginning, educational strategies for change have been important to the women's liberation movement, and indeed many of its earliest manifestations were among students, notably those already involved in the civil rights and anti-war movements in the US. As Juliet Mitchell pointed out at the time, the emerging women's liberation movement shared with the other radical movements of the sixties the context of a greatly expanded higher education sector:

> This was partially a response to demographic pressures – the babies of the post-war birth-boom came of college age in 1964 – and also a result of changing economic demands. In America, Black colleges,

> city and state schools expanded. In England, many technical, educational and art colleges had the greatness of university status thrust upon them.
>
> (1971, p. 28)

Other western countries saw a similar expansion in higher education, and for comparable reasons: education was provided not only for the skills needed in more complex technologies of production but also for the 'expanded consciousness' necessary for advanced consumer capitalism (pp. 29–31). The major contradiction involved here was the likelihood of that consciousness expanding into life-conditions beyond those concerned with consumption, and for young women in particular this consciousness coincided with their preparation in unprecedented numbers to join the skilled workforce, despite the still-prevalent ideology that women's place was in the home (Magarey 1983, p. 163). It is hardly surprising, then, that many of the first groups in the new movement for women's liberation emerged from the institutions of higher education.

Educating themselves was one of the first priorities of the early women's groups, and this took several forms. As an adjunct to campaigns for fertility control, equal pay, childcare, and so on, there was the need to find out about women's health and sexuality, their legal position, their position in the workforce and the family, and the history of earlier feminist campaigns around such issues; and it was the first time for many, despite their involvement in male-dominated movements, that they had to speak in public and deal with the media, draw up submissions, and seek out the kinds of information that their formal education had not prepared them to find. Then there was the passionate desire to find out about the situation of women in other cultures and times – was this situation of subordination which they had become conscious of natural? Was it universal? What were its causes? How did women come to live out the oppressive ideology of feminity? What did theories of social and political change have to say about women? Where were the women activists and writers of the past? Where, for that matter, were descriptions and analyses of ordinary women and their everyday life to be found? And, most importantly of all at the time, there was the process of consciousness-raising, where women met regularly in small groups to explore their own experiences and feelings, to draw out the shared elements in these and to understand the political dimensions of these personal experiences, and finally to learn to respect, trust and even love each other as women. In all these projects of self-education, the new feminists developed processes of small-group interaction which would maximize the participation of all members and, it was hoped, ensure that they did not repeat the power-structures evident in male political groups and the competitive behaviour often found among women who saw their own value primarily in relation to men.

In all these projects, women were educating themselves by acquiring skills and knowledge formerly unavailable to them, even to those who had the privilege of a 'good education'. They were expanding their capacity to intervene in the cultural and political processes of a society in which they were assigned the place of second-class citizens, the place they now challenged at all levels. With this dialectic of self-education and political intervention in mind, I want to propose four broad and overlapping categories of feminist knowledge that have been developed by the women's movement outside of the academy, but which have had a continuing impact on women's studies. The categories include: processes of group interaction, activism as knowledge, women-centred cultural production, and feminist theories of women's oppression.

Group processes

The belief that process is as important as the product it is designed to achieve, whether this be the completion of a task or reaching a decision within a group, is not of course unique to feminism, but it is more strongly emphasized among feminists than in other political movements and is associated particularly with the radical and socialist feminist groups that developed in the 1970s. Some would even argue that contemporary feminism is principally 'a mode of analysis, a method of approaching life and politics, rather than a set of political conclusions about the oppression of women' (Hartsock 1981, p. 35). In this respect, group processes and structures, such as the collective sharing of skills and responsibilities, collective decision-making by consensus, no hierarchies of skills or status, no leaders to speak for others, and so on, became the hallmark of the new feminism. It is difficult to put such principles into action because they are alien to the prevailing structures of the division of labour and to their concomitant hierarchies of power and instrumentalist practices. When feminist objectives are pursued along these lines within larger organizational structures, such as schools, unions, or workplaces, compromises inevitably have to be made. But even in autonomous women's groups there have often been bitter disputes about operating along these lines, and reflections on process (critical or otherwise) have frequently appeared in feminist publications (for example, Rowbotham *et al.* 1979; Bunch and Pollack 1983). Major criticisms have included the tendency of unstructured groups to develop informal and unacknowledged power structures (Freeman 1975), and the privileging of personal experience as the basis for analysis, which can short-circuit awareness of the situations of women not represented in a given group (see chapter 1). All the same, modified versions of these principles still inform the operations of many feminist groups, even those inside institutions, and any account of contemporary feminist knowledge must include an awareness of how group processes and structures shape what we know by shaping how we come to know it.

Activism as knowledge

Women's acquisition of research and organizing skills as part of their political activism has a long tradition. Nineteenth-century feminists were among the earliest social researchers, developing empirical methods of observation and data organization to study social problems – participants, in fact, in the growth of sociology as a branch of knowledge. They also trained themselves as public speakers, at a time when public forums were even more jealously guarded male domains than they are today. Contemporary feminist activism (much of it still voluntary work) in areas of welfare and public policy has involved many women in acquiring such skills, and no longer exclusively from the middle-class perspective of 'helping the less fortunate' but from the point of view that the oppressed should define and organize around their own priorities. Feminist activism in these areas has also produced crucially important new concepts, those new 'namings' of oppressive practices which enable women to perceive as socially constructed realities what they had previously experienced as private misery or failure. New concepts such as 'structural discrimination' and 'sexual harassment', and new analyses of terms such as rape, incest, wife-battering, homophobia, construct political meanings for such experiences and make space for campaigns around them. Much of the work of developing equal opportunity and affirmative-action policies applying to a variety of 'socially disadvantaged groups' has been done by feminists. Women activists in the trade unions have challenged the masculinist values and traditions of the labour movement and demonstrated alternative methods of organization, and the same challenge is being made by women active in political parties and groups. In the area of cultural politics, women attempting to project feminist perspectives in the arts and the media are developing a range of concepts and techniques with which to analyse critically patriarchal ways of seeing and construct new ones. These forms of feminist knowledge have developed beyond older notions of 'agit-prop' cultural interventions because of the increased sophistication of the late twentieth-century culture industry, and because feminist analyses of ideology have demonstrated that it is not simple 'false consciousness' that oppresses women but a more complex system of ideological representations and significant silences.

Women-centred cultural production

Women's silence and the 'hidden history' of women's everyday lives and of earlier feminist movements are major themes in the feminist critique of the dominant culture. In the space opened up by this critique, work by women about women – in history, biography and autobiography, film, art, fiction, poetry, and essays – is produced in profusion. It can be argued, in specifying this kind of feminist knowledge, that where women's silence and absence are the cultural norm, then any instance of women speaking for themselves, or being recorded as speaking for themselves, is an interruption or a disruption of prevailing patriarchal definitions.

Woman-centred feminist knowledge does not necessarily take up the analyses offered by feminist political theory, but it can include all sorts of implied or explicit positions, from celebrations of traditional women's culture to radical separatist speculations like Mary Daly's (1978), to investigations of whole social groups from the perspective of the women in them, such as Beatrix Campbell's work on poverty and working-class politics (1984). Some of this work, such as feminist group processes, runs the risk of false inclusiveness in its appeal to women's sisterhood and shared experience; some of it risks making women the objects of its attention rather than subjects. Yet this growing body of work – stories, images, visions – seems today to be the life-blood of the broad social movement of women's liberation. That political body has, and needs, other substances, organs, processes; but its blood-supply keeps it in movement. These works usually speak to a wider audience than the women's movement itself, yet their production is supported by that movement and they function as part of a wider feminist counter-culture with its own institutions such as presses, bookshops and libraries, theatre and film groups, magazines, information centres, clubs, and pubs.

Feminist theory

> The condition of women became 'political' once it gave rise to a struggle, and when at the same time this condition was thought of as oppression.
>
> (Delphy 1984, p. 217)

Most of the early women's liberation analyses of women's condition as one of oppression were produced outside of the academy, and are still being debated, challenged, and modified in many different arenas. The first book-length studies to have appeared are distinguished by the wide range of issues they address, just as the new movement itself was asking a multitude of questions about women and sexuality, family, housework, paid work, welfare, law, health, politics, popular culture, and the arts. There were no specialisms, and no experts by training. They drew eclectically on the theories of radical politics that were current at the time, notably revisions of Marxism produced by the New Left and revisions of Freud such as the 'politics of experience' propounded by Laing and Cooper; they also sometimes drew on popular psychological and sociological discourses on role theory and social control.

Kate Millet's *Sexual Politics* ([1970] 1972) grew out of a PhD dissertation on literature, but she produced out of her textual and contextual analyses of political theory, sociology, and psychology as well as literature a fledgling theory of patriarchal power and the influential concept of the 'sexual politics' of male/female interactions. Shulamith Firestone (1970) looked to what was available of a pre-existing feminist tradition and named Simone de Beauvoir's classic, *The Second Sex* (1949), as her model. She then proceeded to rewrite Marx and Engels's theory of the dialectics of historical materialism in terms of sex, and to metaphorize the basic tenets of psychoanalysis in terms of the nuclear family as a micro power structure. Aries's *Centuries of Childhood*, Calvin Hernton's theories of the psychology of racism, C. P. Snow on the 'two cultures' of science and humanities, all were grist to her mill. Both these North American works are distinctively marked by the then-current discourse on sexual repression and liberation associated with Marcuse and the Frankfurt School.

In Britain, Juliet Mitchell's *Woman's Estate* (1971) grew out of an earlier essay called 'The longest revolution', whose title echoes that of Raymond Williams's account of the 'long revolution' towards socialist democracy in Britain. Mitchell set out to 'ask the feminist questions but tried to come up with some Marxist answers' (p. 99); she ended up by concluding that both psychoanalysis and Marxism were needed for developing a comprehension of the crucial ideological dimension of women's oppression. Her next book, *Psychoanalysis and Feminism* (1974), set on the feminist theoretical agenda a Freud and a Marx that had been definitively revised by French structuralism (by Lacan and Althusser respectively). In the earlier style of those wide-ranging analyses of women's position, drawing on powerful metaphors rather than specific theoretical traditions, Anne Summers's *Damned Whores and God's Police: The Colonization of Women in Australia* (1975) drew together prodigious quantities of historical and contemporary materials around the structural analogy (now largely discredited in feminist thinking) between women's oppression and imperialism. More recent widely read works of feminist theory have been of necessity more restricted in their subject (e.g. Adrienne Rich, *Of Woman Born: Motherhood as Experience and Institution*, 1976) or in their choice of approach (e.g. Michèle Barrett, *Women's Oppression Today: Problems in Marxist Feminist Analysis*, 1980).

Since the mid-1970s several factors have combined to make encyclopaedic accounts of the situation of women seem less politically acceptable and less intellectually possible. As Elizabeth Grosz demonstrates in chapter 3, radical political theory has changed, through structuralist and post-structuralist revisions of Marx and Freud, and moved away from their totalizing or universalizing tendencies of the past. This change has posed a challenge to feminist theories of women's oppression which seek to understand its origins historically and to explain its apparent universality by a monolithic theory of patriarchal power, or even by a dual-systems theory of patriarchy and capitalism. The distrust of universalizing theories coming from the direction of Paris is matched by the emerging voices of women ignored or marginalized by white middle-class feminism and its preoccupation with heterosexual relations – women who identify as lesbian, black, Third World, or migrant. Feminist politics and feminist theory are in the process of being transformed by their interventions, as Sneja Gunew's discussion in the previous chapter indicates. A third factor which is affecting the modes and substance of feminist theory derives from the subject of this chapter – the development of women's studies within the academy, where the need to counter common-sense understandings of gender difference and to draw attention to the absence of women in analyses of social formations has involved many feminists in the massive task of criticizing established bodies of knowledge – of showing how their basic assumptions assume a masculine universal and of spelling out the implications of this gender-blindness. Feminist theory has become more specific, and arguably more specialist in its concerns, focusing on discrete discourses or problems.

'An insurrection of subjugated knowledges'

This phrase from Michel Foucault's account of the conjunction of power and knowledge is an apt description of these categories of feminist knowledge that have sprung out of the women's movement. They might well be described, in terms borrowed from him, as 'naive knowledges, located low down on the hierarchy, beneath the required level of cognition or scientificity', which are even 'directly disqualified knowledges (such as that of the psychiatric patient . . .)' – or, we might add, that of the pregnant woman, the miner's wife, the urban Aboriginal woman, the daughter of a migrant family. These are popular knowledges – people's knowledges – not in the sense of a 'general common-sense knowledge' but 'on the contrary a particular, local, regional knowledge, *a differential knowledge incapable of unanimity* and which owes its force only to the harshness with which it is opposed by everything surrounding it' (Foucault 1980, p. 82; emphasis added). Another group of 'subjugated knowledges' are identified in this discussion and distinguished from the plurality of local and popular knowledges. These are 'the historical contents that have been buried and disguised in a functionalist coherence or formal systematization' (p. 81). For my purposes here, such learned or erudite knowledges produced by women would include the poetry and fiction that has been left out of the canon of 'great literature' and never reprinted, the buried or misrepresented theoretical work of past feminist thinkers such as Mary Wollstonecraft, and the scholarly work of writers such as Jane Harrison, whose woman-centred perspective in classical studies goes unremarked by male commentators. They would include, too, those parts of feminist history submerged by dominant accounts (Delmar 1986) and evidence of what Adrienne Rich has called 'the lesbian continuum' of primary relationships between women, both in individual lifetimes and throughout history (1980). In Foucault's category of 'subjugated knowledges', what brings together these buried works of learning and those popular, differential knowledges is that 'both were concerned with *a historical knowledge of struggles*' (emphasis in original). In both there 'lay the memory of hostile encounters which even up to this day have been confined to the margins of knowledge' (p. 83). Bringing these knowledges to light in the still-hostile environment of male-dominated institutions of learning has been a major task of women's studies in the 1970s and 1980s.

WOMEN'S STUDIES: POLITICS IN THE ACADEMY

This is not the place to attempt a comparative history of the development of women's studies, yet as an Australian dealing with mainly US materials I inevitably bring a comparative perspective to them. It is clear, too, that the different shapes taken by women's studies depend on the various structures of educational institutions, as well as on national and regional differences in the women's movement. Yet there are certain key issues that recur in the literature on women's studies that will serve as focal points for this discussion. I want to begin by using as a narrative framework on which to comment Marilyn Boxer's indispensable 1982 study, 'For and about women: the theory and practice of women's studies in the United States'. As she points out, the first women's studies courses were attempts to bring the women's liberation movement into the academy. Many were student-led, with short-term goals of setting up study groups along the lines instigated by the free universities, which would provide both consciousness-raising and compensatory learning, as part of women's revolutionary 'struggle for self-determination' (p. 240). Following the model of black studies, the move towards constructing women's studies as a *corrective* to the biases and distortions of the traditional curriculum soon followed, although this was not nearly so strongly evident a direction in early women's studies in Australia, perhaps because it lacked that model. But it was primarily a political movement, raising

> Questions without easy answers about the tensions between academic and political goals of classroom teaching, the responsibility of women's studies to the women's movement, and the implications of organizational structure and program governance for impact on the university.
>
> (p. 243)

While these issues may recur from time to time among United States women's studies practitioners, they are still debated fiercely, it seems, in Britain. There the education system, which has been under attack from a Conservative government for so long, is also much more obviously divided along class lines. Women's studies courses within degree-granting institutions are few, but there are many within the adult education sector (Duelli Klein 1983, p. 255) – which is the 'poor cousin' of educational provision in the British (and Australian) system, and massively used by women (Ramsay 1986, p. 168). In such a situation a defender of this sector, such as Jane Thompson in *Learning Liberation*, is harsh in her criticism of courses elsewhere which are inaccessible to the majority of women, no matter how sound their critique of the patriarchal institutions within which they are situated (1983, pp. 120–6). Mary Evans, associated with one of the few university women's studies courses at the time, the MA at Kent, is acutely aware of such reservations when she writes in defence of academic women's studies that it is a valid form of feminist struggle, and that its intellectual challenge to male control of knowledge is by definition radical (1983). Judicious comments such as the following suggest the same awareness among proponents of women's studies at a polytechnic:

> Working within the constraints of a state institution, we never saw the WS course we offered as a direct part of the autonomous women's movement . . . and we were sensitive to glib assumptions that WS and the women's movement were inevitably identical.
>
> (Brunt *et al.* 1983, p. 284)

In comparison, Boxer's account of the constitution of the National Women's Studies Association (NWSA), formed in 1977 after more than a decade of women's studies courses and conferences in the US, indicates an enterprise far more secure in its 'mission' and its relationship to the wider women's movement:

> Research and teaching at all educational levels and in all academic and community settings would be not only *about* but *for* all women, guided by 'a vision of a world free not only from sexism, but also from racism, class-bias, ageism, heterosexual bias – from all the ideologies and institutions that have consciously or unconsciously oppressed and exploited some for the advantage of others.' . . . By breaking down the divisions that limit perceptions and deny opportunities, by revising pedagogical processes as well as courses and curricula, this educational reform has itself become a social movement.
>
> (1982, p. 238)

The belief expressed here in the power of education to effect social change is distinctively North American. While feminists involved in women's studies in Britain, Canada, New Zealand, and Australia share the vision, they frequently express scepticism about the extent to which educational institutions themselves are implicated in the structures and ideologies of patriarchal capitalism and cannot be transformed without major changes in the society as a whole (e.g. Evans 1983; Magarey 1983; Lowe and Benston 1984). Yet, as Boxer's review goes on to demonstrate, this statement of NWSA's aims followed years of bitter dispute among women's studies practitioners over balancing their commitment to changing specific educational institutions and practices against their responsibility to the women's movement (pp. 245–6), and about the extent to which women's studies programmes, in their governance and classroom practice, should uphold feminist principles of collectivity (pp. 243–4).

However, by the mid-1970s it was possible to envisage women's studies as 'settling in for the long haul, no longer justifying itself as primarily compensatory and ultimately, if successful, self-liquidating' (Boxer 1982, p. 247). Programmes began more aggressively seeking a continuing place in the academy, with adequate and dependable staffing and funding. These demands, when met, have involved significant changes in the relationship between women's studies and the institutions where courses are located, notably a weakened emphasis on challenging structures:

> Commitment to structural innovation declined as the early ties to community women's liberation weakened and as the practitioners of women's studies on campus began to seek the security of stable course offerings for students, tenure-track appointments for faculty, and continuing and adequate funding for programs.
>
> (p. 267)

This tension is still very much in evidence in the literature on women's studies, although the spread of courses and programmes throughout all levels of education has brought with it an appreciation that they will always be shaped by their institutional locations, available resources, and the needs and capacities of those involved, and there is no single ideal model of women's studies (Sheridan 1986, p. 8).

Two contrasting examples from the Australian experience will serve to illustrate some of these issues about institutional location. The Flinders University women's studies course (initiated by a group of students in 1973) was *marginally* located, attached to the Philosophy department by means of a tutorship (fixed-term, low-paid) and thus able to offer courses for credit to enrolled students, but also opening its doors to non-enrolled women from the community. It was thus relatively autonomous, and was able to maintain collective principles in relation to assessment as well as course organization (Helling 1983), but it was dependent on the goodwill of one (all male) department, and the labour of the women's studies tutor was heavily exploited. Its eventual demise, after ten years of strife-torn existence, was the result of a complex of factors, which included a parting of the ways between the tutor and the department over teaching methods, and a lack of support from other parts of the university structure; it has since been replaced by a more conventionally structured, but also more powerfully situated and much more generously staffed, women's studies unit. The contrasting example, the women's studies programme at the Australian National University, was also set up in response to student demands (1975). They succeeded in arguing the case for an independent, interdisciplinary programme against the objection that this would 'ghettoize' women's studies, and agreed to conventional assessment procedures. The original fixed-term lectureship was later – and not without protracted struggle – made a tenurable position, and eventually another was added (Magarey 1986). So, while the programme has since been subject to pressures to 'mainstream' women's studies, and is still partially dependent on other departments administratively, it has survived and grown. It maintains links with local women's groups, and students are encouraged to join their projects, but its location is still firmly within the university's boundaries and any creative marginality it is able to practise is in relation to its interdisciplinary courses rather than assessment practices, etc.

Thus, while debates still surface about the incompatibility of feminist practices with existing methods of teaching and learning (e.g. de Wolfe 1980, p. 49), most academic women's studies courses are obliged to follow more or less conventional assessment methods even while they may attempt to maintain collectivity in the classroom (e.g. Culley and Portuges 1985). Assessment is, it seems, the point at which the division between academic and non-credit courses is cemented. Whether this division will eventually also mean divergent conceptions of the nature and goals of women's studies developing in different sectors remains to be seen.

Boxer has also suggested that:

> Perhaps in the light of the spectacular, and to some extent unforeseen, flowering of feminist scholarship – which has created an increasingly strong foundation and justification for the movement – academic women's studies has become less directly a strategy for institutional change and more specifically an attack on sexist scholarship and teaching.
>
> (1982, p. 252)

The distinction she is making here seems to be between a strategy of marginality where, as we have seen, women's studies had to maintain its capacity to challenge the structure of the academy at the cost of a secure place within it, and a strategy of challenging its ordering and use of knowledge *from within*, ideally both by the example of an independent women's studies programme and by the incorporation of feminist perspectives into the traditional curriculum. Recent experience of the introduction of affirmative action principles and programmes in some universities and colleges suggests that some *structural* changes can be made from within also – that is, that a series of 'revolutionary reforms' within the institution might not only 'shake the conceptual foundations of our knowledge' (Magarey 1983, p. 169), but shake up its material structures as well. Yet however successful such 'revolutionary reforms' might be, these strategies will not necessarily affect the hierarchical structure of education, in particular the relations between elite and newer universities, and between them and adult education/community colleges (Baca Zinn *et al.* 1986). Nor will they necessarily open up further access to post-school education for women from 'socially disadvantaged' class, ethnic, racial, and age groups (Hooks 1984, pp. 107–15). And while this remains the case, is the pacific solution to contending responsibilities – that women's studies will work to reform educational institutions from within (Coyner 1983, p. 128), that academic feminists' primary role is after all 'to serve as teachers and scholars' (Strong-Boag 1983, p. 99) – merely a complacent one? Better at least to remain aware that: 'Existing in between a social movement and the academy, women's scholarship has a mistress and a master, and guess which one pays wages' (Gordon 1986, p. 21).

WOMEN'S STUDIES AND FEMINIST SCHOLARSHIP

As Marilyn Boxer puts it, 'the spectacular, and to some extent unforeseen, flowering of feminist scholarship' has given women's studies 'an increasingly strong foundation and justification' (1982, p. 252). This justification can be used to defend an institutionalized women's studies which, while it cannot successfully challenge the university's hierarchical structures, can still evade containment by demonstrating that it offers 'a clear and explicit challenge to the university's ordering and use of knowledge' (Magarey 1983, p. 168). Yet the inevitable implication of women's studies in institutional structures shapes the feminist knowledge it produces. For instance, much of the literature on women's studies is written from the perspective of its explicit challenge to male knowledge, its critique of what is. While the meaning of that critique has changed radically since the early declarations about women's studies' corrective mission, and claims are frequently made that the feminist critique undermines the very foundations of male knowledge, we need seriously to consider the extent to which we have 'produced new knowledges, and thus reshaped at once the field and the object of knowledge, as well as the conditions of knowing' (de Lauretis 1986, p. 3). We also need to consider that if feminist scholarship 'remains *simply* reactive, *merely* a critique, paradoxically it affirms the very paradigms it seeks to contest' for it remains on the very theoretical grounds it wants to 'question and transform' (Gross 1986, p. 195).

Feminist critiques of the traditional disciplines into which knowledge is divided are highly developed, especially in the US where, as Catharine

Stimpson has pointed out, disciplinary organization is very influential (1986, p. 5), and women's studies programmes commonly consist of voluntary groupings of scholars from several disciplines, sometimes with an appointed convener. One of the first, and most dramatic, demonstrations of the capacity of feminist thought to challenge the whole organization of a discipline was Joan Kelly-Gadol's (1976) claim that women's history shook the foundations of historical study by making problematical three of its key concepts: periodization, the categories of social analysis, and theories of social change. Yet the question of how far such challenges advance feminist knowledge itself depends on the quality of their disciplinary opponents: for instance, reacting against Great Man theories of political and literary history can lead feminists merely to substitute female for male names in the pantheon or canon: although it is true that they will have to produce and defend somewhat different criteria of significance for their choices, there is no necessity in this model to rethink the shapes of history-writing. Alternatively, the impulse to rethink comes sometimes from directions other than feminism, and feminist critics must occupy the high ground of theoretical debate and engage at that level, if their interventions are not to be dismissed or merely tolerated as adding another interesting subject area, as Marilyn Strathern (1985) argues has happened in relation to the discipline of anthropology.[3]

Arguments about whether women's studies should be 'mainstreamed', i.e. incorporated as a 'perspective' within the traditional discipline-based curriculum, become much more complicated in the light of such considerations. Besides, one does not 'simply *add* the idea that the world is round to the idea that the world is flat' (McIntosh and Minnich 1984, p. 140). However, the 'mainstreaming debate', as it is known in the US women's studies literature, is primarily a battle over the carving up of funds available to women's studies projects.[4] There are few voices to be heard now defending the view that women's studies will 'wither away once the curriculum is transformed, should that happy event ever come to pass', while there is a variety of proposals about the kind of autonomous existence it might lead in the future as a discipline or body of knowledge (Rosenfelt 1984, p. 168). Thus the major debate of the 1980s about the nature and scope of women's studies in the academy is an elaboration of the question of its relation to the disciplinary division of knowledge, whether it is to be a transformative critique, 'changing paradigms' within the disciplines, or whether it is to take its place as an independent interdisciplinary 'discipline'.

Such questions are partly urged by the different practical circumstances in which women's studies programmes find themselves within educational institutions, and partly by the desire to clarify concepts of women's studies among the community of feminist scholars. Both impulses can be discerned in the arguments put forward by Sandra Coyner for making women's studies an academic discipline (1983): she proposes that the attempt to transform the existing disciplines is a waste of time and that we would do better to build an independent discipline around the shared literature and priorities of women's studies, offering specialist professional training and other paraphernalia of an academic discipline. Yet the political implications of this project would include, as her paper suggests, a severing of ties with the women's movement and pressure to fix certain concepts as central to the discipline, whereas many would feel that, on the contrary, the shifting variety of feminist concepts is a strength (Harding 1986) and that 'the connection to a political movement is the lifeblood of feminist scholarship, not its tragic flaw' (DuBois *et al.* 1985, p. 8). A fact also to be considered is that the critique of the disciplines is currently producing some of the most innovative and invigorating feminist scholarship, demonstrating that we cannot afford to abandon that ground or indeed to lose touch with advances that may be made there (Sheridan 1986, p. 11).

An important exploration of the way feminist scholarship both challenges and is shaped by disciplinary enquiry is offered by DuBois *et al.* (1985). Their book demonstrates that while many of the subjects addressed 'have their genesis in the concerns of the women's liberation movement and do not readily fall within the purview of any particular discipline' (p. 9), women's studies is shaped by the disciplines as well. Yet they make no clear distinction between 'transdisciplinary' and 'multidisciplinary' studies (neither does Coyner 1983). Such a distinction is crucial, however, argues Magarey (1983). For if a 'multidisciplinary' exercise eclectically draws upon the procedures of many disciplines, it 'will face enormous difficulty in establishing criteria for doing so' and its eclecticism will

> generate teaching and research that is either superficial, or chaotic, and probably reluctant to confront negative evidence. A 'transdisciplinary' enterprise, by contrast, endeavours to transcend a specific range of disciplines, and this means that it establishes criteria for assessing and selecting techniques and procedures from these disciplines.
>
> (p. 167)

The attempt to meet this admittedly tall order will perhaps help women's studies rid itself of the opprobrium that attaches to interdisciplinary teaching and research in the academy. This would be a good thing if it meant that more feminist scholars would support women's studies, yet there is also a sense in which its health depends upon remaining 'a larrikin in the field of learning' (Watson 1987, p. 125). Women's studies differs from other 'fields' that draw on a variety of disciplines, such as urban studies, in that it *is* scholarship for a cause. Further, it involves a critical examination of the academy itself, as one of the power/knowledge institutions which constitute a central problem addressed by women's studies, that of women's social and cultural subordination.

The final issue to be raised here, briefly, concerns the object of women's studies: is it to be, as the name implies, the study of women? In the previous chapter of this book some problems, both theoretical and political, were elaborated around 'women' as a guiding concept for feminism – as an appeal to already constituted, biologically defined women, and also as a mask over those differences among women which are constituted by the intersections of sexism with other orders of domination based on race, class, ethnicity, sexuality. In relation to women's studies, objections to these implications of the name have come from all these groups, for instance the inauguration of black women's studies out of the inadequacies of both (white) women's studies and (male-dominated) black studies (Hull *et al.* 1982, pp. xx–xxi) and proposals for lesbian studies which would add to the feminist curriculum a challenge to the myth of the lesbian as 'other' (Cruikshank 1982, p. xii). The tendency to limit the meaning of 'women's studies' to a concern with the *status* of women has been criticized by an Indian feminist in that it deflects attention from *relationships* of power, not only gender but class as well (Jain 1983, pp. 172–3).

'Gender' is a concept which might focus attention on relationships of power, as Jain proposes. Its increasing currency in feminist studies in the late 1980s suggests fresh intellectual directions – the naming of new journals such as *Genders*, *Gender and History*, and *Differences* (which, also, does not specify 'women' as the subject/object of the enquiry). Linda Gordon has affirmed the value of the concept of gender to indicate the *imposition* of difference, indicating the weakness of a currently popular feminist notion of women's 'difference' which 'can function to obscure domination, to imply a neutral asymmetry' (1986, p. 27). There has been some confusion about what kind of term 'gender' is – an analytical category, or a subject matter? (*Signs* Editorials Spring 1987 and Spring 1988). Joan Scott has argued strongly for the former view in her influential article, 'Gender: a useful category of historical analysis' (1986), yet she also points out its potential to blunt the critical edge of feminist scholarship. 'Gender studies' as a reference to subject matter only can encourage male 'me-tooism' ('gender must include discussions of women *and* men') and the old accusation that the study of women is 'narrowly defined' (*Daedalus*, Editorial, Fall 1987, p. vii). It can – and sometimes usefully – sound like a claim to objectivity and neutrality 'by suggesting a comparative social scientific methodology to examine patterns of masculinity and femininity' (Stimpson 1986, p. 30). But can the title 'gender studies' carry out the more radical intellectual and political task of shifting the emphasis towards a *complex* of socially constructed relationships of domination?

On the other hand, many feminists would regret the failure of 'gender studies' to name the *subjects* of the enterprise – women silenced again. There is after all a happy ambiguity in 'women's studies', as it can mean some or all of 'by, about and for women'. 'Feminist studies', while suggesting the importance of a political position to the enterprise, is often avoided for purely pragmatic reasons, but it could also be objected that the name implies an already constituted and fixed position. There is also an ambiguity about its referent – is feminism to be the object of the study, or the approach(es) adopted towards it? The strength of the latter, of course, is that any issue or object under the sun may be the concern of feminism. But then again, which feminism?

In the end, of course, the name matters less than the meanings we produce from it in particular times and places, particular political contexts. The project of women's studies is diverse and profound, and its implication in the production of feminist knowledge is complex. As we have seen, because of its dual functions of both passing on feminist knowledge from the women's movement and producing more formal feminist knowledge in its teaching and scholarship, women's studies has a dangerous potential to institutionalize that knowledge in the toils of its structures, and to defuse its political force. On the other hand, we have also seen that it has struggles of its own to fight in the academy in order to continue its work of critical and transdisciplinary learning, struggles which keep its crucial political commitments well within view. If, as Linda Gordon puts it, 'existing between a social movement and the academy, women's scholarship has a mistress and a master' (1986, p. 21), then it should point out to the mistress the similarity of their positions in relation to the wage-paying master, and form strategic alliances with other servants of the academy which have similar commitments to opening its doors and radically transforming its formal and material structures.

NOTES

1 This is the most common designation; alternative titles and their implications (gender studies, feminist studies) will be considered below.

2 Women's studies in the Third World has somewhat different origins and implications from those in the west, according to Mies (1986, p. 9); the present discussion is restricted to women's studies in the Anglophone west.

3 A similar incorporation is classically demonstrated by K. K. Ruthven's book, *Feminist Literary Studies* (1985), where feminist discourse is regarded as 'just another way of talking about books'.

4 See G. Bowles and Duelli Klein (1983, Introduction), and the special issue (7:3) of *Women's Studies International Forum* (1984).

REFERENCES

Baca Zinn, M., L. Weber Cannon, E. Higginbotham and B. Thornton Dill (1986) 'The costs of exclusionary practices in women's studies', *Signs*, 11:2, pp. 290–303.

Barrett, M. (1980) *Women's Oppression Today: Problems in Marxist Feminist Analysis*, Verso, London.
Bowles, G. and Duelli Klein, R. (eds) (1983) *Theories of Women's Studies*, Routledge & Kegan Paul, London.
Boxer, M. (1982) 'For and about women: the theory and practice of women's studies in the United States', in N. O. Keohane, M. Z. Rosaldo, and B. C. Gelpi (eds) *Feminist Theory: A Critique of Ideology*, Harvester Press, Sussex, pp. 237–71.
Brunt, R., E. Green, K. Jones and D. Woodward (1983) 'Sell-out or challenge? The contradiction of a masters in women's studies', *Women's Studies International Forum*, 6:3, pp. 283–90.
Bunch, C. and Pollack, S. (eds) (1983) *Learning Our Way: Essays in Feminist Education*, Crossing Press, New York.
Campbell, B. (1984) *Wigan Pier Revisited: Poverty and Politics in the 80s*, Virago, London.
Coyner, S. (1983) 'Women's studies as an academic discipline: why and how to do it', in G. Bowles and R. Duelli Klein (eds) *Theories of Women's Studies*, Routledge & Kegan Paul, London, pp. 46–71.
Cruikshank, M. (ed.) (1982) *Lesbian Studies*, Feminist Press, New York.
Culley, M. and Portuges, C. (eds) (1985) *Gendered Subjects: The Dynamics of Feminist Teaching*, Routledge & Kegan Paul, London.
Daly, M. (1978) *Gyn/Ecology: The Meta-ethics of Radical Feminism*, Beacon Press, Boston.
Delmar, R. (1986) 'What is feminism?', in J. Mitchell and A. Oakley (eds) *What Is Feminism?*, Blackwell, Oxford.
Delphy, C. (1984) *Close to Home: A Materialist Analysis of Women's Oppression*, trans. D. Leonard, Hutchinson, London.
DuBois, E., G. P. Kelly, E. L. Kennedy, C. W. Korsmeyer, L. S. Robinson (1985) *Feminist Scholarship: Kindling in the Groves of Academe*, University of Illinois Press, Chicago.
Duelli Klein, R. (1983) 'A brief overview of the development of women's studies in the UK', *Women's Studies International Forum*, 6:3, pp. 255–60.
Evans, M. (1983) 'In praise of theory', in G. Bowles and R. Duelli Klein (eds) *Theories of Women's Studies*, Routledge & Kegan Paul, London, pp. 219–28.
Firestone, S. (1970) *The Dialectic of Sex*, Morrow, New York.
Foucault, M. (1980) 'Two lectures', in *Power/Knowledge*, C. Gordon ed., Harvester Press, Sussex.
Freeman, J. (1975) *The Politics of Women's Liberation*, McKay, New York.
Gordon, L. (1975) 'A socialist view of women's studies', *Signs*, 1:2, pp. 559–66.
Gordon, L. (1986) 'What's new in women's history', in T. de Lauretis (ed.) *Feminist Studies. Critical Studies*, Indiana University Press, Bloomington, pp. 20–30.
Gross, E. (1986) 'What is feminist theory?', in C. Pateman and E. Gross (eds) *Feminist Challenges*, Allen & Unwin, Sydney, pp. 190–204.
Harding, S. (1986) 'The instability of the analytical categories of feminist theory', *Signs*, 11:4, pp. 645–64.
Hartsock, N. (1981) 'Fundamental feminism: process and perspective', in *Building Feminist Theory: Essays from 'Quest'*, Longman, New York, pp. 32–43.
Helling, R. (1983) 'The personal is political', *Journal of Educational Thought*, 17:2, pp. 172–81.
Hooks, B. (1984) *Feminist Theory. From Margin to Mainstream*, South End Press, Boston.
Hull, G., P. Bell and B. Smith (eds) (1982) *But Some of Us Are Brave: Black Women's Studies*, Feminist Press, New York.

Jain, D. (1983) 'Comment on Shapiro's "Women's studies: a note on the perils of markedness"', *Signs*, 9:1, pp. 172–3.
Kelly-Gadol, J. (1976) 'The social relations of the sexes', *Signs*, 1:4, pp. 809–24.
Lauretis, T. de (1986) 'Feminist studies/critical studies: issues, terms and contexts', in T. de Lauretis (ed.) *Feminist Studies. Critical Studies*, Indiana University Press, Bloomington, pp. 1–19.
Lowe, M. and Lowe Benston, M. (1984) 'The uneasy alliance of feminism and academia', *Women's Studies International Forum*, 7:3, pp. 177–84.
McIntosh, P. and Minnich, E. (1984) 'Varieties of women's studies', *Women's Studies International Forum*, 7:3, pp. 139–48.
Magarey, S. (1983) 'Towards trans-disciplinary learning', *Journal of Educational Thought*, 17:2, pp. 162–71.
Magarey, S. (1986) 'I never wanted to be an administrator of anything', *Women's Studies International Forum*, 9:2, pp. 195–202.
Mies, M. (1986) *Patriarchy and Accumulation on a World Scale*, Zed Books, London.
Millet, K. ([1970] 1972) *Sexual Politics*, Abacus, London.
Mitchell, J. (1971) *Woman's Estate*, Penguin, Harmondsworth.
Mitchell, J. (1974) *Psychoanalysis and Feminism*, Penguin, Harmondsworth.
Ramsay, J. (1986) 'Women's education', *Australian Feminist Studies*, 3, pp. 165–72.
Rich, A. (1976) *Of Woman Born: Motherhood as Experience and Institution*, Virago, London.
Rich, A. (1980) 'Compulsory heterosexuality and lesbian existence', *Signs*, 5:4, pp. 631–60.
Rosenfelt, D. (1984) 'What women's studies programs do that mainstreaming can't', *Women's Studies International Forum*, 7:3, pp. 167–76.
Rowbotham, S., L. Segal and H. Wainwright (1979) *Beyond the Fragments*, Merlin, London.
Ruthven, K. (1985) *Feminist Literary Studies*, Cambridge University Press, Cambridge.
Scott, J. W. (1986), 'Gender: a useful category of historical analysis', *American Historical Review*, 91, 5, pp. 1053–75.
Sheridan, S. (1986) 'From margin to mainstream: situating women's studies', *Australian Feminist Studies*, 2, pp. 1–14.
Stimpson, C. (1986) 'Women's studies: the state of the art', unpublished paper.
Strathern, M. (1985) 'Dislodging a world view: challenge and counter-challenge in the relationship between feminism and anthropology', *Australian Feminist Studies*, 1, pp. 1–25.
Strong-Boag, V. (1983) 'Mapping women's studies in Canada', *Journal of Educational Thought*, 17:2, pp. 94–111.
Summers, A. (1975), *Damned Whores and God's Police: The Colonization of Women in Australia*, Penguin, Ringwood.
Thompson, J. (1983) *Learning Liberation*, Croom Helm, London.
Watson, K. (1987) 'Women's studies in the university: some practical considerations', *Australian Feminist Studies*, 4, pp. 123–32.
Wolfe, P. de (1980) 'Women's studies: the contradictions for students', in D. Spender and E. Sarah (eds) *Learning to Lose*, Women's Press, London.

FURTHER READING

Abel, E. and Abel, E. (eds) (1983) *Women, Gender and Scholarship*, University of Chicago Press, Chicago.

Bristol Women's Studies Group (1979) *Half the Sky*, Virago, London.
Broom, D. (ed.) (1984) *Unfinished Business*, Allen & Unwin, Sydney.
Cass, B., Dawson, M., Temple, D., Willis, S. and Winkler, A. (1983) *Why So Few? Women Academics in Australian Universities*, Sydney University Press, Sydney.
Higgins, S. and Matthews, J. (1979) 'Feminist publishing in Australia', *Meanjin*, 38:3, pp. 321–33.
Howe, F. (ed.) (1975) *Women and the Power to Change*, McGraw Hill, New York.
Howe, F. (1984) *Myths of Coeducation*, Indiana University Press, Bloomington.
Keohane, N. O., Rosaldo M. Z., and Gelpi, G. C. (eds) (1982) *Feminist Theory, A Critique of Ideology*, Harvester Press, Sussex.
Langland, E. and Gove, W. (eds) (1981) *A Feminist Perspective in the Academy*, University of Chicago Press, Chicago.
Rowland, R. (1982) 'Women's studies courses', *Women's Studies International Forum*, 5:5, pp. 487–95.
Sherman, J. and Beck, E. (eds) (1979) *The Prism of Sex*, University of Wisconsin Press, Madison.
Spender, D. (ed.) (1981) *Men's Studies Modified*, Pergamon, Oxford.
Stanley, L. and Wise, S. (1983) *Breaking Out: Feminist Consciousness and Feminist Research*, Routledge & Kegan Paul, London.
Tobias, S. (1978) 'Women's studies: its origins, its organization and its prospects', *Women's Studies International Forum*, 1, pp. 85–97.
Women's Studies Group (1978) *Women Take Issue*, Centre for Contemporary Cultural Studies, Hutchinson, London.
Woolf, V. ([1938] 1977) *Three Guineas*, Penguin, Harmondsworth.

Part II

CONTEMPORARY THEORIES OF POWER AND SUBJECTIVITY

3

CONTEMPORARY THEORIES OF POWER AND SUBJECTIVITY

Elizabeth Grosz

THEORIZING SUBJECTIVITY AND POWER

Theory does not develop out of the air. It is not the result of men of 'great ideas', 'brilliant minds', or 'astute observation'. It is the product of history, and thus requires an understanding of the socio-political and intellectual contexts out of which theories and knowledges develop. It is the result of the interwoven and mutual defining set of relations between one theory or discourse and many others. In this chapter, I will examine a number of recent theories of power (developed by men). This may help to assess the critical and constructive contributions feminism might have to make to the knowledges out of which it is formed and against which it rebels.

Feminist theory must always function in two directions if it is to effectively challenge patriarchal knowledges. On the one hand, it must engage in what could be called a *negative* or *reactive* project – the project of challenging what currently exists, or criticizing prevailing social, political, and theoretical relations. Without this negative or *anti-sexist* goal, feminist theory remains unanchored in and unrelated to the socio-theoretical *status quo*. It risks repeating problems of the past, especially patriarchal assumptions, without recognizing them as such. But if it remains *simply* reactive, *simply* a critique, it ultimately affirms the very theories it may wish to move beyond. It necessarily remains on the very ground it aims to contest. To say something is *not* true, valuable, or useful *without posing alternatives* is, paradoxically, to affirm that it *is* true, and so on. Thus coupled with this negative project, or rather, indistinguishable from it, must be a positive, constructive project: creating alternatives, producing *feminist*, not simply *anti-sexist*, theory. Feminist theory must exist as *both* critique *and* construct.

In other words, feminist theory should consider itself a form of *strategy*. Strategy involves recognizing the situation and alignments of power within and against which it operates. It needs to know its adversary intimately in order to strike at its most vulnerable points. It must also seek certain (provisional) goals and future possibilities with which it may replace prevailing norms and ideals, demonstrating that they are not the only possibilities. They *can* be superseded.

As a series of strategic interventions into patriarchal social and theoretical paridigms, feminism must develop a versatile and wide-ranging set of conceptual tools and methodological procedures to arm itself defensively and offensively. It requires weapons to challenge patriarchal intellectual norms; and by which to protect itself against various counter-attacks from the existing regimes of power. Feminists can ignore the history and current conceptions of theories of human subjectivity only at their own peril. Feminist theory need not commit itself to the values and assumptions governing patriarchal knowledges; but in order to go *beyond* them, it must work through them, understand them, displace them in order to create a space of its own, a space designed and inhabited by women, capable of expressing their interests and values.

Feminist theory must thus undertake a kind of intellectual 'apprenticeship' in patriarchal knowledges in order to understand how they function, what presumptions they make, what procedures they rely upon, and what effects they produce. It must first develop a capacity to recognize patriarchal commitments in their underlying, as well as in more apparent, forms: to be able to recognize how the world is coded according to masculine or feminine attributes and associations, how knowledges, theories, discourses, function by excluding, expelling, or neglecting the contributions of femininity and women, producing lacks, gaps, absences about femininity which are necessary for these theories to operate; and how these theories distribute value according to the privileging of one sex over the other. In short, it must develop the capacity to recognize the patriarchal theories underlying *phallocentrism*. (For further discussion about phallocentrism, see chapter 5.) Phallocentrism occurs whenever the two sexes are represented by a singular – or 'human' (i.e. masculine) – model. The feminine is defined only in some relation to the masculine, and never autonomously, in its own terms. It is represented either as *the opposite* or other; or as a *complement*; or as the *same* as masculinity.

Second, feminist theory needs to address methodological questions, those about how patriarchal theories function and how feminists may utilize them *against themselves*. It is impossible to maintain or develop a theoretical 'purity' untainted by patriarchy for our ideas, values, terminology, repertoire of concepts are all products of patriarchy. Feminism does not necessarily require 'theoretical separatism', which attempts to eliminate patriarchal ingredients by isolation and distance. It can also result from a thorough familiarity with their methods, commitments, and values, and with their blind-spots, contradictory elements, and silences. A viable feminist methodology must be the consequence of an active yet critical engagement with patriarchal methods.

Third, feminists must use whatever remains worthwhile in patriarchal discourses to create new theories, new methods, and values. This may imply taking patriarchal discourses as points of departure, allowing women's experiences rather than men's to select the objects and methods of investigation. By its very existence, such theory demonstrates that patriarchal paradigms are not *universal*, valid for all, but at best represent one point of view.

It is within this general context of the relations between phallocentric and feminist discourses that I will situate the following outlines of four contemporary (male) theorists of subjectivity and power – Louis Althusser, Jacques Lacan, Michel Foucault, and Jacques Derrida. They develop accounts of social, discursive, and individual relations of power that, between them, provide a context and targets for French feminisms.[1]

Althusser and Lacan are major contributors to an anti-biologistic, anti-naturalistic, and, above all, anti-humanist theory of subjectivity. They provide crucial elements in accounting for the *social construction of subjectivity*. Although critical of them, Foucault and Derrida can be seen to contribute a discursive and political dimension to the two earlier theorists. Clearly, none of them could be considered feminist (they do not, for example, raise the question of patriarchal power structures); yet each has provided inspiration for many feminists. Rarely, however, are their works uncritically or wholeheartedly accepted. Generally, feminists have subjected them to critical assessment and use these texts to develop their own.

THEORETICAL BACKGROUND

Althusser, Lacan, Foucault, and Derrida are four French theorists whose works can be related, if not to a common content, then at least to a common context, that of French philosophy. Our first question is thus: *why French theory?* There are two major reasons why, instead of looking at an Anglo-American framework, which would presumably be more relevant to English-speaking feminists, we examine the work of a number of difficult, even esoteric and eccentric, French theorists. First, French philosophy has been extremely, even disproportionately, influential in twentieth-century accounts of human subjectivity and socio-political functioning – in the same way that English and German philosophies transformed knowledge in the nineteenth century (via Liberalism and Marxism respectively). Second, the works of these and other French intellectuals have been extremely influential in the development of feminist theory, beginning with Simone de Beauvoir's landmark text, *The Second Sex* (1972). French feminisms provide a major alternative to American liberal feminism and reveal a more British orientation to Marxist-feminism. It is difficult to see how French feminisms could be assessed by and useful to us without some understanding of the issues and intellectual contexts of twentieth-century thought.

While necessarily schematic and compressed, the following overview positions the four male theorists we are examining in the milieu out of which they developed. The crucial dividing line I will present is May and June 1968,[2] demarcating two generations of French intellectuals. The first generation was preoccupied with a 'debate' between Existentialism, phenomenology, or humanism on the one hand (perhaps best represented by Jean-Paul Sartre); and, on the other, Marxism. Sartre published *Being and Nothingness* in 1943, making explicit the basic commitments of humanism. Humanism is the theory that all value and meaning, history and cultural production are the products of human consciousness and the lived experiences of individuals. Phenomenology and Existentialism espouse the primacy of experiences, subjectivity, and individuality in social and interpersonal life. For Existentialism, the human being is defined by his or her capacity for freedom, to make choices and decisions regarding the meaning and value of one's life (Sartre 1975).

In opposition to humanism, which it denounces as idealist and individualistic, the position of the French Communist Party (the PCF) was defined in economic terms. Class struggle is the motor of history and the explanation of cultural production. Capitalism is a system beyond the control of individuals. It exhibits an internal logic – the dialectic – which inevitably progresses towards the dissolution of class structures, social and economic revolution, and the creation of a new, egalitarian order. Classes are conceived purely economically, the economy being regarded as the cause and explanation of the nature of its cultural and ideological infrastructure. The PCF aimed to lead the working classes in a takeover of the state, the means, and forces of production.

Existentialism and economistic Marxism are two extremes of radical political thought during the Cold War in the 1950s. By 1961, however, Sartre was moving closer to a compromise position. He attempted to embrace Marxism in the texts *The Search for a Method* and *The Critique of Dialectical Reason*. There, he links Marxist and Existentialist concerns through the concept of *praxis*: the practice of individual and group (class) subjects who, through their conscious, concerted efforts, are capable of transforming oppressive structures. Existentialism was itself transformed by Sartre's acknowledgement that class oppression may be a mitigating factor on human freedom (although significantly Sartre seemed to ignore de Beauvoir's re-inscription of Sartre's position by acknowledging women's oppression); as was Marxism, which was 'humanized'. In sum, by the 1960s, Marxism, in both its economistic and its humanist forms, dominated the field of political theory and action.

Coupled with these alliances and interactions was the rediscovery of the 'sacred' texts of the ninteenth century – Hegel, Marx, Freud, and Nietzsche. These figures were instrumental in the emergence of each of our four contemporary theorists. Althusser, with whom we will begin, sees his work as a reading, a reinvestigation of the texts of Marx. Ignored by dogmatic, received interpretations, Marx's work, particularly *Capital*, had not been read as a *scientific* account of historical and economic relations.

ALTHUSSER AND THE THEORY OF IDEOLOGY

Althusser challenges humanism, particularly Sartrean versions, by claiming that consciousness at best provides merely a subjective or 'personal' view of reality, a view which does not usually conform to objective social relations. In order to transform subjective experience into objective knowledge, a scientific analysis, such as Marx provided, is necessary. Althusser's conception differentiates the lived experiences of individuals from the real economic and social relations in which they live. He divides information into the category of science, which is truthful, objective knowledge of social relations; and ideology, which is the personal experience of individuals and/or groups. For him, consciousness is not a reliable index of social reality but its distorted or false representation.

On the other hand, Althusser also rejected determinism and the economic reductionism involved in more dogmatic versions of Marxism: while social and cultural products depend on economic conditions, economic relations are not adequate to explain them. They exert a 'relative autonomy' from economic relations. Althusser utilizes the traditional Marxist metaphor of the social formation as a building which requires a strong base or foundation (provided by the economic forces, the forces and relations of production); on to this foundation two more storeys can be added (jointly constituting the ideological and cultural superstructure). The first floor is the legal and political system, the state and the law; the second floor is made up of various cultural practices, including moral, religious, educational, familial, and ethical systems. The two upper floors are supported, 'in the last instance' by the economic base, but are not directly determined by it.

Ideology mutually defines and interacts with the economic sphere, so that while the economic is the condition for ideology, the ideological also provides a 'relative determination' of the economic. Economistic Marxism assumes that if upheavals at the economic level occur, this *in itself* will provide the conditions for an accompanying ideological upheaval. For Althusser, given the relative autonomy of ideology, this is by no means clear.

His anti-humanism refuses any notion of a pre-given subjectivity, free of ideology, and his anti-economism accords an autonomy to socio-cultural practices. Together these influence a surprisingly large number of feminists. Many saw in Marxist analyses of class relations a striking analogy with women's patriarchal oppression.

Althusser also helped alert feminists, even Marxist-feminists, to the phallocentric assumption that women's identities are somehow *natural*. His anti-humanism and his account of the social construction of subjectivity in and by ideology propelled many feminists away from natural or biological accounts of women's identities towards social, cultural, and historical explanations. His anti-economism, on the other hand, proposed that cultural, artistic, communicational, and representational systems, i.e. ideologies, do not automatically follow economic changes. They themselves must be subjected to a thoroughgoing analysis and subversion, if questions about personal identity, interpersonal relations, or, more generally, about everyday life (such as those asked by feminists about women's everyday experiences of oppression) are to be resolved. In other words, while problematizing personal experience by describing it as ideological rather than truthful, Althusser enables women's experiences to be still taken seriously. He shifts the *status* of experience, so that it is no longer guaranteed a truth-value but acts as *symptom* of a deeper, underlying, or latent structure. His claim is not that of Descartes, that our experiences deceive us, but rather, that we must learn how to 'read' them other than by taking them at their face value.

Althusser aims to develop a *scientific* account of ideology, one that positions ideology and its effects clearly in a socio-economic context. His analysis of ideology has two components. One is epistemological and involves the distinction between science and ideology as ways of knowing; and the other, psychological and sociological, involving his notion that ideology creates or constitutes subjects.

The science/ideology distinction

The distinction between science and ideology is Althusser's attempt to justify Marxism as a scientific account of history and class relations and psychoanalysis as a scientific account of psychical organization, making them stand out against their ideological rivals, liberal political theory, classical and neo-classical economics, and empirical psychologies, respectively. These pseudosciences or ideologies rationalize existing class relations, and thus, ultimately function to obscure rather than reveal real relations. In opposition to these unreflective, ideological knowledges, Althusser claims that Marxism not only provides a truthful account of real class relations, but also explains the ideological investments of competing knowledges – why and where they go wrong.

He argues that Marx's understanding of history – historical materialism – must be distinguished from empiricist and idealist accounts, in so far as historical materialism presumes a revolutionary rupture in classical history, an 'epistemological break', marking itself as scientific and its rivals as ideological. It typifies the inaugurating process involved in all sciences: science is marked by a particular relation to its objects, whether these are numbers (in mathematics), matter (in physics or chemistry), or individual and social behaviour (in the social sciences). A scientific approach is initiated when the evidence provided by observation, the senses, or consciousness is discounted from the status of knowledge. Science, in other words, *constructs* or produces its objects. Ideology, by contrast, takes pre-given objects, objects given to consciousness, as its foundation:

> The critical work performed by Marx upon the texts of English economists may be described as *productive* work in the literal sense of the word – a transformation of raw material culminating in a finished product. Marx produces knowledge . . . by working on a raw material which is not something 'real', revealing itself in phenomenological experience, but an ideological discourse upon the real – the discourse of political economy. We may therefore say that a science is the knowledge of the *ideology* from which it springs . . .; and it *is* this knowledge as a result of its having transformed the ideological material.
>
> (Descombes 1980, p. 121; cf. Althusser 1971, chapter 1)

Althusser does not consider science in empiricist terms. Thus historical materialism is not true or false in terms of what empirically occurs to verify or falsify it. It is scientific because of its *internal* operations, its mode of ordering statements and procedures to produce its investigative objects. Sciences are 'theoretical practices', forms of labour analogous to the production of commodities. Ideologies leave their given objects untransformed. Science, by contrast, is the labour of producing an object, transforming raw materials provided by consciousness or observation into the appropriate object of theoretical analysis. Ideology represents 'objects' according to pre-given class values and power relations; science produces an object that explains the real (i.e. class) basis of ideologies as well.

Althusser draws an analogy between scientific knowledge and economic production. Both are processes involving raw materials, procedures for transforming these materials, and products – commodities in one case, and scientific theories and propositions in the other. Both must be regarded as determinate, concrete, material *practices*. Instead of being construed as a creative, or purely intellectual, accomplishments, Althusser claimed that the sciences are made up of transformed, worked-upon materials, concepts, language, theories, and frameworks. These are not the results of cerebral, 'private', insight or intention, but are processes 'without a subject'. In order to understand science and its production and history, we need make no reference to the individuality or subjectivity of the scientist. The scientist is no more than an agent or single point within a far more complex network of connections making science possible. Historical materialism takes the data of classical economics as its raw materials, transforming them so that they make clear the implicit ideological interests they serve, and developing beyond them a scientific explanation for economic and historical relations.

Scientific theories have a dialectical relation to political practice. Althusser regards knowledge as *prior* to practice, guiding, informing, and directing it appropriately, or providing it with an 'intelligence' or purpose in its goals; and *after* practice, as a mode of reflection and criticism, a form of analysis and assessment. Theory is thus a precondition of *guided*, directed practice *and* a form of retrospective analysis or reflection:

> Philosophy (or theory) represents the people's struggle in theory. In return it helps people to distinguish in *theory*, and in all *ideas* (political, ethical, aesthetic, etc.) between true and false ideas. In principle, true ideas always serve the people; false ideas serve the enemies of the people.
>
> (Althusser 1971, p. 24)

Ideology always operates in the interests of the ruling class and against those of the working class; it obscures social relations, and their bases in class domination, presenting a false or distorted picture of them. It is a system (or several) for distorting the real relations of power.

On the basis of the opposition between science and ideology, Althusser claims that Marxism, in the context of history and class relations, and psychoanalysis, in the context of psychical and individual behaviour, are sciences which are distinct from the ideological functioning of liberal political theory, classical economics, and empirical psychology. These sciences construct and produce class relations and the unconscious as their respective objects of scientific investigation.

Ideology and the production of subjects

Althusser's account of the construction of subjects in and by ideology is found in his paper 'Ideology and ideological state apparatuses' (Althusser 1971). There he examines the ways in which a society ensures the production and reproduction of its necessary conditions of existence. It must reproduce both the material/technical components of production – raw materials, tools, machines, technological instruments – and the labour-power needed to work them. Every society must ensure a relative continuity through successive generations. It must be able to guarantee that a certain kind of subject is produced, with the appropriate skills and capacities needed for the production process.

His interest in the social construction of subjectivity distinguishes his work from economistic and humanist versions of Marxism. For the former, individuality is a determinate effect of economic processes; the socio-cultural and ideological systems are more or less predictable effects of economic relations. For the latter, the subject, the individual, is taken as natural, pre-given, and in no need of explanation. Althusser analyses the processes of socialization that instill attitudes, beliefs, and behaviour as desirable for individuals. Socially appropriate subjects need to acquire various technical and interpersonal skills, the internalization of various attitudes and a submission to dominant value-systems. It requires not just 'know-how', but also 'subjection to the ruling ideology'.

Subjects are not usually subjected to coercive or external forces (although coercive forms of repression do of course occur). Althusser calls these 'Repressive State Apparatuses' (RSAs), and includes military, police, legal, punitive systems under this category; more internalized, less coercive ideological systems – Ideological State Apparatuses (ISAs) – usually produce social subjectivity. The RSAs generally function by violence and force, while the ISAs function by ideas, values, ideologies which, if they rely on violence, are more insidious and less visible than the RSAs. Althusser includes religious, educational, familial, political, communicational, and cultural institutions under the category of ISAs. Between them, these two state apparatuses ensure that there is a harmony between the requirements of a socio-economic system and the subjects it thereby produces.

He distinguishes between ideology in general, and particular ideologies. Particular ideologies are always explicable in terms of specific class positions and the concrete histories of a particular social formation. They are determinate systems of value, rationalizations, for the interests of the dominant class. These ideologies vary widely over time and from culture to culture; they cannot be generally characterized except that they express the interests and values of the dominant class. They must be distinguished from ideology in general which, he claims, 'has no *history*' (Althusser 1971, p. 150).

In this sense, ideology is 'omnipresent' and 'transhistorical', necessary in all cultures. Each must ensure the reproduction of subjects appropriate to its ongoing maintenance and development. Even after a revolutionary upheaval of capitalism and its replacement by socialism, society would require socialized subjects. Each particular culture does this in specific ways which require concrete historical analysis. Althusser himself focuses on the concept of ideology in general. He advances two theses concerning it: 'Thesis I: Ideology represents the imaginary relationship of individuals to their real conditions of existence' (Althusser 1971, p. 153); and 'Thesis II: Ideology has a material existence' (Althusser 1971, p. 155). These will be separately discussed.

As an imaginary representation of 'men's' real social relations, Althusser's model of ideology differs from other accounts: ideology as collusion or as alienation. For him, ideology is not the creation of a ruling clique (capitalists, the media, multinational corporations, etc.) who somehow have access to the truth but can fool the majority into believing false representations. Ideology is thus *not* the result of a conspiracy or collusion of those in power. Nor is it a function of an alienation specific to capitalism that would somehow disappear 'after the revolution', like a veil being removed to reveal the real object underneath. Because ideology is eternal, it cannot be overthrown by liberation or enlightenment. It is a *necessary condition* of existence for all cultures that there be an inculcation of cultural values into its social agents. *Ideology is the system of representation by means of which we live in cultures as their products and agents*. This explains why there must be a naturalizing, neutralizing process by which what is culturally desirable is presented as given or obvious, unquestionable. The contents of consciousness are ideological in this sense; they are composed of what is considered self-evident, inevitable, and natural.

While *lived* as natural, ideological representations cannot be regarded as purely natural, inevitable, merely intellectual, conceptual, or mental processes. Ideas do not come from nowhere, but are produced in concrete material practices, which are themselves products of various institutions, including the ISAs: '[the subject's] . . . ideas are his *material actions inserted into material practices governed by material rituals which are themselves defined by material, ideological apparatus which derive the ideas of that subject*' (Althusser 1971, p. 158; emphasis in the original).

For any individual subject within bourgeois ideology, the individual presumes it thinks for itself, that ideas are the products of its own inspiration, experience, or consciousness. Believing ideas are freely chosen and thus capable of rejection, each will consider itself self-made. This is a subject that regards its social world and interrelations with others as peripheral to its subjectivity or identity. In opposition to this naturalistic self-conception, Althusser maintains that the subject is the (contradictory) product of institutions, practices, and value systems that produce and validate some ideas and denigrate or exclude others. What the subject believes are products of his or her own thoughts are in fact produced elsewhere (in the ISAs) and serve political and class interests in obscured but unconscious form.

If particular ideologies reproduce the values and interests of culturally specific social groups, ideology in general serves one overall function: its task is to constitute or construct individuals as subjects, transforming biological 'raw materials' into social subjects who function in the society in which they are born. *The function of ideology is the transformation or interpellation of biological individuals into social subjects*. On the one hand, ideology creates a pre-designated space into which the future subject will fit, a place in culture as so-and-so's child, a member of such-and-such a class, etc. On the other hand, ideology functions to concretize the future subject by submitting it to various ISAs (Althusser specifies the power of the family–school nexus in contemporary capitalism) so that this subject concretely fills the abstract position to which it was allocated.

To summarize Althusser's understanding of ideology and power relations, we can say:

1 Ideology is not simply a series of empirical events but a highly developed social structure.
2 As a social structure, it distorts and obscures, neutralizes and renders invisible various class or power relations.
3 It is a reflection of the values and interests of dominant social classes.
4 It is a system of ideas, practices, beliefs, and values that are presented as obvious or natural.
5 It is produced in and by various ISAs – the institutions, rituals, and practices comprising the socio-cultural life of any society. In this sense, it is material.
6 It produces social subjects by transforming biological raw materials into social subjects.
7 In this productive process, it obscures the processes by which the subject is constituted, enabling the subject to consider itself self-produced or naturally given.
8 Ideology functions by a recognition and a misrecognition: the subject recognizes/misrecognizes itself in the institutions and practices that constitute it and in the positions that have been pre-designated for it.
9 Ideology has an external existence in so far as all culture must socialize subjects; and
10 Only a scientific, objective analysis of social class and power relations can explain, if not undo, the effects of ideology.

Althusser and feminism

Althusser's work has had a powerful effect on feminist theory, particularly Marxist-feminism, for a number of reasons:

(a) He signals the relevance of Marx's work to feminist concerns, even those outside economic issues. He showed that Marxism was capable of explaining wide-ranging cultural, social, and personal issues. In particular, he situated a major object of feminist interrogation – the nuclear family – in a broader socio-economic framework, so that it could be regarded as *symptomatic* of an underlying economic structure while not being itself economically determined. The family could be analysed in terms of its structural role in producing or reproducing social values, including patriarchal and capitalist values. A whole range of institutions previously analysed discretely – the family, the educational system, the media, religion, and all the ISAs – do not function to benefit or enlighten individuals. They are agencies for the transmission of and inculcation into a series of values that are necessary for various social and power relations to continue. Although Althusser only indicates how the ISAs function, individually or in co-operation, many feminists have found his notions of the 'relative autonomy' of ISAs and yet their determination 'in the last instance' by economic relations extremely fruitful in detailing women's positions within culture. He demonstrated they can be analysed without resorting to empiricist, descriptive, or 'personalized' views of these institutions, or 'objective', 'scientific' analyses based on generalized statistical terms. He showed that the family, for example, could be analysed as a structure which both functions within a larger totality (the social whole) and itself provides a structured framework for smaller sub-elements (the individuals reared by and living within the family). It could be detailed in its analysis without sacrificing the broader perspectives of social and psychological effects.

(b) He showed that Marx's account of society was in principle compatible with a more individualistic, psychologically oriented account, such as that offered by Freudian/Lacanian psychoanalysis. In Lacan's reading of Freud (see next section) he saw an analogous project to his own rereading of Marx: the revelation of a generally repressed *scientific core* misrecognized by more conservative followers. He helped to establish a powerful trajectory also of concern to feminists: the bringing together of a 'macroscopic' social theory with a 'microscopic' theory of individuality; the linking of private and public spheres.[3]

(c) His anti-humanism, his critique of individualism and his adoption of a structural and scientific model of the individual and society have been utilized by many feminists to explain the operations of patriarchal ideology. For example, acts of discrimination against women could be regarded, using Althusser's notion of structural determination, not simply as random actions committed by aggressive individuals, but as an inbuilt feature of an entire social system. Women's oppression need not be seen as a conscious process of oppression perpetrated by a few (or many) misogynists because of their irrational hatred of women. It is the result of various social *structures* unconsciously reproduced by both men and women, independent of their personalities or choice. To blame social structures for supporting and requiring oppression does not absolve capitalists (or men) who benefit from it, even if they did not conspire to create it.

(d) Above all, his understanding of ideology as a systematically integrated co-operation of practices, social rules, ideals, and values as a system of representation of dominant values under the guise of nature or inevitability, provided many feminists with a conceptual framework for analysing patriarchal ideology (and, for some, its integration with bourgeois ideology).

Althusser's wide-ranging impact on feminist theory, both within and beyond France, helped to direct feminists away from humanist and liberal arguments about women's equality, towards a more structural account of oppression. A common tendency of the feminism of the 1960s, the categorization of men as villains and women as their victims, became transformed into examining the social system and its various institutions. Since his revitalization of Marx (although clearly he is not the only one responsible), feminists have had to confront the question of the interrelation of women's oppression and class domination – of patriarchy with capitalism – generating a number of debates about whether a thorough analysis of capitalism could explain the oppression of women, or whether capitalism is a distinct system overlaid on patriarchy. These debates are still strong preoccupations, and form a pivotal point around which Liberal, Radical and Marxist feminisms are distinguished (Kuhn and Wolpe 1978; Eisenstein 1979; Barrett 1980).[4]

However, partly as a result of his own published self-criticisms, partly as a result of his role in the events of May–June 1968,[5] and partly as a result of 'personal' events in his life,[6] his work has fallen into disrepute. Since the mid-1970s, his work has tended to be ignored by Marxists and Marxist-feminists. Yet in spite of being rarely mentioned by name, he remains an important, if unacknowledged, source of contemporary accounts of power. He is the implicit object of many critical and conforming accounts of subjectivity and power, as we will see in outlining Foucault's work.

I will return to Althusser (and the other male theorists discussed here) towards the end of this chapter.

LACAN, THE UNCONSCIOUS AND SEXUALITY

Jacques Lacan is arguably the most controversial and charismatic psychoanalyst since Freud himself. He presents a series of scrupulously detailed readings of Freud's texts, which have proved to be a major source of inspiration for Althusser's account of ideology, as well as for contemporary French feminisms – and, through their influences on Juliet Mitchell's text, *Psychoanalysis and Feminism* (1974), for Anglo-American and Australian feminist theory as well.

English-speaking feminists considered Freud to be the epitome of all that was misogynistic and irksome in patriarchal theories. This antipathy was understandable given that received interpretations of Freud's by-now highly popularized work were largely based on neo-Freudian revisionism. Anglo-American analysis was dominated by 'ego psychology', which Lacan described as a 'psychology of free enterprise'. Ego psychology aimed to strengthen the ego of the patient or analysand, and thereby to strengthen and reinforce the super-ego or conscience through an identification with the figure of the analyst. These versions of psychoanalysis remain fundamentally conservative. Taking the social context for granted, it functions to reintegrate individuals back into these given social contexts. By contrast, Lacan aimed to draw attention to what is most threatening and subversive in Freud's work, especially in his understanding of the unconscious, which is almost completely ignored in ego psychology.[7] Feminists in the 1960s, so Mitchell claimed, had either not read Freud's own texts but had substituted mediated, 'revised', or 'updated' versions or read Freud filtered through the lens of ego psychology. Those forms of theory and therapy criticized by feminists as forms of readapting women (and men) to their preordained social roles were not in fact those developed by Freud.

Feminists may also have ignored Freud's work because, during the 1960s and early 1970s, the question of *how to read a text*, how the politics of interpretation functions, had not been adequately raised. Freud's work can be read in a number of different ways – it can be taken literally/ empirically/ descriptively; it can be read symptomatically, i.e. in terms of what it does not say but must presume; or it could be read 'psychoanalytically', in terms of multiple meaning, ambiguity, indirection, displacement. Mitchell's feminist vindication of Freud consisted in arguing that his work should be read or interpreted other than as an apologist for patriarchal power relations. He does not advocate a patriarchal society; he merely describes it. Mitchell's reading of Freud and the rekindling of feminist interest in Freud's work were largely an effect of Lacan's idiosyncratic yet powerful lectures on and readings of Freud.

Lacan's reading displaces psychoanalysis from the medical moral, biological, and normative framework of ego psychology by placing it within the context of philosophical, literary, and semiotic theory. Viewed from this perspective, Freud's work can be seen as a challenge to the norms governing western knowledges since Descartes. With few exceptions, western reason presumes a unified, rational, and self-knowing or conscious subject. Literary analysis and criticism, and traditional (empiricist forms of) linguistics presume a transparent language that enables communication between subjects and truthful representations of reality. Lacan stresses the subversion of consciousness of the pre-given subject and the problematization of truth and knowledge effected in Freud's account of the 'split subject' – a subject irremediably divided between a consciousness which believes it is the centre of subjectivity, and an unconscious which continually subverts this claim through its existence outside and beyond the awareness of consciousness. Freud demonstrated that the subject is *incapable* of knowing or mastering itself. Placing psychoanalysis within the register of language and signification, he positions Freud's 'discovery' of the unconscious in the explanatory context of language. This is encapsulated in his most famous dictum: 'the unconscious is structured like a language'.

The symbolic and the imaginary

Freud's work rests on two interconnected cornerstones: an account of the unconscious as inaccessible and radically other to consciousness; and an account of the production of sexuality, especially of the psychical distinction between the sexes. These two elements are bound together by Freud's understanding of the Oedipus complex and castration threat.

Lacan regards both as effects of the subject's immersion in and alienation by language and signification. Subjectivity, sexuality, and the unconscious are functions of the material play of language, regulated by what Lacan calls the symbolic order. The symbolic is the domain constituting social law, language, and exchange – the domain of the social. This order is governed, according to Lacan, by the Other (with a capital 'O'). The Other is not a person, but a place, a locus from which language emanates and is given meaning. Misidentified with God, the Other is incarnated in human experience in the figure of the Symbolic Father – the authority that real fathers invoke to institute the law. This law is fundamental to patriarchy, even if it is not, as Lacan claims, a universal cultural condition: the law forbidding (mother–son) incest – the law of exogamy. The Symbolic Father is 'he' who is invoked as castrator when the boy transgresses this law. The symbolic order is the social field, as regulated by the law of the father. When the boy takes up a position within the symbolic, he internalizes this law as the unconscious in an act of primal repression.[8]

Sexuality and desire are not governed by a path of 'natural' development or regulated by instincts. They are structured and organized by the key signifier of the symbolic order – the phallus. For Lacan, the phallus is not an organ, nor the symbol of an organ, but a *signifier*. Signifiers are the material components of language composed of phonemes in speech, or graphemes in writing. The phallus is an element of language, a term within a system which circulates terms, exchanging them between subjects. The phallus is the threshold signifier to the symbolic order, and the crucial signifier in representing the distinction between the sexes. As a signifier, no one can possess, own, or control the phallus for it exists only by virtue of its circulation within the symbolic order. Each sex nevertheless confuses the signifier with a part or the whole of its body, and in doing so acquires a position as having (for the male) or being (for the female) the phallus. The male is construed as having the phallus because of his 'possession' of the penis. Because the female is construed as castrated, as 'lacking' this much-valued organ, she becomes the (passive) object of men's desires, a phallus for him. The woman *is* the phallus and the man *has* the phallus only through the desire of the other. The desire of the other is in fact the desire for meaning and significance to mark and structure the body, constituting it as social (patriarchal). Women's status as the object of the other's desire is a compensation for her perceived status as castrated. Only if women *lack* the phallus can men be considered to have it; and because of her castrated position, she aspires to *be* it.

Lacan's account of the symbolic is dependent on a (logically and chronologically) prior order, the imaginary. His earliest works were directed towards the question of the birth of the ego or sense of self in a phase that he called 'the mirror-stage'. His theory of the mirror-stage is an account of the primal separation of mother and child and the laying of the foundations of social and linguistic identity. It marks the child's entry into the order of images, the imaginary.

The mirror-stage begins at about six months of age. Until this time, the child has no concept of self and no boundaries separating it from the world or from others. The sense of separateness begins only when the ego is being formed. Lacan elaborates Freud's paper 'On narcissism: an introduction' (1914), where Freud outlines the genesis of the ego through the phenomenon of narcissism. Lacan argues that the ego is not the result of maturation or biology but is the specific effect of the child's recognition of the mother's absence, which designates a lack in the child's previously full relation to the world. This phase becomes apparent in the child's joyous recognition of its own image in a mirror. It not only recognizes this as an image of itself, it identifies with the image, internalizing it and investing it with libido. The ego is the result of the child's narcissistic investment in its corporeal image. The internalized image, or *imago*, provides the child with an illusory sense of wholeness or completeness and unity. It is illusory in so far as the child *experiences* a sense of fragmentation and disunity, which Lacan describes as the 'body-in-bits-and-pieces', the uncoordinated, developmentally incomplete organization of its sensory and motor capacities.

Lacan regards the mirror-stage and the imaginary order as sexually undifferentiated, analogous to Freud's account of pre-Oedipal sexuality. Masculinity and femininity and their bases in the anatomical differences between the sexes are not yet understood by the child. The child's acquisition of a determinate sexual identity occurs only with its entry into the symbolic with the Oedipus complex. The mirror-stage introduces the child to an identity and an idea of its separateness from the world of others. It provides a border or boundary defined by the child's skin. But the identity and unity the mirror-stage and the imaginary offer are precarious, for the identity is modelled only on the other, an ego as a function of the alter-ego. If identity is first posed for the child at the time of the mirror-stage, it is not yet stable or definitive. If the self is modelled on the other, it is necessarily interpersonal, based on identifications with others. It is thus, Lacan stresses, a paranoid and alienated construct. The ego is always an other, always split between an illusory stability and unity and a recognition of the power of the other in defining the self.

The imaginary mother–child dyad needs to be mediated for the child to gain a place in the symbolic. This occurs through the intervention of a third party, one outside the imaginary identifications binding the ego to the other. This third term is the Symbolic Father, representing the law prohibiting incest. It ensures that the child gives up the mother to enter the social world of law, language, and exchange. Only at this point does the distinction between the sexes become evident to the child.

Like Freud, Lacan concentrates largely on the boy's symbolic development. The apparently complementary processes in the girl remain obscure. In accepting the father's law, exemplified by the threat of castration, the boy identifies with paternal authority and represses his desire for his mother. In identifying with the father, he establishes a super-ego. With the creation of the super-ego and the (primal) repression of the desire for the mother, the unconscious is formed. He becomes a subject, an 'I' able to function within a (patriarchal) symbolic system.

The girl must also abandon her mother and thus her primary, homosexual attachment, transferring her object of desire from the mother to the phallus, and thus to the father whom she presumes 'has' it. In acknowledging her castration, she desires the phallus she lacks. In this case, Lacan is explicit in asserting that the phallus is *not* a biological organ, but access to the signifier of desire and authority. She comes to acquire the traits associated with femininity under patriarchy – passivity, seductiveness, the renunciation of active, clitoral sexuality and its transformation into passive, vaginal sexuality. She is not constructed, as is the boy, as an active, desiring subject but as a passive, desired object (of the other's desire). *She is positioned in the symbolic order as a spoken exchanged object, not as a subject who is a partner within exchange*.

The unconscious structured like a language

In spite of his claim to be merely deciphering and interpreting Freud, Lacan's reading is a considerable departure from Freud. Lacan claims that if Freud had been aware of linguistics, and especially the work of Ferdinand de Saussure,[9] he could have seen the unconscious in linguistic/semiotic form. The contents and processes of the unconscious can be very precisely charted using the distinctions between signifier and signified, and various rhetorical figures, particulary metaphor and metonymy.[10]

Although we can have no direct access to the unconscious because of repression, nevertheless the unconscious creates compromises through which it can express itself in consciousness. These symptoms – dreams, slips, jokes, accidents, neurotic symptoms – are inexplicable in conscious terms, but can be meaningfully deciphered using the postulate of the unconscious as their 'true' source. The unconscious is an explanatory hypothesis needed to understand those conscious phenomena that consciousness is incapable of explaining.

Freud conceived of the unconscious as a storehouse of wishes, images, fantasies that are unacceptable to consciousness. Its nucleus consists in infantile, usually Oedipal, incestual wishes, sexual impulses directed toward the mother and/or hostile aggressive impulses towards the father. The repression of these Oedipal wishes is the object of *primal* repression, which creates a permanent barrier dividing the unconscious from consciousness, being itself impervious to conscious scrutiny. With primal repression, there is also a retrospective repression of the memory of pre-Oedipal wishes related to the repressed Oedipal wish. As their repository, the unconscious is a permanent storage system governed by its own rules and procedures. In his paper 'The unconscious' (1914), Freud cites four defining features of the unconscious:

(a) It is governed by primary processes (i.e. condensation and displacement). These function according to the pleasure principle, which seeks immediate satisfaction for wishes, independent of their viability in reality. Displacement disguises unconscious wishes by transferring their intensity and meaning to relatively innocuous preconscious ideas, which can thus function as their distorted representatives. Condensation also helps disguise forbidden wishes by representing several unconscious contents through a single preconscious image, effecting great compression using an *economy of omission*. By means of distorting and disguising functions, the forbidden unconscious wish gains some satisfaction. The primary processes have a freely mobile energy or libidinal cathexis, which can be directed to more socially useful outlets when regulated by the secondary processes. These constitute those preconscious and conscious activities dominated by the reality principle. If primary processes aim for immediate discharge and satisfaction of libidinal drives, secondary processes aim to inhibit these energies, deferring their satisfaction for more (socially) approved contexts, using their energies for social production.

(b) The unconscious is thus dominated by the pleasure principle, while the preconscious and consciousness are governed by the reality principle. Indeed, the unconscious is unable to distinguish between fantasy and reality. Its contents and wishes carry no index of their origin. They may never have existed in reality, but because the unconscious is incapable of separating actual from wished-for events, it also contains ideas only fantasized and never experienced in actuality.

(c) There are *no* relations between unconscious contents. Each wish or idea exists side-by-side with others, but is incapable of being modified by them. There are thus no logical or conceptual connections: there is no form of contradiction, no negation, no degrees of doubt or certainty, no probabilities. All these are preconscious forms of qualification or evaluation. In the unconscious, there are only contents, charged with greater or lesser intensity or energy. The absence of an organizing relation between unconscious contents may help explain the ingenious devices (punning, multiple meaning, ambiguity, anagrams, metaphors, etc.) the unconscious wish must utilize in order to gain conscious expression.

(d) The unconscious is non-temporal. Memories do not fade with the passage of time, but retain the force they had at the time they were repressed. Nor is there any chronological organization of unconscious contents, they are not organized in terms of earlier or later. It is for this reason that the unconscious remains largely infantile even if these wishes are inappropriate or impossible in adult life (e.g. where the desired object is dead).

Given these characteristics, the unconscious functions entirely differently to consciousness. Consciousness is hostile and alien to these unconscious wishes; it resists their aim of conscious expression. It is for this reason that the wish requires distortion and disguise to enter the conscious system. Lacan attempts to integrate these Freudian insights into a linguistic framework, distinguishing the unconscious discourse from the discourses of consciousness.

For Lacan, while consciousness is articulated by means of grammatical and syntactical organization, the unconscious is a system which does not obey these rules. Through repression, signs are reduced to signifiers – i.e. they are quite literally robbed of their meaning, detached from their signifieds. *Repression is thus the robbery of meaning; it is the severing of the significance of the sign*. Freud himself described repression as a failure of translation. Lacan expresses this failure as the splitting of a signifier from signified. The unconscious is thus unable to speak in its own voice and vocabulary. It can only speak through and by means of conscious discourse. It is not the smooth, continuous unfolding of meaning; rather, it is expressed as silence, verbal slips, stutterings, gaps, and puns.

Freudian primary processes, condensation and displacement, are explained by Lacan using Roman Jakobson's distinction between metaphor and metonymy. For Lacan, condensation is explicable as metaphor. It consists in utilizing terms related by similarity so that one is capable of taking the place of the other, the first, now latent, signifier delegating its meaning to the second. Displacement can be regarded on the model of metonymy, which consists in utilizing terms related by contiguity, one transferring its intensity to the other. As a movement from one contiguous signifier to the next, metonymy is the model for the movement of *desire*. (Desire is the substitutability of one object for another, the capacity to displace the (lost) original object of desire – the mother, the mother's breast – by a potentially infinite chain of alternatives.) Metaphor and metonymy enable the unconscious to be mapped using only the discourses of the analysand. It is for this reason psychoanalysis has been described as 'the talking cure': its methods, objectives, and procedures are all features of language.

Lacan and feminism

Lacan's work has generated a good deal of controversy in feminist circles. Many French feminists remain unswervingly loyal to his work, arguing that he presents one of the most astute analyses of patriarchal social requirements, and one of the most stringent criticisms of mainstream, logocentric, and phallocentric knowledges (e.g. Clement, Lemaire, Kristeva). Others, while taking his work seriously, remain highly critical, seeing it as a less obvious but equally insidious version of Freud's phallocentrism. This range of attitudes is also reflected in Anglo-American feminisms. Clearly in the limited space available here, this intricate debate cannot be adequately discussed, let alone resolved. Nevertheless, some of the ways in which his work continues to be relevant to contemporary feminist theory can be outlined in point form. More critical remarks will be developed at the end of this chapter.

(a) Lacan elaborates the major role that language, metaphor, metonymy, and the play of signification exert in the formation of the unconscious and in the principles governing its interpretation. The unconscious, desire, and sexuality are not effects of nature, biology, or some human essence, but are consequences of the human subject's constitution in and by the symbolic and the imaginary. His reformulation of Freud in terms of language has made psychoanalysis more palatable for feminists. It is no longer a biological account of women's lack or castration, but a socio-historical analysis of the transmission of meanings and values across generations.

(b) He 'decentres' dominant notions of human subjectivity unquestioningly assumed by philosophy, sociology, psychology, and linguistics. He challenges the presumption of an autonomous, ready-made subject by elaborating his view that the subject is socio-linguistically constituted. The subject is the end-result of processes that constitute it as an ego or unified self (the imaginary); and as a social and speaking subject (the symbolic). The subject is constructed by its necessary dependence on others and on the Other. This is significant for feminist theory for, on the one hand, it provides a critique of commitments to a pre-given or pre-social subject, common to both patriarchal and feminist theory; while on the other, it explains the construction of subjects as masculine/phallic or feminine/castrated, and their scope for change.

Not providing a socio-economic account of patriarchy, Lacan's work has been used to provide an account of the psychic components of social subjectivity.

(c) His account of sexuality indicates the crucial role language plays in the construction of personal identity. The (male or female) subject is produced as masculine or feminine by constituting and then prohibiting the desired (primal) object. Social needs are thus met because of the inscription of the body with meanings, encoding it with significances and values of the parents. Masculine and feminine identities are not 'natural' but products of a *rift* in the natural order, a gap into which language insinuates itself. As the key signifier of the symbolic, the phallus marks male and female bodies and sexualities in different ways. This has important implications for feminist theory: for one thing, it signals the end of universalist, or 'humanist', sexually neutral models of subjectivity. Such models can be seen as phallocentric, exerting a power of representation and authority to male models. While a number of feminists have levelled this charge at Lacan himself (Irigaray 1985b, 1985c; Gallop 1982), his work is still useful for making clear that sexuality is not incidental or contingent, but necessary for the constitution of subjectivity.

(d) His grounding of psychoanalysis within a history of thought in which Freud is a moment of radical subversion, effects a serious challenge to the presumptions and framework of received knowledges. Freud showed that the knowing subject cannot be identical to the object known. As subjects, we are not transparent to our own introspective gaze. Our ideals of a direct access to reality, a clear, solid foundation for knowledges and objectivity, are questioned by Lacan's positioning the unconscious in the context of knowledge. It has enabled a number of feminists, even those critical of Lacan, to question not only the repressions and evasions exercised by individuals but also those effected by knowledges, texts or discourses (e.g. Irigaray 1985b; Le Doeuff 1980).

(e) His emphasis on the question of language, law, and symbolic exchange as founding structures of society signals key points of investment by patriarchal culture, which feminists need to understand in order to be able to subvert. This may help explain why there is so much discussion in recent feminist literature on infantile development, the mother–child relation, the imaginary order, and their unacknowledged roles in the operation of culture.

Largely as a result of the interpretive techniques developed by Lacan and Althusser, Freud and Marx became the ambivalent sources for current feminist theory. Lacan is a difficult and controversial writer, yet his audacious style and highly critical contextualizing of Freud's work where it can function at its most subversive, reinvigorated psychoanalysis, making it the major source for radical accounts of subjectivity.

FOUCAULT'S ANALYTICS OF POWER

Foucault's prolific works were written before and after the impact of Althusser and Lacan. He came to prominence, however, in the period after Althusser and Lacan were subjected to political criticisms. They seemed to fill a void left by the absence of self-styled intellectual masters, given his awareness of and hostility towards the kinds of Freudo-Marxist project with which both were involved.

His writings can be arbitrarily but conveniently divided into two phases, marked by the year 1970, and the publication of his inaugural address at the College de France, 'The discourse on language' (1972). His earlier works rely on what he calls an 'archaeological' method, while the later texts, following Nietzsche, are described as 'genealogical'. While I will focus mainly on his later works, it may be worth briefly describing the differences between these two methods, not only in relation to his conception of power, but also to help locate his work relative to Althusser and Lacan. This schematic comparison and contrast may also help clarify his move away from more traditional notions of power towards his own productive concept. It will become clear that while his work is indirectly relevant to feminism, his later works are more directly influenced by and influential on feminist theory, gay liberation politics and their impact on day-to-day and interpersonal politics.

The archaeological method

Even in his first archaeological text, *Madness and Civilization* ([1961] 1973) there is a marked difference between Foucault's approach and that of a more conventional historical and political analyst. This text highlights a continuing object of investigation in all his work: the concept of reason, so highly esteemed in science and philosophy, that is based on the exclusion of unreason, the passions, the body, concepts of power, etc. His archaeological texts investigate a history of unreason, silenced in its own language and the creation of unreason as the object of investigation for the newly formed 'sciences of man' out of which psychiatry, psychology, criminology, and all the modern social sciences are born. Foucault claims that the conditions for the emergence of psychiatry and psychology as sciences were based on the silencing, exclusion and containment of madness by reason:

> The language of psychiatry, which is a monologue of reason *about* madness, could be established only on the basis of such a silence.

> I have not tried to write a history of that language, but rather the archaeology of that silence.
>
> (Foucault [1961] 1973, pp. xii–xiii)

His objects of investigation are not fixed and established bodies of knowledge, but the rules of formation and the conditions of possibility of specific discourses, world-views, or *epistemes:* the discourses of psychology, psychiatry, medicine, models of representation – peripheral knowledges when compared to the natural sciences.

Madness and Civilization inaugurated a new and highly eclectic method – that of the archive, the forgotten document, the seemingly trivial document and record surrounding and traversing social practices, information considered theoretically unimportant. The information of documents, reports, judicial inquiries, files, plans that were previously seen as beneath the 'dignity' of scientific and philosophical knowledges. He also showed that there were histories waiting to be written on largely neglected areas of political concern. He showed that not only was it possible to write a history of madness, of the gaze (*The Birth of the Clinic*, [1963] 1975), of true knowledges (*The Order of Things*, [1966] 1970), of punitive practices (*Discipline and Punish*, [1975] 1979), of procedures of putting sex into discourse (*The History of Sexuality*, 1978), but also that these studies were necessary for understanding the operations of power. While trivial from the point of view of macroscopic theories of economic subordination, objects such as madness, prisons, desire, sexuality, asylums, poor houses, hospitals, institutions, which were forgotten by Marxism, were given a prominent place in analysing power in Foucault's work. Foucault himself claims that although he does not appear, in the archaeological texts, to be analysing power, in retrospect, he sees all of his work contributing to outlining the intricate and highly variable forms of power in discursive and non-discursive practices.

In schematic form, some of the main features of the archaeological method can be outlined:

(a) Archaeology differs from traditional forms of history, political theory and philosophy in its objects of investigation. Instead of dealing with the 'rigorous' science, such as physics, cosmology, mathematics – 'pure' sciences revealing a progressive movement towards 'truth' – Foucault is interested in the less certain, more conjectural 'sciences of man'. He focuses on knowledges that are still more or less in their infancy, and have direct or indirect relations to social rules and powers, 'non-formal' knowledges that are nevertheless organized according to rules of formation and evaluated by their own criteria.[11]

(b) Archaeology does not seek out lineages, continuous lines of development and progress in knowledges, but the spaces in between interlocking domains. For example, instead of looking at the connections between eighteenth- and nineteenth-century biology, Foucault sought epistemic connections between ninteenth-century biology and its contemporary knowledges, linguistics, economics, philology. He sought lateral connection, oblique influences and relations, rather than causal or chronological connections.

(c) While more traditional researches refer to the individuality of the scientist, beliefs, practices, training, context, in seeking an explanation of the formation of knowledges – at what the knowing subject means or intends, or at influences outside the subject's awareness, archaeology avoids any explanation of science which refers to the subject. He attempts to analyse the rules of formation of knowledges, rules defining the objects, techniques and processes of validation in science – science as a complex activity. Like Althusser, he maintains that science is a process 'without a subject'.

(d) Archaeology avoids traditional explanations developed in the history and philosophy of science – such as those based on concepts of causality, development, continuity, discontinuity, and the founding subject. Foucault questions their value as explanatory tools; while they may be relevant at particular times and contexts, they are not *a priori* explanations. The rules of formation of knowledges are specific, not generalizable.

(e) Instead of relying on 'Great Texts', 'grand discoveries', or 'master thinkers' for his arguments, he turns to archives, the texts of minor officials usually neglected in political theory.

The archaeological period in his work uses and attempts to explain an underlying concept of power that was to be clearly differentiated from his later, genealogical concerns. But before turning to the genealogical texts, we will examine the differences between his project(s) and those of either Marxism or psychoanalysis, as represented by Althusser and Lacan.

Foucault, Althusser, and Lacan

In his paper 'Truth and power' (in Morris and Patton 1978), Foucault makes a number of critical objections to Marxism as theory and practice, which he augments in *The History of Sexuality* (1978). He argues that Marxism distinguishes between a unified, homogeneous economic level and a heterogeneous state and its organs, which function to represent and disseminate power relations accrued economically. He claims that Marxists have ignored the detailed operations of power by focusing largely on its global forms. As a result, major manifestations of power, such as penal or psychiatric incarceration, are either ignored or politically minimalized: 'As long as one posed the question of power while subordinating it to the economic instance and systems of interest this ensures, one is led to regard these problems as of little importance' (Foucault, 'Truth and power', in Morris and Patton 1978, p. 34). For Foucault, power does not simply take on a massive form: even if it did, it would still require minute or micropolitical channels to disseminate it throughout the whole of the social body. Marxism's understanding of non-economic power is questioned because it is reduced to being representations of central or macropolitical power. The non-economic ultimately functions in the interests of the economic. Moreover, Foucault objects to the conception of ideology developed in Marxism, and especially in Althusser's version: ideology as a distorted representation of 'men's' real relations. While Althusser is not mentioned by name, his work seems the implicit target of Foucault's arguments. Against the Althusserian account, Foucault raises three concerns:

(a) Ideology is defined in opposition to science and truth, a form of distortion or falsehood. It is politically problematic for Althusser precisely because of its lack of truth. This enables Marxism, Foucault suggests, to consider truth and knowledge as somehow outside of power, value-free or objective, and thus to focus only on the power relations manifested in ideology. Foucault, by contrast, argues that power is even more effective when it uses truth and knowledge than when it relies on ideology or falsehood. The science/ideology distinction enables knowledge and truth to evade political scrutiny.
(b) The theory of ideology necessarily refers to a subject who is both its 'object' and its bearer. While this subject is not necessarily considered natural or pre-given, nevertheless, given the tenacity and inevitability of ideology, the category of the subject is made permanent and eternal. It is simply the details of this subject that are considered historically variable instead of its very form.
(c) The operation of ideology is secondary to an economic order. Ideology is a reflection or superstructural effect of a primary, determining level. Instead of ideology – a term he rarely, if ever, uses – Foucault looks at institutions, bodies of knowledge that are both scientific and/or practical, without one being privileged over the other by being regarded as outside of power.

Foucault opposes a commitment common to Marxism and psychoanalysis, that power exists as a form of inhibition or repression. Both rely on a negative concept of power which prevents the expression of impulses, wishes, libidinal energies, political opposition, class consciousness, and so on. Power here is a form of suppression, preventing undesired effects. For Foucault, however, repression or inhibition is, at best, a 'terminal' form of power, power in its frustrated form rather than in its typical functioning. He regards power as a productive, creative force. Power creates knowledges, methods, and techniques, and this, for Foucault, is its major significance. To pose power in terms of the state and its repressive and ideological functions, or in terms of the Oedipus complex and the Symbolic Father's prohibitive power over the son is to pose power in terms of sovereignty or law. It is to understand power juridically, in forms that are both anachronistic and reductionist. Power is not so much a law that says no as a proliferative, productive series of forces that creates new objects, properties, subjectivities, and knowledges.

In *The History of Sexuality*, Foucault questions three major features of psychoanalysis. First, he claims that as a self-styled 'talking cure', psychoanalysis is one of the major forms of current knowledge advocating and institutionalizing the techniques of *confession*. The analysand is encouraged to confess, to elaborate verbally all the details of his or her psychic and sexual life. Foucault regards confession as one of the major procedures of modern punitive powers by which the individual is tied to processes of normalization. He regards it as perhaps the most effective form of gaining information about the individual subjects. It is a relay between the formation of knowledges and the operation of power over the bodies and lives of individuals. Psychoanalysis has developed the ancient technique of extracting confessions into a fine art. It binds the subject's desire into a desire to speak, to tell all, as if confession could in itself be liberating. Liberation and discourse are tied together by psychoanalysis in ways which obscure the relations between confession and power.

Second, in conjunction with Deleuze and Guattari (1972), Foucault objects to the *a priori*, universal explanatory grid of Oedipal relations that psychoanalysis imposes as a general mode of explanation. This Oedipal grid does not so much explain individual psychologies as impose on them a socializing and normalizing function. In explaining individual development, sexuality, neurotic symptoms, and the kernel of the unconscious in terms of Oedipalization, psychoanalysis reduces the concrete specificities and positive actions of individuals to a form of re-enacement of an infantile drama. Like Marxism's use of macrolithic state power evidenced everywhere in the social, psychoanalysis explains psychical structures in terms of a monolithic power of refusal, the father's castrating Oedipal prohibitions. And like Marxism's indifference to the more 'marginalized' sites of power (asylums, prisons, hospitals, etc.), psychoanalysis thus ignores phenomena that are not reducible to or explicable by an Oedipal (or economic) model.

Third, as the analysis of the transference relations between analysand and analyst, psychoanalysis is unable to examine the power invested in the therapeutic and training processes. The relation between analyst and analysand, and between master and disciple is uncritically assumed.[12]

In other words, Marxism and psychoanalysis, or their offspring, Freudo-Marxism, are blind to their own investments in power. Marxists remain blind to their 'will to power', their desire to represent an ideologically motivated, more or less ignorant mass whom they claim to represent or lead in the coming revolution (cf. Foucault, 'Powers and Strategies', in Morris and Patton 1978). While focusing on the patient's desire, psychoanalysis too is unable to investigate the analyst's desire for power and knowledge.

In spite of his wide-ranging objections to Marxism and psychoanalysis, Foucault cannot be regarded as anti-Marxist or anti-Freudian. Neither a Marxist nor a Freudian, his works can be considered 'post-Marxist' and 'post-Freudian', acknowledging their profound effects on concepts of power, and attempting to supersede them.

The genealogical method

Discipline and Punish ([1975] 1979) and *The History of Sexuality* (1978) best represent Foucault's genealogical method. These texts are foreshadowed in the transitional text between the archaeological and genealogical writings, 'The discourse on languge' (in Foucault 1972). To briefly characterize this 'new' method, we can say the following.

(a) Although Foucault claims that the archaeological texts were analyses of the relations between power and knowledge (even without his being aware of it at the time), they relied on a concept of power that was primarily negative, inhibitive or repressive:

> Now I believe that this is a wholly negative, narrow and skeletal conception of power . . . If power was anything but repressive, if it never did anything but say no, do you really believe that we should manage to obey it? What gives power its hold, what makes it accepted, is quite simply the fact that it does not weigh like a force which says no, but that it runs through, it produces things, it induces pleasure, it forms knowledge, it produces discourse; it must be considered as a productive network which runs through the entire social body much more than as a negative instance whose function is repression.
>
> (Foucault, in Morris and Patton 1978, p. 36)

While archaeology remains tied to a silencing, forbidding power, genealogy sees power as a productive network of forces that make connections, produce objects for knowledge, and utilize the effects of knowledges:

> The case of penalty convinced me that the problem (of power) was not so much to be seen in terms of right, law, but in terms of tactics and strategies and it was this substitution of a technical and

strategic grid for a juridical and negative grid that I tried to set up in *Discipline and Punish*.

(Foucault, 'Interview with Lucette Finas', in Morris and Patton 1978, p. 68)

(b) Along with a change in his conceptions of power also came a shift of emphasis in Foucault's objects of investigation. He became more interested in the ways in which technologies of power operate on human bodies to shape, organize, and inscribe them in particular ways. This later emphasis on bodies seems to be directed against Althusser's account of ideology as a system of inculcated ideas and beliefs. Foucault turns to the analysis of the inscription of power on bodies, without recourse to the mediation of mental or conceptual systems.

(c) Foucault concentrates more on those techniques, institutions, and practices where power is invested in his later texts than in the earlier ones. For example, his focus on disciplinary practices, procedures, and institutions in *Discipline and Punish* signals a more openly pragmatic and political concern than his earlier concentration on the coherence of a corpus of texts, truths, or statements. Not that the latter was conceived outside of power; it is just that Foucault's emphasis has significantly shifted.

(d) Genealogy is more concerned with current, local, regional, and marginal struggles than archaeology. The later works are more 'histories of the present', histories of present sites of struggle than the earlier texts. For example, one of his motivations for writing *Discipline and Punish* was his involvement in the prisoner's movement (Groupe d'Information sur les Prisons) in 1971–3. It now seems clear that *The History of Sexuality* was at least partially a response to sexual liberation movements – the women's movement and gay politics.

Foucault's conception of power

Given his critique of the investments of power and knowledge, it is hardly surprising that Foucault does not claim the status of truth or science for his own work. He considers them 'useful fictions', that is, tools or tactics of challenge. They are oppositional discourses to those which aspire to truth, authority, and power. Thus he does not present a *theory* of power, but develops a series of methods for examining the truth-effects of knowledges. Each of his books is an examination of quite specific forms of knowledge within their historical and geographic context. Instead of a theory of power, he describes his work as an 'analytics of power' – a series of methods that make no claim to lasting or eternal value (as does truth) but which may be useful at some times, and within some struggles, and is eventually disposable once strategic goals have been accomplished.

While he does not consider power a uniform and homogeneous thing and does not develop a theory of power, we can nevertheless extract several methodological theses from his work to help us examine power relations. He generally begins by spelling out what power is *not* – that is, in what ways his own view differs from other positions. He argues that:

(I) Power is not a thing, an entity, property, quality, or commodity. This proposition challenges most prevalent views of power shared by Marxism and Liberalism. Both see power as something that some individuals, groups, or classes have, and wield over others who lack it. Liberal political theorists (Hobbes, Locke, Mill) maintain that power is a social and legal right, established through social contract whereby individuals agree to give up some of their personal power for the good of society as a whole. All are able to equally participate in social organization. Marxism also sees power as a property or right that one class exercises over another in order to keep it subjugated. Many versions of feminism too regard (patriarchal) power as something men, as individuals or as a group, exercise over women; in a different social organization, power would be shared equally. Liberal, Radical, and Marxist-feminists shared the view that power is something men have and that women lack. It is often equated with physical strength, or with decision-making capacities. For Foucault, however, power is not possessed, given, seized, captured, relinquished, or exchanged. Rather, it is *exercised*. It exists only in actions. It is a complex set of ever-changing relations of force – a moveable substratum upon which the economy, mode of production, modes of governing and decision-making, forms of knowledge, etc., are conditioned:

> Power is not possessed, it acts in the very body and over the whole surface of the social field according to a system of relays, modes of connection, transmission, distribution, etc. Power acts through the smallest elements: the family, sexual relations but also: residential relations, neighbourhoods, etc. As far as we go in the social network we always find power as something that 'runs' through it, that acts, that brings about effects. It becomes effective or not, that is, power is always a definite form of momentary and constantly reproduced encounters among a definite number of individuals. Power is thus not possessed because it is 'in play'; because it risks itself.
>
> (Foucault, 'Interview with Lucette Finas', in Morris and Patton 1978, p. 60)

He refuses to equate power with a social structure (such as patriarchy), or with social institutions and practices (such as the family or the practices of socialization exercised by it), or with interpersonal force or strength (as in heterosexual sexual and aggressive relations). Rather, power is both (a) historical systems aligned across structures, institutions, rituals, practices, and individual lives, bringing them together in some contexts, and dividing them in others – a 'substratum' of force relations; and (b) the particular use of the products of these alignments (e.g. knowledges, practices) to interrogate, regulate, supervise, observe, train, harness, and confine the behaviours and subjectivities of individuals and groups.

He does not deny feminist concepts of women as an oppressed group, nor the Marxist postulate of the oppression of the working class. He demassifies, localizes, the categories 'women' and 'the working class', so that these concepts are no longer universal categories. They are localized, made specific, placed in a socio-historical and discursive framework. Their oppression is not explained by general structures of oppression – patriarchy and/or capitalism – but in terms of a tactical utilization of the bodies and speech of women and/or the working class for the extraction of knowledges, labour, service, and so on; and a non-complete, non-hegemonic domination – a domination that, by its nature, breeds resistance, a domination never succeeding in total subjugation.

(II) Power is not centralized, global, or uniform. It is not massified into a core, such as the economy, the state, the power of elites, the Oedipal structure, the family, etc.; nor is it re-presented, filtered down through subsidiary agencies, such as state apparatuses. Power is more like a continually changing grid that runs unevenly through the whole of society, creating points of intensity as well as sites of resistance. Power has no single source (the law of the father, the accumulation of wealth), but is based on a large number of localities which are homogeneously linked, which do not necessarily serve the same function and cannot be regarded as representatives of one another (the father as head of the household exerts a different authority to that of the head of state; the former does not reflect the latter). The family, for example, cannot be regarded simply as a microcosm of state power, reflecting the interests of the macrocosm. It exerts specific powers of its own, which may or may not be allied with the various powers exercised by the state. Power does not guarantee a mode of production or reproduction, as Althusser claims. It functions through and across a mode of production, making it possible and utilizing its effects. It runs through ideologies, truths, discourses, institutions, practices without being equated with any one of them.

Foucault suggests three different orders of events invested with power relations:

(a) the orders of discourse, including the texts of 'High Theory', the notes and memos of small-time officials, diaries, court records, documents, or archives which, through their roles in establishing practices and institutions, are part of a regime of power;

(b) the orders of non-discursive practice, including systems of education, punishment, confession, etc., which, while enmeshed with discourses, are material processes concretely marking human bodies; and

(c) the *effects* of these discursive and non-discursive events; the creation of docile, observable, quantifiable, or resistant bodies, groups, populations.

At the level of discourses, power utilizes strategies for the production of truth and the disqualification of non-truth (see 'The discourse on language', in Foucault 1972); at the level of non-discursive events, power establishes technologies that direct themselves towards the bodies and behaviours of subjects; and at the level of *effects*, power establishes programmes, forms of extraction of knowledge and information that help constitute, at particular moments in time, overarching, more global systems.

(III) Because power runs *unevenly* through social formations, no event can be regarded as outside its grid. Knowledges, truths, and sciences are as much instruments and effects of power as are ideologies, propaganda or falsehood. Power is not exterior to knowledge or to social relations, but is their condition of existence. Because power can be conceptualized as an ever-changing grid with specific points of intensity, sites of greatest force, it can also be seen as a grid that necessarily *generates* points of resistance. This implies that knowledges, methods, procedures which at one time support forms of power, at another time or in a different context, can act as sites of resistance, struggle and change.

His approach questions the advisability of conceptualizing political struggle and change on the model of unified, organized mass action. Marxism, he suggests, maintains the necessity of an organized mass movement of workers in overthrowing capitalism. Many forms of feminism are also committed to an organization of the mass of women united together by a common oppression and a common struggle against patriarchy. Foucault makes it clear that even if such mass movements were possible, they may not be the most effective forms for change. Smaller groups of militants, well-positioned and strategically armed, may well be more successful in effecting change than large-scale mass organizations. These groups may align themselves over issues they share in common, but at other times, may develop hostile, or intimate, relations. In opposition to seeing two megalithic groups – women/men; workers/capitalists – Foucault suggests a model based on guerilla warfare; a plural, multiple and multidimensional series of encounters of non-aligned groups, each struggling for self-determination.

(IV) Power cannot be conceptualized as a global phenomenon, as a macroscopic form of domination. While acknowledging a distinction between global and local forms of domination, Foucault claims that power is not imposed by the global on the local; it comes 'from below', from the (temporary) alignments of local forms of power. The local and the global mutually condition each other. No global form can gain a grip on bodies and subjects, on the behaviour of individuals and groups, without the support of local forms – the 'fine links' running through a social order. No local form of power can sustain itself for any length of time without the broader context of global, overarching alignments (Foucault 1980a, p. 94).

(V) Foucault claims that although power has intentions – i.e. aims, goals, objectives – it can never be entirely successful in achieving them. The very forms that power takes create the possibility of resistances. Power and resistance need each other. While one can never escape the grids of power, it is not necessary to always remain in a position of support to power: 'Power relationships . . . depend on a multiplicity of points of resistance: these play the role of adversary, target, support or handle in power relations. The points of resistance are present everywhere in the power network' (Foucault 1980a, p. 95). Power is both intentional and non-subjective. It has specific aims and objects which, however, cannot be reduced to or explained by the aims and aspiration, conscious or unconscious wishes of its agents. The strategic deployment and uneven distribution of power ensure that resistance is its condition of existence.

Foucault and feminism

In the year before his death, Foucault's interests shifted again. In *The Use of Pleasure* ([1984] 1985) and *The Care of the Self* (1986) he is more concerned with the question of the ways in which subjects develop modes of (ethical) self-production and self-surveillance through the regulation of their sexualities. Once again, he claims that this interest has always been there in his works, even if not formulated in these terms. It is indeed true that he is interested in the genealogical texts with the question of the formation of (determinate types of) subjectivity through the functioning of regimes of knowledge–power. However, his concern with ethical self-regulation, the ways in which the self plans its own good health, well-being, and social position through various ethical procedures, is certainly a major shift in orientation. Yet it makes even more clear the fact that his work is highly suggestive for feminist theory. The problem at present seems to be that few feminists analyse or criticize his work as feminists. In spite of Lacan's obscure and difficult style, and politically problematic relation to phallocentrism, much more time and attention has been devoted to his work than Foucault's. Nevertheless there are a number of issues that may, in the future if not the present, prove significant to feminism:

(a) He problematizes the aspiration to truth, as an objective, verifiable, eternal value; and his adoption of a notion of theory as strategy both confirms and supplements many feminists' suspicions about the epistemological politics invested in truth. He does not focus on the relationship between statements and their reference to a 'real' world, but on relations (of alliance or conflict) *between* statements. This has strengthened feminist interrogations of theory, especially since the 1970s. While still analysing and challenging the positions occupied by *real women* (an indispensable feminist commitment, but one that is of limited success unless undertaken with deeper investigations), feminists have also begun to question the implicit or sometimes explicit misogny of theories, disciplines, and intellectual frameworks, criticizing them and attempting to avoid their pitfalls. With his critique of the concept of truth, and his suggestion of theory as a strategy or tool, Foucault has contributed to the developing sophistication of feminist counter-researches in the sciences and humanities. It is significant, for example, that a number of French feminists do not claim a truth-status for their writings, but position them between fiction and theory; various challenges to phallocentrism do not necessarily aim to replace patriarchal falsehoods with feminist truths, but to reveal the investments patriarchal knowledges have in both representing and excluding women. They are also involved in exploring and experimenting with new kinds of speaking/writing, forms of experience, and perspectives on the world. These do not necessarily claim a universal, objective value; but may openly see themselves as particular views, written from specific perspectives (e.g. Irigaray 1977; Pateman and Gross 1986).

(b) Foucault's notion of knowledges and truths as the bearers of power has raised a number of relevant questions for those feminists involved in institutional practices (whether these are educational, welfare, social work, management, or informational). Feminist practices are neither no more nor less neutral and value-free than any other. Feminist research, for example, is as implicated in power relations as any other. Foucault implies that there are some situations in which it may be wiser to remain silent than create truth, for knowledge of these areas may be utilized against the interests of those who speak. For example, his discussion of the procedures developed for putting sex into discourse makes it clear that to speak out about sexuality, desire, one's innermost feelings, etc., may provide data for even greater social control. In some contexts, speaking/writing may provide a key to liberation or self-determination, while in others, it may provide one's adversaries with new, more effective strategies of control.

(c) In his emphasis on the body as the ever-intensified locus of power and resistance, he signals a site that feminists have long struggled around (e.g. in campaigns associated with birth-control, abortion, body-images, and so on) but have not analysed in theoretical terms. The specificity of women's bodies and the provision of a theoretical space in which to discuss them, outside of phallocentric regimes of representation has become more urgent in feminism. Among others, Foucault suggests how the body may be viewed as an object of power and resistance, without being committed to biologistic, naturalistic or essential notions. Nevertheless, we should note in passing that Foucault himself does not specify the sexual particularity of bodies, and the implications of this for understanding regimes and technologies of power. Male and female bodies may well entail two different forms of control, modes of knowledge and forms of resistance.

(d) Foucault's account of marginal political struggles and subjugated discourses confirms the practices and systems of organization of various women's groups, which have generally refused hierarchical organization or representative leaders. Specific groups and issues enable women's groups to come together for strategic purposes. These groups do not represent others, less fortunate (as some Marxists claim), but only themselves and the positions or experiences that link them with other women. While Foucault's marginalized, localized struggles rule out the concept of 'The Revolution', smashing patriarchy in one fell swoop, he makes clear that a revolution of sorts is already under way. Patriarchal relations can be transformed, not through reformism, but in strategically located strikes at power's most vulnerable places. In this sense, his work confirms methods and ideals already developed by feminists, thus providing a theoretical justification for some or many of them.

DERRIDA AND DECONSTRUCTION

Like Foucault, Jacques Derrida has been classified as 'post-structuralist', indicating that while his intellectual roots may be based in structuralism, such as developed by Althusser and Lacan, he goes beyond them to question its assumptions, methods, and values. Also like Foucault, Derrida follows Nietzsche in the latter's denunciation of truth, objectivity, and neutrality in knowledge. He examines the intellectual commitments that knowledges – particularly philosophy – make to power relations. Unlike Foucault, Derrida's concern (shared with Lacan) is with power relations, not between discursive and non-discursive practices, but within the order of discourse. More directly than Althusser or Lacan, Derrida takes as his object or critical investigation central texts within the history of philosophy; he concentrates on texts associated with the 'Proper Names' of philosophy – Plato, Rousseau, Hegel, Nietzsche, Heidegger, Freud. These 'Proper Names' form a history of metaphysical or idealist thought that Derrida attempts actively to destabilize (Derrida 1976).

Derrida's avowed aim is not to eliminate metaphysics but to push it to its limits, forcing it to acknowledge the oppositions, exclusions, dichotomies, and distinctions which characterize it. He analyses, or rather, deconstructs, texts within the history of philosophy to show how they attain a position of dominance and what they must suppress, leave unacknowledged, for this dominance to be assured. However, extracting a general deconstructive method from his work, or even summarizing it, is very difficult. Unlike Foucault, moreover, he seems relatively reluctant to discuss his own work in interviews. Each of his papers is a close reading of other texts, an exercise in inter-textuality, a marginal reading, which requires not only a detailed knowledge of the 'primary' (metaphysical) text, but also of his particular modes of reading.

A number of French feminists follow Derrida in his claim that western metaphysics is usually structured in terms of dichotomies and binary oppositions. Within such a conceptual structure, one of the terms, the dominant one, defines the terrain of the other, placing it in a position of subordination or secondariness. This dichotomous structuring of concepts has figured strongly in our history since ancient Greece, guiding both philosophical and everyday thought: good/bad, mind/matter, being/nothingness, presence/absence, truth/error, identity/difference, signified/signifier, culture/nature, speech/writing, man/woman are only some examples. Derrida argues that these binary pairs do not define two equal and independent terms. In each pair, the first represents a positive and the second, a negative value, a deprived or lacking version of the first.

Derrida's critique consists above all in demonstrating that the positive terms – unity, identity, immediacy, presence, etc. – are in fact intimately dependent on, and can themselves be defined by, their opposition to the 'negative' terms – difference, distance, deferment, and dissimulation. Presence, for example, is inevitably bound up with, but unable to accept its dependence on, absence. Rather than seeing absence as the deprivation of presence, Derrida shows that absence *can* be seen as the primary term and presence as its negative counterpart.

He claims that western metaphysics is dominated by the belief in our ideal of the self-presence and the immediacy of concepts like truth, reality, knowledge, identity: the ideal of a truth that presents itself directly to consciousness in 'pure' form, without the mediation of anything extraneous haunts western knowledges. This (impossible) ideal provides one of the criteria by which western reason judges discourses, ignoring some at the same time as elevating others to the status of knowledge. Derrida gives the name 'logocentrism' to this obsession with presence (*logos* = speech, logic, reason, the word, God). His work consists in various deconstructive readings of logocentric texts, those which presume that the word, the text, language, are self-evident, clearly delimited, independent, neutral media for the transmission of pre-given or pure concepts.

Philosophy has an investment in seeing itself as a discipline unaffected by language, independent of its own textuality and materiality, unhampered in its exploration of ideas by the limits and nature of the linguistic tools upon which it relies. Philosophy refuses its dependence on the 'frailties', imprecisions, fluctuations, and changes that occur within languages. It will not acknowledge that it is a concrete, material process involved in and surrounded by other practices which influence it and will not acknowledge that it is a site for more or less vicious struggles for power.

Especially in its typical Anglo-Saxon forms, philosophy designates language usage as 'style', which is then considered as an effect of individual idiosyncrasies, an ornamental embellishment that can easily be replaced by a neutral, technical, accurate (non-'stylish') mode of expression. For philosophy, any truth must be seen as independent of the particular way it is formulated, translatable into other terms without a loss of meaning.

In opposition to logocentrism, but ironically spawned by it, Derrida develops a series of deconstructive techniques which seek out the traces and marks of textuality and materiality that are crucial if unacknowledged elements of the various texts he explores. These elements are key phrases, metaphors, and images necessary for the text to function. But they fall outside of the logic of the text's avowed aims; they exert a textual resistance to logocentric assumptions implicit in the text. These figures of speech, turns of phrase, etc., indicate points of possible paradoxes in the logocentric order. Terms such as 'differance', 'supplement', 'trace', 'pharmakon', 'hymen', 'dissemination', and even 'woman' (Derrida 1979; 1981a, pp. 173–286) challenge the primacy of presence and are used as pivotal points to question the logocentric texts within which they were embedded.

'Grammatology', 'the science of writing', 'dissemination', 'the science of difference', 'textuality' are all terms that signal an excessiveness or supplement that escapes the logic of the self-present subject, the presumed master of meaning. Difference eludes the grasp of the subject and indicates not the impossibility of meaning but its endless deferral and displacement (Spivak 1976; Cousins 1978; Derrida 1981b).

Difference/differance

The concept of difference has been extremely powerful in French feminist theory. Many so-called 'feminists of difference', who struggle for recognition and validation of feminine autonomy and specificity rely on the notion of difference – 'pure difference', difference without positive terms (Saussure) – to undermine the phallocentric definition of woman as the binary opposite of man. On the other hand, there are a number of attacks from feminist quarters over his use of the term 'woman' as a metaphor for style (Jardine 1980, 1985; Bartowski 1980; Spivak 1983).

In his earlier work, Derrida attempts to deconstruct the texts of phenomenology (especially those of Husserl and Heidegger) to make clear the reliance of metaphysics upon the logic of presence. Phenomenology needs concepts such as presence, consciousness, immediacy, the privilege of speech over writing (phonocentrism), signified over signifier. It is a philosophy of sameness, of presence, of a given subjectivity. Derrida attempts to reveal the dependence of the text on displacement, mediation, unconsciousness. He shows that phenomenology depends on repressed terms, oppositions and hierarchies it can't acknowledge. Similarly, while remaining close to Lacanian and Freudian psychoanalysis, Derrida also attempts to deconstruct their logocentric commitments (Derrida 1978a, pp. 196–231; 1978b, pp. 19–22). Psychoanalysis may well effect a deep and far-reaching subversion of the metaphysics of presence, subjectivity, and truth; it is nevertheless still part of a logocentric tradition. Structuralism and semiotics are also seen as moments of rupture or subversion which, almost in spite of themselves, remain committed to binary pairs (signifier/signified, langue/parole, structure/event, etc.). Saussure, for example, carefully distinguishes signifier from signified, claiming that neither term has an identity except in terms of its opposite. While rupturing logocentrism, he also privileges the signified or concept, explaining the signifier in terms of it.

If we take sameness/difference, presence/absence, speech/writing as typical examples, Derrida shows that the privileged term derives its position from a suppression or curtailment of its opposite or other. He argues that these oppositions and the distribution of values they effect, is not *given* but is an effect of an uncontrolled play of terms. Sameness and difference are both dependent on difference. But this difference is not the same difference as that which exists in the binary structure. To designate this difference within difference Derrida coins the neologism, 'differ*a*nce' with an 'a'. This term signals the primacy of the repressed term over the dominant term. For example, it signals the primacy of writing over speech (the 'a' only has value in reference to the absent 'e' it presumes and plays with), of matter over mind (it is a series of material traces, textual marks, of which the signified or concepts are the effect). The play of difference is the unspoken condition of logocentrism. It functions as an equivocal term, irresolvably duplicit:

> On the one hand, it indicates difference as distinction, inequality or discernibility; on the other, it expresses the interposition of delay, the interval of *spacing* and temporalizing . . . (T)here must be a common, although entirely different root within the sphere that relates the two movements of differing to one another. We provisionally gave the name *differance* to this sameness which is not *identical*.
>
> (Derrida 1973, p. 129)

Derrida uses the term 'differance' to designate:

1. An active and passive movement that consists in deferring, delaying and substituting. This delay is not the delay of a given presence (whether of the subject, meaning or truth); it is *originary*. Lack or absence marks the origin itself, not simply the things substituted for the (lost) object.
2. A movement at the basis of different things. In this sense, differ*a*nce is the condition of differ*e*nce, and of the binary oppositional structure itself. Differance is thus the condition for *both* difference *and* sameness.
3. A differance that is the condition of linguistic difference, and thus, of signification. This differance consists in the recalcitrance of a text in terms of its author's intentions – the fact that the author (or reader) cannot control the totality of the text he or she produces, and thus over the meaning intended.
4. The activity designed to reveal difference, a 'provisional' name (like 'grammatology') for analysing the unfolding of discourses. The concept of differance, the movement of difference, the challenge to binary logic that these pose are gathered together under this one term.

Deconstruction

Deconstruction is always a double procedure, a 'double science' or double writing, one that simultaneously occupies a space both inside and outside of texts. It is a double procedure, a duplicit use of a system's own weapons against themselves.

Its double processes consist in a reversal of dichotomous terms *and* a displacement of the system within which they function. If one simply reverses philosophical/political dichotomies, placing the subordinate term – absence, writing, difference, woman – into the dominant position previously occupied by presence, speech, identity, man, a (reverse) logocentrism still operates. Moreover, the force and violence that gave the dominant term its primacy is in effect ignored. Reversal must counter this force. If, on the other hand, one merely displaces dichotomies, one cannot understand their historically necessary structuring role within the history of knowledges. One must both reverse the dichotomy and displace the excluded, negative term, moving it from its oppositional role into the very heart of the dominant term. This move makes clear the violence of the hierarchy, and its unspoken debt to the subordinated term. It also makes clear the non-reversible, unequal roles given to the two terms. The simultaneous reversal and displacement makes it clear that the dichotomous structure *could* be replaced by other modes of conceptualization. Although they are historically necessary, they are not logically necessary.

Deconstruction thus involves not two, but three 'phases': reversal, displacement, and the creation of a new term – which Derrida calls a 'hinge word' – such as 'trace' (simultaneously present and absent), 'supplement' (simultaneously plenitude and excess); 'differance' (sameness and difference); 'pharmakon' (simultaneously poison and cure); 'hymen' (simultaneously virgin and bride, rupture and totality), etc. These are terms which are both *preconditions* of the oppositional structure and terms *in excess* of its logic (Derrida 1981b, pp. 41–42).

These 'hinge words' (in Irigaray, the two lips, fluidity, maternal desire, a genealogy of women,[13] in Kristeva, semanalysis, the semiotic, polyphony, etc.[14]) function as undecidable, vacillating between both oppositional terms, occupying the ground of their 'excluded middle'. If strategically harnessed, these terms rupture the systems from which they 'originate' and in which they function. Derrida's deconstructive 'double science' aims to undo the history of logocentrism in order to allow differance its space of free play.

This is both an *impossible* but *necessary* project: impossible because, on the one hand, it can only use logocentrism to challenge logocentrism (witness the parallel with feminism, which must use patriarchal terms to challenge patriarchy); and on the other hand, deconstruction reveals only what is absent, no-thing, non-sense, a difference, gap, or trace. A deconstructive reading does not so much demonstrate the errors, flaws, and contradictions in texts, but tries to reveal the *necessity* with which what a text says is bound up with what it cannot say.

Difference: sexuality and textuality

While Derrida's work has been extremely influential for some French and, more recently, Anglo-Saxon feminists – especially because of his development of deconstructive reading strategies and the concept of difference, it has also aroused considerable controversy within feminist circles, especially for his use of the term 'woman' and 'becoming woman' as metaphors for the demise of truth, and the play of difference. While a number of feminists have defended Derrida,[15] others have accused him of co-opting, de- or re-politicizing women's struggles for self-determination in ways he may not be prepared to accept.

While the metaphor of 'woman' as style circulates in a number of Derrida's texts, his position is most detailed in his readings of Nietzsche in *Spurs: Nietzsche's Styles* (1979). Here, through a reading of Nietzsche's pronouncements on woman, Derrida signals Nietzsche's radical break with phallocentric traditions of speculation on 'the woman question', as well as Nietzsche's commitment to and involvement in the history of misogynist thought.

His paper 'La double séance', translated as 'The double session' (1981a, pp. 173–286), is his first detailed discussion of the use of the metaphor of femininity. The term 'hymen' functions as one of his hinge words, undecidable within binary logic, baffling the either/or choice demanded by logocentrism. The hymen is neither identity nor difference, neither confusion nor distinction, neither inside nor outside, neither the veil nor the unveiling, neither consummation nor virginity, but the condition of both. It is the metaphor Derrida uses for a certain folded space of writing, the virginal/consumed space of the white page on which the pen/phallus disseminate (his pun on *seme*, the minimal unit of meaning, and semen). A dissemination that is a seed sown in futility, a non-reproduction, an insemination that does not produce within a genealogy of patronyms. The patronym is patriarchy's stamp upon the subject, the Proper Name (of the father) (*propre* = clean, own, proper, property, propriety) paying homage to his authority. Neither directed from a past (the origin in the father's genealogy), nor to a future (a teleology of reproduction, through dutiful sons, of the father's law), dissemination is fruitlessly expended:

> The fold folds (itself): its meaning spaces itself out with a double mark, in the hollow of which a blank is folded. The fold is simultaneously virginity, what violates virginity and the fold which, being neither one nor the other and both at once, undecidable, *remains* as a text, irreducible to either of its two senses. . . . The masculine is turned back upon the feminine: the whole adventure of sexual difference.
>
> But in the same blow, so to speak, the fold ruptures the virginity it marks as virginity. . . . It differs from itself, even *before* the letter opener can separate the lips of the book. It is divided from and by itself, like the hymen. After the consummation more folded up than ever, the virginity transforms the act that has been perpetrated into a simulation, a 'barbarous simulacrum'.
>
> (Derrida 1981a, pp. 258–9)

Paradoxically duplicit, the hymen is the space of imitation, mimesis, or artifice, a space of mime (Derrida's paper, 'The double session' is a reading of Mallarmé's *Mimique*) that is traditionally attributed to women.

Derrida's 'homage' to femininity, in many respects similar to Lacan's in its chivalrous rivalry, attributes the possibility of dissimulating dissimulation (not dissemination) to femininity: femininity is the possibility of feigning the truth. In being imitated – imitation is not here, as it was for Plato, a form of debasement or impurity – truth is supplementary, making up for an originary absence: 'Woman is but one name for that untruth of truth' (Derrida 1979, p. 51). His 'homage' is a reading of Nietzsche's proposition from *The Gay Science:* 'Finally – if one loved them . . . what comes of it inevitably? that they 'give themselves', even when they – give themselves. The female is so artistic' (Nietzsche, 1974, p. 317). Women mime or impersonate orgasm even at the moment of orgasm – the implication being that this contrasts with men's clear-cut orgasm, a 'real' one which cannot be faked.

Derrida's reading involves the triple process of deconstruction. Nietzsche's proposition of woman-as-truth, woman and truth, can be resolved in three broad phases: in the first, woman is seen as a liar, the figure of faslehood and misrepresentation, in opposition to the 'credulous man, who, in support of his testimony, offers truth and his phallus as his own proper credentials' (Derrida 1979, p. 97). In the second phase, woman is truth, but a truth which is not to be trusted, a dissimulating truth. As truth, woman does not believe in the truth. She is guileful, play-acting, which is her truth. But, as Derrida points out: '[T]he woman, up to this point, then, is twice castration: once as truth and once as untruth' (Derrida 1979, p. 97). The woman proposed is castrated – defined only by reaction to or as the negation of a purity measured by man. In the third phase, however, Nietzsche, deconstructs his own position:

> beyond the double negation of the first two (propositions), woman is recognised and affirmed as an affirmative power, a dissimulatress, an artist, a dionysiac. And no longer is it man who affirms her. She affirms herself, in and of herself, in man. Castration, here again, does not take place. And anti-feminism, which condemned woman only so long as she answered to man from the two reactive positions, is in its turn overthrown.
>
> (Derrida 1979, p. 97)

Woman ultimately affirms the untruth of truth, the impossibility of identity, the unsubstantiated faith in truth, being and presence. She is neither the veil over truth, nor truth as an unveiling of nothing-to-see (Freud's description of female genitals); but the truthfulness of truth, the unveiling which veils another veil: 'The hymen is therefore not the truth of unveiling. There is not *aletheia* [truth as unveiling], only a blink of the hymen' (Derrida 1981a, p. 293). Woman is the metaphor of truth's dissimulation – and with it the demise of a (logocentric) philosophical pretension to provide 'answers':

> There is no such thing as the essence of woman because woman averts, she is averted of herself. Out of the depths, endless and unfathomable, she engulfs and distorts all vestige of essentiality, of identity, of property. And the philosophical discourse, blinded, founders on these shoals and is hurled down these depthless depths to its ruin. There is no such thing as the truth of woman, but it is because of the abyssal divergence of the truth, because that untruth is 'truth'.
> (Derrida 1979, p. 51)

The invaginated, hymeneal text is the space of the dissemination of meaning and truth, woman as the impossible, deceiving, seductive, unveiling of a truth that does not exist, woman as paradox and enigma. Such is Derrida's use of metaphors of femininity. As metaphor, *Woman* has the potential to dislodge the operation of a tyrannical dichotomous structure; but as *name* (and not even a 'proper' name at that!), woman is the term referring to wom*e*n. This play with the name/metaphor may well shake the foundations of a logocentric and phallocentric intellectual tradition; but it will also exact its price – from women.

Derrida and feminism

Derrida's destabilization of logocentrism and binary logic challenged many of the same targets to which feminists have directed their energies. I will simply outline some of the ways in which Derrida's work has been utilized in feminist research.

(a) Phallocentric theory has relied on various dichotomous characterizations of man and woman. One of the problems faced by feminists has been how to question these structures. At first, it appeared that the most useful strategy would be a reversal of the positions of the binary terms. But, as has been recognized, this strategy remains within binary logic. Derrida's deconstructive techniques make it clear that if feminist theory is to succeed in its challenge to phallocentric discourses, it cannot do so from a position outside of phallocentrism. Deconstruction is an attempt to negotiate with this dilemma: to remain outside a (logocentric, phallocentric) system is to leave it intact; to remain only within its terms, on the other hand, is to risk absorption, to be unable to go beyond it. Working from within logocentrism, deconstruction is a method for dealing, within texts, with the text's limits; it is to play with the positions inside and outside of that text:

> The movements of deconstruction do not destroy structures from the outside. They are not possible and effective, nor can they take accurate aims except by inhabiting those structures. Inhabiting them *in a certain way*, because one always inhabits and all the more

> when one does not suspect it. Operating necessarily from the inside, borrowing all the strategic and economic resources of subversion from the old structure, borrowing them structurally . . . the enterprise of deconstruction always in a certain way falls prey to its own work.
>
> (Derrida 1976, p. 24)

His deconstructive project parallels and refines the feminist challenge to phallocentrism (phallocentrism is a sub-category of logocentrism, where the phallus takes on the role of the logos). Logocentrism is implicitly patriarchal; the very structure of binary oppositions is privileged by the male/non-male (i.e. female) distinction. Given the co-operation of these 'centrisms', deconstruction and the play of difference it engenders may be of strategic value to feminists.

(b) His stress on the material processes of reading (and writing) and the violent, coercive force necessary for terms to function as they have, provides a politically, as well as intellectually, useful trajectory for feminist researches. Not only does he make explicit the powers invested in discourses (whether these are knowledges, sciences, truths, or not), indicating further objects of feminist interrogations, but also the active, political role of reading and interpretation. This confirms and adds depth to feminist projects, especially in literature or in reading/writing differently. 'Deconstruction' is a much-used term in various critical theories. However, Derrida's term involves very precise reading practices that problematize the very grounds on which various discourses base themselves.

(c) Deconstructive techniques inform the work of Luce Irigaray and Julia Kristeva, among others. Derrida's mode of deconstruction, which instead of creating a new truth aims to unveil the political commitments of various prevailing discourses, has provided one of Irigaray's major interpretive techniques in her critical/lyrical evaluations of texts within psychoanalysis and the history of philosophy (1984; 1985b; 1985c). His more substantive arguments about a difference inhabiting all identity have inspired Kristeva's analysis of the symbolic and the semiotic, whose interrelation can be understood on the model of a difference *within* (personal and sexual) identity.

(d) His commitment to the concept of difference has become emblematic of a powerful critical force within feminist theory. Clearly Derrida is not the first or the only theorist of difference. (See for example, the prefigurative writings of Blanchot, Bataille, and Levinas, who wrote decades before Derrida.) Yet, with the exception of feminists themselves, his work is probably the most politically motivated. He adds a political dimension to Saussure's concept of pure difference to make it more incisive in challenging metaphysical adherences to identity. In distinguishing difference from 'differance', he shows that difference need not function within the logic of identity as its excluded element. On the contrary, it implies a mode of autonomy, not independent of and in isolation from other elements, but functioning with reference to them.

(e) His analysis of the metaphor of woman and femininity, whatever its problems, still makes explicit a procedure common within phallocentric texts – their necessary dependence on an either implicit or explicit metaphor of femininity as excess, materiality or instability. He makes clear how these metaphors have been necessary for phallogocentric texts to continue their dominance. In spite of Derrida's relevance to feminist theoretical projects, even those sympathetic to his work have expressed alarm at his use of femininity as a deconstructive tool.[16] Irigaray, for example is scathing about his metaphor of 'becoming woman' which, he claims, makes sense only if one is *not* a woman. Moreover, taking on the metaphor of woman as revolutionary upheaval is an act of political appropriation. It is significant that at precisely the moment when women begin to speak of themselves as subjects, as women, men begin to moralize about the politics of 'becoming feminine':

> As for men, it is up to them to speak for themselves. I have no desire to speak for them as they have spoken for us, nor to speak 'universal'. . . . They ask themselves certain types of questions which, as such, must not be confused with women's questions because many men at the moment say: 'Now we are becoming women . . .'. As soon as something worthwhile manifests itself concerning women, men want to become women. What interests me is the difference. Why, all of a sudden, should one be in a reversal of power, in a problematic of the Same? Above all, don't become women, sirs!
>
> (Irigaray 1981, trans. C. Sheaffer-Jones and E. Gross)

In acknowledging deconstruction as a strategic tool or device for feminist readings, Gayatri Spivak suggests an ambivalent attitude may be most appropriate:

> My attitude to deconstruction can now be summarized: first, deconstruction is illuminating as a critique of phallocentrism; second, it is convincing as an argument against the founding of a hysterocentric order to counter phallocentric discourse; third, as a 'feminist' practice itself, it is caught on the other side of sexual difference.
>
> (Spivak 1983, p. 184)

She remains wary of Derrida's metaphorics of femininity, which hovers dangerously close to other variants of male (self-) representations which use woman as a reflective mirror:

> If women have always been used as the instrument of male self-deconstruction, is this philosophy's newest twist? . . . a bold description of the feminist's problem of discourse after the critique of the old ways of knowing. . . . Yet, with respect, we cannot share in the mysterious pathos of the longing: for a reason as simple as the question of woman in general, asked in this way, is *their* question, not *ours*.
>
> (Spivak 1983, pp. 183–4)

Feminists today refuse the passive positions of metaphor and speculative object of art and theory for men. Instead of being metaphor, women affirm the right to *make* metaphor, to become the subjects of discourse instead of its objects. It is by no means clear whether Derrida, and for that matter Althusser, Lacan, or Foucault, provide this space for women's self-representations, even if their works can be strategically used by feminists in attempting to counteract, decentre, or deconstruct patriarchal theory.

FEMINISM, MASCULINITY AND POWER

Without detailing criticisms of the foregoing texts, I think it is important to recognize what feminist theory has learned from the male theorists, and in what ways it must depart from them. Each of the theorists discussed develops a complex theoretical system(s) or method(s) in his work, and each defines his own work both in relation to and in disagreement with each other. Each adopts a theoretical and political position that is, in part at least, a response to political activities, movements of resistance and rebellion, including feminism. We need to look at what their positions are on the question of sexual difference, as well as what relations feminism sees between their discourses and feminist aims and goals. Given the limits of space here, I will not discuss those criticisms and objections to their works developed outside feminist perspectives. I will concentrate only on the relevant relations each has to feminism.

Before briefly outlining the complex, reciprocal interactions between feminism and radical theory, it is worth pointing out that, while they are often acknowledged as sources of inspiration in feminist texts, it is rare to find feminist sources acknowledged there. At best, women are eulogized or treated as metaphors; at worst they are ignored or actively silenced under the general category, 'man' or 'humanity'. For example, where Lacan and Derrida mention feminism, it is in a caricatured form:

> Feminism is nothing but the operation of a woman who aspires to be like a man. And in order to resemble the masculine dogmatic philospher this woman lays claim – just as much claim as he – to truth, science and objectivity in all their castrated delusions of virility.

> Feminism too seeks to castrate. It wants a castrated woman. Gone the style.
>
> (Derrida 1979, p. 65)

Which feminism is Derrida referring to? But he is at least prepared to raise feminist issues, as Foucault and Althusser do not.

Each has a certain blindness to the specificity of female subjectivity, the interests of feminist theory and politics, and the concrete particularities of the (culturally inscribed) female body. Althusser, for example, does not neglect to mention that the crucial ISA in the construction of subjectivity is the nuclear family. Yet, he does not make the point that it is not the nuclear family *per se* that socializes subjects. It is significant that the father generally plays only an indirect role in socialization, which proceeds even in his absence or death. Althusser neglects the formative role of the *mother* in the various processes producing subjects, and the fact that it is only the father's *authority*, not his presence, that is required. The mother bears the child, nurtures, educates, loves, and cleans it; and ensures that the child adequately reproduces socially acceptable behaviour. The nuclear family could not function as such except through its unrecognized debt to the mother's services. Althusser is blind to the fact that if there are 'capitalist ideologies', then these have always functioned in pre-capitalist cultures as and through patriarchal systems. The ways in which capitalism and its agencies function is not randomly or accidentally male dominated; such domination is one of its integral features.

Althusser tries to absolve himself of responsibility for neglecting the psychical and sexual components of bourgeois ideologies by claiming that psychoanalysis explains this dimension of social existence. Coupled with psychoanalysis, Marxism, it seems, need not pay any serious attention to the sexual division of labour, or various economic forms of women's oppression, for psychoanalysis serves this purpose! Clearly the ideologies which function to interpellate individuals as subjects within culture do so in sexually bifurcated, sexually distinguished ways – the subjects produced are not sexually neutral, but have masculine or feminine attributes. Whatever other objections may be levelled against his understanding of ideology, he not only ignores the sexually specific effects of ideologies; he leaves no theoretical space in his account for patriarchal power relations, and their effects on and interactions with capitalist power relations.

If Althusser is blind or indifferent to the effects of sexual relations on ideology, and ideology's relation to the structuring of sexual distinctions as relations of domination and subordination, his work has nevertheless provided a series of useful questions and critiques that feminists may be able to utilize in projects quite different from his own. His anti-humanist critique of notions of the pre-given subject, his claims that cultures, institutions, and practices materially produce subjects, his conception of ideology as a web of interrelated ideas, practices, values, behaviours, and social institutions and structures, his mode of relating socio-economic issues to epistemological and cultural questions, have all proved fruitful and suggestive for many contemporary feminists (see Barrett, Spivak, Mitchell, and Rose). Yet, in terms of the critiques of his work developed by feminists and non-feminists (e.g. Hirst), ideology considered as a distorted reflection of reality, in opposition to truth or science, remains a problematic framework in which to develop feminist theory.

With analogous blindness, Lacan fails to specify that the phallus, the threshold signifier of the symbolic, is not merely a signifier, an empty trace, but is 'filled' or given meaning with reference to the penis. Women cannot be regarded as *lacking the phallus* (and thus attempting to be it) unless this is the sign of the presence or absence of the penis. Lacan claims to have radically separated biology (the penis) from psychic and symbolic orders (the phallus); yet he also continually collapses them together whenever the question of femininity, female sexuality or women's identities arises (see 'A love letter', in Mitchell and Rose 1982). He seems to want it both ways: women are 'produced as castrated' only through phallic inscription; yet, there is something of/in the woman that predisposes her to the side of 'not-all', the negative, or supplementary side ('A love letter', in Mitchell and Rose 1982). In other words, Lacan is unable to explain why it is the *phallus* and not any other signifier that operates as the 'signifier of signifiers' to the symbolic or social order, why the law must be the father's, why masculinity provides the norms of femininity, and why female sexual pleasure is considered either as phallic or as supplementary to the phallus.

It is not simply that Lacan ignores feminist questions about the differential values of the two sexes, but also that he renders the structures and power relations between the sexes eternal and universal, conditions of the very existence of language and sociality. Lacan is, as usual, very difficult to pin down. But some of his followers are a little more explicit. One of the most 'authorized' of his 'disciples', Moustafa Safouan, openly discusses the question of the universality of the Oedipus complex (Safouan 1981, p. 87):

> We know what a storm has been unleashed by Freud's thesis as to the phallicism of the girl. But in the end, over and above anything that might be said about one person's feminism and another's misogny, we are dealing with an indubitable analytic fact, even if it is not easy to make it intelligible because after all, the penis is not such a wonderful thing as to force the girl to want to sacrifice her own nature.
>
> [Castration] . . . lays the foundations for the object relation in the human being, insofar as it imposes not mourning for the primordial object, which is rather a matter of the law, but a *restriction on the*

> *narcissism* into which the relation to the object as such would otherwise set.

In other words, it is not so much the Oedipus complex as the castration threat he claims is universal. This is because the child must find a way of detaching itself from the mutually defining relation to the mother, which it can only do with respect to a third party who *has* an access to the mother that the child (of either sex) *lacks*. The child's genital desires must be subordinated, that is, not to another, a successful rival, but to a law which directs its desire to substitutes. Yet neither Safouan nor Lacan can explain why the *phallus* takes on this role, why the mother must be construed as lacking, and why children must abandon the primordial love relation according to the *presence* or *absence* of anatomical organs and the threat or 'reality' of their loss. Nor indeed, why it is the woman who functions as the nurturer, the imaginary other from whom the child must detach itself. We must ponder whether, if fathers or men nurtured and reared children from their earliest years, the child would be detached from him by the postulate of the *father's* anatomical lack. Or whether the mother would consequently be regarded as 'possessing' what he lacks. It seems doubtful, given the fact that many fathers, especially lone fathers, do act as nurturers. I am suggesting that Lacan, Safouan, and indeed Freud, take what are the prevailing norms of our culture and ontologize them to enable them to function universally. This then provides a perfect justification for the necessary maintenance of patriarchal values of the two sexes in their present, oppressive forms. As universal conditions of culture itself (both Lacan and Safouan refer to Lévi-Strauss here), women's castration and the phallic attributes of masculinity become unquestionable.

If, however, psychoanalysis is a powerful source of inspiration to many feminists, in most cases this is not because these problems are unrecognized. On the contrary, many feminists have turned to psychoanalytic texts precisely because they articulate in explicit fashion the ideals and values underlying all cultural and theoretical practice within patriarchy. Psychoanalysis remains useful to feminism because, to date, it is the most sophisticated and intricate account of psychological processes and structures functioning in our culture for the reproduction of male and female social and sexual positions. Concepts like the unconscious, desire, drive, identification, etc., seem necessary for explaining the transmission of sexual roles, and, moreover, for attempting to challenge or subvert their transmission and reproduction.

In spite of its problems Lacan's work has been effective in focusing attention on the powerful subjective effects of language and systems of signification in producing the socio-symbolic subject. Through his theory and writings, Lacan demonstrated the tenacity, power, and playfulness of language, and its primacy over experience. He has revealed an unconscious dynamic of articulation that has inspired new modes of listening/reading/reception of texts, in which what is not spoken is as significant as what is said. Ironically, while it was Althusser who attempted to develop a materialist theory of subjectivity that integrated psychic and socio-economic orders by means of the concept of ideology, it was in fact Lacan who, through his materialist understanding of language, was more successful in linking the individual to the social. This is an insight that feminists cannot afford to ignore.

Lacan's subversion of philosophical categories – the subject, truth, reality, certainty, knowledge – is a powerful tool against phallocentric traditions governing all the academic disciplines. His insights about the ways in which the strange 'texts' of the unconscious may be deciphered, his linguistic explanation of the unconscious, are all trajectories which feminists could develop one way or another for their own purposes without necessarily remaining committed to more problematic features of psychoanalysis. Above all, Lacan's work has been most fruitfully interpreted (by, for example, Irigaray and Gallop) as providing a detailed analysis of the operations of masculine desire, men's socio-symbolic construction and positioning, the constitution of masculine, phallic sexuality and the ways in which men's fantasies of and desires for women are projected on to women. But what it leaves untouched is the specificity of women's positions. If Lacan elaborates collective masculine fantasies about women that are actively imposed on to women, he does not provide any account of the ways in which women do or do not live up to these expectations.

While clearly more sensitive to issues raised by feminist theory and politics than Lacan or Althusser, Foucault also seems to be unaware of the impact that recognizing sexual difference would have on his work. Although he carefully disclaims any speaking *on behalf of* or in the name of others, such as women (in 'The political function of the intellectual', 1977), he neglects the fact that the various technologies of power he outlines operate in quite different ways acording to the sex of the bodies they take as their objects. Power inscribes male and female bodies in quite different ways, with different goals and consequences. The body is not a sexually neutral or indifferent, pliable, flesh; it is a body that is sexually concrete (even if it does not, as with *Herculine Barbin* (1980b), conform to a binary classificatory schema).

Technologies and instruments of power are not neutral with respect to sexual difference. While it may be true that these technologies actively contribute to the production of the body as male or female – i.e. explain the modes of *categorization* of bodies – Foucault does not explain the fact that different technologies and instruments inscribe male and female bodies. The material practices surrounding them in familial and residential relations, the different institutions – educational, legal, medical, and religious – and the different tasks male and female bodies are expected to perform, are all neglected by Foucault.

While his work may prove useful to feminists in signalling the centrality to and production of bodies by power and in pointing out the modes of material inscription cultures must use in producing and regulating its members, he remains ignorant of the sexual specificity of processes he considers universal to a culture. While he demassifies the megalithic notion of patriarchy as a system of totalizing completion, he does not thereby explain the tangible effects of patriarchal domination on the bodies and lives of the two sexes. Given the concepts he employs, he has no way of explaining these differences.

Until *The History of Sexuality* (1978) the question of sexuality was barely raised by him. In this text, in which the question of the two sexes seemed difficult to avoid, Foucault devotes only one small section to women's specificity when he discusses the hystericization of women's bodies. In *The Use of Pleasure* ([1984] 1985), the second volume of an incomplete history of sexuality, he openly acknowledges that the modes of ethical self-regulation are relevant only to men:

> women were generally subjected . . . to extremely strict constraints, and yet this ethics (of self-regulation) was not addressed to women; it was not their duties, or obligations, that were recalled, justified, or spelled out. It was an ethics for men: an ethics thought, written, and taught by men – to free men, obviously. A male ethics, consequently, in which women figured only as objects or, at most, as partners that one had to train, educate and watch over when one had them under one's power, but stay away from when they were under the power of someone else (father, husband, tutor) . . . it was an elaboration of masculine conduct carried out from the viewpoint of men in order to give form to *their* behaviour.
>
> (Foucault [1984] 1985, pp. 22–3)

Even if it is not for women, such an ethics is still not irrelevant to them. Women are still affected by men's sexual ethics, even when it is directed to a paederastic object. It is not clear whether women have a (different) sexual ethic, a question he doesn't raise. One wonders whether his studies on power and knowledge are simply descriptions of techniques regulating, punishing, supervising, and knowing *men's* bodies, not women's.

In Derrida's case, his focus on the power or force vested in concepts and discourses has inspired feminists to challenge the most basic philosophical or theoretical assumptions of universal or neutral validity by virtue of their self-evidence. Yet, like his colleagues, Derrida too occupies a position in phallocentric discourses. While advocating the subversiveness of the metaphor of femininity, he neglects the effects of his own enunciative position as masculine. He himself acknowledges that not only is *what* a discourse says, important, but also *how* it is said, the specific terms in which it is articulated. We must also add to this the *position* from which it is said – who speaks and from what position. In speaking for or as women, he takes away the space which women have (re-) defined for themselves. He uses women as metaphors of a subversion of truth and order, while not recognizing women as subjects and the positions from which *they* might speak.

Each of these male theorists of power draws attention to notions of power and human subjectivity. Yet each ignores the masculinity or phallocentrism of his textual point of view. In different ways, each ignores the question of sexual difference, specificity, and autonomy by claiming some kind of sexual generality or universality, for their leading terms are presented as if sexuality is an irrelevant issue. Yet all theory, all knowledge is produced from sexually specific positions and with sexually specific effect. In so far as these are relevant to men's work as much as women's, what is needed is not just the *inclusion* of women within their various investigations, but also the acknowledgement that their works are also the effects of specifically masculine points of view and interests.

Male theorists should, in other words, speak *as men*, speak while acknowledging their positions as masculine subjects. *The more 'woman' exists as metaphor in men's texts, the less energy and subversive power do women have to speak in their own names.*

CONCLUSION

Each of these male theorists has problems in coming to terms with the status and scope of his discourses. While all (perhaps with the exception of Lacan) claim to be open to questions of historical, geographical, and cultural diversity, they do not seem to be able to question their own works in terms of *sexual* specificity. This does not mean that their works are useless or irrelevant to feminist theory. They retain a relevance partly because they are implicated in patriarchy as much as any texts are. They provide *objects* of feminist investigation and procedures and methods or strategies feminists may harness in their projects. Clearly, feminist theory is itself implicated in patriarchal paradigms. These theories of power and subjectivity, instead of providing overarching frameworks or criteria for judging feminist theory, can instead become the objects of feminist scrutiny. Feminists need to maintain something of a theoretical distance from their frameworks and commitments in order to be able to use what is of value while rejecting the more problematic structure of each. This will be difficult, given the demanding, difficult texts that each has produced.

These male theorists do not simply provide routine objects for feminist analysis. Their works have been particularly instrumental in developing and adding sophistication to feminist theory over the last two decades.

They have provided a number of crucial insights that, it could be argued, helped shape the form and range of feminist theories circulating today. Feminist theory has come to maturity, however, when it can both acknowledge these sources and also go beyond them in producing its own perspectives. This will involve a three-pronged approach to phallocentric texts: first, a critical immersion in (male) theory is necessary, to the extent of understanding its commitments, contributions, and vulnerable points; then, an anti-sexist critique of the kind that I discussed at the beginning of this paper: a project involving the assessment of these theories from outside their frameworks, that is, from a feminist perspective; a third phase in the development of feminist theory involves departing from either phallocentric discourses or their critiques, the development of different types of theory, different perspectives and interests to those which prevail.

This chapter has been an exercise in the first and second phases of a self-determined feminist theory. It has consisted in an outline, summary, and discussion of the work of four key male thinkers in French (political) theory, in which the merits and problems of each were noted; it has also begun the process of anti-sexist critique, although clearly feminist objections to their various texts could have been further detailed. The task of developing feminist theory, the third phase described above, has yet to be developed, at least in academic circles. This is the task most urgently facing feminist intellectuals today.

Each of these 'Proper Names' has been a point of reference and a point of departure for feminism. Marxist-feminism gained much of its impetus from Althusser's reading of Marx; those feminists now concerned with psychoanalysis have developed either through object-relations theory (especially American feminists, e.g. Chodorow and Dinnerstein) or through Lacan's reading of Freud. Yet given the convincing political critique of neo-Freudianism articulated by Lacan, it is not clear how feminists committed to radical social change can continue to utilize accounts with such conservative underlying commitments. Between them, Marx and Freud have become virtually indispensable reference points for informed feminist theories.

Foucault and Derrida, and, through their readings of him, Nietzsche, have been used to problematize Althusser's separation of science and truth from ideology, and Lacan's postulate of a single organizing structure in symbolic identity, the phallus. Foucault and Derrida, as post-structuralists, owe an intellectual debt to the structuralist projects of Althusser and Lacan; yet they have both developed beyond the structural traditions in which each was trained to develop critical alternatives, 'genealogy' in Foucault's case and 'deconstruction' in Derrida's. In conflicting ways, they raise the question of the materiality of discursive and non-discursive power relations, and the precarious dependence of dominant forms on repressed, subjugated, or subordinated terms. (Their differences seem, among other things, to be located in the scope each gives to the discursive domain: for Derrida, 'there is no outside' of discourses. To leave one discourse is to enter another; while, for Foucault, the discursive is identified only with written or spoken texts, texts which are to be located in a non-discursive space.) Feminist theory has the advantage of putting these various discourses to work *against each other*, allowing one patriarchal discourse to challenge another; in this process it may also develop new techniques and values, so that different types of knowing may become possible:

> we ought to be prepared for what I call the 'affirmation of the difference', not a kind of wake about the corpse of the mummified woman, nor a fantasy of woman's decapitation but something different: of her power, her potency, her ever-dreaded strength, of the regions of femininity. Things are starting to be written, things that will constitute a feminine Imaginary, the site, that is, of identifications of an ego no longer given over to an image defined by the masculine but inventing forms for women on the march, or as I prefer to fantasize, 'in flight', so that instead of lying down, women will go forward by leaps in search of themselves.
>
> (Cixous 1981, p. 52)

ACKNOWLEDGEMENTS

All cultural production, including writing, is a collective product. This usually remains unacknowledged in most patriarchal texts. At best, a note of acknowledgement thanking *x* and *y* for typing and/or proof-reading may appear. Production, especially the production of theory, is more profoundly collective than this indicates, for texts are the results of a thinking and a writing or speaking that are effects of our interactions with others (other texts, other people, other women). I have no way of acknowledging all those who contributed to the production of this paper: I discussed the ideas and texts used here with literally scores of others, in a variety of contexts. Lists of names thus do not adequately represent collective contributions, although they may notch up 'credit points' for the more career-oriented. However I would like to single out Moira Gatens, Sneja Gunew, and Cecily Williams for special mention as major sources of inspiration, ideas, and support.

NOTES

1 Throughout this chapter I avoid, where possible, references to sources unavailable in English translation. This means that some of the more relevant textual sources have not been cited. But I think this is counterbalanced by an accessibility of texts to a non-French reader.

2 This was a period when, for a few days and without preplanning, students,

workers, professionals, and radicals seemed on the verge of a major social revolution. A national strike by students, full-scale street fighting, and strikes in factories and offices facilitated a socio-political crisis that signalled a period of transition and upheaval in French political and intellectual life. For further details, see Hirsch (1981, pp. 139–54) and Guattari (1984, pp. 208–17).

3 The earliest explorations of Freudo-Marxism were undertaken by Marcuse (1969) and Reich, especially in 'Dialectical materialism and psychoanalysis' (1972). The project of linking Marx and Freud was revitalized in the late 1960s and early 1970s. There are numerous examples, but perhaps some of the more well-known include Mitchell (1974), Barrett (1980), Chodorow (1980), and Mitchell and Rose (1982).

4 For a feminist critique of Liberal Feminist arguments about equal treatment, see Gatens (1983).

5 He urged solidarity with the PCF, which maintained a basically conservative position. They claimed that the time for revolution was not then, and that it was important to wait for the right moment, when the party itself could lead workers in a united struggle.

6 In 1979 Althusser murdered his wife, a well-known feminist. He was not charged but confined to a psychiatric institution for many years.

7 Because of his provocative relations with the International Psychoanalytic Association, which was and is dominated by ego psychology, Lacan was expelled in 1964. See Turkle (1978) and Clément (1983) for details.

8 The boy is threatened with castration by the Symbolic Father, and, fearing the loss of his penis, he gives up his sexual attachment to the mother. He converts his aggression towards the father into an identification, introjecting his father's authority in the form of the super-ego. With the newly formed super-ego, he performs the first act of primal repression by repressing the desire for his mother. This act provides the first contents for the unconscious, which is constituted as such only as a consequence of primal repression.

9 Saussure, arguably the founder of modern linguistics and semiotics, lectured on linguistics in Geneva between1908 and 1911; his work (with one exception) was posthumously published from lecture-notes compiled and edited by his students, under the title *Course in General Linguistics* in 1916. Freud published *The Interpretation of Dreams* in 1900 and his metapsychological account, 'The unconscious' in 1914.

10 Jakobson and Halle (1956) argues that the two essential poles of language are similarity (or metaphor) and contiguity (metonymy). Impairment in these linguistic functions, such as occurs in aphasias, results in an inability to participate in language. Similarity is based on our ability to select from a series of similar terms the one appropriate to our purposes. It is a function of selection. Contiguity is the ability to combine the units thus selected into a higher-order linguistic unit. It is thus a function of combination.

11 Foucault elaborates these rules and powers in 'The discourse on language' (1972).

12 Turkle (1978) and Roustang (1982) elaborate in considerable detail the plots, struggles for power, and back-biting involved in the history of the most self-aware of master–disciple relations, psychoanalysis.

13 'But if [feminist projects] were to aim simply at reversing the order of things – let us admit even that it were possible – history would finally return to the same thing. To phallocratism. In which neither their sex, nor their imaginary, nor their language would (re)discover their place of occurrence' (Irigaray 1978, p. 167).

14 Like Derrida's hinge terms they are undecidable, ambiguous, paradoxical terms, baffling binary categorization.

15 For example, Spivak's preface to *Of Grammatology* (1976) and her interview in *Thesis Eleven*, 10/11, 1984–5, where she defends Derrida against certain criticisms; but in her paper in *Displacement* (1983) she is much more critical of his relations to feminism.

16 See, for example, Irigaray (1981); Spivak (1983); and Jardine (1985).

REFERENCES

Althusser, L. (1971) *Lenin and Philosophy and Other Essays*, New Left Books, London.

Barrett, M. (1980) *Women's Oppression Today: Problems in Marxist-Feminist Analysis*, New Left Books, London.

Bartowski, F. (1980) 'Feminism and deconstruction', *enclitic*, 4:2, pp. 70–7.

Beauvoir, S. de (1972) *The Second Sex*, Penguin, Harmondsworth.

Chodorow, N. (1980) 'Gender relations and difference in psychoanalytic experience', in H. Eisenstein and A. Jardine (eds) *The Future of Difference*, G. K. Hall, Boston.

Cixous, H. (1981) 'Castration or decapitation', *Signs*, 7:1, pp. 41–55.

Cousins, M. (1978) 'The logic of deconstruction', *Oxford Literary Review*, 3:2, pp. 70–7.

Deleuze, G. and Guattari, F. (1972) *Anti-Oedipus: Capitalism and Schizophrenia*, Athlone Press, London.

Derrida, J. (1973) *Speech and Phenomena*, Northwestern University Press, Evanston, Ill.

Derrida, J. (1976) *Of Grammatology*, tr. G. C. Spivak, Johns Hopkins University Press, Baltimore, Md.

Derrida, J. (1978a) *Writing and Difference*, Routledge & Kegan Paul, London.

Derrida, J. (1978b) 'Speculations – on Freud', *Oxford Literary Review*, 3:2, pp. 78–97.

Derrida, J. (1979) *Spurs: Nietzsche's Styles*, University of Chicago Press.

Derrida, J. (1981a) *Dissemination*, University of Chicago Press (contains 'The double session').

Derrida, J. (1981b) *Positions*, Athlone Press, London.

Descombes, V. (1980) *Modern French Philosophy*, Cambridge University Press.

Eisenstein, Z. (ed.) (1979) *Capitalist Patriarchy and the Case for Socialist Feminism*, Monthly Review Press, New York.

Foucault, M. ([1966] 1970) *The Order of Things: An Archaeology of the Human Sciences*, Random House, New York.

Foucault, M. (1972) *The Archaeology of Knowledge and the Discourse on Language*, Harper & Row, New York.

Foucault M. ([1961] 1973) *Madness and Civilization: A History of Insanity in the Age of Reason*, Tavistock, London.

Foucault, M. ([1963] 1975) *The Birth of the Clinic: An Archaeology of Medical Perception*, Vintage Books, New York.

Foucault, M. (1977) 'The political function of the intellectual', *Radical Philosophy*, 17, pp. 12–14.

Foucault, M. (1978) *The History of Sexuality: An Introduction*, Pantheon Books, New York.

Foucault, M. ([1975] 1979) *Discipline and Punish: The Birth of the Prison*, Pantheon Books, New York.

Foucault, M. (1980a) *Power/Knowledge: Selected Interviews and Other Writings*, ed. C. Gordon, Harvester Press, Sussex.
Foucault, M. (1986b) *Herculine Barbin: Being the Recently Discovered Memoirs of a Nineteenth-Century Hermaphrodite*, Pantheon Books, New York.
Foucault, M. ([1984] 1985) *The Use of Pleasure*, Pantheon Books, New York.
Foucault, M. (1986) *The History of Sexuality*, vol. 3, *The Care of the Self*, Campion Books, New York.
Freud, S. (1900) 'The interpretation of dreams', in *The Standard Edition of Complete Psychological Works* (24 vols, 1953–74), Hogarth Press and the Institute of Psychoanalysis, London, vol. 5.
Freud, S. (1914) 'The unconscious', in *The Standard Edition of the Complete Psychological Works* (24 vols, 1953–74), Hogarth Press and the Institute of Psychoanalysis, London, vol. 14.
Gatens, M. (1983) 'A critique of the sex/gender distinction', in *Beyond Marxism? Interventions after Marx*, Intervention Publications, Sydney.
Gallop, J. (1982) *Feminism and Psychoanalysis: The Daughter's Seduction*, Macmillan, London.
Guattari, F. (1984) *Molecular Revolution: Psychiatry and Politics*, Penguin, Harmondsworth.
Hirsch, A. (1981) *The French New Left: From Sartre to Gorz*, South End Press, Boston.
Irigaray, L. (1977) 'Women's exile', *Ideology and Consciousness*, 1, pp. 62-76.
Irigaray, L. (1978) 'The sex which is not one', in P. Foss and M. Morris (eds) *Language, Sexuality and Subversion*, Feral Publications, Sydney.
Irigaray, L. (1981) *Le Corps-a-corps avec la mère*, Editions de la Pleine Lune, Montreal.
Irigaray, L. (1984) *L'ethique de la difference sexuelle*, Editions de Minuit, Paris.
Irigaray, L. (1985a) *Speculum of the Other Woman*, Cornell University Press, Ithaca, NY.
Irigaray, L. (1985c) *This Sex Which is Not One*, Cornell University Press, Ithaca, NY.
Jakobson, R. and Halle, M. (1956) *The Fundamentals of Language*, Mouton, The Hague.
Jardine, A. (1980) 'Theories of the feminine: Kristeva', *enclitic*, 4:2, pp. 5–15.
Jardine, A. (1985) *Gynesis: Configurations of Woman and Modernity*, Cornell University Press, Ithaca, NY, and London.
Kuhn, A. and Wolpe, A. (1978) *Feminism and Materialism*, Routledge & Kegan Paul, London.
Lydon, M. (1988) 'Foucault and feminism: a romance of many dimensions', *Feminism, Foucault: Reflections on Resistance* in I. Diamond and L. Quimby (eds) Northeastern University Press, Boston.
Marcuse, H. (1969) *Eros and Civilization*, Beacon Press, New York.
Mitchell, J. (1974) *Psychoanalysis and Feminism*, Allen & Lane, London.
Mitchell, J. and Rose, J. (eds) (1982) *Feminine Sexuality: Jacques Lacan and the Ecole Freudienne: Feminine Sexuality*, Macmillan, London.
Morris, M. and Patton, P. (eds) (1978) *Michel Foucault: Power, Truth, Strategy*, Feral Publications, Sydney.
Nietzsche, F. (1974) *The Gay Science*, Vintage Books, New York.
Pateman, C. and Gross, E. (eds) (1986) *Feminist Challenges: Social and Political Theory*, Allen & Unwin, Sydney.
Reich, W. (1972) *Sex-Pol*, Vintage Books, New York.
Roustang, F. (1982) *Dire Mastery: Discipleship from Freud to Lacan*, Johns Hopkins University Press, Baltimore, Md.

Safouan, M. (1981) 'Is the Oedipus complex universal?', *m/f*, 5 and 6, pp. 83–90.
Sartre, J. P. (1958) *Being and Nothingness*, Methuen, London.
Sartre, J. P. (1968) *The Search for a Method*, Vintage Books, New York.
Sartre, J. P. (1975) 'Existentialism is a humanism', in W. Kaufmann (ed.) *Existentialism from Dostoevsky to Sartre*, New American Library, New York.
Sartre, J. P. (1976) *The Critique of Dialectical Reason*, New Left Books, London.
Saussure, F. de (1906–1911), *Course in General Linguistics*, McGraw-Hill Book Co. (1966), New York.
Spivak, G. C. (1976) 'Translator's preface', in J. Derrida, *Of Grammatology*, Johns Hopkins University Press, Baltimore, Md.
Spivak, G. C. (1983) 'Displacement and the discourse of woman', in M. Krupnick (ed.) *Displacement: Derrida and After*, Indiana University Press, Bloomington.
Spivak, G. C. (1984–5) 'Criticism, feminism and the institution', *Thesis Eleven*, 10/11, pp. 175–87.
Turkle, S. (1978) *Psychoanalytic Politics: Freud's French Revolution*, Basic Books, New York.

FURTHER READING

Althusser, L. (1969) *For Marx*, Penguin, Harmondsworth.
Althusser, L. and Balibar, E. (1970) *Reading Capital*, New Left Books, London.
Andermatt, V. (1981) 'Helene Cixous and the uncovery of a feminine language', *Women and Literature*, 7:1, pp. 38–48.
Argyros, A. (1980) 'Daughters of the desert', *Diacritics*, 10:3, pp. 27–35.
Benveniste, E. (1971) *Problems in General Linguistics*, University of Miami Press.
Berg, E. (1982) 'The third woman', *Diacritics*, 12:2, pp. 11–20.
Bersani, L. (1977) 'The subject of power, *Diacritics*, Fall, pp. 2–19.
Botsman, P. (ed.) (1982) *Theoretical Strategies*, Local Consumption, Sydney.
Bové, P. (1983) 'Intellectuals at war: Michel Foucault and the analytics of power', *Sub-Stance*, 37/38, pp. 36–55.
Bowie, M. (1979) 'Jacques Lacan', in J. Sturrock (ed.) *Structuralism and Since: From Lévi-Strauss to Derrida*, Oxford University Press.
Boyne, R. (1981) 'Alcibiades as the hero: Derrida/Nietzsche', *Sub-Stance*, 28, pp. 25–36.
Certeau, M. de (1984) *The Practice of Everyday Life*, University of California Press, Berkeley.
Certeau, M. de (1986) *Heterologies. Discourses on the Other*, Manchester University Press.
Chodorow, N. (1978) *The Reproduction of Mothering: Psychoanalysis and the Sociology of Gender*, Universityof California Press, Berkeley.
Cixous, H. (1976) 'Interview', *Sub-Stance*, 13.
Cixous, H. and Clément, C. (1986) *The Newly Born Woman*, University of Minnesota Press, Minneapolis.
Cixous, H. (1979) 'Rethinking difference: an interview', in G. Stambolian and E. Marks (eds) *Homosexualities in French Literature: Cultural Contexts/Critical Texts*, Cornell University Press, Ithaca, NY.
Cixous, H. (1980) 'Arrive le chapitre-qui vient (come the following chapter)', *Enclitic*, 4:2, pp. 45–59.
Cixous, H. (1983) 'Portrait of Dora', *Diacritics*, Spring, pp. 2–36.
Clément, C. (1983) *The Lives and Legends of Jacques Lacan*, Columbia University Press, New York.

Collins, J., Green, J. R., Lydon, M., and Skoller, E. H. (1983) 'Questioning the unconscious: "The Dora Archive"', *Diacritics*, Spring, pp. 37–46.
Conley, V. (1977) 'Missexual Misstery', *Diacritics*, Summer.
Coward, R. (1976) 'Lacan and signification', *Edinburgh Review*, 1, pp. 6–20.
Coward, R. and Ellis, J. (1977) *Language and Materialism*, Routledge & Kegan Paul, London.
Culler, J. (1983) *On Deconstruction: Theory and Criticism After Structuralism*, Routledge & Kegan Paul, London.
Davis, R. C. (ed.) (1981) *The Fictional Father: Lacanian Readings of the Text*, University of Massachusetts Press, Amherst.
Davis, R. C. (1983a) 'Lacan, Poe and narrative repression', *Modern Language Notes*, 98:5.
Davis, R. C. (1983b), 'Introduction: Lacan and narration', *Modern Language Notes*, 98:5.
Davis, R. C. (1983c) (ed.) *Lacan and Narration*, Johns Hopkins University Press, Baltimore, Md.
Derrida, J. (1972–3) 'Interview', *Diacritics*, Winter 1972 and Spring 1973.
Derrida, J. (1977) 'Fors', *Georgia Review*, Spring.
Derrida, J. (1978a) 'Becoming woman', *Semiotext(e)*, 3:1, pp. 128–37.
Derrida, J. (1978b) 'The retrait of metaphor', *enclitic*, 2:2, pp. 5–33.
Derrida, J. (1978c) 'Coming into one's own, in G. Hartman (ed.) *Psychoanalysis and the Question of the Text*, Johns Hopkins University Press, Baltimore, Md.
Derrida, J. (1978d) 'Speculations – on Freud', *Oxford Literary Review*, 3:2, pp. 78–97.
Derrida, J. (1981a) 'Title (to be specified)', *Sub-Stance*, 31, pp. 5–22.
Derrida, J. (1981b) 'Economimesis', *Diacritics*, Summer, pp. 3–25.
Derrida, J. (1982) 'Signsponge 1 & 2', *Oxford Literary Review* 5:1/2.
Derrida, J. (1983a) 'The time of a thesis: punctuations', in A. Montefiore (ed.) *Philosophy in France Today*, Cambridge University Press.
Derrida, J. (1983b) 'The principle of reason', *Diacritics*, Fall, pp. 3–21.
Derrida, J. (1984a) 'Of an apocalyptic tone recently adopted in philosophy', *Oxford Literary Review*, 6:2, pp. 3–37.
Derrida, J. (1984b) 'No apocalypse, not now (full speed ahead, seven missiles, seven missives)', *Diacritics*, Summer, pp. 20–32.
Derrida, J. and McDonald, C. (1982) 'Choreographies', *Diacritics*, Summer, pp. 66–76.
Dinnerstein, D. (1976) *The Mermaid and the Minotaur: Sexual Arrangements and the Human Malaise*, Harper & Row, New York.
Le Doeuff, M. (1977) 'Women and philosophy', *Radical Philosophy*, 17, pp. 2–11.
Le Doeuff, M. (1979) 'Operative philosophy: Simone de Beauvoir and existentialism', *Ideology and Consciousness*, 6, pp. 47–58.
Dreyfuss, H. L. and Rabinow, P. (1983) *Michel Foucault: Beyond Structuralism and Hermeneutics*, University of Chicago Press.
Duren, B. (1981) 'Cixous' exorbitant texts', *Sub-Stance*, 32, pp. 39–51.
Evans, M. N. (1982) 'Portrait of Dora: Freud's case history as reviewed by Hélène Cixous', *Sub-Stance*, 36, pp. 64–71.
Felman, S. (1975) 'Women and madness: the critical phallacy', *Diacritics*, Winter, pp. 2–10.
Felman, S. (1981a) 'Rereading femininity', *Yale French Studies*, 62, pp. 19–44.
Felman, S. (ed.) (1982) *Literature and Psychoanalysis: The Question of Reading: Otherwise*, Johns Hopkins University Press, Baltimore Md.
of Defense and Poetic Will, Yale University Press, New Haven, Conn.

Felman, S. (ed.) (1982) *Literature and Psychoanalysis: The Question Of Reading: Otherwise*, Johns Hopkins University Press, Baltimore Md.
Felman, S. (1985) *Writing and Madness (Literature/Philosophy/Psychoanalysis)*, Cornell University Press, Ithaca.
Felman, S. (1987) *Jacques Lacan and the Adventure of Insight*, Harvard University Press, Cambridge, Mass.
Forrester, J. (1980) *Language and the Origins of Psychoanalysis*, Columbia University Press, New York.
Foucault, M. (1971a) 'A conversation with Michel Foucault', *Partisan Review*, 38, pp. 192–201.
Foucault, M. (1971b) 'Monstrosities in criticism', *Diacritics*, 1, Fall.
Foucault, M. (1974) 'Michel Foucault on Attica: an interview', *Telos*, 19.
Foucault, M. (1975a) *I, Pierre Riviere, Having Murdered My Mother, My Sister and My Brother . . . A Case of Parricide in the Nineteenth Century*, Pantheon Books, New York.
Foucault, M. (1975b) 'Prison talk', *Radical Philosophy*, 16.
Foucault, M. (1977b) 'Power and sex: an interview', *Telos*, 32, pp. 152–61.
Foucault, M. (1978a) 'Politics and the study of discourse', *Ideology and Consciousness*, 3, pp. 7–26.
Foucault, M. (1978b) 'The eye of power', *Semiotext(e)*, 3:2, pp. 6–19.
Foucault, M. (1978c) 'The west and the truth of sex', *Sub-Stance*, 20, pp. 5–8.
Foucault, M. (1979) 'My body, this paper, this fire . . .', *Oxford Literary Review*, 4:1, pp. 9–28.
Foucault, M. (1980a) 'The history of sexuality: an interview', *Oxford Literary Review*, 4:1.
Foucault, M. (1980b) 'War in the filigree of peace', *Oxford Literary Review*, 4:1, pp. 9–26.
Foucault, M. (1980c) 'George Canguilhem, philosopher of error', *Ideology and Consciousness*, 7, pp. 51–62.
Foucault, M. (1981) 'Questions of method: an interview', *Ideology and Consciousness*, 8, pp. 3–14.
Foucault, M. (1983a) *This Is Not A Pipe*, University of California Press, Berkeley.
Foucault, M. (1983b) 'How we behave', *Vanity Fair*, November, pp. 62–9.
Foucault, M. (1983c) 'Structuralism and post-structuralism: an interview with Michel Foucault', *Telos*, 55, pp. 195–211.
Funt, D. P. (1973) 'The question of the subject: Lacan and psychoanalysis', *Psychoanalytic Review*, 60, pp. 397–405.
Gallop, J. (1980a) 'Psychoanalysis and feminism in France', in H. Eisenstein and A. Jardine (eds) *The Future of Difference*, G. K. Hall, Boston.
Gallop, J. (1980b) 'Sade, mothers and other women', *enclitic*, 4:2, pp. 60–8.
Gallop, J. (1982a) '"Nurse Freud": class struggle in the family', *Hecate*, 3:1, pp. 26–31.
Gallop, J. (1982b) 'Writing and sexual difference: the difference within', in E. Abel (ed.) *Writing and Sexual Difference*, University of Chicago Press.
Gallop, J. (1983) 'Lacan's "mirror-stage": where to begin', *Sub-Stance*, 37/38, pp. 118–28.
Gallop, J. (1984) 'Why does Freud giggle when women leave the room?', *Hecate*, 10:1, pp. 49–53.
Gallop, J. (1985) *Reading Lacan*, Cornell University Press, Ithaca.
Gallop, J. (1988) *Thinking through the Body*, Columbia University Press, New York.
Gasché, R. (1979) 'Deconstruction as criticism', *Glyph*, 6.

Gashé, R. (1986) *The Tain of the Mirror. Derrida and the Philosophy of Reflection*, Harvard University Press, Cambridge, Mass.
Gordon, C. (1977) 'The unconscious of psychoanalysis', *Ideology and Consciousness*, 2.
Gordon, C. (1978) 'The birth of the subject', *Radical Philosophy*, 17, pp. 15–25.
Gordon, C. (1981) 'The subtracting machine', *Ideology and Consciousness*, 8, pp. 27–40.
Grisoni, D. (1982) 'The onomatopeia of desire', in P. Botsman (ed.) *Theoretical Strategies*, Local Consumption, Sydney.
Hartman, G. (1975) 'Monsieur texte: on Jacques Derrida, his Glas', *The Georgia Review*, pp. 759–75.
Hartman, G. (ed.) (1978) *Psychoanalysis and the Question of the Text*, Johns Hopkins University Press, Baltimore, Md.
Hartman, G. (1983) 'Psychoanalysis: the French connection', in E. Kurzweil and W. Phillips (eds) *Literature and Psychoanalysis*, Columbia University Press, New York.
Heath, S. (1978) 'Difference', *Screen*, 19:3, pp. 51–113.
Heath, S. (1982) *The Sexual Fix*, Macmillan, London.
Hirst, P. Q. (1976) 'Althusser and the theory of ideology', *Economy and Society*, 5:4, pp. 385–412.
Hussein, A. (1981) 'Foucault's *History of Sexuality*', *m/f*, 5/6, pp. 169–91.
Hyde, M. J. (1980 'Jacques Lacan's psychoanalytic theory of speech and language', *The Quarterly of Speech*, 66:1.
Irigaray, L. (1980) 'When the goods get together', in Marks and Courtivron, 107–10.
Irigaray, L. (1981) 'And one doesn't stir without the other', *Signs*, 7:1, pp. 60–7.
Irigaray, L. (1983) 'Interview with Luce Irigaray', *Hecate*, 9:12, pp. 192–202.
Jardine, A. (1982) 'Gynesis', *Diacritics*, Summer, pp.54–65.
Johnson, B. (1978) 'The critical difference', *Diacritics*, Summer.
Johnson, B. (1980) *The Critical Difference. Essays in the Contemporary Rhetoric of Reading*, The Johns Hopkins University Press, Baltimore, Md.
Johnson, B. (1982) 'The frame of reference: Poe, Lacan, Derrida', in S. Felman (ed.) *Literature and Psychoanalysis: The Question of Reading: Otherwise*, Johns Hopkins University Press, Baltimore, Md.
Jones, A. R. (1981) 'Writing the body: toward an understanding of écriture féminine', *Feminist Studies*, 7:1.
Judovitz, D. (1979) 'Freud: translation and/or interpretation', *Sub-Stance*, 22, pp. 29–38.
Kofman, S. (1980a) 'The narcissistic woman: Freud and Girard', *Diacritics*, Fall, pp. 36–45.
Kofman, S. (1980b) 'Ex: the woman's enigma', *Enclitic*, 4:2, pp. 17–28.
Kofman, S. (1981) 'No longer full-fledged autobiogriffe', *Sub-Stance*, 29, pp. 3–22.
Kristeva, J. (1981a) 'Women's time', *Signs*, 7:1, pp. 13–35.
Kristeva, J. (1981b) 'The maternal body', *m/f*, 5/6, pp. 158–63.
Kristeva, J. (1981c) 'Interview', *m/f*, 5/6, pp. 164–8.
Kristeva, J. (1982a) 'Approaching abjection', *Oxford Literary Review*, 5:1/2, pp. 125–49.
Kristeva, J. (1982b) *Powers of Horror. An Essay in Abjection*, Columbia University Press, New York.
Kristeva, J. (1984) *The Revolution in Poetic Language*, Columbia University Press, New York.
Kristeva, J. (1987) *Tales of Love*, Columbia University Press, New York.

Krupnik, M. (ed.) (1983) *Displacement: Derrida and After*, Indiana University Press, Bloomington.

Lacan, J. (1970) 'Of structure as an inmixing of otherness . . .', in R. Macksey and E. Donato (eds) *The Languages of Criticism and the Sciences of Man: The Structuralist Controversy*, Johns Hopkins University Press, Baltimore, Md.

Lacan, J. (1972) 'Seminar on "The Purloined Letter" ', *Yale French Studies*, 48, pp. 39–72.

Lacan, J. (1977) *The Four Fundamental Concepts of Psychoanalysis*, Hogarth Press, London.

Lacan, J. (1980) 'Seminar Paris 10th, 12th June, 1980', *Papers of Freudian School of Melbourne*, pp. 97–108.

Lacan, J. (1981a) 'Ste Anne . . .' *Semiotext(e)*, 10, pp. 208–18.

Lacan, J. (1981b) 'The Oedipus complex', *Semiotext(e)*, 10, pp. 190–202

Lacan, J. (1982) 'Desire and the interpretation of desire in *Hamlet*', in S. Felman (ed.) *Literature and Psychoanalysis: The Question of Reading: Otherwise*, Johns Hopkins University Press, Baltimore, Md.

Lacan, J. and Granoff, W. (1956) 'Fetishism: the symbolic, the imaginary and the real', in M. Balint (ed.) *Perversions, Psychodynamics and Therapy*.

Laplanche, J. (1976) *Life and Death in Psychoanalysis*, Johns Hopkins University Press, Baltimore, Md.

Lemaire, A. (1977) *Jacques Lacan*, Routledge & Kegan Paul, London.

Lemert, C. and Gillan, G. (1982) *Michel Foucault: Social Theory and Transgression*, Columbia University Press, New York.

Lingis, A. (1983) *Excesses: Eros and Culture*, SUNY Press.

Lingis, A. (1986) *Libido. Six Existential Thinkers*, SUNY Press.

McCabe, C. (ed.) (1981) *The Talking Cure*, Macmillan, London.

Macey, D. (1978) 'Review of Jacques Lacan', *Ideology and Consciousness*, 4, pp. 113–28.

Macey, D. (1988) *Lacan in Contexts*, Verso Press, London.

Major-Poetzl, P. (1983) *Michel Foucault's Archaeology of Western Culture: Towards a New Science of History*, University of North Carolina.

Marks, E. (1978) 'Women and literature in France', *Signs*, 3:4, pp. 832–42.

Marks, E. and Courtivron, I. de (eds) (1980) *New French Feminisms*, University of Massachusetts Press, Amherst.

Megill, A. (1979) 'Foucault, structuralism and the ends of history', *Journal of Modern History*, 51.

Montefiore, A. (ed.) (1982) *Philosophy in France Today*, Cambridge University Press.

Moi, T. (ed.) (1986) *The Kristeva Reader*, Blackwell, Oxford.

Moi, T. (ed.) (1987) *French Feminist Thought*, Blackwell, Oxford.

Muller, J. P. (1982) 'Ego and subject in Lacan', *Psychoanalytic Review*, 69:2, pp. 234–48.

Muller, J. P. and Richardson, W. J. (1981) *Lacan and Language: A Reader's Guide to the Ecrits*, International University Press.

Mykyta, L. (1983) 'Lacan, literature and the look: woman in the eye of psychoanalysis', *Sub-Stance*, 39, pp. 49–57.

Norris, C. (1983) *The Deconstructive Turn*, Methuen, London.

Pajakowska, C. (1981) 'Introduction to Kristeva', *m/f*, 5/6, pp. 149–57.

Raceviskis, K. (1983) *Michel Foucault and the Subversion of Intellect*, Cornell University Press, Ithaca, NY.

Ragland-Sullivan, E. (1986) *Jacques Lacan and the Philosophy of Psychoanalysis*, University of Illinois Press, Urbana.

Rajchman, J. (1977) 'Analysis in power', *Semiotext(e)*, 2:3.
Rajchman, J. (1983) 'Foucault and the ends of modernism', *October 24*, pp. 37–62.
Ramas, M. (1985) 'Freud's Dora, Dora's hysteria: the negation of a woman's rebellion', in C. Bernheimer and C. Kahane (eds) *In Dora's Case, Freud-Hysteria-Feminism*, Columbia University Press, New York.
Ryan, M. (1980) 'Self-evidence', *Diacritics*, 10:3.
Ryan, M. (1982) *Marxism and Deconstruction*, Johns Hopkins University Press, Baltimore, Md.
Schaffer, E. (1978) 'Review of *The History of Sexuality*', *Signs*, 5:4, pp. 812–20.
Schneiderman, S. (ed.) (1980) *Returning to Freud: Clinical Psychoanalysis in the School of Lacan*, Yale University Press, New Haven, Conn.
Schneiderman, S. (1983) *Jacques Lacan: The Death of an Intellectual Hero*, Cambridge University Press.
Seltzer, M. (1984) 'Reading Foucault: cells, corridors, novels', *Diacritics*, Spring, pp. 78–87.
Smith, J. and Kerigan, W. (1984) *Taking Chances: Derrida, Psychoanalysis and Literature*, London.
Spivak, G. (1979) '*Glas*-piece: a compte rendu', *Diacritics*, pp. 22–43.
Spivak, G. (1980) 'Revolutions that as yet have no model. Derrida's Limited Inc.', *Diacritics*, Winter.
Spivak, G. (1981) 'French feminism in an international frame', *Yale French Studies*, 62, pp. 154–84.
Spivak, G. C. (1982) 'The letter as cutting edge', in S. Felman (ed.) *Literature and Psychoanalysis: The Question of Reading: Otherwise*, Johns Hopkins University Press, Baltimore, Md.
Spivak, G. (1987) *In Other Worlds. Essays in Cultural Politics*, Methuen, London, pp. 39–58.
Ulmer, G. (1981) 'The post-age', *Diacritics*, Fall.
Wilden, A. (1981) *Speech and Language in Psychoanalysis*, Johns Hopkins University Press, Baltimore, Md.

4

FEMINISM, SUBJECTIVITY, AND SEXUAL EXPERIENCE

Philipa Rothfield

INTRODUCTION

In this chapter, I will discuss the question of subjectivity in relation to the issue of modernity. I will look at some of the implications of the writings and emphases of the early women's liberation movement, then trace some of the theoretical trajectories of subjectivity and sexual difference. This will incorporate an investigation of humanism, anti-humanism, the unconscious, and sexuality. The final section will move on to a less-charted territory, and articulate some thinking on the role of the body/our bodies within subjectivity. I will discuss the philosophical tendency to focus upon consciousness at the expense of the body, performance art, and the recognition of the body's place in the work of art itself, and finally sex as a social practice.

Subjectivity has been theorized within philosophy, political theory, and sociology for some time, and in the case of philosophy, for a very long period. The whole idea that we are subjects has developed within particular historical circumstances. Hence, how subjectivity is both understood and experienced has changed over time. In particular, it was the Enlightenment which generated our modern sense of self and what we have come to call humanism. Charles Taylor charts the impact of radical Enlightenment thought which, he argues, produced the modern subject as a self-defining being, that is, as someone who creates him-/herself (Taylor 1975)[1]. The self-defining subject of modern epistemology is said to form the basis of the atomic subjectivity of psychology and politics which arose out of this movement (Taylor 1975, p. 7). Taylor writes:

> But the modern notion of the subject has left no one untouched and unchanged in European society, or indeed the world. In part we can see this as the result of changes, political, economic, social which spread under the influence of minorities first over Western society as a whole, and then over alien societies.
>
> (1975, p. 9)

This modern notion of the self has been the subject of critical examination. At a political level, the New Left, having departed from Soviet orthodoxy, has come to interrogate subjectivity via developments in the theory of ideology.[2] To theorize on these matters in anti-humanist terms, such as Althusser proposes, is not merely critically to revise the conceptual framework of subjectivity but is to threaten radically the entire capacity of the subject to know itself. This is why the general terrain of anti-humanist work is seen to figure 'the death of the subject'. Anti-humanism has a further implication for forms of social analysis such as feminist theory, for it denies the possibility of articulating the social sphere in terms of the subject as a ground of explanation. Like Taylor, Foucault also looks at the growth of the human subject in modern discourse. Foucault further makes certain predictions regarding the lifespan of such a subject whose development he critically traces. He writes of the subject ('man'; the *male* subject):

> One thing in any case is certain: man is neither the oldest nor the most constant problem that has been posed for human knowledge. Taking a relatively short chronological sample within a restricted geographical area – European culture since the sixteenth century – one can be certain that man is a recent invention within it, . . . As the archeology of our thought easily shows, man is an invention of recent date. And one perhaps nearing its end.
>
> (Foucault 1970, pp. 386–7)

In a comparable vein, Marx predicted the death of capitalism. Yet he later wrote that he had mistaken the birth-pangs of capitalism for its death-throes. If one were to give a feminist response to Foucault's eschatology in a manner equally grandiose, it would be that Man will not die until the birth and death of Woman. However, the birth of any such Woman is attended by a host of theoretical and discursive influences not present at the birth of Man. Feminist theorists have given some insight to the notions of subjectivity developed within modernity. For instance, the notion that 'man' is just that, and not woman also. However, a feminist critique of that monolithic concept, Man, need not pose a similarly giant foil, Woman. The development of woman-centred theory is not a contemporary of but an heir to modernity's birth of 'man'. Such theories at once both bear the mark of modern thought and are subject to critiques of modernity and the (modern) subject.[3] As Alice Jardine writes:

> The result has been that 'woman' (as well as that which has connoted the female) has been *problematized* in new ways as both concept and identity. In the search for new kinds of legitimation, in the absence of Truth, in anxiety over the decline of paternal authority, and in the midst of spiraling diagnoses of Paranoia, the End of Man and

> History, 'woman' has been set in motion both rhetorically and ideologically.
>
> (Jardine 1985, p. 36)

The question of subjectivity covers a highly complex concatenation of problems which are always in part determined by socio-historical factors. A heterogeneity of other contemporary fields has also speculated on what it is that makes up our identity; from neurology, biology, and physics, to the relationship between mind and brain (see Bergland 1985), electromagnetic circuitry, and the body (see Becker and Seldon 1985), to questions of performance, the entry of the body into performance art (see Lippard 1976), and postmodernism (see Kelly, 1983). Because of the political nature of feminism, one of the most pertinent fields of inquiry regarding subjectivity is that of social and political thought, for it is centrally concerned with notions of agency subjectivity, social practice, and structures. At a most general level, the impact of feminism in social and political theory has been to introduce questions regarding the *relationship between gender and subjectivity*. As Stuart Hall writes:[4]

> A theory of culture which cannot account for patriarchal structures of dominance and oppression is, in the wake of feminism, a non-starter. . . . The problematics of these theories have had to be profoundly recast, their very premises brought into radical question, because of their absence, in their very theoretical structure, of the question of sexual difference.
>
> (Hall *et al.* 1980, p. 39)

I think one central consideration here concerns the way in which gender is considered a fundamental determinant of subjectivity. There are two extreme ways of representing this relationship: (1) that gender is a social construct, a social level, which is attached to a given identity, or (2) that gender is a basic given such that there are *masculine subjects* and *feminine subjects*, and these are the intrinsic categories of subjectivity. How is one to account for subjectivity/identity here? Humanist forms of theory suggest that we are all fundamentally equal, rational, conscious beings, whose autonomy incorporates the potential to make informed, free choices. This position underlies both liberalism and liberal feminism. Now,the role of gender for the liberal subject lies 'outside' the neutral, autonomous self. According to this paradigm, gender will be a secondary characteristic – one which somehow arises at a later moment in the production of one's identity. This is why much of the emphasis of liberal feminism is upon the elimination of discrimination and the availability of equal opportunities of which the rational (in the first instance), female (in the second) subject is able to avail herself.

On the other hand, a distinct approach towards subjectivity, one which utilizes the unconscious and psychoanalytic theory, locates the presence of gender differences at a much deeper, inaccessible level, that is, where certain determinants of sexual difference are said to be outside the immediate scrutiny of one's conscious mind. This is a very different view of gender and subjectivity from the liberal position. The movement away from a liberal account of the self, towards one involving the unconscious, is more generally represented in the contrast between *humanism* and *anti-humanism* (although liberalism is but one variant of humanism). Since the advent of structuralism and its successors, a contrast has been asserted between humanist forms of explanation and either decentred or anti-humanist accounts.

One of the earliest influences on structuralism was Saussure's linguistics.[5] Saussure argued that individuals 'slot' into a given language which is structured outside of them. In this sense, language prefigures the individuals who speak it. This is significantly different from other linguistic accounts. The contrast lies between thinking that *we* create meaning through intending to say something, and seeing meaning as already part of a system (language) of which we are able to partake. Such diverse traditions as empiricism and phenomenology are centred upon the individual, and this is reflected in their theories of language. Saussure's work signifies a radical break with this tradition, for he stresses the system of language as having priority (over individual usage of it) for any attempt to explain signification. This break has had a great influence in differing areas of the humanities, for example, anthropology, literature, and sociology. What characterizes this influence is a *decentred* form of explanation. At its most general level, one can observe an explanatory focus upon the social, the systemic, that which is outside the individual as a means to account for any phenomena, whether meaning, behaviour, sexual difference, or *anthropos*. The emphasis is upon the underlying conditions of a social system which makes individual participation possible. Culler writes:

> In all cases where we are dealing with what Saussure calls values, that is to say with the social significance of objects and actions, the subject takes on a crucial role, in that the facts one is seeking to explain come from his intuitions and judgements. However, once the subject is in place, once he is firmly established at the centre of the analytical domain, the whole enterprise of the human sciences becomes one of deconstructing the subject, of explaining meanings in terms of systems of convention which escape the subject's conscious grasp.
>
> (1976, pp. 77–8)

This is completely at odds with Taylor's depiction of the self-defining subject of modern epistemology. The shift from that which the individual can know, towards the social/external elements which condition the subject is fundamental. Culler refers to the construction of explanation outside the subject's knowledge. *Once such a method is adopted, we leave the epistemological realm of modern subjectivity and move towards a decentred form of explanation*. Within social theory this is elaborated in terms of a tension between *human agency* – self-chosen action and the ability to effect change – and *socio-structural conditions*. The former represents an emphasis on the individual's ability to act, the latter upon the social conditions which prefigure, if not determine, individual action. The two emphases can be characterized in terms of humanism and anti-humanism. Although I am tracing the development of humanism as an outgrowth of the Enlightenment, and anti-humanism as the product of semiotics and structuralist thought, there are other sources of a 'non-centred' perspective. Heidegger's work has served to inspire an anti-humanist perspective, especially in the writings of Derrida and poststructuralism.[6] Also Freud, Nietzsche, and Marx represent thinkers who did not focus their work on the consciousness of the individual but who have been instead described as three *masters of suspicion* (see Ricoeur 1970). The usage of suspicion here has to do with whether the consciousness of the subject is a sufficient ground for analysis, and, ultimately, objectivity. The contemporary force of anti-humanism derives from the general decentred character of recent French thought which has found inspiration from the writings of these earlier authors amongst others.[7]

Humanism and anti-humanism differ according to the way in which the structural nexus between self and society is posited. A form of humanism is involved where the individual is seen to be fundamental, and society the resultant sum of individual actions. For humanism, the self is both distinct and whole. The humanist subject is self-constitutive. According to anti-humanism, the self is not the most fundamental element. The subject within anti-humanism is always secondary for any social explanation, which will draw on factors outside of – beyond – the individual. In this sense, there are factors outside the self which make possible the acts, speech, and thinking of the human subject. The emphasis upon that which is both outside of and prior to the subject leads to a focus upon a whole variety of social determinants and orders of determination. Within feminism, there has been a great deal of interest in looking at sexual difference, and the ways in which patriarchy determines male and female subjectivity. The anti-humanist stance leads to a focus upon the social determination of the individual. In the case of feminist theory, this can be seen in the use of psychoanalytic or ideological/materialist forms of explanation which stress the role of the unconscious in the social production of gender/sexual difference.[8] The shift away from the consciousness of the fe(male) subject as a ground for explanation is at the same time a focus upon the structural determinations of patriarchy and the forms of symbolic/representational orders which prefigure (if not construe) the male and female person. Hence, we witness an emphasis upon the role of ideology in the cultural production of gender or upon the phallocentric symbolic order wherein male and female subjects are positioned.[9]

The above discussion represents one general level of approach towards, and debate surrounding, subjectivity. It is the attempt to give a socio-structural account of the way in which subjects are constituted. Social theory is concerned to explicate notions of agency, subjectivity, social practices, and social structures.[10] The socio-structural account bears upon the question of how are we to theorize subjectivity, and the nature of the relationship between gender and subjectivity. Michèle Barrett writes of feminism's challenge to Marxism, and the Marxist development beyond economism both yielding a new emphasis on the potency of ideology (1980, p. 31). The role of ideology in the oppression of women, and the relationship of this to gender's role in the social formation, has allowed the oppression of women to be understood as a 'relatively autonomous element of the social formation' (p. 31). This has enabled discussion around the *construction of masculine and feminine subjects*. Barrett writes:

> This influence has been demonstrated in the emphasis given in recent Marxist feminist work to the ideological construction of gendered subjects and the attempt to rethink psychoanalytic theory from a Marxist feminist perspective. This work has taken two major directions: the exploration of familial relations and the development of masculine and feminine subjectivity, and the analysis of representations of gender diffence in cultural production.
>
> (p. 31)

Another approach which might be explored, is to take a more discursive path via the issues/characteristics of ourselves which have bearing upon questions of subjectivity. Such an approach allows for the introduction of new and as yet untheorized considerations. For instance, if feelings are not thought to be important, it is unlikely that they will be considered pertinent for any theoretical rendition of the subject. The women's liberation movement (WLM) began with protests and writings about all sorts of features of women and women's experience that had not been considered important before. It is possible to see the variety of theoretical reverberations which exist as responses to the political radicalization of sexual difference we call feminism.

THE WOMEN'S LIBERATION MOVEMENT: OPENING GAMBITS

The theoretical terrain of subjectivity has undergone much change in the last twenty years, and has opened up in particular respects, not least because of the unsettling impact of feminism. Henriques *et al.* write of the WLM that:

unlike traditional forms of resistance, it was insisted that subjective transformation was a major site of political change. . . . It is the impact of the Women's movement, with an increasingly strong network of publications, which provides impetus for much recent theoretical work on subjectivity.

(1984, p. 7)

Personal praxes

The WLM has effected an enormous shift as regards the domain and processes of socio-political activity. This shift is signified by the feminist slogan, 'the personal is political'. Historically the Left had embraced what had come to be understood as Marxist orthodoxy, one which correlated political activity with the class struggle, that is, the political praxis (practice) of the working class. The worker's struggle was focused upon the workplace as the arena in which the capitalist mode of production operated and around which the battle against exploitation would be conducted. Trade unions were regarded as the vanguard of the worker's struggle, and the history of their formation involved both the effective exclusion of women from their hierarchies (working women also had the prime responsibility for childcare and domestic labour), and the political battle for a 'a working man's family wage'. As an example, the battle in Victoria, Australia, for the eight-hour working day had the slogan:

EIGHT HOURS LABOUR
EIGHT HOURS RECREATION
EIGHT HOURS REST
(from the first eight-hour banner used in Victoria, Australia, 16 April 1856)

Notice that childcare and domestic labour don't feature in the above reckoning. Either the campaign referred only to working men, or unpaid domestic labour is recreation! Family life was regarded as private, a refuge, a 'haven in a heartless world'.[11] Politics had to do with the public sphere, and personal relationships, intimate matters, were not the concern of any Leftist orthodoxy, then or more recently.

Doris Lessing's fictional writings could be related to the personal difficulties she experienced as someone of the Left in both Africa and England. Written prior to the WLM (first published in 1962), *The Golden Notebook* is itself divided into notebooks, which function as categories, whereby her protagonist's personal questions are separated from her political thoughts on the (Communist) Party. The 'golden notebook' (within the novel) is a synthesis of the separate(d) categories, and one can see her narrator's attempt to deal with the problems inherent in such a separation. The WLM witnessed a burst of writings on the inequities within the Left and the civil rights movement, which draw attention to the importance of personal relations in the political realm. In 1969, Marge Piercy wrote 'The Grand Coolie Damn', in which the sexual manipulations, narcissism, and exploitations by the men in the movement were acidly documented (in Morgan 1970). It is vital that the personal realm, a hitherto ignored region of political activity, is seen to be a legitimate domain of political concern.

Women and privacy

At the onset of the WLM, much critical attention was directed to the primary identification of women as wives and mothers. The forms of social practice associated with this notion of identity are within the confinement of the home. Sex, personal relationships, family life – all private affairs.

Feminists have written on the public/private split, and its attendant notions of selfhood within the area of social and political theory. In her discussion of liberal feminism, Zillah Eisenstein traces the history and constitution of the public and private spheres alongside women's relegation to the home, the archetype of privacy. In classical Athens, men spent their time in the marketplace, the gymnasium – public areas – whilst women laboured indoors (Eisenstein 1981, p. 22). It is interesting to note also that Plato and Aristotle began to *theorize the citizen*: a male participating in the public domain, the subject of political life. *Vis-à-vis* women's association with the private sphere, women have not universally and transhistorically lived and worked only within the home. In Europe, peasant women worked in the fields, and after the industrial revolution, proletarian women worked in the factories. Yet the growth of sociology in the nineteenth century is one which mirrors the separation of spheres of public and private in relation to industrial society. Janet Wolff notes the appearance of women in the classic texts of sociology only inasmuch as they 'relate to men, in the family, or in minor roles in the public sphere' (Wolff 1985, p. 43). She writes:

> But the literature of modernity ignores the private sphere, and to that extent is silent on the subject of women's primary domain. This silence is not only detrimental to any understanding of the lives of the female sex; it obscures a crucial part of the lives of men, too, by abstracting one part of their experience and failing to explore the interrelation of public and private spheres. . . . Moreover, the public could only be constituted as a particular set of institutions and practices on the basis of the removal of other areas of social life to the invisible arena of the private.
>
> (p. 44)

The absence of women from the texts of modernity, along with a generalized lack of sociological theorization on the private sphere, does not signify a complete absence of women from working life/the paid workforce. The industrialization of Europe also led to the entry of women into the workforce in a mode of production that was out of the home (Heller 1982, p. 61). What we do see in classical sociological works is the presence of women to the extent that they figure in the recognizable arenas of public life and productive labour. Wolff argues that the modern era clearly affected women's experience of home and work, and that there is a need for a yet-to-be-articulated feminist sociology. She writes:

> The recovery of women's experience is part of the project of retrieving what has been hidden, and attempting to fill the gaps in the classic accounts. The feminist revision of sociology and social history means the gradual opening up of areas of social life and experience which to date have been obscured by the partial perspective and particular bias of modern sociology.
>
> (Wolff 1985, p. 45)

Consciousness-raising

In this section, we will discuss notions of experience, consciousness, the unconscious, and in particular, make some points regarding the pertinence of consciousness-raising (CR) to questions of subjectivity. At the time of its emergence in the late sixties, CR performed the vital function of allowing women to reassess the popular beliefs and misconceptions about women and a woman's place (Morgan 1970, pp. xxiii–xxiv; Eisenstein 1984, chapter 4). It also served to highlight the importance of inner feelings. The practice of CR has enabled women to articulate a broad range of personal concerns – such as body image, appearance, sexuality, sexual relationships, motherhood – which gained recognition as 'valid' issues. The emphasis and legitimation of interest in the personal has since provoked much writing in feminist theory which is centred upon sexuality, the body, desire, and the female subject. Similarly, the notion of sexual difference has emerged in the past twenty years as a central pivot for much feminist writing. So, the first point to be made is that all of these concerns have gained a sense of importance as a result of CR. In this sense, it is possible to say that CR functioned historically to help feminists flesh-out the content of their subjectivities, and to perceive connections in relation to their shared/common experience.

Second, the development of CR groups was a strategic innovation, allowing women to explore their experience and to become politicized within the one process. The process of CR itself was also seen to constitute political action *per se*, a form of political activity wholly distinct from those traditionally associated with the Left.

The third point I wish to make concerns the place of consciousness within a theory of subjectivity. The stress on consciousness within CR carries with it a certain epistemological trajectory which looks towards the conscious mind as a source of knowledge. Now, this model embodies a certain framework, which suggests that:

1 The contents of our conscious minds are accessible and amenable to introspection.
2 In principle we only have to look inside to uncover that which is present to consciousness.
3 One can look towards consciousness for evidence of women's experience under patriarchy.

Alternatively, feminist theorists have made the attempt to introduce *the unconscious as a central feature of our subjectivity*. This represents a move away from the epistemological priority accorded consciousness as shown above. A feminist theory which utilizes the unconscious need not wholly reject the attention paid to consciousness within CR, but it does signify an interest in a domain which is not accessible to the subject's own reflections. Politically, there is an associated question of emphasis. It is possible to observe a focus on consciousness and CR in the earlier period of the WLM allied to voluntaristic forms of polemic, whereas more recently, there has been a growth of feminist theory which incorporates notions of the unconscious. Henriques *et al*. write:

> This voluntarism accords with much of the traditional left's approach to change and we have criticized it explicitly with respect to the liberatory politics of the 1960s and early 1970s. . . . Furthermore, we have argued that the political crises of the present time make it imperative that we develop a clearer understanding of what militates against change, what accounts for reaction and for resistance. This has been recognized particularly within feminism. The task of working out what, exactly, a personal politics might consist of has forced women to recognize limitations in what can be achieved through consciousness-raising. This has proved to be particularly so in the area of sexuality, where . . . the intransigence of desires defies any simple rationalistic manipulation.
>
> (1984, p. 207)

From an initial hostility, to wary critical adaptation, the entry of theories of the unconscious upon feminist views of the subject has produced the following consequences:

1 Our subjectivity consists of more than that which we know through our conscious minds.
2 The question of sexuality is intrinsically bound up with our psychological make-up.

3 Sexual difference is a central feature of our identity.
4 We are no longer seen to be rational, autonomous beings, or unitary selves.

Juliet Mitchell and Jane Gallop attempt to explore sexuality and sexual difference fromn a psychoanalytic viewpoint, where they make the connection between *the workings of patriarchy in the construction of masculine and feminine identity* (see Mitchell 1974; Gallop 1982). Teresa Brennan has highlighted the crucial importance of the role of the historical in the social/psychical determination of sexual difference and femininity (Brennan 1989). If one subscribes to some form of psychoanalytic theory within feminism, the political question arises as to whether the unconscious is tied to particular historical forms, namely, the ubiquitous yet concrete existence of patriarchy at given moments, or whether the unconscious is universal and immutable. The latter option does not recommend itself for a theory of social change, for one would confront an antinomy between the possibility of social change against the impossibility of individual change (since the individual's unconscious is fixed). Consider also the initial reasoning behind introducing a theory of the unconscious into feminist theory – in order to help explain the operations of patriarchy (a concrete social form, not some immutable trans-social structure) in the determination of subjectivity. Henriques *et al*. note the importance of paying attention to that which mitigates against social change, not to that which renders change impossible. This question also has relevance for the theory of subjectivity in that it demands a further articulation of the nature of the unconscious and sexual difference.

The sex/gender distinction was fairly prominent in feminist texts of the 1970s. I mention it here because it betrays a certain emphasis on the external façade of the social production of gender which parallels the centrality of consciousness for CR. The sex/gender distinction generally represented discussions around the social construction of gender. The initial tenor of feminist writings on sex-role differences went to suggest that basically men and women were the same, and that society produced notions of gender difference which were then somehow melded on to concrete sexual differences. The ideals of androgyny, the intent to procure the 'annihilation' of sex-roles, and the debates with sociobiology (see chapter 7), all tended to regard gender difference as a social construct which could in principle be peeled off one's identity. This is the view that gender differences are external to one's identity or subjectivity. As Moira Gatens notes: 'for theorists of gender, the mind of either sex is a neutral, passive entity, a blank state, on which is inscribed various social "lessons"' (1983, p. 144). Also, the notion of socialization is central for the sex/gender distinction, for it is used to explain the inscription of masculinity and femininity upon the given physical, sexed body. Boys and girls are socialized differently; at school, home, and via the media. Gatens argues that the sex/gender distinction presupposes that the body, upon which is inscribed gender, is a neutral, passive entity, and that consciousness is both primary and determinant (Gatens 1983, p. 147). She denies that the body is neutral, passive, and 'inert', and argues instead that *the body is situated*. The implication of this point is that our identity is not centred upon consciousness, but involves the body also in a complex configuration of 'signification and its historical, psychological, and cultural manifestations' (Gatens 1983, p. 152). This is at the same time to take a position against humanism, one which we will now address.

BEYOND HUMANISM: THEORETICAL DIRECTIONS

Liberal feminism and humanism – freedom and the closet male

The concept that the subject is an autonomous, self-constitutive being is articulated within the framework of liberal humanism, and therefore appears in the discourse of liberal feminism. The identity contained in the liberal paradigm would appear to be an abstract individual. However, the tradition of liberal humanism has been critically reviewed by feminist authors who tease out the implicitly male gender of such an 'abstract' individual (see Lloyd 1984; Grimshaw 1986; Tapper 1986). Toril Moi further argues that humanism is actually part of patriarchal ideology: 'At its centre is the seamlessly unified self – either individual or collective – which is commonly called "Man". . . . Gloriously autonomous it banishes from itself all conflict, contradiction and ambiguity. In this humanist ideology the self is the *sole author* of history' (1985, p. 8). Yet some feminists still wish to incorporate some of the ideals of liberalism such as equality, freedom of the individual, the right to minimal state interference, and this is most generally known as liberal feminism.

The dichotomy between humanism and anti-humanism differentiates French and Anglo-American theory. In feminist terms, it represents a difference in the ways in which the female subject of emancipation is represented and articulated. For humanism, the individual is fundamental, and is an entity whose social freedom is the ultimate end of liberation. Anti-humanism does not have a simple opposite, for the conception of 'the self' becomes problematized in decentred modes of discourse. The self is no longer regarded as self-constitutive, but rather as a production of, variously, ideology, discourse, the structure of the unconscious, and/or language. In its extreme form, the subject of anti-humanism is completely determined, and those determining factors are likely to be social in nature, if discursive in form. Such a determinist conception of the self need not subscribe to an essentialist view of the subject as the same subject throughout history, but does regard subjectivity as completely determined at any particular historical juncture or discursive position. Thus, there may very well be different kinds of subjectivity, e.g. male and female, in different socio-historical periods and geographical locations. What the determinist form of anti-humanism maintains is that the production of subjectivity occurs outside the subject via social determinants. This manner of production is the same for all subjects, though the societal factors which enter upon such determinations will vary, and hence the subjects of different epochs will also differ.

In the political discourse of humanist feminism, women are both able to have a unified voice and to be universally addressed.[12] What have the theoretical trajectories of anti-humanism done to 'the' subject of feminism? The dissolution of the universal subject has also led to heterogeneity of theoretical discourses within feminism. It is no longer possible to assume a univocal epistemological project for women.[13] The ensuing fracturing of subjectivity, from within and without, has led to certain shifts in orientation in feminist discourse. What are the political implications of this? Angela McRobbie argues that we live within social forms of this fragmentation, within postmodernism, and its attendant social schizophrenia and ruptured subjectivity (McRobbie 1986, p. 55). Yet she does not view this social state of radical incoherence as necessarily implying political reaction, but claims that it has appeal to social groups, black, female, working class, who are experiencing the 'enforced fragmentation of impermanent work' (p. 58). Lucy Lippard is concerned with the question of the political potential of the 'post-everything' art of the 1980s (1984, p. 165). She looks at the positive potential in the techniques of distance and social irony such as Yvonne Rainer employs. She further cites a show held in New York, which expressed no single, political line but a 'social and philosophical cacophony':

> Distancing techniques were used against themselves in self-referential hooks into content from art, as in Barbara Kruger's contribution which began: 'We are reading this and deciding whether it is irony or passion/We think it is irony/We think it is exercising a distancing mechanism – '
>
> (Lippard 1984, p. 168)

The smooth and harmonious face of subjectivity has become pitted with a series of historical and semantic productions, and overdeterminations. Feminist excursions into the terrain of sexuality and sexual difference have come to ascribe an ensemble of levels to the female subject, such that networks of desire, conscious thought, unconscious repressions, and complexes may be interwoven, producing paradoxes, tensions, and ruptures. Mary Kelly's work is an expression of this theoretical complexity. In her work *Post-Partum Document*, she utilizes 'multiple representational modes' which also interrogate Lacanian theory in relation to motherhood.[14] Kelly's more recent work, *Interim*, is concerned with women ageing, against a background of fashion, romantic fantasy and popular medicine, elements she sees as involved in the fixing of femininity and which are able to be contested (Nairne *et al.* 1987). *Interim* uses both text written on acrylic and a photograph of a leather jacket, an item of fashion, which is not shown as worn by any one subject/woman. One could say that both devices at once construct or imply a feminine subject, yet nowhere make explicit her presence. There is a certain ambiguity in all of this, in that one sees the means by which (a) female identity is suggested, yet we never 'see' her. Kelly denies the existence of a single theoretical discourse which can exhaustively explain all social forms and relations (Kelly 1982, p. 33). In discussing her work, Kelly notes that:

> My aim is to establish that there might be another postmodernist strategy which doesn't simply have to do with reviving the traditional practices concerned with a specific medium. . . . It's actually an intervening moment when one becomes aware of something that's grating – a dissonance between how one feels and how one appears. . . . How I organise the first section around the body is to take that theme, and in a sense to parody their presentation in the discourses like fashion or popular medicine. . . . So in the piece, the movement that's being set up is one shifting between image and text, between looking and hearing; and then considering the image of woman again from a new perspective.
>
> (Nairne *et al.* 1987, pp. 148–9)

The multiplicity of subject-positions implied in various discourses might be said to have dissolved the notion of the subject altogether. But I don't think this is the case. The women artists cited above (Kruger and Kelly) both dislocate given forms of female sexuality,and suggest new forms. To say that there is no *a priori* subject is not to deny the very real historical productions of any particular conjuncture and within specific contexts. Nor is it to rule out the possibility of generating new forms of subjectivity. Let us consider the work of Althusser, discussed in chapter 3. The central feature of Althusser's account is that the subjects produced by ideology are real by virtue of their inscription and participation in the social process. For Althusser, we become subjects through the forms of address inherent in social practice(s). This represents the workings of ideology, which has both a material existence, and which operates so as to interpellate (constitute) individuals as subjects. Our sense of identity as women in advanced capitalist society is given, for example, through the variety of social practices in which we find ourselves inscribed and in which we act. The different class, race, and national characteristics we possess also imply different senses of subjectivity which are produced according to social context and forms of practice. This, for Althusser, ensures the reproduction of capitalism, and, we might say, of patriarchy.

Whilst Althusser pointed out the efficacy of ideology as the means by which subjectivity is produced, his work does not pay adequate attention to the *productions of meaning* inherent in the various forms of social interaction. The sense of identity and configurations of sexual difference present in all manner of cultural practice, such as on television, in films, magazines, books, and newspapers, requires some account of signification so as to supplement the work of Althusser. Although Althusser's theory of ideology gives a very specific framework for the production of subjectivity, it does not consider the representations through which one may be addressed as subject which are intrinsic to the meaning/significance of social practice. For instance, the codes of behaviour and appearance in everyday life are socially inscribed with meaning, such that a woman doing the shopping in a working-class suburb is likely to be addressed in a certain way in the course of her activities because of the social significance of her clothing, demeanour, and apparent social status (Barthes 1973). A woman dressed in expensive apparel is likely be addressed in a more deferential way, signifying both that she is a member of the ruling class, and a woman. The ways in which these women will implicitly take their subjectivity to be addressed will incorporate the social meaning of the social actions they find themselves in. To wear fur and jewels, to talk in particular ways, has a certain significance in advanced capitalist society, and the social systems of meaning which give such things significance are integral to an understanding of the role of ideology in these forms of social practice. As Stuart Hall has remarked:

> Semiotics has greatly contributed to our understanding of how signification systems work, of how things and relations signify. But . . . it tends to halt its investigation at the frontier where the internal relations of 'languages' articulate with social practices and historical structures. The materialist theory of ideology has considerably advanced our understanding of the nature of the economic and socio-historical determination on ideas – but it lacks an adequate theory of representation without which the specificity of the ideological region cannot be constituted.
>
> (1978, p. 28)

The theory of ideology then also needs an account of the operations of discourse in the social formation. Althusser's work does not look at the signifying relations within which all forms of social practice are inscribed. Hall's point is that the theory of ideology needs to be combined with one of representation/signification.[15]

Where does this leave us in our perusal of subjectivity? We have moved from a discussion on the impact of the politics of the personal on notions of subjectivity, through the raising of consciousness, to its decentring via the unconscious and anti-humanism. The entry of questions of discourse, and the forms of signifying and cultural relations, enables a certain emphasis upon *the subject position inscribed in representations and social practice*. This enables a feminist analysis of the images and representations of women, and 'the feminine' in the social formation. Feminist film theory has utilized such a theoretical framework to investigate the ways in which women are both represented in the medium of film and addressed as viewing subjects of the film (see Kaplan 1983; Kuhn 1985). What is sometimes called 'the subject-in-process' could be seen to be the person in active and collaborative relation to the film. It is through ideology that one's subjectivity is at once both addressed and produced, and via the social production of meaning that this process occurs.

The link between material forms of social practice, economic determinants, and semantic configurations in the ideological production of subjectivity is an important one. But is it enough for an account of subjectivity? Foucault writes:

> Indeed I wonder whether, before one poses the question of ideology, it wouldn't be more materialist to study first the question of the body and the effects of power on it. Because what troubles me with these analyses which prioritise ideology is that there is always presupposed a human subject on the lines provided by classical philosophy, endowed with a consciousness which power is then thought to seize on.
>
> (1980, p. 58)

The movement away from humanism need not dwell in the terrain of decentred *consciousness*, but may involve a reconceptualization of the self as more than consciousness.

THE MINDFUL BODY/THE EMBODIED MIND: BEYOND DUALISM

The classical philosophical episteme to which Foucault refers is given through both the traditions of empiricism and rationalism. In Plato's work, the denial of sensual experience, in the broadest sense, as food for either the soul or the growth of rational knowledge, we see the beginnings of the western Judaeo-Christian vilification of flesh and the carnal. The construction of rationality upon the exclusion of the senses – whose organ of experience is the body – has had a profound influence upon the development of western philosophical thought.[16]

It is in Cartesian dualism, however, that we experience both the split between mind and body and the *privileging* of the mind over body. Descartes's axiomatic discovery that 'I think therefore I am' expresses the view that our identity is to be characterized through thought. The ensuing privilege given to consciousness in nearly all the human sciences has deprived us of an understanding of the body. Bryan Turner argues that 'the body is absent in social theory, especially in sociological theory' (1984, p. 6). This is despite the fact that our bodies are clearly central for our social interactions, perceptual abilities, sexual encounters, rituals of eating, and excretion.

Unlike the Hindu belief that the body is a temple for the soul, where the dance is considered one of the most spiritual forms of devotion, our bodies are socially inscribed in a myriad of ways which enable them to participate in the 'free' market of commodity forms. The body beautiful, the packaged rituals in the production of fitness (if it hurts it must be doing you good), have particular pertinence to women, for the development of reason and the privilege of consciousness has been a male preserve. In contrast, the possession, persecution, and control of *women's* bodies has enjoyed historical continuity in form if not content. Women have been identified with the carnal, the physical, one of whose contemporary manifestations can be seen in the representation and treatment of women as sex objects. If the human sciences have generally and historically been androcentric in form, and patriarchal in social context, it should come as little surprise that the couplet woman/body has been devalued in a hierarchical logic of binary difference. As Foucault has gone to great lengths to explore, western society has practised a history of disciplinary inscriptions on our bodily participation in the world via configurations of power and the constitution of knowledge.

The history of feminism reveals some crucial struggles over the control and determination of women's bodies. The issues of rape, abortion, reproductive technology, and sexuality are all instances of these struggles. Women's particular identification with the body, and the feminist interest in 'bodily issues', also indicates possibilities for exploration and new work on these concerns within feminist discourse and practice. Two books have been recently published on art and the women's movement (Parker and Pollock 1987) and on images of femininity in art and the media (Betterton 1987). Both these edited collections are interested in questions of representation in relation to the female body. The arena of women's health has seen some innovative links between mind and body, and women's spiritual or intuitive experience. Jeannine Parvati writes:

> What I have explored in the process of making this book is the relationship between the feminine and the healing. . . . So I see this creative project, the book Hygieia: A WOMAN'S HERBAL, as an attempt to translate from the soul's point of view the phenomenon of holistic health as it relates to women, and many aspects of the feminine.
>
> (1978, pp. iv–v)

The concept of holistic health is predicated on a desired harmony and unity between mind, body, and soul. It is clearly non-dualistic, and challenges some of the categories of western medicine. Similarly, yoga blurs the traditional boundaries between mind, body, and spirit via the breath.

What, then, does the western privileging of consciousness indicate about subjectivity? Firstly, that *we witness an instance of the law of uneven development*. The centring of theories of subjectivity on consciousness has distorted the very framework by which we attempt to understand subjectivity. Gatens articulates and argues against the dualistic assumption that whilst: 'the body is neutral and passive with regard to the formation of consciousness, consciousness is primary and determinant – implicitly a rationalist view' (1983, pp. 146–7). In recent years, there has been a good deal of interest in the body within feminist theory.[17] Gatens discusses the different kinds of body which are central for an adequate understanding of subjectivity. She rejects the notion of the body as a passive and neutral, and claims that there are at least two kinds of body, male and female (p. 148). Furthermore, she discusses the body as situated, lived, and animate (p. 150).

The realms of contemporary dance, performance art, Feldenkrais and Alexander techniques have produced some interesting insights for our sense of selves and our bodies. Both Alexander technique and the work of Moshe Feldenkrais, whilst utilized by some dancers, have arisen from therapeutic and movement-oriented origins. Both techniques aim to extend our awareness and experience of the body, of our habitual yet unconscious movement qualities and patterns. Sometimes this involves the attempt to 'think into' or concentrate upon different areas of the body. This may enable a growth of awareness of, or sensitivity towards, these regions as we inhabit them. For instance, I might do a series of exercises that give me the experience of the roundness of my head, of its positioning on the spine and so on. This may lead to the perceptual experience of both the three-dimensionality of my head, and its movement through space along with my own movement. This could be contrasted with my more habitual experience of my head as largely constituted by my face (the front of my head), and with not much regard as to the back of my skull or its placement on my spine. In this sense, one might say that such an exercise enables the expansion of one's experience of one's own body, if not of other's. Louise Steinman cites Bonnie Bainbridge Cohen: 'I would say that I'm in a state of awareness. If I'm working with any area of someone else's body, I will go into that area of my own body to see. In the process I become more open also. It becomes like two bells ringing on the same pitch. We can resonate each other' (in Steinman 1986, p. 19). I want to say that this extension or heightening of awareness represents an experience of our bodies in a more subjective fashion. Often we pay little or no attention to many areas of our bodies, whilst, as Gatens points out, some bodily sites are privileged or emphasized, for example, the mouth, anus, and genitals (Gatens 1983, p. 152). That we can experience our bodies in a subjective fashion, rather than as reified objects, allows for the expansion of awareness and understanding in and through our bodies. This kind of approach is at odds with a strictly dualistic conception of mind and body, for *it tends towards the development of a mindful body*. We are inclined to locate consciousness in the brain, as the subject of our thinking. Thinking is thought to emanate from the mind-centred eye of consciousness. But the experience of feeling, breathing, even thinking into areas of our own bodies says something about the possibilities for our sense of subjectivity and our understanding of consciousness – that it can be expanded from the realm of consciousness through to a world of conscious bodies. Allison Caddick writes of the desire to develop an account of 'embodied subjectivity' (1986, pp. 60–88). This is in contrast to the notion of bodies as objects, almost foreign to ourselves. In recent writings on performance art and the entry of the artist's body into the art work itself, there is a recognition that 'the artist's body becomes both the subject and the object of the action' (Barber 1979). Lucy Lippard writes of women's body art: 'When women use their own bodies in their art work, they are using their selves; a significant psychological factor converts these bodies or faces from object to subject' (1976, p. 124).

FINAL WORDS

The reification of the body is one thing – the tendency to call my own body 'it', a locution I could not easily ascribe to my mind or my self – but its inscription at the level of power is something further. The discursive configurations of power on the body spill over into our experience of sexuality, sexual expression, and relationships. In *The History of Sexuality*, Foucault looks at pleasure, sex, and bodies, but the very ascription of *sexual contact* to an interaction carries with it certain demarcations with respect to our modes of contact. The sensual, considered distinct from the sexual, would certainly impoverish the realm of the latter. Yet, the intrusion of the sexual into the sensual is a social transgression of the kind that features in the work of Georges Bataille. Bataille's work on transgression, and the radical eroticism of his writings, undermines the strict separation of the sexual from other forms of social activity. Kristeva also looks at our disgust for bodily wastes, blood, death, and decay in her work on abjection, *Powers of Horror* (1982). She looks at abjection as transgression, exclusion, that which is beyond the realm of acceptability (Kristeva 1982, p. 17).

Does sex operate so separately from other modes of interaction? Angela Carter writes about sex in *The Sadeian Woman* (1979, p. 9):

> But our flesh arrives to us out of history, like everything else does. We may believe we fuck stripped of social artifice; in bed, we feel we touch the bedrock of human nature itself. But we are deceived. Flesh is not an irreducible human universal. Although the erotic relationship may seem to exist freely, on its own terms, among the distorted social relationships of a bourgeois society, it is, in fact, the most self-conscious of all human relationships, a direct confrontation of two human beings whose actions in bed are wholly determined by their acts when they are out of it.

The supposed seclusion of the boudoir is already permeated by the social, external world, and it too is subject to political, economic, and gendered determinants. The mere fact that western sexual relations are sequestered means that an explicit expression of sexual feelings is both kept out of all our other social interactions, and is intensely expressed within the sexual encounter. Also, the purported privacy of sexual interaction makes feminist mobilization against sexual abuse, rape, and incest all the more difficult since these occur in what are supposedly domains of social non-intervention. Of course, a host of forms of sexual repression may well be acceptably expressed, and *sex* is one of the most powerful devices in selling capitalism's latest commodity form. These forms of separated social practice say something about our subjectivity – if one subscribes to an Althusserian account, our subjectivity arises only through the various forms of address inherent in the forms of social practice in which we participate. Thus, the rigid separation of sexual contact from other forms of communication in terms of social action may mean that we also separate sexuality from the rest of our subjective feelings and sensations. This contributes to the divide between the sexual and the sensual, and the general prohibitions on public touching. However, the body and our experience through our bodies may well pose certain tensions and contradictions to any rigid separation which may be mirrored in our consciousness. In this sense, we might learn things through our bodies which go against what our minds tell us. We sometimes talk of falling ill as a sign from our bodies that we need a rest. Perhaps we can learn other things from listening to our bodies.

This is obviously not an end, but a beginning for an understanding of subjectivity. I cannot finish with any definitive conclusions. Women's bodies have born the brunt of patriarchy, but perhaps also, through them we can learn to experiment and move beyond the conceptions of subjectivity so caught within patriarchy's socio-discursive net. And retrace and reform the theoretical configurations of the body theory on the subject. Louise Steinman writes in *The Knowing Body* (of performers):

> In their very live presence, with their movement and their breath, they affirm the life that is in exquisite balance with the process of

death. The transformations they undergo are a metaphor for the constant process of change which brings food to our tables, our bodies to our graves, our babies from the womb. Experience which comes from 'wisdom, the epic side of truth', is dying out, proclaimed Walter Benjamin. But there are reassuring signs today that wisdom is present, that experiences are being shared with skill and with passion, and the story which begins in our bodies is the fundamental sign of life. We just have to listen.

(Steinman 1986, p. 144)

NOTES

1 See also John Rundell's *Origins of Modernity* (1987).

2 In the work of Althusser, we see the development of a theory of subjectivity within his own structuralist version of historical materialism. This kind of account represents the attempt to explain the creation of people as subjects with reference to the determinations of economic or productive forces; see Althusser and Balibar (1983), Althusser (1971; 1982). Althusser's own project was to articulate an anti-humanist Marxism. We will consider his work in this chapter in the context of a discussion on humanism and anti-humanism. For an interesting discussion of Althusser's own political/theoretical context, see Hirsch (1981).

3 These critiques are largely to be found in the work of French poststructuralism, semiotics, and postmodernism; see, in particular, Lyotard (1984).

4 Hall was Director of the Birmingham Centre for Contemporary Cultural Studies, which has produced a number of works on gender, class, and race understood through cultural analysis. The analyses in these works show the influence of Marxist thinkers, such as Althusser and Gramsci, a semiotically informed perspective, and an interest in contemporary cultural forms such as the media.

5 Saussure was a Swiss linguist working at the turn of the century. His emphasis on the systematic nature of language, and its arbitrary social character has been taken up by Lévi-Strauss, Barthes, Eco, and many others in a variety of fields, either directly, or in terms of the general project he articulated – semiotics, as 'a science that studies the life of signs within society' (Saussure 1966, p. 16).

6 Heidegger wrote on the question of humanism in 1946, in response to Sartre's famous essay, 'Existentialism as a humanism'. In a published letter on humanism, Heidegger subjects to critical examination the metaphysical assumptions of humanism which he rejects in favour of his own discourse on language and Being (Heidegger, 1978).

7 For example, Foucault has written on Nietzsche, genealogy, and history (1977), Derrida on Heidegger (1982), and Kristeva on anti-humanism (1987).

8 Juliet Mitchell was one of the first to combine an anti-humanism with a feminist analysis (1974). Michèle Barrett's work *Women's Oppression Today* also exhibits an anti-humanist character (1980). Both of these authors have drawn upon Althusserian theory. More recently, Jacqueline Rose has produced an interesting discussion on sexuality, feminism, and politics where the question is posed as to the role of psychoanalysis and the unconscious for feminist theory (1986).

9 See chapter 3 of Barrett (1980) and both Introductions by Mitchell and Rose (1982).
10 Giddens argues in his work *Central Problems in Social Theory* that the notion of action and structure are central for social theory. He further claims that one must also rework these terms, along with the related notions of structure, system, incorporating his own theory of structuration (Giddens 1979).
11 This phrase is cited in the work of historian, Christopher Lasch, in his book of the same name (1977). See also Barrett and McIntosh's *Anti-Social Family* (1982) wherein they argue against the social utility of the modern nuclear family configuration.
12 The notion of universality and universal solutions (arising from the work of Kant) is severely criticized in Lyotard's *The Postmodern Condition* (1984). However the point against the hegemony and imperialist tendencies of western feminism masquerading as universal, speaking for all women, was given recognition through the choice of Nairobi as the location for the UN Decade for Women Conference in 1985. See also Hamilton and Barrett (1986).
13 See ch. 1.
14 See Owens's (1985) discussion of Kelly's *Post-Partum Document*.
15 The work of Michel Pêcheux represents a combination of these two regions, ideology and discourse. Pêcheux invents the concent of *interdiscourse* to represent the complex interface between ideology, subjectivity, and discourse; see Pêcheux (1982).
16 Genevieve Lloyd (1984) has further discerned the ways in which reason, as conceived within western philosophy, has developed along an implicitly male-identified trajectory.
17 See the work of Kristeva, Irigaray, Grosz, and Gatens.

REFERENCES

Althusser, L. (1971) *Lenin and Philosophy*, tr. Ben Brewster, Monthly Review Press, New York.
Althusser, L. (1982) *For Marx*, tr. Ben Brewster, Verso, London.
Althusser, L. and Balibar, E. (1983) *Reading Capital*, tr. Ben Brewster, Verso, London.
Barber, B. (1979) 'Indexing conditionalism and its heretical equivalents', in Bronson and Cale (eds) *Performance by Artists*, Art Metropole, New York.
Barrett, M. (1980) *Women's Oppression Today: Problems in Marxist Feminist Analysis*, Verso, London.
Barrett, M. and McIntosh, M. (1982) *The Anti-Social Family*, Verso, London.
Barthes, R. (1973) *Mythologies*, Granada, London.
Becker, R. and Seldon, G. (1985) *The Body Electric: Electromagnetism and the Foundation of Life*, Quill, New York.
Bergland, R. (1985) *The Fabric of Mind*, Penguin, Melbourne.
Betterton, R. (ed.) (1987) *Looking On: Images of Femininity in the Visual Arts and Media*, Pandora Press, London.
Brennan, T. (1989) *Between Feminism and Psychoanalysis*, Routledge, London and New York.
Caddick, A. (1986) 'Feminism and the body', *Arena*, 74, pp. 60–88.
Carter, A. (1979) *The Sadeian Woman*, Virago, London.
Culler, J. (1976) *Saussure*, Fontana/Collins, Glasgow.
Derrida, J. (1982) *Margins of Philosophy*, University of Chicago Press, Chicago.

Eisenstein, H. (1984) *Contemporary Feminist Thought*, Allen & Unwin, Sydney.
Eisenstein, Z. (1981) *The Radical Future of Liberal Feminism*, Longman, New York.
Foucault, M. (1970) *The Order of Things*, Tavistock, London.
Foucault, M. (1977) *Language, Counter-Memory, Practice*, Cornell University Press, Ithaca, NY.
Foucault, M. (1980) 'Body/power', in *Power/Knowledge*, Harvester Press, Sussex.
Gallop, J. (1982) *Feminism and Psychoanalysis: The Daughter's Seduction*, Macmillan, London.
Gatens, M. (1983) 'A critique of the sex/gender distinction', in *Beyond Marxism? Interventions after Marx*, Intervention Publications, Sydney.
Giddens, A. (1979) *Central Problems in Social Theory: Action, Structure and Contradiction in Social Analysis*, Macmillan, London.
Grimshaw, J. (1986) *Feminist Philosophers: Women's Perspectives on Philosophical Traditions*, Wheatsheaf, Sussex.
Hall, S. (1978) 'The hinterland of science: ideology and the sociology of knowledge', in *On Ideology*, Centre for Contemporary Cultural Studies, Hutchinson, London.
Hall, S., Hobson, D., Lowe, A., and Willis, P. (1980) *Culture, Media and Language*, Hutchinson, London.
Hamilton, R. and Barrett, M. (1986) *The Politics of Diversity: Feminism, Marxism and Nationalism*, Verso, London.
Heidegger, M. (1978) *Basic Writings*, Routledge & Kegan Paul, London.
Heller, A. (1982) 'On feminism and socialism', *Thesis Eleven*, 5/6, pp. 59–71.
Henriques, J., Holloway, W., Urwin, C., Venn, C., and Walkerdine, V. (1984) *Changing the Subject: Psychology, Social Regulation and Subjectivity*, Methuen, London.
Hirsch, A. (1981) *The French New Left: An Intellectual History from Sartre to Gorz*, South End Press, Boston.
Jardine, A. (1985) *Gynesis: Configurations of Woman and Modernity*, Cornell University Press, Ithaca, NY.
Kaplan, E. A. (1983) *Women and Film: Both Sides of the Camera*, Methuen, London.
Kelly, M. (1982) 'No essential femininity: a conversation betwen Mary Kelly and Paul Smith', *Parachute*, 26.
Kelly, M. (1983) *Post-Partum Document*, Routledge & Kegan Paul, London.
Kristeva, J. (1982) *Powers of Horror: An Essay in Abjection*, Columbia University Press, New York.
Kristeva, J. (1987) *The Kristeva Reader*, ed. Toril Moi, Blackwell, Oxford.
Kuhn, A. (1985) *The Power of the Image: Essays on Representation and Sexuality*, Routledge & Kegan Paul, London.
Lasch, C. (1977) *Haven in a Heartless World*, Basic Books, New York.
Lippard, L. (1976) *From the Center: Feminist Essays on Women's Art*, E. P. Dutton, New York.
Lippard, L. (1984) *Get the Message? A Decade of Art for Social Change*, E. P. Dutton, New York.
Lloyd, G. (1984) *The Man of Reason: 'Male' and 'Female' in Western Philosophy*, Methuen, London.
Lyotard, J.-F. (1984) *The Postmodern Condition: A Report on Knowledge*, Manchester University Press.
McRobbie, A. (1986) 'Postmodernism and popular culture', in *ICA Documents 4: Postmodernism*, Institute of Contemporary Arts, London.

Mitchell, J. (1974) *Psychoanalysis and Feminism*, Penguin, Harmondsworth.
Mitchell, J. and Rose, J. (1982) *Feminine Sexuality: Jacques Lacan and the Ecole Freudienne*, Macmillan, London.
Moi, T. (1985) *Sexual/Textual Politics: Feminist Literary Theory*, Methuen, London and New York.
Morgan, R. (1970) *Sisterhood is Powerful: An Anthology of Writings from the Women's Liberation Movement*, Vintage Books, New York.
Nairne, S., Dunlop, G., and Wyver, J. (1987) *State of the Art: Ideas and Images of the 1980s*, Chatto & Windus and Channel 4, London.
Owens, C. (1985) 'The discourse of others: feminists and postmodernism', in H. Foster (ed.) *Postmodern Culture*, Pluto Press, London.
Parker, R. and Pollock, G. (1987) *Framing Feminism: Art and the Women's Movement 1970–1985*, Pandora Press, London.
Parvati, J. (1978) *Hygieia: A Woman's Herbal*, Freestone Collective Publishing, California.
Pêcheux, M. (1982) *Language, Semantics and Ideology*, Macmillan, London.
Ricoeur, P. (1970) *Freud and Philosophy: An Essay on Interpretation*, Yale University Press, New Haven, Conn.
Rose, J. (1986) *Sexuality in the Field of Vision*, Verso, London.
Rundell, J. (1987) *Origins of Modernity: The Origins of Modern Social Theory from Kant to Hegel to Marx*, Polity Press, Cambridge.
Saussure, F. de (1966) *Course in General Linguistics*, McGraw-Hill, New York.
Steinman, L. (1986) *The Knowing Body: Elements of Contemporary Performance and Dance*, Shambhala, London.
Tapper, M. (1986) 'Can a liberal be a feminist?', *Supplement to Australian Journal of Philosophy*.
Taylor, C. (1975) *Hegel*, Cambridge University Press, Cambridge.
Turner, B. (1984) *The Body and Society: Explorations in Social Theory*, Blackwell, Oxford.
Wolff, J. (1985) 'The invisible flaneuse: women and the literature of modernity', *Theory, Culture and Society*, 2:3, pp. 49–68.

Part III

DISCOURSES OF DEFINITION

5

PHILOSOPHY

Elizabeth Grosz

> A woman does not *want* the truth; what is truth to women? From the beginning, nothing has been more alien, repugnant and hostile to woman than the truth – her great art is the lie, her highest concern is mere appearance and beauty.
>
> Friedrich Nietzsche[1]

INTRODUCTION: LANGUAGE, DEFINITIONS AND POWER

Since its emergence as a separate discipline in ancient Greece, western philosophy has exerted a powerful influence on conceptions, ideals, and values in everyday life as well as in the production of discourses and knowledges. It is ironic that it emerges approximating many of its modern contemporary features only when it is divided from poetry and myth (Homer's *The Iliad* and *The Odyssey* are simultaneously philosophical, psychological, poetic, theological, and narrational); only then do its propositions gain precise, unambiguous formulation and a truth-function: only, that is, when philosophy carefully controls language, clears up 'poetic' ambiguities, is cast into a propositional form, placed within the structure of the logical syllogism and assessed in terms of truth and validity will a statement be considered philosophical. These requirements emerge gradually over the period between the fifth and the third centuries BC.

From this time, philosophy has developed around a series of issues and central questions. It has concerned itself with the nature of reality and subjectivity (ontology), knowledge and truth (epistemology), morality and the good (ethics), and rights and responsibilities (politics). These classical divisions, while never universally accepted, have nevertheless provided the broad categories dominating philosophy up to the present. As an intellectual discipline, philosophy has provided concepts, arguments, methods, and criteria by which elements of everyday life are understood; and it has formed a context and rationale by which other knowledges and other theories have justified themselves. It has, for example, provided social and political relations with a number of conceptual tools (or rather, weapons): reason, truth, knowledge, and other terms provide individuals and groups, both oppressors and oppressed, with discourses and frameworks by means of which they understand their relative positions and rationalize or transform them. The 'politics of philosophy' are manifested in and produced by political and social relations, from which it is never free.

If philosophy can be *used* for overtly political purposes – as Hitler used Nietzsche, or Reagan referred to J. S. Mill, and male chauvinists refer to accounts of 'human nature' – we must ask whether philosophy in *itself* (in its own terms and not in the extremes of abuse to which any theory is liable) participates in power relations. Is the way it develops and uses concepts and methods implicated in power relations? Do its claims and assertions function, create, maintain, or reflect power relations? To ask these kinds of questions of knowledges, including philosophical knowledges, is to subject philosophy itself to a political analysis.

Because philosophy is implicated in how men and women, or masculine and feminine, are defined, it is clear that philosophy must be amenable to feminist analysis and assessment. Philosophy defines the 'nature' of human beings, the range and variety of subjects, the capacities and skills attributed to them, and the ideal forms of social organization – which coincide exactly with historical representations of sexual differences. Moreover, philosophy provides general rules, methods, and procedures linking women and femininity to marginal, ignored, subordinated, silenced, or repressed positions relative to men. In taking philosophy as its critical object, feminist theory focuses on one of two elements in patriarchal philosophical texts: either on what philosophical texts or philosophers have written about women, sexuality, and relations between the sexes – overt pronouncements about sexual differences; or on the apparently 'eternal' questions raised by philosophy, questions, concepts, and issues that seem indifferent or neutral to sexuality – like truth, reason, existence, virtue, knowledge, etc. – which are nevertheless implicitly or indirectly related to or coded by femine or masculine attributes. Valued philosophical concepts, in other words, gain their privileged positions because a series of other terms have been isolated from or expelled by the privileged terms. These terms (e.g. unreason, the irrational, evil, fantasy, illusion, instability) are identified with femininity as the unspoken condition of the primary terms, which, in turn, are defined as and help to define the attributes of masculinity.

Philosophy, then, in spite of its aspiration to a pure, neutral, unmotivated, and disinterested reason, is as susceptible to a feminist critique as any other form of knowledge. It has defined women as secondary, subservient, peripheral, dependent, irrational, bound to nature, emotional, and so on. In collaboration with other knowledges, it has rendered women, femininity, and their characteristics irrelevant, invisible, or incapable of representation, and thus outside the philosophical or theoretical realm. Woman and femininity serve as the unacknowledged supports or foundations of a patriarchal and masculine body of knowledge.

PHILOSOPHY AND WOMEN'S OPPRESSION

To represent adequately the range and scope of women's oppression in patriarchal culture, three distinct types or levels of oppression can be distinguished. These three types of oppression correspond to three broad forms of philosophical misogyny or woman-hating. This correspondence is not entirely surprising, given that philosophy, like other forms of knowledge, is not immune to pervasive social beliefs; it both reflects and helps to produce them. These three types of oppression consist in:

(a) The operation of *sexism*. Sexism resides in a series of individual or collective acts of discrimination against women. There are a vast number of sexist behaviours ranging from pejorative, negative comments and assumptions about women, to their active exclusion from certain social spheres or activities, to conscious intimidation, harassment, and overt violence, including rape. Sexism is an empirical phenomenon. It is visible, designatable, material, a set of actions (including language) which treats women in unequal ways to men. It is thus the *unwarranted* differential treatment of the two sexes, to the benefit of one and at the expense of the other.

Arguably, sexist discrimination is *in principle* reversible. Women *could* behave in a sexist manner towards men. But in the context of our culture, where women as a social group lack the positions and power to enforce female supremacism, this cannot occur. It is certainly true that women can intimidate and victimize men, but this remains the action of an individual. Women *as women* do not oppress men *as men*. This is because oppression consists in *more than* discriminatory acts or unfair treatment; these empirical actions are regulated, supported, and given meaning by an underlying structure. Men, for example, can rely on the ways that social institutions, customs and agencies, laws, rituals, and day-to-day presumptions function to support their discriminatory acts in ways that women cannot. It is for this reason that although women can discriminate against individual men, women as a group cannot oppress men as a group. This requires the support of a second form of oppression which makes sexism possible; it is

(b) an underlying system which I will call 'patriarchal' to distinguish it from sexism. Above and beyond particular, concrete sexist acts is a structure that systematically evaluates masculinity in positive and femininity in negative terms. Patriarchy is thus a structural mode of organization placing men and women in different positions in social, economic, and interpersonal relations. It does not consist in empirical acts; it is a latent structure which makes possible and organizes these individual acts into systematic form, providing the context and the meaning(s) for sexist inequalities. It is for this reason that, even if all examples of sexism were removed, women's oppressed position would remain unchanged. This is made up of not only different, unequal treatment of the two sexes, but also of the different meanings and values accorded to the two sexes, even in cases where they behave in the same ways. What is considered forceful in men may be considered aggressive in women, even if they behave identically.

Patriarchy is a regulated system which positions men and women in superior and inferior social positions and grants different meanings and values to them. It is all-pervasive in so far as it affects all aspects of interpersonal and social life. Patriarchal structures are not immutable, but are historically variable, operating in specific ways in socio-geographically specific cultures; yet it always retains the primary commitment to upholding and maintaining male supremacy.

(c) If sexism operates empirically and observably, and if patriarchy operates structurally, a third level of social misogyny can be discerned that is of major significance for those interested in the operation of theory, representations, and discursive systems. The proliferation of oppressive images and representations of women and the feminine is not entirely distinct from sexist or patriarchal power relations; each requires representational systems. This mode of oppression could be described as 'phallocentric'.

Phallocentrism is a specifically discursive series of procedures, a strategy for collapsing representations of the two sexes into a single model, called 'human' or 'man', but which is in fact congruent only with the masculine. It is the universalization of particular features of masculinity, as if these were genuinely representative of both sexes. The masculinity of the 'human' goes unrecognized. In other words, phallocentrism effaces the autonomous representation of femininity (cf. Irigaray 1977a, 1978, 1984). Within phallocentric paradigms femininity can only be represented in some necessary relation to masculinity.

As a textual or discursive strategy, phallocentrism provides for patriarchal relations. It leaves women no conceptual space for developing autonomous interests and points of view other than or different from men's. Women are constricted to three possibilities, each confirming the primacy of the masculine and the subordination of the feminine. Whenever women or femininity are conceived in terms of either an identity or sameness with men; or of their opposition or inversion of the masculine; or of a complementarity with men, their representation is phallocentric.

Sameness or identity (as is conceived in all universal or 'human' models of subjectivity), opposition or binary categorization (as occurs when feminine attributes are considered the negative or inverse of masculine ones), and complementarity (where the sexes are seen as a form of completion of the lacks in each other) privilege and take as given the qualities attributed to masculinity. Each takes the male as primary and measures and defines the female only in her relation to the male. Sameness, identity, or equivalence implies a given norm or standard according to which one term is measured and judged as the same (cf. Thornton 1986). Opposition is simply the negative of positively conceived properties or predicates; negation always involves a prior affirmation, on which it thus depends. And likewise, complementarity implies taking one term as the standard and assessing to what extent the other completes it. In each case, the male or masculine is granted an autonomous, self-defined position while the female or feminine is taken as secondary and defined according to the attributes suited to the masculine.

WOMEN'S OPPRESSION IN PHILOSOPHY

The distinction between sexist, patriarchal, and phallocentric forms of women's oppression may prove useful in describing and assessing the ways in which philosophy actively participates in that oppression. These types of oppression are, of course, not mutually exclusive – one text or philosophical position may be implicated in all three. Nevertheless given the range and scope of philosophical misogyny, they may provide a way of systematically understanding this misogyny.

Philosophy's *sexism* takes two forms. The first consists in openly derogatory or discriminatory remarks about women and femininity, designed to keep women's participation in philosophy at a minimum. Like other social practices, philosophy has historically confined women's professional involvement in teaching, research, and publishing. Before the twentieth century, it was rare to find women studying, let alone working, within the dsicipline (cf. Le Doeuff 1977), although there are isolated cases where women have achieved some form of recognition: Hypatia, Diotima, Heloise, Christine de Pisan, Princess Elizabeth, and Lou Andreas-Salome.

In other words, this first form of sexism is based on the exclusion of women as philosophical agents and producers. Such an exclusion may well have had dire effects on the nature and type of philosophy that has developed and is practised today.

A second form of sexism is provided by a vast mass of philosophical material on the topic of women. Few philosophers, it seems, can resist making some remarks about women, their 'natures', functions, social roles, and relations to men (cf. Mahawald 1978; Clarke and Lange 1979;

Okin 1980; Finn and Miles 1982). These remarks range from the most hostile diatribes against women's inferiority, weaker moral sense, and intellectual frailties (e.g. Aristotle) to patronizing comments about their charm and their 'unsuitability' for philosophical tasks (e.g. Kant, Rousseau) to apparently even-handed treatment (e.g. J. S. Mill).

Philosophy's *patriarchal* investments become clear in focusing, not on what philosophers say about women and femininity, but on what they *do not* say, what is unarticulated or left out of philosophical reflection. Rather than being the subjects of negative remarks, women and femininity are ignored, treated metaphorically, and severed from their connections to women's lived experiences (cf. Le Doeuff 1977; 1980; Mackenzie 1986). The feminine is disembodied, woman is etherealized and rendered metaphoric (see Thiele 1986) in order to harness, while not acknowledging what women may have to offer, (male) knowledges.

Philosophy's patriarchal orientations help to reproduce male supremacy. It does not openly participate in affirming the masculine and denigrating the feminine; instead, it elevates certain concepts at the expense of others. These terms are only *indirectly* related to or associated with masculinity and femininity, but they actively contribute to the creation of a bedrock of values and assumptions which ground more open forms of discrimination.

On the level of *phallocentric* representational models in philosophy, there are a number of procedures by which femininity is represented only in relation to masculinity and never in autonomous terms. The feminine, conceived as nature in relation to man's culture, body as opposed to mind, lack in opposition to presence, irrational and unknowable in relation to reason, is always reduced to a position subordinate to and dependent upon the male, positioning the female only in relation to him (cf. Jay 1981). The feminine becomes the unacknowledged support of philosophy, its repressed other, a limit beyond which it dares not transgress or even represent.

Philosophical phallocentrism is possible because of a two-fold process. On the one hand, there is a *levelling* procedure, in which all differences and distinctions between subjects are ignored, or reduced to a common denominator, implicitly defined by masculine interests. This reduction to sameness is necessary if one sex is to be compared with and judged by the other. On the other, there is a process of *hierarchization*, where one sex is judged better than its counterpart. As a consequence of this dual process, woman can be regarded as a 'deformed man' (Aristotle), a 'lesser man' (Augustine) or a 'castrated man' (Freud) that is, as a being who is defined by the presence or absence of the characteristics valued in and by masculinity.

The categories of sexism, patriarchy, and phallocentrism may help to overview the range of philosophical forms of misogyny. Philosophy does not use one method for denigrating or excluding femininity, but several. In section 4 we will cite some examples of this misogyny from the history of philosophy; and in section 5 we will discuss the responses made by feminists in recognizing the range and extent of this misogyny. In the final section, we will examine the possibilities of a non-sexist, non-patriarchal, and non-phallocentric philosophy consistent with feminist aims and values.

PHILOSOPHY VERSUS FEMININITY

Feminists have focused on three related areas in their interrogations of the history of philosophy. They are:

1 What philosophers have said about women and the feminine.
2 What philosophers have not said about women and the feminine – the exclusions and silences surrounding women's specificity and autonomy. That is, what philosophers *should* have said but left out of their work.
3 The methods and assumptions, frameworks and commitments philosophers have relied on to ensure men's theoretical dominance and privilege.

Feminist research has made it clear that certain presumptions and misconceptions about women have marked the philosophical endeavour since its inception. Philosophy is not simply neutral towards or ignorant about women; rather, it is actively complicit in providing definitions and interrogative techniques by which western cultures judge and value women.

The 'birth' of philosophy somewhere between the works attributed to Homer and Plato's writings already bears traces (and anticipations) of misogynistic philosophies. Long before Plato – in, for example, the work of the Ionians in the sixth century BC – philosophy is already deeply marked with openly misogynistic statements and rationalizations justifying patriarchal power relations (Garside 1975; Lange 1979, 1983; Lloyd 1979, 1983, 1984a, 1984b, 1985; Spelman 1983).

The Pythagorians introduced the following table of philosophical oppositions, a list of paired terms that are mutually exclusive and exhaustive: limit/unlimited, odd/even, one/many, right/left, male/female, rest/motion, straight/curved, light/dark, good/bad, square/oblong (cf. Adkins 1970a; Lloyd 1984a). In these binary pairs, the first term represents a positive value. It contributes to the order, form, and harmony of the world (*cosmos*). Significantly it is associated with masculinity. The second term is the negative or lack of the first. As an unlimited, disordering, and erratic set of terms, it threatens the stability and order of the *cosmos*. Not surprisingly, it is associated with femininity (see Jay 1981).

This ancient list of oppositions remains even today one of the most succinct summaries of the values philosophy espouses. It is rare to find philosophical texts which refuse these conceptions (even reductionism – whereby one term is seen to be 'really' a form of the other – which is dominant today, affirms the binary terms). The oppositional structure is still among the more insidious procedures we have inherited from the pre-Socratics. The earliest philosophical texts are already hostile to women. Their exclusions are not accidents, or based on individual ignorance but are *constitutive* of the discipline of philosophy. The advent of philosophy coincides with the exclusion of women (Le Doeuff 1977) and its developments and refinements constitute increasingly sophisticated modes of control over women's rights to self-definition.

Among the most influential philosophers within the history of the discipline are Plato and Aristotle. They formulated and formalized a number of central techniques and presumptions still prevalent today. Plato's work, for example, is the forerunner of liberal arguments about the equality of the sexes. His notion of the ideal form of social organization, represented in *The Republic* and *The Laws*, is among the first to afford women the possibility of a position socially equal to men. On his understanding, if women are given the same education and training as men, they should be as capable of governing as men, and thus capable of becoming members of the guardian class (cf. Lloyd 1979, 1983, 1984a, 1984b, 1985; Elshtain 1974, 1980; Thornton 1986; Okin 1980).

Enlightened as his position appears, he does not claim that men and women are or should be equal. He is interested in constructing the most rational form of social organization so that each individual can maximize his or her potential and provide the most useful contributions to the republic (Thornton 1986). The question of the injustices and inequalities between the sexes does not concern him; he is interested only in the most efficient and rational forms of organizing social life (cf. Part 6, *The Republic*, Plato 1974a). For Plato, women can only be granted a position equal to men in so far as they overcome their femininity and become more like men (Thornton 1986). Masculine skills and qualities are the norms for women as well: 'The female sex must share with the male, to the greatest extent possible, in both education and in all else' (*The Laws*, quoted in Okin 1980, pp. 43–4). Plato's position exhibits the same problems as more recent versions of liberalism which grant women equality with men. Both imply the prior evaluation of masculine qualities in forming the criteria of equality. Yet the most serious problems lie, not in his sexism, which, compared to most others, is relatively minor, but in his patriarchal commitments. It is not simply what he says about women that is problematic, but what he does not say. His privileging of reasoned, philosophical methods of argument, his notions of truth and rigour, reason, virtue, and knowledge – equivalents for Plato – are based on the expulsion of those characteristics associated with femininity. Reason, for example, is defined by excluding the body, passions, desires, contingent events, everyday matters, and the empirical world. It is purged and purified and distanced from materiality, which threatens it with contamination. Reason hierarchically subordinates the terms it excludes. It is privileged over all other kinds of knowing, those based on experience, on pragmatic skills, imitation, and apprenticeship. It becomes limited to the capacity to reflect upon and abstract from concrete experience or particulars to create a general or universal concept (Adkins 1970a; Guthrie 1978; Lloyd 1979, 1984a, 1984b; Okin 1980).

As Plato is the predecessor of modern liberal theory, so Aristotle (384–322 BC) can be regarded as the forebear of contemporary forms of conservative and biologistic anti-feminism. Aristotle's misogyny is profuse and infiltrates his notions of biology, ethics, and politics, as well as logic, truth, and reason. Unlike Plato, he is not interested in the question of women's nature but in the question of women's function. This is defined in terms of women's usefulness or purpose relative to men's needs and interests. By contrast, men are defined by their potentialities and the exercise of their capabilities (cf. Elshtain 1981). For Aristotle, women's functions are their nature. Indeed, he sees women as those beings lacking the capacities which define men. To be a woman is *a priori* to be deprived and secondary (see *On the Generation of Animals*, Aristotle 1971b, II, 728a; also Elshtain 1974, 1980; Okin 1980).

In his biological texts (Aristotle was trained in biology), he posited a unity of living being, which is a compound of form and matter. The body provides the matter for which the psyche or soul is the form. The soul is the active animating force for the body. They have an active/passive relation, form actively imposing itself on the passivity of matter. Consequently, he is at least consistent (if not accurate) in claiming that, even in the sphere of reproduction traditionally presumed to be under women's control, women's contribution is merely the provision of inert, shapeless matter; while men's consists in the active, creative soul to give form to disorganized matter. In herself, she is unable to provide any psychical input for the regeneration of species, for she lacks the principle of active reason.

Aristotle presupposes natural differences between individuals that support and necessitate relations of domination and subordination, or hierarchized systems of order. This applies as readily to the distinction between Greeks and barbarians as it does to the distinction between men and women. These relations of *natural superiority* reflect the 'natural' dominance of reason over the body, and the master over the slave (Okin 1980; Harding and Hintikka 1983). Because men and women have different natures, different virtues are appropriate to each. Virtue is the creation of an ideal harmony or ratio between one's nature and the disposition fulfilling that nature (see *Ethics*, Aristotle 1971a, Book 2, chapter 6).

Aristotle's writings on women's nature and virtue are filled with sexist and discriminatory remarks; but more insidiously, his work in logic, ontology, and epistemology is also implicated in patriarchal power (Mahwald 1978; Lloyd 1979, 1983, 1984a, 1984b, 1985). Logic, for example, is defined in opposition to and isolation from material, corporeal, empirical, contingent, and even factual elements. It refuses validity to any statement not in propositional form; it cannot conceptualize groups (being limited to either universal or particulars); and it is incapable of accommodating history or change. Not bound by nature, reason is still based on it. If it does not consist in abstraction, which distances the particular from the universal as Plato affirms, and as Aristotle himself does in his biological classificatory systems (i.e. Porphry's tree), he advocates an instrumental or pragmatic intelligence as well, one which calculates the most efficient and appropriate means of attaining a given end or telos. Given his beliefs about the (active and passive, physical and corporeal) natures of men and women, it follows that reason and virtue must also be different (i.e. structured in terms of superior and inferior).

By the third century BC, a number of major tendencies within both the history and contemporary forms of philosophy had been established. This suggests that philosophy may have been put on a path where women are systematically excluded from positions of autonomy and knowledge. Women and femininity are associated with the qualities that reason, truth and knowledge, validity, virtue, etc., must expel. Implicitly and explicitly, women are disqualified from philosophical activities. In Plato, their exclusion is a consequence of his belief that pederastic love relations – the love of a boy for an older man – provide the path and motivation for the love of wisdom that is philosophy (*The Symposium*, Plato 1974b; Le Doueff 1977). In Aristotle, this occurs because woman is *a priori* disqualified from access to the same kinds of reason and virtue as men.

In the space I have available, it is clearly not possible to elaborate in further detail the influences of Platonic and Aristotelian philosophies on the history of philosophy. Yet it is significant that, perhaps more than any others, they helped generate the central preoccupations of western reason. The complicity of Greek thought in women's oppression has only recently been analysed (e.g. Elshtain 1974, 1980; Lloyd 1979, 1983, 1984a, 1984b, 1985; Okin 1980). Until it can be understood how this misogyny seeps into and affects the very frameworks of philosophy, the residues of this deep-seated hostility to women may never be erased from the discipline.

FEMINISM VERSUS PHILOSOPHY

Although inestimably important in defining the history of philosophy, Plato and Aristotle are merely two examples of a philosophical misogyny that pervades this history. The types and effects of its misogyny are highly variable and widespread. Yet there are two consistent results that emerge from its male-centred alignments. On the one hand, women as a category are excluded from the profession of philosophy. Until the nineteenth century, it was rare for women to even study the texts of philosophy, let alone earn their livelihoods from it. There have been some women who, for various reasons, have entered institutions, but they are clearly exceptions (Le Doeuff 1977). On the other hand, women and femininity are the silent supports that cannot be acknowledged for philosophy to develop as it has. It is a truism that any discourse must exclude elements, and in this respect, philosophical discourses are no exception. Yet it is also the case that philosophy differs from other discourses in so far as the elements it excludes are generally associated with femininity.

Since the late 1970s, there has been an increasing volume of feminist literature on philosophy. Rather than summarize this growing body of work, I will, for the sake of brevity, divide feminist responses to the recognition of philosophy's misogyny into three categories: 'egalitarian feminism', 'conservative feminism', and 'radical feminism'. Clearly there are other ways in which this material could be divided (e.g. Kristeva 1981; Gatens 1986a), but the division I propose may make this volume of material more manageable.

Egalitarian feminism

Feminist philosophers face difficulties in reconciling feminism with philosophy. On the one hand, it is difficult for feminists to accept and agree with the sexism so visible in source texts. On the other, philosophical training, its terminology, goals, and procedures are also difficult to reconcile with feminist emphases on women's lived experiences, especially of oppression. They thus appear to be inarticulable, 'private' experiences outside the frame and interests of philosophy.

In recognizing philosophy's involvement in patriarchal power relations, one of the first reactions on the part of feminists was 'an ostrich approach': to ignore the tensions between the two, conceiving of them as two separate issues. Philosophy may be what one does; feminism is how one lives. But as early as Simone de Beauvoir's *The Second Sex* (1972), feminists have tried to establish a peaceful reconciliation or integration of these two commitments. Earlier egalitarian feminists – Wollstonecraft, Taylor, Mill (cf. Thompson 1983, 1986; Gatens 1986a) – made similar attempts to bring together the capacity to reason, think, and philosophize and a commitment to women's equality.

Egalitarian feminists usually undertake one of two projects: to eliminate all barriers preventing women's equal inclusion in philosophy; or to develop already existing philosophical systems so that they become relevant to and cognisant of women's experiences of oppression. De Beauvoir's relation to Sartrean existentialism (Le Doueff 1977; Gatens 1986a); Firestone's relation to humanist (Marcusian) Freudo-Marxism;[2] numerous Marxist feminists in relation to Marx's texts (cf. Allen 1983; Gatens 1986a) are all examples of feminist renegotiations of patriarchal texts from feminist perspectives. Whatever their considerable differences, egalitarian feminists share an adherence to the values of masculinist and patriarchal thought coupled with the goal of including women as men's equals.

To take de Beauvoir as an example, she explores the oppression of women in an impressively detailed examination of the various social, biological, and economic factors contributing to women's subordinate position. She relies on the framework of Sartre's *Being and Nothingness* (1969) which paradoxically uses an indifferent (at best) or positively hostile (at worst) conception of women and of oppression (Le Doueff 1977; Gatens 1986a; MacKenzie 1986). What is most puzzling about de Beauvoir's text is not her reliance on existentialism but her inability to see that her work effects major modifications of Sartre's position. She enables a highly individualistic theory about freedom and choice which is resolutely ignorant of any social factors mitigating freedom (for Sartre, even the slave is, in a sense, free) to explain the complexities of a structural oppression experienced by women. Feminists claim that not only does de Beauvoir modify Sartre's understanding of human relations, she creates a superior account, one able to explain oppression as Sartre's cannot.[3]

Yet, because she avoids a critical encounter with existentialism, de Beauvoir remains blind to Sartre's passive aggression to women and to the female body (see the final sections of *Being and Nothingness* for his accounts of 'holes' and 'slime'; see also Peirce, in Gould and Wartofsky 1976). She unwittingly reproduces Sartre's hostile representations of femininity in her own accounts of women's oppression, in her discussion of female biology and in her explanation of women's lack of transcendence by the vulnerabilities of the female body. She implies that only if women can overcome their bodies can they achieve equality with men – that is, only when women are no longer women! (cf. Firestone 1979; Gatens 1983).

Egalitarian feminists demand a greater share for women in the rights, duties, privileges, and responsibilities of men. Their goal is to empower women to participate as men's equals in theoretical, political, social, and interpersonal life.

However, as many egalitarians have discovered, it is not possible to easily adjust theoretical frameworks so that women are treated the same as men (women's exclusion is constitutive of theory); and it is moreover of questionable value (there is the assumption that what men do is in fact worthwhile for women as well). There are a number of major problems about this aspiration to equality, including:

1 Women *can* be included as men's equals, but only at the expense of recognizing and validating women's specificity. Equality, then, involves a neut(e)ralization of the feminine.
2 Women remain the objects of male reflection and speculation. Egalit-

arianism leaves the basic frameworks, methods, and assumptions of male theory unquestioned, even if it condemns the more visible, sexist forms of discrimination.

3 Ideally within egalitarianism, the categories of male and female become irrelevant, being displaced by a neutral concept such as 'individual' or 'person'. Egalitarianism is closely allied with individualism and is thus implicated in a problematic split between the individual and the environment where the modification of one (the environment) leads to the equivalence of the other. Such a position makes it difficult, if not impossible, to see the more structural operations of patriarchy. Moreover, it presumes the individual is a pliable substance, whose form is environmentally imposed (cf. Gatens 1983).
4 Even if it remains desirable for women to struggle towards equality with men, it is simply not possible to include women in those theories (and daily tasks) from which they have been excluded. To do so would be to radically alter or transform the theories (and tasks) being examined.

Many working on male texts in order to include women as men's equals have, through bitter experience and frustration, recognized that it is not possible to achieve equality between the sexes within the structural power relations constituting patriarchy. Even if men and women are equally treated, they do not have the same meaning. It is not possible, for example, to substitute the words 'men and women' wherever 'men' occurs without becoming self-contradictory or incoherent. Theories can be 'fiddled' or seen selectively so that women could be included; but this usually involves ignoring those elements of theories incompatible with feminism instead of analysing their relations to the egalitarian components.

Many egalitarians were drawn to what I will describe as 'radical feminism' in seeing the limits of their equalizing strategies. The failure of or disillusionment with, liberal or egalitarian ideals also leads to a more conservative position, a kind of backlash to the advances made by egalitarianism. It is to these I will now turn.

Conservative feminism

In response to the tensions apparent between feminism and traditional philosophy, a number of women and men have attempted to subordinate feminism to the rigour of philosophical scrutiny. Instead of trying to reconcile the two, conservatives (some of whom describe themselves as feminists) use philosophy as a tool to criticize and even 'rectify' problems in feminism. While remaining dubious about the description 'feminist', I will follow the practice of these writers themselves in describing them thus.

Especially within the analytic tradition of philosophy dominant in Britain, America, and Australia, a carefully controlled range of 'women's issues' readily incorporated into the discipline is relatively well tolerated, and in some cases, even encouraged. The abortion issue, for example, has become a controversial 'topic' for discussion within ethics and moral philosophy. Yet far from questioning philosophy's misogyny, its appropriation of 'women's issues' has produced new objects of speculation and new issues for philosophers to debate. Feminism can be used to prove philosophy's credentials of contemporary relevance and modernity in the face of its diminishing power in everyday life. 'Women's issues' can be readily isolated from the really important philosophical concerns, those of the ontology and epistemology, posing no threat to philosophy's self-representations.

Two of the most powerful examples of conservatism in this respect are Carol MacMillan's *Woman, Reason and Nature* (1982) and Janet Radcliffe Richards's *The Sceptical Feminist* (1982). These texts gain a measure of plausibility in feminist terms because at first glance they appear to develop internal critiques of feminism. However, under the guise of a critical self-scrutiny, they develop rationalizations for the philosophical status quo, acting as its female guardians. Their objections are in fact external to feminist interests and are forms of co-option and control of the radical potential feminism implies.

MacMillan challenges the distinction between private and public and its correlation with the distinction between nature and culture in her book. The sphere of private activities is presumed to be equivalent to the biological and natural order. It is an equation commonly used to explain women's exclusion from social and public life. Richards also challenges the concept of nature as it is used in both philosophy and in what she calls 'feminist ideology'. She queries the superimposition of the cultural on the natural, as if this left the natural sphere somehow intact under its social form.

But as we read on, the object of critical analysis is not philosophy but feminism. Her role is not really to liberate women from naturalist definitions but to correct both philosophers and feminists in their mistaken notions. In other words, she continues the mainstream philosophical tradition of criticism, not a specifically feminist intervention.

MacMillan and Richards both assume that feminism is a political movement aimed at achieving equality of the sexes. As a result, both caricature the range and variations within feminist theory. MacMillan ascribes to feminists the aim of establishing a pure, essential woman outside of social and cultural influences: 'Feminists assume that our knowledge of femininity can be legitimate only if it is totally independent of any cultural bias' (MacMillan 1982, p. 62). This is a puzzling description of feminism; but it is no more staggering than Richards's claim that feminism is *not* about women, their experiences or oppression, although it is often conflated with them, but about *social justice*: 'feminism should not even regard itself as a movement to *support women who suffer from injustice*. . . . Feminism is not concerned with a *group of people it wants to benefit*, but with a type of injustice it wants to eliminate' (Richards 1982, pp. 17–18; emphasis in the original). These characterizations neutralize feminism's radical threat, dissolving or making bland the challenge it poses to traditional forms of philosophy. They also neuter, or desexualize the specific points of view that feminist theory articulates.

MacMillan and Richards retain an uncritical acceptance of particular (male) philosophical frameworks, using them to assess, explain, and correct feminism. MacMillan relies on the work of Peter Winch's *The Idea of a Social Science* (1972), while Richards uses the work of John Rawls, especially *The Theory of Justice* (1971). In neither case is the relevance of feminist criticisms to these male sources noted; only feminism is subjected to their criticisms.

Winch attempts to explain and justify various methods used in the social sciences. He claims that social, theoretical, and political relations can be validly examined only in the context of 'a way of life'. Winch does not concern himself with feminist questions, but MacMillan uses the idea to assert that the roles women play in culture today are precisely the roles women *should* be performing. Rather than using *biology* to justify women's social positions, she uses the needs and exigencies of 'a way of life'. She asserts that feminists have confused sex roles and the different social skills developed by men and women with oppression. They have mistakenly conflated authority with power instead of seeing authority as a constitutive feature of any way of life. In other words, she replaces biologistically conceived arguments with arguments about 'social necessity'. The unequal access of women to work, their privatization and isolation by maternity and the responsibilities of child-raising, their role in domestic production, and their association with emotions and feelings are all rationalized by MacMillan as reasonable and fair in social terms.

Similarly, Richards is not prepared to question the works of Rawls, who provides her with her central concepts and basic arguments. She readily accepts the timeless, unquestionable values of reason, logic, truth, and validity. Like MacMillan she chastizes women who question the Great (male) Thinkers or the basic presumptions of philosophical argument. This means accepting and leaving unquestioned the worth of men's knowledges as universally valid. Unlike some egalitarians who are prepared to discard accounts incapable of including women, the conservatives leave philosophy in a privileged and unscrutinized position. They achieve acceptance within male philosophical circles in so far as they act as watchdogs guarding against unwelcome feminist incursions into philosophy.

Spawned in reaction to egalitarian feminists, the conservatives are in fact most threatened by the work of those I call 'radical feminists', those who are prepared to put the entire philosophical project into question.

Radical feminism

Radical feminists are more concerned with the broader conceptual and methodological commitments that philosophy makes to patriarchal power relations than with the sexism of philosophy. These feminists should not be confused with the radical feminists within the political movement of feminism, although there may be some connections between them. Philosophical radical feminisms have emerged as a response to the failure of egalitarian aspirations. In seeing that women could not be readily included as men's equals in many/most theoretical systems, they also saw that there was *no space* there for women's inclusion.

Feminists were thus faced with a choice. They could continue to work in the terms of their chosen (male) discourses (Freud and Marx being probably the most heavily used). Or they could begin to scrutinize these privileged discourses from a critical feminist perspective. The first alternative implies the continuation of the egalitarian approach. The second involves both the critical analysis of and separation from male approaches and the positive construction of feminist alternatives. Among those who could be classified as radical feminists in this sense are Luce Irigaray and Michele Le Doeuff in France, Jane Gallop and Mary Daly in the United States, Mary O'Brien in Canada, and Genevieve Lloyd and Moira Gatens in Australia.

In spite of their diversity, these radical feminists share a number of features and commitments, including:

1 A strong intellectual grounding in traditional forms of philosophy, their norms, methods, and central terms;
2 A primary allegiance to the significance of women's experiences of oppression and their perspectives on the world;
3 A willingness to question, and possibly to reject the underlying assumptions and values of philosophy from the point of view of its adherence to misogyny.

I will here use only a few brief examples. In Lloyd's *The Man of Reason* (1984a), she argues that central philosophical terms – reason in particular – are defined so as to affirm masculinity and to silence or exclude femininity. She analyses the history of conceptions of reason through their opposition to a series of excluded terms, such as passion, faith, emotion, and observation. Her careful analysis of the masculinity vested in a variety of philosophical positions ranging from Plato to Sartre reveals a masculinity that parades itself as universal:

> Our trust in a Reason that knows no sex has . . . been largely self-deceiving. To bring to the surface the implicit maleness of our ideals of Reason is not necessarily to adopt a 'sexual relativism' about rational belief and truth; but it does have important implications for

> our contemporary understanding of gender difference. It means, for example, that there are not only practical reasons, but also conceptual ones, for the conflicts many women experience between Reason and femininity. The obstacles to female cultivation of Reason spring to a large extent from the fact that our ideals of reason have historically incorporated an exclusion of the feminine, and that femininity itself has been partly constituted through such processes of exclusion.
>
> (Lloyd 1984a, pp. ix-x)

For Lloyd, philosophical misogyny is not confined to a few easily ignored remarks about women; nor is reason contingently or accidentally related to masculinity. Misogyny is at the very heart of the philosophical enterprise. The history of philosophy is the history of forms of male theoretical dominance, reflecting and producing patriarchal social relations.

Instead of abandoning philosophy altogether, leaving it to men, Lloyd claims that the future of philosophy is open to the kinds of interventions and critical reformulations feminists seek: 'Fortunately, philosophy is not necessarily what it has in the past proudly claimed to be – a timeless, rational representation of the real, free of the conditioning effects of history' (Lloyd 1984a, p. 109). If Lloyd challenges the ways reason is formulated, and aims to render it genuinely *gender-free*, Michele Le Doeuff's work can be seen as a further step along the path to a feminist deconstruction of philosophy. In *Recherches sur l'imaginaire philosophique* (1980), she analyses the unacknowledged images – the imaginary, which philosophy cannot recognize but must rely upon. While she is not interested specifically in analysing woman or femininity, she is oriented to forcing philosophy to confront its own limits, its languages and imagery. She raises a number of central issues relevant to revealing and superseding philosophy's phallocentrism. With one exception (1977) her work focuses not on women but on philosophy.

Philosophy values precision, accuracy, clarity, and objectivity and regards metaphor, imagery, and allusion a merely decorative and dispensable device for individual expression. While philosophy abounds with image and metaphors, it deceives itself about its own purity and freedom from them: 'Philosophical discourse is registered – it posits itself as philosophical – by distancing itself from the myth, the fable, the poetic, and all that is image-making. The thoughtform is the only form appropriate to philosophy' (Le Doeuff 1980, Preface, p. 9). In its simplest form her argument is that philosophy is based on the containment and (fantasized) expulsion of textual elements that have been labelled poetic, visionary, or even mad. These act as philosophy's other, its supposedly non-philosophical borders or limit. The other of philosophy is both its foundation and what philosophy must expel: 'I wish to consider how some fragments of the imaginary function in places where, as rule, they do not belong, but where, on the other hand, nothing would be accomplished without them' (le Doeuff 1980, p. 10). Her point is in both including and excluding these imaginary elements, philosophy's self-images must generate tender or weak points which, if pressed, threaten to bring the entire structure of the discipline down with them. The imaginary is not alien to or outside of philosophy; it is its underside, its necessary accompaniment.

Its inability to recognize its reliance on textuality and language is what Le Doeuff has described as the 'shameful face of philosophy', its internal scandal. Le Doeuff analyses a series of concrete metaphors in selected texts, including the metaphor of the island in More's *Utopia*, the building in Descartes, the siren in Rousseau, and the island in Kant's *Critique of Pure Reason*. These metaphors are not unrelated to the concept of sexual difference, although Le Doeuff does not explicitly spell out their connections. More's Utopian island is peopled by a mythical race of androgynes who have no need to account for differences between the sexes. Kant's island is also a sexualized metaphor, more related to passion and sexuality than reason or truth. The island of truth is bounded by, and gains its sustenance from, the fruits of the forbidden ocean, the ocean that entices, as does woman, yet must be kept under the control of the island's population.

Le Doeuff's point is that these metaphors *cannot* be eliminated or transcribed into a non-metaphorical form. These metaphors indicate points of intense interest within texts, where what is at stake may not be clear even to the author. This is why these points must remain unspoken and unacknowledged. They are necessary for a text to function for they spell out the conditions necessary for that text. More's Utopia cannot accommodate sexual difference; Kant's pure reason is contingent upon the separation of reason from lived, bodily pleasures and sexual desires.

These metaphors indicate a position the author cannot own up to, marking a place in the text where the text exceeds itself, where it says more than it means. This place is not inscribed by reason but by desire, excess, pleasure, dreams. It is the locus where the philosophical subject is produced by discourse and becomes its agent and support. It is a site of intensity and attraction, love and desire. It indicates that philosophy is bound up with fantasy as much as truth. The desire for philosophy is also related to other desires (for power, otherness, status, etc.). Philosophy is thus not based, as Descartes claimed, on the exclusion of the dream (in *The Meditations*); nor is it composed of incommensurable discourses. It is the product of the collusion of discourses which are neither unrelated nor integrated to each other.

> Philosophical work is not automatically the extension of phantasy or vice-versa. . . . The notion of a dialectical link between dream-

> formation and theoretical work can only lead, for me, to the study of the peculiarities of a social minority, of its points of contact with other forms of thought, other discourses. It also takes into account the tension that exists between what we would like to believe, what is necessary to think and that about which it is possible to be logical. There is no enclosure of discourse, given that discourse is already a compromise, an arrangement between what we can legitimately say, what we would like to put forward, and what we are forced to recognise.
>
> (Le Doeuff 1980, p. 30)

She analyses the strategies of self-definition and evaluation, the ways philosophy evades its sources and its none-too-pure history, leaving unacknowledged its desires so that it can maintain its own image of purity. In 'Women and philosophy' (1977) Le Doeuff outlines the way in which philosophy ensures that only a select few enter the profession; and that those who do have the requisite skills, attitudes, and allegiances, the appropriate degree of reverence and respect, and a disciple-like adherence to a philosophical master. In other words, she analyses philosophy's 'bad faith': the unacknowledged debt it owes to what it must exclude.

Excluded yet metaphorically incorporated elements are related to femininity, materiality, maternity, history, myth. Femininity here is opposed to masculine phallocentrism, order, thought, paternity, the Proper Name, lineage, and descent. She signals a major shift in feminist research. Feminist theory is no longer content to play the handmaiden to Great Male Minds; it is now prepared to challenge existing criteria of greatness. It no longer strives to emulate masculine models of knowledge, validity, and truth but to create new models, styles of argument, and forms of reason.

For Le Doeuff, a new kind of philosophy, more amenable to and accepting of its own limits and gaps, needs to be developed. Instead of seeking a flawless truth, complete and final, she seeks a philosophy capable of accepting its open-endedness and its conceptual and historical limits – philosophy as an 'unfinished play' with its final act yet to be written (Le Doeuff 1977; Gatens 1986a). In her conception, such a philosophy is the product of collective collaboration rather than individual genius (le Doeuff 1977, p. 11). While recognizing its past, the heritage of terms from which it must draw, philosophy should, she claims, recognize its relations to other discourses.

This does not efface the specificity and history of philosophy by blurring it in an undifferentiated interdisciplinary study, but seeks out the specific connections, the borrowings and feedback relations between philosophy and its theoretical others.

Lloyd, Le Doeuff, Irigaray, Daly, and others have questioned philosophy's commitments to the following patriarchal beliefs.

1 The belief in a single, eternal, universal truth independent of the particularities of observers, history, or social conditions. In aiming towards a truth based on correspondence between a proposition and a part of reality, philosophy seeks a position outside of history, politics, and power.
2 The belief in objective, that is, in observer-neutral, context-free knowledge. Objectivity is conceived as a form of substitutability or interchangeability of suitably trained observers. The same results should be achieved by different observers. Such an ideal implicitly introduces socio-political, historical, and local values in the proposal of an interchangeability of suitably trained observers. Suitable training consists of neutralizing and eliminating differences, in reducing them to a common measure which accords with socially privileged (masculine) attributes.
3 The belief in a stable, reliable, transhistorical subject of knowledge, that can formulate true statements and construct objective knowledge. This subject is assumed to be able to separate himself from feelings, emotions, ambitions, personal interests, socio-economic and political values, the past, etc., a subject distanced from the object known and that thus can reflect on the object. But while it is granted unproblematic access to the object, it has no access to its own history, production, and materiality. The philosophy presumes a disembodied, perspectiveless, sexually indifferent subject.
4 The belief in a transparent language and discursive forms that are open to the pure transcription of thought, seeing itself as the play of ideas, concepts, beliefs. Philosophy denies its status as textual and literary by denying its own material dependence on representation.

Instead of abandoning philosophy altogether because it is male-dominated, many radical feminists have voiced opposition to these (and other) underlying assumptions within prevailing forms of philosophy. Rather than accept its present forms, it engages with and challenges the tradition, opening it up to femininity and to the various philosophical paradoxes this may generate.

FEMINIST PHILOSOPHY

There is considerable disagreement among feminists about which approach to take in questioning philosophy's sexist, patriarchal and phallocentric assumptions. They are divided over whether to accept philosophy on its own terms, to undertake a revision of it in the light of feminist knowledges, to abandon it or actively to undermine it. Radical feminists challenge philosophy's orientation around *oneness*, unity, or identity – one truth, one method, one reality, one logic, and so on. Many have insisted that there are a plurality of perspectives and a multiplicity of models on which philosophy could base itself.

In their endorsement of plurality and multiplicity, feminists such as Le Doeuff, Irigaray, and Lloyd are not, however, committed to relativism. Relativism is the belief that there are no absolute positions of judgement or knowledge. There are many positions, each of which is *equally valid*. Relativism or pluralism implies the existence of frameworks and positions which each have their own validity and standards; and the belief that none of these positions is comprehensive or all-inclusive.

Pluralism and relativism imply abandoning the right to criticize actively other positions, even those we find offensive and disturbing – phallocentric or racist statements, for example – and to accept them as having equal validity to our own positions. Radical feminists instead aim to expand and multiply the criteria for what is considered true, rational, or valid and to reject or condemn those they perceive to be discriminatory. They insist on retaining the right to judge other positions, to criticize them, and also to supersede them. Radical feminists are not absolutists nor objectivists nor relativists nor subjectivists. They advocate a *perspectivism* which acknowledges other points of view but denies them equal value.

It is at this time impossible to specify what a philosophy compatible with feminism would be like; given that it does not exist as a definite body of texts, any definition or description would be overly prescriptive. Nevertheless, some general tendencies can be briefly outlined.
Among the features a feminist philosophy may develop are the following.

(a) Instead of a commitment to truth and objectivity, it can openly accept its own status (and that of all discourses) as context-specific. It accepts its *perspectivism*, the fact that all discourses represent a point of view, have specific aims and objectives, often not coinciding with those of their authors. Rather than seeing itself as disinterested knowledge, it can openly avow its own political position: all texts speak from or represent particular positions within power relations.
(b) Instead of regarding philosophy as the unfolding of reason, a sure path of progress towards truth, a feminist philosophy can accept itself as the product of a specific socio-economic and textual-discursive history. Neither relativist nor subjectivist, it aims to render these and other binary oppositions problematic. A feminist philosophy defies modes of conventional evaluation. This is not, however, to claim that it cannot be evaluated in any terms; simply that the criteria used must be different. A theory's validity is not judged simply according to its adoption of a fixed or pre-given form, but it may be judged according to its *intersubjective* effects, that is, its capacity to be shared, understood, and communicated by those occupying similar positions; and also by its *intertextual* effects, that is, its capacity to affirm or

undermine various prevailing or subordinated discursive systems, and the effects it has on other discourses.

(c) Instead of separating the subject and object of knowledge, a feminist philosophy may instead assert a continuity or contiguity between them. The gulf necessary for objectivity is an attempt to guarantee a knowing subject free of personal, social, political, and moral interests (a Cartesian subject), unimplicated in a social context, and uninfluenced by prior ideas and knowledges. A feminist philosophy would need to reconceptualize their interrelations so that reason and knowledge include history, context, and specificity. A feminist philosophy could accept, as patriarchal discourses cannot, that subjects occupying different positions may develop different types of theory and have different investments in their relation to the object. Above all, it can accept that all knowledge is *sexualized*, that it occupies a sexually coded and structured position. However, the sexual position of the text cannot be readily identified with the sexual identity of its author; a female author, for example, does not in any way guarantee a feminine text.

(d) Instead of the dichotomous, oppositional structure, which separates subject and object, teacher and pupil, truth and falsity, etc., a feminist philosophy may regard these terms as continuities or *differences*. Distinctions or oppositions imply that two binary terms are mutually exclusive and exhaustive of the field; that one term defines the other as its negative; that this other can have a place in the binary structure; however, when terms are conceived as two among many others, they are neither contradictory nor all-inclusive. If anything, the relation of difference is based on contrariety not contradiction.

(e) Instead of aspiring to the status of truth, a feminist philosophy prefers to see itself as a form of *strategy*. Strategies are not abstractions, blueprints, or battle-plans for future action. Rather, they involve a provisional commitment to goals and ideals; a recognition of the prevailing situation, in opposition to which these ideals are erected; and an expedient relation to terms, arguments, and techniques which help transform the prevailing order into the ideal. To deny that a feminist philosophy aspires to truth is not to claim it is content with being regarded as false; rather, the opposition between truth and falsity is largely irrelevant for a strategic model.

(f) Instead of dividing theory from practice – so that practice is located chronologically before and after theory (construed as either a plan or a *post facto* reflection, respectively) – a feminist philosophy may regard theory *as* a form of practice, a textual, conceptual, and educational practice, one involved in struggles for theoretical ascendancy, where dominant and subordinated discourses battle with each other. Theory is not privileged by its isolation from practice and its relegation to a pure conceptual level. When it is seen as a material process, theory can be seen as a practice like any other, neither more nor less privileged in its ability to survey and assess other practices. As a material labour or practice, theory relies on concepts, words, and discursive 'raw materials', processes of theoretical production (e.g. the form of argument, narrative, or linguistic structure needed to make coherent discourses) and a determined product (a text or theory). It is not hierarchically privileged over other practices, reserving the right of judgement; rather it is itself capable of being assessed by other practices.

(g) Instead of opposing reason to its others, a feminist philosophy expands the concept of reason. It has analysed how reason as we know it is allied with masculinity and relegates feminine attributes to a repressed or subordinated status (cf. Lloyd 1984a). A feminist philosophy would not reverse the relation between reason and its others, but would expand reason so that its expelled others are now included. In beginning with women's lived experiences in the production of knowledge it seeks a reason that is not separated from experience but based upon it, that is not opposed to the body but accepts it, not distinct from everyday life but cognisant of it.

(h) Instead of accepting dominant models of knowledge (with their logic, binary structure, desire for precision and clarity) a feminist philosophy can accept its status as material, textual, and institutional. As such, it can accept the provisional, not eternal, status of its postulates. It aims for the production of new methods of knowing, new forms of analysis, new modes of writing, new kinds of textual objects, new texts. No *one* method, point of view, position for subjects and objects is the norm or model for all philosophy.

Rather than a norm, a feminist philosophy seeks a new space in which women can write and think as women and not as men's imperfect counterparts or approximations. This space may be capable of sustaining several types of discourse, many perspectives and interests (even contradictory ones). No one form dominates the others.

In short, a feminist philosophy could accept its position as historically grounded in patriarchal texts; yet its future involves a movement beyond this history. It would no longer be confined to women's issues, issues concerning only or largely women, but be free to range over any issue. What makes it feminist is not its object but its perspective. It would no longer accept concepts, terms, methods that have prevailed for millennia but would create new ones appropriate to women.

It proposes arguably one of the most serious upheavals in philosophy since its inception: the claim that the eternal, objective, valid, and true ideals and universal aspirations of philosophy are masculine, not human, interests. Patriarchal philosophies are forced to accept their limits, to recognize that their specific methods and orientations cannot be universal. Feminism threatens philosophy with its own sexualization. The implications of the threat posed by a feminist philosophy have yet to be understood, but they are bound to be devastating to philosophy as it is currently practised.

NOTES

1 Para. 232 'Our virtues', in *Beyond Good and Evil* (Nietzsche 1966, sec. 163).
2 Gatens and Thiele discuss the techniques by which philosophy, and other discourses render women's contributions to knowledges invisible; see their chapters in Pateman and Gross (1986).
3 Her position is that of hybrid sexual liberationist theory from the 1960s (where orgasm was the primary objective) and class analysis. Marcusian Freudo-Marxism is a shorthand notation for theories linking Freudian accounts of sexual liberation with Marxist accounts of the overthrow of capitalism.
4 Sartre has two problems de Beauvoir avoids. First, his account of radical freedom, which posits a freedom that cannot be limited, even in the confines of prison or the shackles of slavery; and second, his individualism. These prevent him from recognizing and accounting for pervasive social structures, power relations, and the constraints imposed by relations of domination and subordination on the subordinated.

REFERENCES

Adkins, A. W. H. (1970a) *From the Many to the One*, Constable, London.
Adkins, A. W. H. (1970b) *Merit and Responsibility: A Study in Greek Values*, Oxford University Press, Oxford.
Allen, J. (1983) 'Marxism and the man question: some implications of the patriarchy debate', in J. Allen and P. Patton (eds) *Beyond Marxism? Interventions After Marx, Intervention*, 17, pp. 91–111.
Aristotle (1971a) *The Ethics of Aristotle*, tr. S. A. K. Thompson, Penguin, Harmondsworth.
Aristotle (1971b), *On the Generation of Animals*, Clarendon Press, Oxford.
Clark, L. and Lange, L.(eds) (1979) *The Sexism of Social and Political Theory: Women and Reproduction from Plato to Nietzsche*, University of Toronto Press.
Elshtain, J. B. (1981) *Public Man, Private Woman, Women in Social and Political Theory*, Princeton University Press, Princeton, NJ.
Finn, G. and Miles, A. (eds) (1982) *Feminism in Canada: From Pressure to Politics*, Black Rose Books, Montreal.
Firestone, S. (1979) *The Dialectic of Sex*, Women's Press, London.
Garside, C. (1975) 'Plato women', *Feminist Studies*, 2.
Gatens, M. (1983), 'A critique of the sex/gender distinction', in J. Allen and P. Patton (eds), *Beyond Marxism? Intervention after Marx*, Intervention Publications, Sydney, pp. 143–61.
Gatens, M. (1986) 'Feminism and philosophy or riddles without answers', in C. Pateman and E. Gross, *Feminist Challenges*, Allen & Unwin, Sydney.
Gatens, M. (1986b) 'Rousseau and Wollstonecraft: nature vs. reason', *Australasian Journal of Philosophy*, Special Issue on Women and Philosophy.

Gould, C. and Wartofsky, M. (eds) (1976) *Women and Philosophy: Toward a Theory of Liberation*, G. P. Putnam, New York.
Guthrie, W. K. C. (1978) *The Greek Philosophers: From Thales to Aristotle*, Methuen, London.
Harding, S. and Hintikka, M. B. (eds) (1983) *Discovering Reality: Feminist Perspectives on Epistemology, Metaphysics, Methodology and Philosophy of Science*, D. Reidel, Dordrecht.
Irigaray, L. (1977) 'Women's exile', *Ideology and Consciousness*, 1.
Irigaray, L. (1978) 'The sex which is not one', in P. Foss and M. Morris (eds), *Language, Sexuality and Subversion*, Feral Publications, Sydney.
Jay, J. (1981) 'Gender and dichotomy', *Feminist Studies*, 7:1, pp. 38–56.
Kristeva, J. (1981) 'Women's time', *Signs*, 7:1, pp. 5–19.
Lange, L. (1979) 'The function of equal education in Plato's *Republic* and *Laws*', in L. Clark and L. Lange (eds), *The Sexism of Social and Political Theory: Women and Reproduction from Plato to Nietzsche*, University of Toronto Press.
Lange, L. (1983) 'Woman is not a rational animal: on Aristotle's biology of reproduction', in S. Harding and M. B. Hintikka (eds), *Discovering Reality: Feminist Perspectives in Epistemology, Metaphysics, Methodology and Philosophy of Science*, D. Reidel, Dordrecht.
Le Doeuff, M. (1977) 'Women and philosophy', *Radical Philosophy*, 17, pp. 2–11.
Le Doeuff, M. (1980) *Recherches sur l'imaginaire philosophique*, Payot, Paris.
Lloyd, G. (1979) 'The man of reason', *Metaphilosophy*, 10:1.
Lloyd, G. (1983) 'Masters, slaves and others', *Radical Philosophy*, 34, pp. 2–9.
Lloyd, G. (1984a) *The Man of Reason: 'Male' and 'Female' in Western Philosophy*, Methuen, London.
Lloyd, G. (1984b) 'History of philosophy and the critique of reason', *Critical Philosophy*, 1:1, pp. 5–23.
Lloyd, G. (1986) 'Selfhood, war and masculinity', in C. Pateman and E. Gross (eds), *Feminist Challenges: Readings in Social and Political Theory*, Allen & Unwin, Sydney.
MacKenzie, C. (1986) 'Simone de Beauvoir: philosophy and/or the female body', in C. Pateman and E. Gross (eds), *Feminist Challenges: Readings in Social and Political Theory*, Allen & Unwin, Sydney.
MacMillan, C. (1982) *Women, Reason and Nature*, Blackwell, Oxford.
Mahawald, M. B. (ed.) (1978) *The Philosophy of Women : Classical to Current Concepts*, Hackett, Indianapolis.
Nietzsche, I. (1966) *Beyond Good and Evil*, Vintage Books, New York.
Okin, S. M. (1980) *Women in Western Political Thought*, Virago, London.
Pateman, C. and Gross, E. (eds) (1986) *Feminist Challenges: Readings in Social and Political Theory*, Redress, Sydney.
Plato (1974a) *The Republic*, Penguin, Harmondsworth.
Plato (1974b) *The Symposium*, Penguin, Harmondsworth.
Rawls, J. (1971) *The Theory of Justice*, Clarendon Press, Oxford.
Richards, J. R. (1982) *The Sceptical Feminist: A Philosophical Enquiry*, Penguin, Harmondsworth.
Sartre, J. P. (1969) *Being and Nothingness*, Methuen, London.
Spelman, E. (1983) 'Aristotle and the politicization of the Soul', in S. Harding and M. B. Hintikka (eds), *Discovering Reality: Feminist Perspectives on Epistemology, Metaphysics, Methodology and Philosophy of Science*, D. Reidel, Dordrecht.
Thiele, B. (1986) 'Vanishing acts in social and political thought: tricks of the trade', in C. Pateman and E. Gross (eds), *Feminist Challenges: Readings in Social and Political Theory*, Allen & Unwin, Sydney.

Thornton, M. (1986) 'Sex equality is not enough for feminism', in C. Pateman and E. Gross (eds), *Feminist Challenges: Readings in Social and Political Theory*, Allen & Unwin, Sydney.
Thompson, J. (1983) 'Women and the high priests of reason', *Radical Philosophy*, 39.
Thompson, J. (1986) 'Women and political rationality', in C. Pateman and E. Gross (eds), *Feminist Challenges: Readings in Social and Political Theory*, Allen & Unwin, Sydney.
Weinbaum, B. (1978) *The Curious Courtship of Women's Liberation and Socialism*, South End Press, Boston.
Winch, P. (1972) *The Idea of a Social Science and its Relation to Philosophy*, Routledge & Kegan Paul, London.

FURTHER READING

Agonito, R. (ed.) (1977) *History of Ideas on Women*, Putnam's, New York.
Annas, J. (1986) 'Plato's *Republic* and feminism', *Philosophy*, 51, pp. 307–21.
Baker, R. and Elliston, F. (eds) (1975) *Philosophy and Sex*, Prometheus, Buffalo.
Barrett, M. (1980) *Women's Oppression Today: Problems in Marxist-Feminist Analysis*, Verso, London.
Beard, M. (1962) *Women as a Force in History*, Collier, New York.
Bishop, S. and Weinzeig, M. (eds) (1979) *Philosophy and Woman*, Wadsworth, Belmont.
Burke, C. (1978) 'Report from Paris: women's writing and the women's movement', *Signs*, 3:4, pp. 843–55.
Burke, C. (1981) 'Irigaray through the looking glass', *Feminist Studies*, 7:2, pp. 287–306.
Campioni, M. and Gross, E. (1983) 'Love's labour's lost: Marxism and feminism', in J. Allen and P. Patton (eds), *Beyond Marxism? Interventions after Marx*, Intervention Publications, Sydney, pp. 113–41.
Chesler, P. (1978) *About Men*, Women's Press, London.
Coward, R. (1983) *Patriarchal Precedents*, Routledge & Kegan Paul, London.
Daly, M. (1978) *Gyn-Ecology: The Metaethics of Radical Feminism*, Beacon Press, Boston.
Dodds, E. R. (1951) *The Greeks and the Irrational*, University of California Press, Berkeley.
Eisenstein, H. and Jardine, A. (eds) (1980) *The Future of Difference*, G. K. Hall, Boston.
English, J. (1977) *Sex Equality*, Prentice-Hall, New York.
English, J. (1978) 'Philosophy', *Signs*, 3:4.
Feral, J. (1980) 'The powers of difference', in H. Eisenstein and A. Jardine (eds), *The Future of Difference*, G. K. Hall, Boston.
Feyerabend, P. K. (1978) *Against Method: Outline of an Anarchistic Theory of Knowledge*, Verso, London.
Finn, G. (1982) 'On the oppression of women in philosophy – or, whatever happened to objectivity', in G. Finn and A. Miles (eds), *Feminism in Canada: From Pressure to Politics*, Black Rose Books, Montreal.
Flax, J. (1979) 'Women do theory', *Quest*, 5:1.
Flax, J. (1980) 'Mother–daughter relationships: psychodynamics, politics and philosophy', in H. Eisenstein and A. Jardine (eds), *The Future of Difference*, G. K. Hall, Boston.

Flax, J. (1983) 'Political philosophy and the patriarchal unconscious: a psychoanalytic perspective on epistemology and metaphysics', in S. Harding and M. B. Hintikka (eds), *Discovering Reality: Feminist Perspectives on Epistemology, Metaphysics, Methodology and Philosophy of Science*, D. Reidel, Dordrecht.
Foss, P. and Morris, M. (eds) (1978) *Language, Sexuality and Subversion*, Feral Publications, Sydney.
Foucault, M. (1978) *The History of Sexuality: An Introduction*, Penguin, Harmondsworth.
Gallop, J. (1982) *Feminism and Psychoanalysis: The Daughter's Seduction*, Macmillan, London.
Gould, C. (1976) 'Philosophy of liberation or liberation of philosophy', in C. Gould and M. Wartofsky, *Women and Philosophy: Towards a Theory of Liberation*, G. P. Putman, New York.
Griffiths, M. and Whitford, M. (eds) (1988) *Feminist Perspectives in Philosophy*, Indiana University Press, Bloomington.
Grimshaw, P. (1982) 'Feminism: history and morality', *Radical Philosophy*, 30.
Grimshaw, P. (1983) 'Review of C. MacMillan's *Women, Reason and Nature*,' *Radical Philosophy*, 34, pp. 33–6.
Grimshaw, P. (1986) *Feminist Philosophers. Women's Perspectives on Philosophical Traditions*, Wheatsheaf Books, London.
Hegel, G. W. F. (1973) *The Philosophy of Right*, tr. T. M. Knox, Oxford University Press.
Irigaray, L. (1974) *Speculum de l'autre femme*, Editions de Minuit, Paris.
Irigaray, L. (1977) *Ce sexe qui n'en est pas un*, Editions de Minuit, Paris.
Irigaray, L. (1980) 'The sex which is not one', in E. Marks and J. Courtivron (eds), *New French Feminisms: An Anthology*, Harvester Press, Sussex.
Jaggar, A. and Struhl, P. (eds) (1978) *Feminist Frameworks*, McGraw-Hill, London.
Janeway, E. (1975) 'On the power of the weak', *Signs*, 1:2.
Jardine, A. (1982) 'Pre-texts for the transatlantic feminist', *Yale French Studies*, 62, pp. 220–36.
Jardine, A. (1982) 'Gynesis', *Diacritics*, Summer, pp. 54–68.
Kahn, C. (1982) 'Excavating "those dim Minoan regions": maternal subtexts in patriarchal literature', *Diacritics*, Summer, pp. 32–41.
Keat, R. (1983) 'Masculinity in philosophy', *Radical Philosophy*, 34, pp. 15–20.
Le Doeuff, M. (1981/2) 'Pierre Roussel's chiasmas', *Ideology and Consciousness*, 9, pp. 39–70.
Marks, E. (1978) 'Women and literature in France', *Signs*, Summer.
Mitchell, J. (1974) *Psychoanalysis and Feminism*, Penguin, Harmondsworth.
Morris, M. (1988) *The Pirate's Fiancée*, Verso, London.
O'Brien, M. (1981) *The Politics of Reproduction*, Routledge & Kegan Paul, London.
Pomeroy, S. (1975) *Goddesses, Whores, Wives and Slaves: Women in Classical Antiquity*, Schocken, New York.
Power, E. E. (1975) *Medieval Women*, Cambridge University Press.
Sachs, H. (1971) *The Renaissance Woman*, McGraw-Hill, New York.
Schwarzer, A. (1984) *Simone de Beauvoir Today*, Chatto & Windus, London.
Stanton, D. (1980) 'Language and revolution: the Franco-American dis-connection', in H. Eisenstein and A. Jardine (eds), *The Future of Difference*, G. K. Hall, Boston.
Stiehm, J. H. (1983) 'The unit of political analysis: our Aristotelian hangover', in S. Harding and M. B. Hintikka (eds), *Discovering Reality: Feminist Perspectives*

on Epistemology, Metaphysics, Methodology and Philosophy of Science, D. Reidel, Dordrecht.
Vetterling-Braggin, M. (ed.) (1982a) *'Femininity', 'Masculinity' and 'Androgyny': A Modern Philosophical Discussion*, Littlefield Adams, Totowa, NJ.
Vetterling-Braggin, M. (ed.) (1982b) *Sexist Language: A Modern Philosophical Analysis*, Littlefield Adams, Totowa, NJ.
Vetterling-Braggin, V., Elliston, F., and English, J. (eds) (1977) *Feminism and Philosophy*, Littlefield Adams, Totowa, NJ.

6

PSYCHOANALYSIS AND FEMINISM

Hazel Rowley and Elizabeth Grosz

Feminists have had a long and ambivalent relation to psychoanalysis, since its inception at the turn of this century. Freud's work tended, between the 1930s and the 1970s, to be regarded as misogynist, ahistorical, and acultural. Many feminists saw it as a rationalization and justification of relations of domination and subordination between the sexes, for they claimed that Freud explains men's and women's relative social and psychical positions in terms of their anatomy. Nevertheless, instead of simply abandoning psychoanalytic theory and seeking alternative models of psychical development and functioning, feminists have remained committed to the reform, rereading, or reinterpretation of psychoanalytic doctrine in an attempt to use it to describe and explain the ways in which males and females acquire their socially ordained sexual roles and their correlative psychical attitudes and structures. This chapter will explore some of the complex, changing relations between psychoanalysis and feminist theory over the last fifty years or so, paying particular attention to the ways in which recent feminists have made psychoanalytic theory an accepted and necessary part of the feminist accounts of the relations between the sexes.

WHAT IS PSYCHOANALYTIC THEORY?

Sigmund Freud originally trained as a neurologist. Before the advent of psychoanalysis proper (around 1900), Freud was moderately well known as an innovative scientist of endocrinology, experimental biology, and pharmacology. His experiments in the sex glands of the male eel, and his speculations on the anaesthetic properties of the cocoa plant in eye surgery had given him an enviable reputation as a medical practitioner. However, after his researches on the treatment of hysterical patients in the 1880s under Janet and Charcot, his interests moved into the area of psychology and psychotherapy. Fascinated by the ways in which Charcot was able to use hypnosis and suggestion to alter, alleviate, and transform hysterical symptoms, over the next fifteen years Freud developed a mode of therapeutic interpretation, deciphering hysterical and neurotic symptoms in terms more literary or hermeneutic than scientific or causal. The origins of psychoanalysis in the two disparate modes of explanation – interpretive and scientific – result in a productive and at times problematic tension in Freudian analysis, a tension between biological and psychological modes of explanation.

For the sake of convenience Freudian psychoanalysis can be divided into two closely related domains: it provides a theory of the genesis and development of human (male and female) *sexuality*; and it gives an account of the operations of a physical *unconscious*. These two cornerstones or foundational principles of psychoanalytic theory are the most contentious points in Freud's work, as well as being the keys to a feminist explanation of the relations between men and women in patriarchal culture. Freud's theory of sexuality had the advantage (in feminist terms) of seeing human sexuality not as naturally heterosexual, genital, or reproductive, but as the consequence of a long and tenuous process of development, in which heterosexual or genital sexuality is but one possible outcome. For Freud, sexuality exceeds and refuses to be subordinated to reproduction. It is not an effect of a predetermined nature, or a response to the species' need for reproduction. It is a set of psychical or meaningful responses to the multiple possibilities of pleasure that the whole of the child's body affords it. It is an effect of the structures of fantasy and signification rather than instincts or biological needs. Moreover, heterosexual genitality, if it is the end-point of the child's psychosexual development, is never secure or definitive, and always betrays its origins in the multiple, 'polymorphous perverse', non-hierarchical pleasures of the infant's body.

> It is always psycho-sexuality, a system of conscious and unconscious human fantasies involving a range of excitations and activities that produce pleasure beyond the satisfaction of any basic physiological need. It arises from various sources, seeks satisfaction in many different ways and makes use of many diverse objects for its aim of achieving pleasure. Only with great difficulty and then never perfectly does it move from being a drive with many component parts – a single 'libido' expressed through very different phenomena – to being what is normally understood as sexuality, something which appears to be a unified instinct in which genitality predominates.
>
> (Mitchell and Rose 1982, p. 2)

Psychoanalysis explores the complex ways in which psychosexuality is bound up with unconscious processes. This is how Juliet Mitchell describes the unconscious:

> The unconscious contains all that has been repressed from consciousness, but it is not co-terminous with this. There is an evident lack of

> continuity in conscious psychic life – psychoanalysis concerns itself with the gaps. Freud's contribution was to demonstrate that these gaps constitute a system that is entirely different from that of consciousness: the unconscious. The unconscious is governed by its own laws, its images do not follow each other as in the sequential logic of consciousness but by condensing onto each other or by being displaced on something else. Because it is unconscious, direct access to it is impossible but its manifestations are apparent most notably in dreams, everyday slips, jokes, the 'normal' splits and divisions within the human subject and in psychotic and neurotic behaviour.
>
> (Mitchell and Rose 1982, pp. 2–3)

You will see that Mitchell, like Freud, treats the unconscious as a special realm, as if it is actual and tangible, able to contain things like a receptacle or an organ. Empiricist critics remind us that this is an illusion: Freud did not discover the unconscious, in the way that Columbus discovered a continent which already existed; what he did was to postulate its existence in order to explain certain phenomena.

SIGMUND FREUD (1856–1939)

Because of the impact of Freud's work on feminism, it is often thought that Sigmund Freud wrote much more about women than he actually did. He himself never claimed expertise about the sexual life of women, which he referred to as a 'dark continent' for psychology. He wrote only three major essays about women – all near the end of his life. They were 'Some Psychical Consequences of the Anatomical Distinction between the Sexes' (1925), 'Female Sexuality' (1931), and 'Femininity' (1933). There are also a number of related essays[1] and three detailed case studies of women, but this is not a great deal given his total output – twenty-four volumes of collected works in the English translation. Freud (unlike Lacan and Kristeva) makes good reading; he has all the flair associated with the Jewish storyteller. Rather than summarizing him here, I'd like to point readers to Freud's work itself.

The first of these papers – the 1925 essay – is short but extremely important, containing the germs of all Freud's later thoughts on the subject. It represents a turning point in Freud's thinking. Until then, he had always described the development of boys and girls as parallel, taking the little boy as his model. Thus he had assumed that a girl's first affection was for her father and a boy's first desires for his mother. Now he outlined a fundamental asymmetry. In the 1931 paper he outlines another important discovery, based on his recent case material: the intensity and duration of the girl's first attachment, her exclusive relationship with her mother:

> Our insight into this early, pre-Oedipus phase in the little girl's development comes to us as a surprise, comparable in another field with the effect of the discovery of the Minoan–Mycenaean civilization behind that of Greece.
>
> (Freud 1931)

The Oedipus complex and the castration complex are fundamental to psychoanalytic theory and practice. (A complex is 'the totality of repressed unconscious ideas that surround an emotionally coloured event'; Mitchell 1974, p. 63.) They are seen as the nucleus of desire, repression, and sexual identity. It is important to grasp Freud's understanding of this process in the formation of the individual's psyche, for the terms will recur throughout this chapter.

Freud called the super-ego 'the heir to the Oedipus complex' for it is formed when the Oedipus complex is resolved and ensures that the values it represents are internalized, regulating the subject from within (Freud 1940, p. 62). Its repressive force reflects the degree of the struggle against the temptation of the Oedipus complex. Hence, Freud suggests, it is stronger in men than in women. To understand this, we must remember that the boy's Oedipus complex is literally shattered by his fear of castration. He abandons incest and enters patriarchal culture in which the power and authority of the father is embodied – a power which he one day aspires to have himself. The girl's Oedipus complex is not resolved as definitively nor to the same extent. She does not fear castration for she is to believe she is castrated already. She does not identify with the father's law in the same way as a boy, for she cannot anticipate having the power herself one day. Hence her super-ego – her sense of conscience and morality – is not as fully developed, says Freud.

The girl's path is much more complex than the boy's. According to Freud she has to undergo two major transferences. Her primary love-object changes from her mother to her father (whereas the boy's remains the mother). And her primary erotic organ must change – Freud says – from the clitoris to the vagina. This is the 'very circuitous path' which she takes to arrive at the 'final normal female attitude' (Freud 1931, p. 230). In his paper 'Femininity' Freud comments that in analytic practice he frequently had the impression that whereas a 30-year-old man seemed youthful and somewhat unformed, a woman of the same age tended to frighten him by her 'psychical rigidity and unchangeability'. He speculates that 'the difficult development to femininity had exhausted the possibilities of the person concerned' (Freud 1933).

It must be noted that Freud did not conceive of the terms 'masculine' and 'feminine' in anatomical terms. Rather, he understood them in terms of three other oppositions: active and passive; subject and object; phallic and castrated. The masculine is equivalent to the first of these terms, and the feminine to the second (Freud 1933, pp. 114–15). This correlation is crucial in understanding how Freud saw the relations between anatomical sex and socio-cultural gender: these are not, as many feminists assume, arbitrarily connected, although the behaviour and attitudes of some men could be described as feminine, and analogously, those of some women could be described as masculine. Masculinity and femininity are neither determined by anatomical and biological factors, nor are they purely arbitrary: they are the consequences of the *socio-cultural meaning of the sexed body*. Freud understood the attribute of masculine and feminine as the consequence of the ways each sex resolves (or fails to resolve) the Oedipus complex. In so far as the boy emerges from his Oedipus complex as an active, phallic subject, he can be described as masculine; in so far as the girl emerges from her Oedipus complex (and that she always does so is not clear from Freud's account) as a passive, castrated (love-) object, she can be described as feminine. Freud made it clear, however, that not all children resolve their Oedipal attachments in such a clear-cut, sexually bifurcated fashion. This insight enables him to suggest that some boys may identify with a passive or castrated position, and some girls may refuse the status of castrated object (most notably, those suffering from the 'masculinity complex') and thus may identify with a passive, 'feminine' position, and an active 'masculine' position, respectively. Masculine and feminine are thus not tied to the child's biological *sex*, but to the ways in which the child is able to resolve, and identify with, the social expectations surrounding the *meaning* of its sex.

THE FEMININITY DEBATE WITHIN PSYCHOANALYSIS

During the 1920s and 1930s there was considerable discussion about the question of femininity – a debate which anticipated the feminist critique of Freud in the 1960s and early 1970s. Karen Horney, Melanie Klein, and Ernest Jones objected to Freud's account of sexual difference because of its postulation of female inferiority. It is important to bear in mind that there has never been a monolithic psychoanalytic view of woman's psychosexuality.

Karen Horney (1887–1952) argued that from a biological point of view woman's capacity to reproduce constituted an undeniable physiological superiority. It was male envy of reproduction which drove men to set up cultural values which devalued women. Given the social subordination of women, the girl's penis envy was quite realistic. Horney observes that: 'the girl begins to measure herself by pretensions and values that are foreign to her specific biological nature and confronted with which she cannot but feel herself inadequate' (Horney 1967, p. 67).

Interested in environmental and social conditions rather than biological drives as determinants of women's behaviour, Horney was dismissed in her own time as a 'culturalist' or revisionist. In 1941 she was expelled from the New York Psychoanalytic Institute. In the 1960s, with the rise of a sociologically oriented feminism, she was taken up with some enthusiasm. Juliet Mitchell, however, claims that Horney merely gave a 'sociological gloss' to a stance which was actually biological determinism (Mitchell 1974, p. 130). (Interestingly, Freud himself spoke out against psychoanalysis becoming bogged down in questions of human 'nature' supposedly based on biology.)

Melanie Klein (1882–1960), who has had considerable impact on contemporary British psychoanalysis, engaged less directly with the debate on femininity, although her ideas had some influence in the area. She emphasized the pre-Oedipal stage in the development of the personality and the child's relationship with the mother in the first year or so of life. Great emphasis was placed on the importance of maternal functions and on the breast, and the existence of breast envy in men. She posited a primordial infantile feminine sexuality, based on the girl's biological sex, which was then modified according to the girl's relations with others (see Klein, in Mitchell 1986).

Ernest Jones (1879–1958), best known as Freud's official biographer, endorsed some of both Horney's and Klein's views in his own work (E. Jones 1948). Like Horney and Klein, he tended to fall back upon a biologistic position in his concern with the *nature* of femininity. For all three the fundamental distinction between the sexes was not a psychosocial construction but a natural given. They envisaged people as *born* masculine or feminine, independent of their subsequent interaction with society.

THE EARLY FEMINIST HOSTILITY TO FREUD: A RADICAL HUMANIST CRITIQUE

> Of all the factors that have served to perpetuate a male-orientated society, that have hindered the free development of women as human beings in the Western world today, the emergence of Freudian psycho-analysis has been the most serious.
>
> (Figes, 1970 p. 148)

Until the early 1970s most feminists (for example, Simone de Beauvoir, Eva Figes, Betty Friedan, Shulamith Firestone, Germaine Greer, and Kate Millett) regarded Freudian psychoanalysis with hostility. Because this attitude was so general, and because it has changed quite dramatically since, at least in some quarters, it is worth considering their objections to Freud in order to see why these are no longer considered relevant in the recent reappraisal of psychoanalysis by certain feminists.

The existentialist, Simone de Beauvoir, writing in 1949, said that she valued some of the insights of psychoanalysis; it was with the psychoanalytical method that she quarrelled. She argued in *The Second Sex* (1949, 1972) that psychoanalytic theory needed to be placed within a historical and philosophical context.The intrinsic weakness of the psychoanalytical framework was that it rejected the idea of freedom, choice, and value. Existentialism is a philosophy which claims that the individual is alone in the world, burdened by a freedom from which she or he cannot escape since it is the precondition of all her or his acts, and for which she or he must take full responsibility. Hence, Freud's emphasis on the unconscious, on drives, instincts, and complexes, ran counter to de Beauvoir's own fundamentally rationalistic position.

Freud's vision, de Beauvoir protested, was male-centred. He had set up a masculine model of individual development and merely adapted this account, with slight modification, to women. (She does not add that Freud himself was aware of this shortcoming in his work.) Indeed, she claimed that psychoanalysis, more than most systems of thought, had been guilty of defining man as a human being and woman as a female – the other.

While de Beauvoir does not discuss Karen Horney's ideas, her own argument is similar. Like Horney, she accused Freud of asserting an account of the development of femininity which failed to take the patriarchal social context into account. If the girl desires a penis, she retorts, 'it is only as the symbol of privileges enjoyed by boys' (de Beauvoir 1972, p. 74), a symbol representing male dominance and the perceived superiority of males. One could argue, however (as Alice Jardine suggests in her interview with de Beauvoir), that she is using a completely different framework, so that many of her objections are invalid (Jardine 1979).

A similar misunderstanding can be found in Betty Friedan's book *The Feminine Mystique* (1963): that Freud was largely responsible for the way in which the mystique of femininity had flourished in America since the 1940s. Although it is Freud himself whom Friedan condemns, she is actually writing about his influence – the fact that his ideas were seized upon, almost in slogan-style, by 'popularizers, sociologists, educators, ad-agency manipulators, magazine writers, child experts, marriage counsellors, ministers, cocktail-party authorities' (p. 93).

Her argument, a commonplace even as she advanced it, is that what Freud observed was peculiar to middle-class Viennese society at the turn of the century and not remotely applicable to American women several decades later. His attempts to universalize his observations merely show the extent to which Freud was 'a prisoner of his own culture' (p. 93).

But Betty Friedan was herself very much the product of her culture. Trained in psychology, she was influenced by the 'ego psychology' popular in the 1950s and 1960s, which saw the ego as the centre of the self and emphasized the healthy adaptation of inner psychic organization to outer social organization. (Erik Erikson, a well-known ego psychologist who entered into the debate himself with his essay 'Womanhood and the inner space' (1968), taught Betty Friedan at Berkeley.) Freud had not paid enough attention to the ego; women's psychic disturbances were not primarily of a sexual nature but rather frustrations caused by blocked growth, as social pressures and material obstacles virtually denied women the possibility of realizing their full potential.

Freud's own life was marked by paternalism and puritanism. Friedan suggests that Freud's focus on sexuality resulted from his own sexual inhibitions. 'One is reminded of the puritanical old maid who sees sex everywhere', she writes (p. 99). This is an *ad hominem* argument, of course, classically condemned as a rhetorical trick, an error of logic. Yet a psychoanalytic approach reopens such questions. Perhaps it is now not only relevant but necessary, turning its own scrutinizing method on the question of its very genesis. Certainly it is a legitimate aspect of the feminist argument that the personal is (also) political.

By contrast, in *The Dialectic of Sex* (1971), Shulamith Firestone appears at first to approach Freud rather benevolently. In fact, however, Firestone's technological pragmatism transposes Freud's analysis to a completely different ground – commonsensical and rational – and she ignores the reigning idea on which psychoanalysis pivots: the hypothesis of the unconscious. While agreeing with the importance Freud places on sexuality, her own approach is quite different. In advocating a freeing of sexual mores in order to liberate individuals, she approaches the libertarian ideas of Reich and Marcuse, which, although Freudian in a general sense, reduce psychoanalysis to merely a biological or sociological analysis (respectively).[2]

An explicit feminist attack on what she saw as Freud's biological determinism was mounted in some detail, and in mocking tones, by Kate Millett in *Sexual Politics* (1969). Pointing out how invidious is his use of such terms as 'the boy's far superior equipment' and 'her inferior clitoris', she accused Freud of a 'gross male-supremacist bias' (p. 182). Why, anyway, asks Millett, would girls assume that the penis is superior to the clitoris, that bigger is better? Why is it not a trauma that one sex has breasts and the other does not?

As for the girl's discovery of her 'castration', Millett comments sardonically: 'It is interesting that Freud should imagine the young female's fears centre about castration rather than rape – a phenomenon which girls are in fact, and with reason, in dread of, since it happens to them and castration does not' (p. 184). (See Kaplan's critique (in Evans 1982) of *Sexual Politics*.)

Kate Millet attempts to refute Freud with sociological evidence. Arguably, however, this places everything Freud says in an entirely different context, involving a denial of the unconscious, desire, and fantasy. This is Juliet Mitchell's argument, one which shows the influence of Louis Althusser. In his essay 'Freud and Lacan' (1984) he argued that psychoanalysis is a special discipline because it has its own object: the unconscious.

> History, 'sociology' or anthropology have no business here, and this is no surprise for they deal with society and therefore with culture, i.e. with what is no longer this small animal [this small biological being] – which only becomes human-sexual [a human child] by crossing the infinite divide that separates life from humanity, the biological from the historical, 'nature' from 'culture'.
>
> (Althusser 1984, p. 158)

JACQUES LACAN: A REREADING OF FREUD

Some twenty years after the controversy surrounding female sexuality had died down within psychoanalysis, Jacques Lacan reopened the debate. He stressed that Freud's disciples and heirs had taken false directions, and that they had been asking the wrong questions.

Jacques Lacan's work is highly obscure, as the Mitchell and Rose (1982) anthology reveals. Whether or not it is justified, the difficulty of Lacan's writing is a deliberate strategy on his part. His texts are a labyrinth of puns, alliterations, and neologisms. Colloquialisms, slang, and coarse humour appear beside highly abstruse allusions. Since Lacan's subject is the unconscious, he attempts to imitate its processes in his writing, to write as the unconscious. His style reinforces his claim that unambiguous meaning in language is a pre-Freudian illusion. Lacan's style – as well as the content of his writing – has had a great influence on French feminist writing.

Let us try to summarize here those aspects of his work which have been most useful to feminism.

By placing Freud within the new framework of linguistics, Lacan reopened the case for psychoanalysis within feminism. The unconscious and sexuality are not seen by Lacan as natural or biological essences, but as products of the subject's constitution in language, within what he calls the imaginary and symbolic orders. (The term 'subject' is used in psychoanalytic theory to avoid running into the very concepts of selfhood, personhood, and individuality which Lacan and other structuralists argue are ideological remnants of humanism and bourgeois individualism.) These orders – or structures – are symbolic systems which produce meaning, and Lacan is concerned to describe the construction of the subject in relation to meaning. For Lacan there is no natural being outside society – outside language. There is no natural sexuality. Its existence is a socially specific construction.

Lacan carefully avoids any commitment to individualism, which is usually based on two underlying assumptions: the (logical) separation of one subject from another (i.e. atomism) and the distinctness of the subject from the social order, which, consequently, needs to be imprinted, learned, internalized, reproduced by the subject. According to Lacan's model, the child is not born a subject, who then bit by bit acquires the appropriate social characteristics: rather, it becomes a subject only through a specific social intervention (the Oedipus complex or the Name-of-the-Father), through which it at one and the same time becomes a social and speaking subject; a being definitively separated from others, particularly the mothers; and acquires a sexual identity and position. In other words, it becomes a (symbolic or social) subject only in taking up either a masculine or feminine position and identity.

For Lacan, as for Freud, the distinction between the sexes is a psychical question: it is not an effect of nature or anatomy, but of the child's resolution of the castration complex. Freud sees this process in terms of the self-evidence of vision (the 'invisibility' of the girl's sexual organ enables both sexes to construe the girl as castrated). Lacan, by contrast, sees it not in the presence or the absence of the penis (the anatomical organ) but in terms of the subject's relations to the *phallus*. (In so far as the subject *has* the phallus, he is masculine; in so far as the subject *is* the phallus, she is feminine). The phallus is clearly understood by Lacan not as an organ, but as a *signifier*, the key signifier of the symbolic order. By this he means that it is only in so far as the phallus is missing, detachable, removable that it has any physical significance: the boy's having a phallus is predicated upon the girl's not having it. Like the signifier itself, it is the presence of an absence. Like a signifier, it does not exist as a thing in itself but only through its circulation and exchange with other signifiers – that is, it exists only by virtue of a circuit in which the other has a vital place. It is only through the other (a woman), that man can be affirmed as having the phallus; and it is only through the other (a man) that a woman can be affirmed as being it. Lacan removes the question of sexual identity from the realm of biology to place it crucially in the field of signification: the subject's sexual identity is an effect of its position in the symbolic order.

Where Freud distinguishes between two forms of sexuality and pleasure for each sex – the pre-Oedipal and the Oedipal – Lacan reformulates these developmental terms in his distinction between the imaginary and the symbolic. The imaginary order is roughly coincident with the pre-Oedipal. However, the term does not refer simply to a sexual orientation (polymorphous perversion), a sexual object (the child's own body in auto-eroticism), or a set of bodily zones (the child's erotogenic zones), the three defining characteristics of infantile sexuality. The imaginary refers above all to the genesis of the ego. It refers to what Freud calls 'ego instincts' rather than to the 'sexual instincts'. The imaginary is the order in which the ego strives to see itself reflected in its relations with the other. The imaginary is the order of the child's identification with images. The other acts as a kind of mirror for the child's newly formed ego, providing the form and limits of its notion of the self. However, because it is fundamentally an image of the other with whom the child identifies, the ego or identity it bestows on itself through its identifications is a necessarily alienated one: the self is always an other. This notion of the imaginary relations between the self and other, the child and the mother, forms the centre of Lacan's account of the mirror-stage, which is based on a careful reading of Freud's account of primary narcissism. For Lacan, the ego is an illusory unity: it takes the other to be an image of self, which means the self-image it forms is always inter-subjective. This is at the basis of his scathing condemnation of ego psychology, a powerful school within revisionist Freudianism.

Ego psychology (of the kind practised by Erikson, Hartman, and the object-relations theorists so powerful in American psychoanalysis) is scathingly condemned by Lacan. He sees it as a repression of Freud's understanding of the unconscious. Ego psychologists take the role of analysis to be the strengthening of the analysand's ego. The analyst takes on the function of acting as an ego-ideal for the analysand – which Lacan sees as an insidious form of moral control, whose end-result is the unified and integrated 'person'. The analyst acts as a kind of role model for the analysand on the presumption that his own values, ideals, and morality are those on which the analysand should also base his or her identity. Lacan sees this as a form of consumerism and voluntarism which simply confirms existing social relations and values instead of seeking out the unconscious desires of the subject. The problem for him with ego psychology is that it mistakes the imaginary for the symbolic.

Freud's notion of the Oedipus complex is recast by Lacan in his notion of the symbolic. The symbolic is the domain of law, language, and exchange. Through the child's resolution of the Oedipus complex (or, in Lacan's terminology, through its accession to the Name-of-the-Father) the cripplingly close identification between mother and child can be mediated, and the child can establish independent relations with others and with the social in general. The symbolic order is regulated by the father's law, the law which prohibits incest. Its key term is the phallus. The phallus becomes the first and definitive object of exchange, and thus initiates the child in a realm of socio-economic and symbolic exchange which is characteristic of each culture. The symbolic order is also the domain of language or signification. It is the order in which the child exchanges the immediacy of its lived experiences for language, for the ability to signify. It is the domain in which the child has access to the verbal 'I', the term by which it can make language refer to itself, the term which enables it to appropriate language for its own purposes. While clearly the child begins to learn to speak long before its access to the symbolic, its use of language is not governed by the *laws* of grammar and syntax, and it is unable to say (and mean) 'I'. It is not yet positioned as a speaking subject. Only when it is separated from its stultifying identification with the (m)other can it use the 'I' to refer to itself. The imaginary is the order of signifiers, of *pure difference*, difference without distinction or regulation; the symbolic, by contrast is the order of signs, of distinction, law, and regulation.

Unlike other Freudian revisionists, Lacan insists that Freud's account of the unconscious is his most threatening and repressed insight. Freud, Lacan claims, knew exactly what he was doing in ascribing a precise structure, methods, and modes of operation to the unconscious, that 'other scene' of thought and desire in subjectivity.

> For Lacan, the unconscious undermines the subject from any position of certainty, from any relation of knowledge to his or her psychic processes and history, and simultaneously reveals the fictional nature of the sexual category to which every human subject is none the less assigned. In Lacan's account, sexual identity operates as a law – it is something enjoined on the subject. For him, the fact that individuals must line up according to an opposition (having or not having the phallus) makes that clear. But it is the constant difficulty, or even impossibility, of that process which Lacan emphasised.
>
> (Mitchell and Rose 1982, p. 29)

The subject attains its sexual identity and position, not simply through enacting the behaviours appropriate to its sex, or from holding appropriate beliefs or attitudes. Its sexual identity is more an effect of the structure of its unconscious, which is formed at precisely the moment when the child takes up its symbolic position as a sexed subject.

The subject is necessarily split, internally ruptured. In the first instance, this is an effect of its imaginary identification with the image of another as the model for itself in the mirror-stage. This means that the subject is incapable of resolving the tension between the fragmentation and disorganization of its lived experiences and the unity, wholeness, and totality of the image with which it identifies. This split in subjectivity is retraced and further exacerbated with the advent of the unconscious as a result of the resolution of the Oedipus complex: the subject is here split into (at least) two distinct physical agencies, the conscious and the unconscious (mediated by a third, the preconscious). Consciousness is radically incapable of knowing the unconscious, which is permanently removed from conscious scrutiny through the processes of repression. Repression ensures that consciousness cannot be identified with the whole of subjectivity: there is more to the subject than consciousness. Repression is the means by which what Freud called the 'reality principle' – the principle of social order – is instilled in the child in place of the primacy of the pleasure principle. Repression removes unconscious memories and wishes from access to consciousness; at the same time, it permanently preserves unconscious contents, which, from this time, are not subject to the normal processes of wear and decay. Repression and the various other techniques for the inhibition of anti-social or pleasure-seeking impulses – disavowal, denial, negation, repudiation, reversal – ensure that what is socially intolerable about the subject's desires remains apparently unrelated to its conscious motives and actions. At the same time, these psychical defences instill the process deferring and delaying pleasure at the behest of social reality, regulating the psychical primary processes (which seek immediate gratification and pleasure) through the imposition of the secondary processes (which inhibit the attainment of pleasure so that satisfaction is sought only when reality can provide an appropriate object for desire):

> Society's injunction that desire must wait, that it must formulate in the constricting word whatever demand it may speak, is what effects the split between conscious and unconscious, the repression that is the tax exacted by the use of language.
>
> (Wright 1984, p. 109)

Lacan's account of the formation of masculinity and femininity is crucially dependent on his understanding of language. In his complex and idiosyncratic discussion of female sexuality and pleasure (Mitchell and Rose 1982), he analyses the ways in which the notion of an 'Eternal Feminine' or 'Woman' (with a capital 'W') is the fantasy or construct of the masculine subject, not a truthful representation of an essential feminity. Hence his claim 'The Woman does not exist'. He presents a brilliant analysis of the lures and forms of self-deception the masculine subject projects on to the Woman who is defined as his complement or self-completion, who will make him 'All'. Romantic love, in his view, is a masculine ideal of woman's subjection: in Woman, man seeks access to the Other (with a capital 'O'), the law, the symbolic father, or God. Romantic love relations are not two-person relations, but always involve five 'parties': the self, the other, the self's image of the other, the other's image of the self, and the Other, who functions as the obstacle to the fulfilment of each party.

Lacan's understanding of femininity is more complex and sophisticated than Freud's: for him femininity is always in an ambiguous relation to the phallus. On the one hand, femininity is defined as the lack (of a phallus). The woman does not have the phallus, for which she may compensate by attempting to become the phallus, making the whole of her body into the erotic object of (men's) desire. Her sexuality and identity are capable of characterization only with reference to the phallic signifier. Yet, on the other hand, Lacan acknowledges that the phallus can in no way adequately contain and capture female sexuality: there is always a residue, an unabsorbed excess which defies reduction to male models. He posits a peculiarly feminine '*jouissance*', a term which undecidably refers to orgasm in particular, and pleasure in general, a kind of non-localized ecstasy (which, incidentally, Lacan asserts, should not be translated). There is something in female sexuality which is always 'beyond the phallus'.[3]

However, in granting women a potential autonomy and a pleasure uncontained by phallic models, Lacan also denies women the ability to know or say in what their pleasure consists. In being 'beyond the phallus', this pleasure cannot be symbolized: it is unrepresentable. This enables men to confuse female sexuality with distinct sexual zones (vaginal or clitoral), to speculate about women, to find them enigmatic and alluring. It justifies the interventions of the analyst, who can with some legitimacy speculate on and attempt to articulate something of this pleasure:

> The woman can only be written with *The* crossed through (~~la~~ femme). There is no such thing as *The* woman, where the definite article stands for the universal. There is no such thing as *The* woman since her essence – having already risked the term, why think twice about it? – of her essence, she is not all. . . .
>
> There is woman only as excluded by the nature of things which is the nature of words, and it has to be said that if there is one thing they themselves are complaining about enough at the moment, it is well and truly that – only they don't know what they are saying, which is all the difference between them and me.
>
> It none the less remains that if she is excluded by the nature of things, it is precisely that in being not all, she has, in relation to what the phallic function designates of *jouissance*, a supplementary *jouissance*. . . .
>
> There is a *jouissance*, since we are dealing with *jouissance*, a *jouissance* of the body which is, if the expression be allowed, *beyond the phallus*.
>
> (Lacan, 'God and the Jouissance of The Woman', in Mitchell and Rose 1982, pp. 144–5)

We will return to this question of an excessive or supplementary feminine *jouissance* later. We now need to explain how a Lacanian reading has persuaded feminists to return to Freud.

MITCHELL AND CHODOROW

Juliet Mitchell's text, *Psychoanalysis and Feminism* appeared in 1974. It became a major force in convincing feminists that even if psychotherapy is a patriarchal institution, the writings of Freud himself provided a detailed description of the psychical operations of patriarchal social reproduction: it explains how sex roles and their values are transmitted from one generation to the next in unconscious form.

As author of an influential article, 'Women: the Longest Revolution', which had appeared in *New Left Review* in 1966, and the book *Woman's Estate* (1971), Mitchell was already known and respected as a Marxist feminist. *Psychoanalysis and Feminism* did not indicate a change of position; it was a call for feminists to reconsider Freud's work in order to develop a materialist feminist theory of gender and sexuality.

The book opens by arguing that 'psychoanalysis is not a recommendation *for* a patriarchal society, but an analysis *of* one' (Mitchell 1974, p. xv). Because of its focus on ideology and sexuality, feminism could not afford not to make use of the insights of psychoanalysis:

> The way we live as 'ideas' the necessary laws of human society is not so much conscious as *unconscious* – the particular task of psychoanalysis is to decipher how we acquire our heritage of the ideas and laws of human society within the unconscious mind, or, to put it another way, the unconscious mind *is* the way in which we acquire these laws. [. . .] where Marxist theory explains the historical and economic situation, psychoanalysis, in conjunction with the notions of ideology already gained by dialectical materialism, is the way into understanding ideology and sexuality.
>
> (pp. xvi, xxii)

Feminist studies of Freud up to that time had provided a necessary critique of a 'Freudianism' which had become popularized and debased. However, Mitchell considers that feminists had performed a disservice by placing Freud's ideas in a false context, outside the psychoanalytical framework. They had systematically denied the two pivotal notions of psychoanalysis: the unconscious and infantile sexuality. Here she echoes Jacques Lacan's criticism of post-Freudian psychoanalysis.

Like Lacan, Mitchell is selective in the parts of Freud she takes up, distinguishing between what she calls the 'Freudian Freud' – the thinker in advance of his time – and the 'pre-Freudian Freud' (not meant in a temporal sense, of course), who was unable to break away completely from the thought, concepts, and terminology of his time. In this sense, 'Freud was as capable as anyone else of being pre-Freudian' (p. 323).

The 'Freudian Freud' who interests Mitchell was concerned not with social reality but with psychical reality, with mental representation. What Freud says about femininity relates to how it is lived in the mind – in the unconscious.

The Oedipus complex, we are reminded, is not predicated on the *actual* family situation nor are the desires associated with it conscious ones – it is about repressed ideas. The actual parent figures are not necessarily even present. It is similar to the threat of castration – the actual threat need not occur, but the idea of it is still there. As for penis envy, Mitchell writes that 'we are talking not about an anatomical organ, but about the ideas of it that people hold and live by within the general culture, the order of human society' (p. xvi). This view is convenient, but not altogether historically convincing. Michèle Barrett (1980, p. 56) writes that Freud, when describing penis envy, poses the question 'in exclusively physical rather than mental terms'. She suggests that, from a feminist point of view, Juliet Mitchell might be offering 'an unduly charitable reading of his position'.

While it is strongly influenced by Mitchell's feminist re-vindication of Freud, Nancy Chodorow's use of psychoanalysis, unlike Mitchell's, is heavily based on object-relations theory. This gives it a peculiarly American flavour. Chodorow's work is presented from a generally sociological, empirical, and descriptive perspective. Object-relations theorists – Chodorow cites Balint, Fairbairn, Winnicott, and Guntrip as examples – stress the crucial role that the child's concrete social environment plays in the formation of its 'personality'. The subject is conceived as a 'person-ego', which is 'the person, self, subject in relationship, with conscious and unconscious motives and intentions' (Chodorow 1979, p. 49) – conceived, that is, on a wholist or totalized model, as an integrated being. Using this conceptual framework, Chodorow sees an isomorphism between the child's physical organization and the requirements of the social order:

> A child . . . comes to channel libido and aggression in patterned ways as a result of its relational experiences and its interactions with caretakers, that is, the id becomes patterned and constructed. Thus, society constitutes itself psychologically in the individual not only in the moral strictures of the superego. All aspects of psychic structure, character, and emotional and erotic life are social, constituted through a 'history of object-choices.' This history, dependent on the individual personalities and behaviour of those who happen to interact with a child, is also socially patterned according to the family structure and prevalent psychological modes of a society.
>
> (p. 50)

Chodorow argues that psychoanalysis may provide an explanation for how mothering is reproduced from generation to generation, how, that is, women from one generation to the next take on the role of nurturing and caretaking without observable coercion or social pressure. One of the major preoccupations of Chodorow's book is her analysis of the gender-specific transmission of nurturance. She locates this socio-psychical transmission of 'gender roles' in the child's primary and formative relation to the mother. Like Freud, she claims that the origins of the child's later social identity are based on two unclearly separated relations – to its own corporeality and bodily sensations, and to the world of objects. The first relation derives from 'an inner physical experience of body integrity and a more internal "*core* of sense"' (p. 67), while the second is the result of a 'sense of personal psychological division from the rest of the world' (p. 68).

If its primary, given relations to the mother are based on a symbiosis, then the child only gains some measure of independence and autonomy from the mother through frustration. This creates the possibilities of separation and thus of identity and a viable sense of self. The infant is impelled by two contradictory impulses, one which strives for a merger with the mother, which sustains its dependence on her; and the other which strives for independence and its own autonomous place in the world. These processes of the acquisition of a sense of self or identity are, in Chodorow's opinion, dependent on the child's resolution of the Oedipus complex, in which the roles of mother and father have different effects on the two sexes. For both sexes the mother is the primary caretaker and representative of love, care, and well-being; the father is only a secondary representative of love, being more emotionally and physically distant from the child, and in a sense, he comes to represent the separateness of the external world. Boys and girls will develop different degrees of merging and separation, according to the relative degree of attachment to each of the parents:

> Relational capacities that are curtailed in boys as a result of the masculine oedipus complex are sustained in girls. Because of their mothering by women, girls come to experience themselves as less separate than boys, as having more permeable ego boundaries. Girls come to define themselves more in relation to others.
>
> (p. 93)

If women's attachment to their mothers (and consequently, to other women) remains intense and cannot be directly transferred to the father because of his relative distance and separateness from the child, Chorodow finds the explanation she has been seeking for the reproduction of mothering. The girl's resolution of the Oedipus complex will in general imply a heterosexual object-choice. The girl will take the father as a model for her later relations with men, but she retains her need for the mother's warmth and closeness which she finds difficult to satisfy with men. Chodorow implies that if women could become sexually involved with other women, this may more readily satisfy the daughter's need for erotic and emotional attachment. However, given that most women are in fact heterosexual, there is a rupture in their erotico-affectionate relations with men which can only find compensation in the close physical and affectionate relation with a child. In this way the structure of the daughter's family is reproduced in turn for her daughter.

Mitchell and Chodorow represent two different feminist approaches to psychoanalysis: Chodorow's use of it is largely clinical: for her, psychoanalysis is a set of clinical and empirical insights about the ways in which men and women live, experience, and behave in our culture. For Mitchell, psychoanalysis is more an interpretive grid, a theoretical construct of explanatory, rather than merely descriptive, value. Mitchell carefully distinguishes between psychoanalysis as practice and as theory: as practice, it may well serve the prevailing values of patriarchal culture. But as theory, it provides an explanation for patriarchal power relations that is profoundly threatening to those relations. That, she believes, is why psychoanalysis has, for her, been so easily misrepresented. Chodorow, on the other hand, takes it as a descriptive (and possibly predictive) set of truths.

Mitchell's work is vulnerable to quite different criticisms than Chodorow's. Given Mitchell's debt to a Marxist (or Althusserian) account of ideology, and to a structuralist analysis of social relations, she remains committed to creating an integrated Marxist-feminist model of the class–gender structure. However, if one questions the presumptions of Althusserianism and ideology-based models of social power, her feminist justification of Freud becomes less convincing. Moreover, she remains entirely uncritical of the many feminist problems or tensions in Freud's (and Lacan's) work, wholeheartedly accepting the inevitability of the positions of mother as the object from which the child must be severed, and the father as the necessary condition and support for the child's entry into civilization. In short, she eternalizes patriarchy, making it equivalent to culture itself. In Chodorow's case, there are problems associated with her naturalism and wholism. She presumes that there are stable identities and unities in psychical life that are prefigured biologically and physiologically. A stable ego, a secure sense of belonging, and a well-regulated relation to objects become moral ideals. One danger here is that she risks generalizing the values of a bourgeois culture as unquestionable ideals. She is committed to notions of individualism that are not merely bourgeois; she conceives of the individual and the social as two logically distinct orders; and thus her primary question is the connection between them. But perhaps most problematically, she operates within a framework that takes the equality of the sexes as its unquestioned goal. To put it crudely, for her the solution to the problem of the reproduction of mothering lies in some notion of shared parenting, in which both sexes participate equally in the nurture and care of children. However, such an equality, even if it is possible, will not provide a solution to patriarchal power relations, in so far as the same behaviour in the two sexes will retain a different (unequal) meaning unless the very structures of significance and meaning, and not just social practices, are tackled. Chodorow's position does not adequately address the intermeshing and interdependence of social and significatory practices.

PSYCHOANALYSIS AND FRENCH FEMINISMS

Lacan's rereading of Freud has had enormous influence on French intellectuals; this may explain its status as presumed background knowledge in the work of a number of French feminists. While there are few French feminists who are entirely uncritical of Lacanian analysis, nevertheless, even those highly critical of his positions have tended to develop their criticisms in terms more or less internal to his framework. In particular, they tend to remain critical of his pronouncements regarding the force and inevitability of paternal law, and the ways in which he ties the privilege of the phallus to the child's entry into the symbolic, and thus to language and social exchange. This may explain the unexpected ways (for English-speaking feminists) in which language, sexuality, and pleasure are linked in the work of many French feminists.

Julia Kristeva, Luce Irigaray, Hélène Cixous are prominent amongst French feminists who challenge 'phallogocentrism' and who share a common interest in a feminine language.[4] From there, each takes a different direction, so we will look at each separately.

Julia Kristeva

A Bulgarian linguist who arrived in Paris in 1966 at the age of 25, Julia Kristeva made a rapid impression on French intellectual life. Today she is a practising psychoanalyst as well as a literary theorist and cultural critic. Her thinking has been much influenced by Lacan, but she has shifted away from him in her celebration of what she calls the 'semiotic'. Closely allied to the unconscious, the 'semiotic' is a sort of residue of the pre-imaginary, pre-Oedipal, pre-symbolic realm. Whereas the symbolic is associated with the paternal – the realm of Lacan's Name-of-the-Father – the semiotic is linked with the maternal. Kristeva sees it as a site of resistance to the symbolic, for it constantly undermines rational discourse. As Carolyn Burke explains, the symbolic and the semiotic are 'two closely related modalities of signification, which, in our cultures, tend to be related as master and slave' (Gallop and Burke 1980, p. 111).

> If the semiotic expresses itself in the infant's world as babble, rhythm, melody, and gesture, then in the adult's it returns in word play, prosodic effects, nonsense, and laughter – all relatively uncensored traces of the unconscious.
>
> (Gallop and Burke 1980, p. 120)

If Kristeva links the semiotic with the maternal, it is because she associates this realm with the stage in psychic development when the child experiences the world through the rhythms and gestures of the mother's body. It is not innately female. Indeed, the writers who interest her – avant-garde writers whose fluid and often ungrammatical writing disrupts conventional discourse – are mostly men: Mallarmé, Artaud, Joyce, Beckett. She has paid some attention to Virginia Woolf, but claims that Woolf does not engage in the systematic dissection of language which she sees in Joyce's work.

What Kristeva considers 'the feminine', then, is not something specific to women, but a psychic position – a realm preserved in the unconscious, a realm marginal to the symbolic. That is what she means when she says:

> In 'woman', I see something that cannot be represented, something that is not said, something above and beyond nomenclatures and ideologies. There are certain 'men' who are familiar with this phenomenon; it is what some modern texts never stop signifying.
>
> (Kristeva 1981a, pp. 137–8)

Kristeva argues that women are not fundamentally different from men, but that the semiotic mode is more dominant in the female psyche than in the male psyche. This is basically due to the different meaning of castration in the female and the male unconscious – and the different ways in which the genders accept castration.

Both the semiotic and the symbolic constitute the subject – whether a masculine or feminine subject. The symbolic is established through the repression of the semiotic, but the semiotic re-emerges continually in the symbolic, challenging it, undermining it, and keeping it open.

As you see, the direction of Kristeva's work is to develop the Lacanian theory of subjectivity by reversing various categories. Jane Gallop makes an interesting comment on this:

> In thinking about Kristevan theory, there arises the question of the relation between 'the semiotic' and the Lacanian 'imaginary'. Both are defined in contradistinction to 'the symbolic'. Both are associated with the pre-Oedipal, pre-linguistic maternal. But whereas the imaginary is conservative and comforting, tends towards closure, and is disrupted by the symbolic; the semiotic is revolutionary, breaks closure, and disrupts the symbolic. It seems there are two kinds of maternals; one more conservative than the paternal symbolic, one less. It is noteworthy that the male theorist sees the paternal as disruptive, the maternal as stagnant, whereas the female theorist reverses the positions.
>
> (Gallop 1982, p. 124)

Kristeva maintains that any politics will fail unless it takes the pre-symbolic realm into account. She writes: 'The subject of a new political practice can only be the subject of a new discursive practice' (cited in A. R. Jones 1984, p. 61). In a recent interview (Kristeva 1984), she expresses disillusionment with political discourses, as she claims they consistently fail to take account of individuals and subjectivity. For this reason, she advocates political marginality, and is critical of feminism as a collective movement.[5]

A number of questions are raised by Kristeva's position, which, of course, we have barely gone into here, hardly doing her justice. For example, is avant-garde writing *necessarily* revolutionary? Some questions which Ann Rosalind Jones raises in an article on Kristeva (1984) are important:

> What is the relationship, exactly, between textual and political revolution? Which comes first, a shift in subjectivity or in the social structures that enclose it? Do ruptures in literary discourse have any necessary connexion to other social transformations?
>
> (A. R. Jones 1984, p. 61)

Toril Moi, editor of *The Kristeva Reader* (1986), argues that 'many of Kristeva's most valuable insights draw at times on highly contentious forms of subjectivist politics' (Moi 1985, p. 169).

Luce Irigaray

Luce Irigaray, a Belgian, studied linguistics and philosophy before she went to Paris and trained to become a psychoanalyst. Taken under Lacan's wing, she taught in his department – the department of psychoanalysis at the University of Vincennes, a university with progressive ideals, formed after 1968. However, after the publication of her book *Speculum of the Other Woman* (1985a), Jacques Lacan abruptly dismissed her from her teaching post.

One of the central theses in Irigaray's work is that language and the systems of representation cannot express female desire (Irigaray 1977, p. 71). Having studied the language of male and female schizophrenics, Irigaray observes that men have an ability for meta-language (language which talks about language) which women do not have. A man in a state of madness can distance himself from himself whereas in women the delirium is suffered within the body itself, and cannot be expressed in another mode.

Irigaray claims that this phenomenon is not specific to madness. Women, she says, are unable to express their desire through the language that is imposed upon them when they enter the symbolic order:

> As Freud admits, the beginnings of the sexual life of a girl are so 'obscure,' so 'faded with time,' that one would have to dig very deep indeed to discover beneath the traces of this civilization, of this history, the vestiges of a more archaic civilization that might give some clue to woman's sexuality. That extremely ancient civilization would undoubtedly have a different alphabet, a different language . . . Woman's desire would not be expected to speak the same language as man's; woman's desire has doubtless been submerged by the logic that has dominated the West since the time of the Greeks.
>
> (Irigaray 1985b, p. 25)

In *Speculum of the Other Woman*, she looks at why this should be, analysing the history of western theoretical discourse from Plato to Hegel. In this tradition (to which Freud belongs), the feminine is defined as 'nothing other than the complement, the other side, or the negative side, of the masculine' (Irigaray 1977, p. 63).

Irigaray is not interested in anatomy as such, but in its morphology – in the way it has been represented, conceptualized, and produced as such in discourse. She expresses this idea in the following terms:

> all Western discourse presents a certain isomorphism with the masculine sex: the privilege of unity, form of the self, of the visible, of the specularisable, of the erection (which is the becoming in a form). Now this morpho-logic does not correspond to the female sex: there is not 'a' female sex. The 'no sex' that has been assigned to the woman can mean that she does not have 'a sex', and that her sex is not visible, or identifiable, or representable in a definite form. There is indeed a visible exterior of the female sex, but that sex can in no way lend itself to the privilege of the form: rather what the female sex enjoys is not having its own form.
>
> When one says, or believes that this sex is a 'hole', it is a way of indicating that it cannot represent itself in either the dominant discourse or 'imaginary'. Thus I have tried to find out what the specific modes of functioning of the female sex and 'imaginary' could be.
>
> (Irigaray 1977, p. 64)

The question of what the female imaginary (as opposed to the phallic symbolic) could be is tackled by Irigaray in *This Sex Which Is Not One* (1985b). In this book, which affirms the positive potential of sexual difference, Irigaray constructs an elaborate metaphor around feminine sexuality. The word play in the title indicates her project: feminine sexuality (the sex that isn't) is not one but plural:

> Fondling the breasts, touching the vulva, spreading the lips, stroking the posterior wall of the vagina, brushing against the mouth of the uterus, and so on. To evoke only a few of the most specifically female pleasures. Pleasure which are somewhat misunderstood in sexual difference as it is imagined – or not imagined, the other sex being only the indispensable complement to the only sex.
>
> But *woman has sex organs more or less everywhere*. She finds pleasure almost everywhere. Even if we refrain from invoking the hystericization of her entire body, the geography of her pleasure is far more diversified, more multiple in its differences, more complex, more subtle, than is commonly imagined – in an imaginary rather too narrowly focused on sameness.
>
> (Irigaray 1985b, p. 28)

Female genitalia, she writes, could be positively represented in terms quite different from their patriarchal representations, representations which are polarized around two distinct zones, clitoris or vagina: the image of the two lips renders this opposition laughable – and makes clear what is at stake for men in wanting a single zone to define women.

> Woman 'touches herself' all the time, and moreover no one can forbid her to do so, for her genitals are formed of two lips in continuous contact. Thus, within herself, she is already two – but not divisible into one(s) – that caress each other.
>
> (Irigaray 1985b, p. 24)

A feminine use of language (which is repressed) would, according to Irigaray, have a similar form, or rather formlessness, to the female sexual morphology: plural, ambiguous, playing with itself, diffuse, and polymorphous. Given free rein, it would subvert the dominant discourse which, based on a privileging of the phallus, is single, unified, visible, and definable.

In her emphasis on heterogeneity, play and difference in language, rather than unity, Irigaray is influenced by the work of Jacques Derrida. As well as exploring 'the specific morphological characteristics of the feminine' (Todd 1983, p. 237), Irigaray's feminist project, again influenced by Derrida, is to 'deconstruct' phallogocentric discourse – 'to show that the so-called universal discourse, whether it be philosophic, scientific, or literary, is sexualized and mainly in a masculine way'. She adds: 'It is necessary to unveil it, to interpret it, and at the same time to begin to speak a language which corresponds better to, and is in continuity with, our own pleasure, our own sensuality, our own creativity' (Todd 1983, p. 242).

Hélène Cixous

Hélène Cixous founded women's studies at the University of Vincennes in 1975. She was a spokeswoman for the feminist group 'Psychanalyse et Politique' (popularly known as 'Psych et Po'), and her prolific output of experimental novels was published by this group's publishing house, Des Femmes. In 1982 she stopped publishing with them, claiming that it impaired her freedom as an artist. She sees her writing as political: to question language, to break up character and unity linked to a linear concept of time, to write from what she considers a feminine border.

Cixous has been a passionate proponent of 'feminine writing' – texts which subvert the dominant phallogocentric logic. By 'feminine', Cixous does not mean female; she criticizes Freudian psychoanalysis for its 'thesis of a "natural" anatomical determination of sexual difference–opposition' (Cixous 1981a, p. 93). She is not interested in the sex of the author – she endorses Freud's belief in the *bisexual* nature of all human beings – but in the kind of writing.

'Masculine writing' is seen by Cixous as systematic, closed, and limited by laws, whereas 'feminine writing' comes from the imaginary.

> Cixous argues for a new kind of production, a writing from the imaginary, with its infinite multiplicity of identifications precluding a stable subject. She urges for figuration, not characterization, with possibilities of reading in different directions. The new 'subject', which as true subject of the unconscious is always on the run, explodes codes and social orders, undoes censorships and repression. It frees, gives birth to writer and reader, breaks the contract, displaces debt and recognition. The author's signature is always multiple.
>
> (Conley 1984, p. 26)

It is because she claims to be writing from the imaginary that Cixous writes: 'I am where the unconscious is speaking'. Cixous's famous manifesto for feminine writing, called 'The Laugh of the Medusa' (written in 1975), is a utopian picture of female creative powers:

> To write. An act which will not only 'realize' the decensored relation of woman to her sexuality, to her womanly being, giving her access to her native strength; it will give her back her goods, her pleasures, her organs, her immense bodily territories which have been kept under seal; it will tear her away from the superegoized structure in which she has always occupied the place reserved for the guilty (guilty of everything, guilty at every turn: for having desires, for not having any, for being frigid, for being 'too hot'; for not being both at once; for being too motherly and not enough; for having children and for not having any; for nursing and for not nursing . . .) – tear her away by means of this research, this job of analysis and illumination, this emancipation of the marvelous text of her self that she must urgently learn to speak.
>
> (Cixous 1981b, p. 250)

CONCLUSION

This chapter aimed to introduce an important debate and to indicate new directions which have directly resulted from the productive clash between femininism and psychoanalysis.

Certainly there are problems for feminism in all this. English-speaking feminists, in particular, seem to feel ambivalent – excited, disorientated, and also wary about that French feminist theoretical writing which validates the 'feminine'. There is an interesting discussion between Anglo-American academic feminists in the introduction to a special issue of *Yale*

French Studies (1981, no. 62), called 'Feminist readings: French texts/ American contexts'. To pinpoint some feminists' reservations, here is a collage of their reflections:

> *Mary Jacobus*: It seems to me that the emphasis on the body and on the Dark Continent in authors like Cixous and Irigaray is something we should be very suspicious of and that such essentialism does have a conservative implication. But it depends on where these things are coming from. When Father Ong says that women are to do with motherhood and with the feminine and with peace and nurturance, it's coming from a very conservative direction. When Cixous says women are to do with the body and that the hysterical symptom is a way of refusing to be exchanged, refusing the Law, then it's quite a different kind of intervention.
>
> *Susan Gubar:* There's also a nervousness about validating the 'feminine' and the extent to which that is really a conservative move. Is that an entrapment in a stereotype, or is it some genuinely new step? . . .
>
> I wonder whether part of my suspicion of the French scene is how much we are still dealing with the problem of Milton's daughters: we have Lacanian daughters: and we have Lévi-Straussian daughters, . . . and what other daughters do we have? . . . and I really do wonder whether buying into theoretical discourse doesn't mean buying into just the kind of abstract language that so much of feminism has been opposed to. So I do sense a division between practice and theory, between history and theory.
>
> *Sandra Gilbert:* But there is another problem for me with a lot of French feminist theoreticians. My sense of their 'otherness' has something to do with a way in which their theory is detached from what we have to struggle with. It has to be said that people like Irigaray and Cixous in particular are anti-empirical. They are involved in a kind of word play: interrogating absences in Freud often becomes a sort of wistful fantasy . . .
>
> *Elizabeth Abel:* As a feminist I'm still, perhaps in a very naive way, looking for answers about female identity, and I don't want it all to be word play. I feel that's a male privilege. It isn't what I want to do with texts. I want to figure out what the forms of female experience are.
>
> *Yale French Studies* (1981)

Susan Rubin Suleiman, another American academic, also expresses some reservations about the work of the French radical feminists:

> To recognize that women, mothers, have been excluded from the order of patriarchal discourse, and to insist on the positive difference of maternal and feminine writing in relation to male writing, can only be beneficial at this time. But it would be a pity if the male gesture of exclusion and repression of the female 'other' were to be matched by a similar gesture in reverse. I do not mean by that only the obvious exclusion of men, for some French feminists . . . are willing to admit that certain male poets have attained a 'feminine' status in their writing. Rather, I mean the exclusion of a certain *kind* of writing and discourse arbitrarily defined as 'male', repressive, logical, the discourse of power, or what have you. Such a gesture necessarily places 'feminine' writing in a minority position, wilfully ex-centric in relation to power. I am not wholly convinced that this is the best position for women to be in.
>
> I also have reservations about what might be called that fetishization of the female body in relation to writing. It may be true that femininity and its quintessential embodiment, motherhood, can provide a privileged mode of access to language and the mother tongue. What would worry me would be the codification, on the basis of this insight, of women's writing and writing style.
>
> (Garner *et al.* 1985, pp. 371–2)

Rosi Braidotti, on the whole enthusiastic about current trends in French feminism, suggests that while feminists should be aware of certain risks, such as the risk of essentialism, it is one we must take. We must use the women's movement as a 'laboratory of ideas, a place of experimentation'.

> How do we explore the unconscious? How do we explore the feminine? I think it's a question that we have to keep asking, and it is almost my perverse hope that we can go on asking the question without answering it because that's the only way, it seems to me, to talk about the politics of subjectivity without falling into the trap of either sociological feminism or essentialist feminism. Staying in between these two positions implies that we suspend our belief in ultimate identities while at the same time acquiring, almost like Descartes, provisional morality. We acquire a feminist identity insofar as we are fighting oppression but we know it's not enough to stop there.
>
> (Braidotti 1986, p. 13)

NOTES

1 The most important related essays are: 'Three essays of the theory of sexuality' (1905); 'On narcissism' (1914); 'The psychogenesis of a case of homosexuality in

woman' (1920); 'The dissolution of the Oedipus complex' (1924); 'The question of lay analysis' (1926); 'An outline of psychoanalysis', ch. VII (1940).

2 Herbert Marcuse (1898–1978) rejected the contrast Freud made between sexuality and civilization. Whereas Freud believed that if the repression of libidinal gratification were lifted society would collapse, Marcuse envisaged a possible social order in which desires were liberated. To Wilhelm Reich (1897–1957), what was known in psychoanalysis as 'sublimation' was in fact the rationalized product of bourgeois sexual inhibitions. As a psychoanalyst, he held that many adult problems would not occur if sexual expression was not prematurely stifled.

3 'The verb *jouir* (to enjoy, to experience sexual pleasure) and the substantive *la jouissance* (sexual pleasure, bliss, rapture) occur frequently in the texts of the new French feminisms. . . . This pleasure, when attributed to a woman, is considered to be of a different order from the pleasure that is represented within the male libidinal economy often described in terms of the capitalist gain and profit motive. Women's *jouissance* carries with it the notion of fluidity, diffusion, duration. It is a kind of potlatch in the world of orgasms, a giving, expending, dispensing of pleasure without concern about ends or closure' (Marks and Courtivron 1981, pp. 36–7).

4 Other names are Michèle Montrelay, Sara Kofman, and Eugénie Lemoine-Luccioni.

Phallogocentrism' is a term used by the philosopher Jacques Derrida. Carolyn Burke explains it as follows: 'His word weds "phallocentrism" to "logocentrism": it implies that psychoanalytical discourse is guilty of identifying the phallus with the *Logos* as transcendent, and therefore, unexamined (and unexaminable) grounds of signification, of assigning meaning' (Burke 1981, p. 293).

5 Kristeva's political trajectory closely mirrors the positions taken by the journal *Tel Quel*, with which she has been closely associated. The political evolution of the journal is outlined by Dews: '1966–8, rapprochement with the *PCF* (Communist Party of France) and strong influence of Althusser; after 1968, the long detour through "Maoism" . . .; 1976, disillusionment with China and beginning of a realignment of theoretical "pluralism of the text" with political pluralism; 1978, emergence of an ideology of "dissidence" and discovery that Christianity and literature . . . are the true bastions against totalitarianism and "the political view of the world"' (1979, p. 130).

REFERENCES

Althusser, L. (1984) 'Freud and Lacan', in *Essays on Ideology*, Verso, London, pp. 141–71.

Barrett, M. (1980) *Women's Oppression Today*, Verso, London.

Beauvoir, S. de (1972) *The Second Sex*, Penguin, Harmondsworth.

Braidotti, R. (1986) 'Interview', *Refractory Girl*, May 1986, pp. 9–13.

Brake, M. (ed.) (1982) *Human Sexual Relations*, Penguin, Harmondsworth.

Burke, C. (1981) 'Irigaray through the looking glass', *Feminist Studies*, 7, pp. 288–306.

Chodorow, N. (1979) *The Reproduction of Mothering: Psychoanalysis and the Sociology of Gender*, University of California Press, London.

Cixous, H. (1981a) 'Sorties', in E. Marks and I. de Courtivron (eds) *New French Feminisms*, Harvester Press, Sussex, pp. 90–8.

Cixous, H. (1981a) 'The laugh of the Medusa', in E. Marks and I. de Courtivron (eds) *New French Feminisms*, Harvester Press, Sussex, pp. 245–64.
Conley, V. (1984) *Hélène Cixous: Writing the Feminine*, University of Nebraska Press.
Dews, P. (1979) 'The nouvelle philosophie and Foucault', *Economy and Society*, 8:2, pp. 127–71.
Erikson, E. (1968) 'Womanhood and the inner space', in J. Strouse (ed.) (1974) *Women and Analysis*, Dell Publishing Co., New York, pp. 333–64.
Evans, M. (ed.) (1982) *The Woman Question: Readings on the Subordination of Women*, Fontana, London.
Figes, E. (1970) *Patriarchal Attitudes*, Faber & Faber, London.
Firestone, S. (1971) *The Dialectic of Sex*, Bantam, New York.
Freud, S. (1953–74) *The Standard Edition of the Complete Psychological Works* (24 vols), Hogarth Press and the Institute of Psychoanalysis, London.
The Standard Edition includes the following works:
(1900) 'The interpretation of dreams', IV and V.,
(1905) 'Three essays on the theory of sexuality', VII.
(1924) 'The dissolution of the Oedipus complex', XIX.
(1925) 'Some psychical consequences of the anatomical distinction between the sexes', XIX.
(1931) 'Female sexuality', XXI.
(1933) 'Femininity', XXII.
(1940) 'An outline of psychoanalysis', XXIII.
Friedan, B. (1963) *The Feminine Mystique*, Penguin, Harmondsworth.
Gallop, J. (1982) *Feminism and Psychoanalysis: The Daughter's Seduction*, Macmillan, London.
Gallop, J. and Burke, C. (1980), 'Psychoanalysis and feminism in France', in H. Eisenstein and A. Jardine (eds) *The Future of Difference*, G. K. Hall, Boston.
Garner, S. N., Kahane, C., and Sprengnether, M. (eds) (1985) *The (M)other Tongue*, Cornell University Press, Ithaca, NY, and London.
Hall, S. (1980) 'Recent developments in theories of language and ideology: a critical note', in S. Hall, D. Hobson, A. Lowe, and P. Willis (eds) *Culture, Media, Language*, Hutchinson, London.
Horney, K. (1967) *Feminine Psychology*, Routledge & Kegan Paul, London.
Irigaray, L. (1977) 'Women's exile', *Ideology and Consciousness*, 1, pp. 24–39.
Irigaray, L. (1985a) *Speculum of the Other Woman*, Cornell University Press, Ithaca, NY.
Irigaray, L. (1985b) *This Sex Which Is Not One*, Cornell University Press, Ithaca, NY.
Jardine, A. (1979) 'Interview with Simone de Beauvoir', *Signs*, 5:2, pp. 224–36.
Jones, A. R. (1984) 'Julia Kristeva on femininity: the limits of a semiotic politics', *Feminist Review*, 18, pp. 56–74.
Jones, E. (1948) 'Early female sexuality', in *Papers on Psychoanalysis*, Baillière, Tindall & Cox, London.
Kristeva, J. (1981a) 'La femme, ce n'est jamais ca', in E. Marks, and I. de Courtivron (eds) *New French Feminisms*, Harvester Press, Sussex, pp. 137–41.
Kristeva, J. (1984) 'Histoires d'amour; Julia Kristeva in conversation with Rosalind Coward', *Desire*, ICA documents, London.
Marks, E. and Courtivron, I. de (1981) *New French Feminisms*, Harvester Press, Sussex.
Millett, K. (1969) *Sexual Politics*, Abacus, London.
Mitchell, J. (1971) *Woman's Estate*, Penguin, Harmondsworth.
Mitchell, J. (1974) *Psychoanalysis and Feminism*, Allen Lane, London.

Mitchell, J. (ed.) (1986) *The Selected Melanie Klein*, Penguin, Harmondsworth.
Mitchell, J. and Rose, J. (1982) *Feminine Sexuality: Jacques Lacan and the École Freudienne*, tr. J. Rose, Macmillan, London.
Moi, T. (1985) *Sexual/Textual Politics: Feminist Literary Theory*, Methuen, London and New York.
Moi, T. (ed.) (1986) *The Kristeva Reader*, Columbia University Press, New York.
Plaza, M. (1978) '"Phallomorphic power" and the psychology of "woman": a patriarchal chain', *Ideology and Consciousness*, 4. Reproduced in *Human Sexual Relations: A Reader*. ed. M. Brake, Penguin, Harmondsworth, 1982, pp. 323–59.
Todd, J. (ed.) (1983) *Women Writers Talking*, Holmes & Meier, New York and London.
Wright, E. (1984) *Psychoanalytical Criticism: Theory in Practice*, Methuen, London.
Yale French Studies (1981) 62, 'Feminist readings: French texts/American contexts'.

FURTHER READING

Barker, F., Hulme, P., Iversen, M., and Loxler, D. (eds) (1983) *The Politics of Theory*, University of Essex, Colchester.
Brown, B. and Adams, P. (1979) 'The feminine body and feminist politics', *m/f*, 3, pp. 35–50.
Chodorow, N. (1980) 'Gender, relation, and difference in psychoanalytic perspective', in H. Eisenstein and A. Jardine (eds) *The Future of Difference*, G. K. Hall, Boston.
Coward, R. and Ellis, J. (1977) *Language and Materialism*, Routledge & Kegan Paul, London.
Eagleton, T. (1983) *Literary Theory*, Blackwell, Oxford.
Eisenstein, H. and Jardine, A. (eds) (1980), *The Future of Difference*, G. K. Hall, Boston.
Jardine, A. (1981) 'Introduction to Julia Kristeva's "Women's Time", *Signs*, 7:1, pp. 5–12.
Jones, A. R. (1981) '"Writing the body": toward an understanding of "l'écriture féminine"', *Feminist Studies*, 7:2, pp. 247–63.
Kristeva, J. (1981b) 'Women's time', tr. A. Jardine and H. Black, *Signs*, 7, pp. 13–20.
Lacan, J. (1968) *The Language of the Self: The Function of Language in Psychoanalysis*, tr. A. Wilden, Johns Hopkins University Press, Baltimore, Md.
Lacan, J. (1977a) *Ecrits: A Selection*, Tavistock, London.
Lacan, J. (1977b) *The Four Fundamental Concepts of Psychoanalysis*, Hogarth Press, London.
Mitchell, J. and Rose, J. (1983) 'Feminine sexuality: interview with Juliet Mitchell and Jacqueline Rose', *m/f*, 8, pp. 3–17.
Ragland-Sullivan, E. (1982) 'Jacques Lacan: feminism and the problem of gender identity', *Substance*, 36, pp. 6–20.
Rose, J. (1983) 'Femininity and its discontents', *Feminist Review*, 14, pp. 5–22.
Salleh, K. (1984) 'Contribution to the critique of political epistemology', *Thesis Eleven*, 8, pp. 23–43.
Strouse, J. (ed.) (1974) *Women and Analysis*, Dell, New York.
Turkle, S. (1978) 'French psychoanalysis: a sociological perspective', in A. Roland (ed.) *Psychoanalysis, Creativity and Literature: A French–American Inquiry*, Columbia University Press, New York, pp. 39–71.

Turkle, S. (1981) *Psychoanalytic politics: Freud's French Revolution*, MIT Press, Cambridge, Mass.
Wolff, J. (1981) *The Social Production of Art*, Macmillan, London.

7

THE DEFINITION OF MALE AND FEMALE

Biological reductionism and the sanctions of normality

Gisela T. Kaplan and Lesley J. Rogers

Biology has been used in debates of great social, political, and economic relevance for as long as there have been discussions of 'human nature', and today it is very much at the centre of the nature–nurture debate. The biological sciences are concerned with human behaviour at the physiological, psychological, and social levels. The interests of power, class, and status, as well as traditions of norms and values, interact with scientific findings and the theoretical constructs which produce them. Like any other field of knowledge, biology is not 'value-free' (see Lewontin *et al.* 1984). Thus, any debate on 'human nature' that has been propelled or proposed by biology has been surreptitiously underscored by a host of assumptions, arguments, values (and prejudices) which are part of the biologist's social construction of reality.

What is important about biology to feminists can be seen by asking one simple question: what is a male and what is a female? One may take certain things about males and females for granted. These may have little to do with scientific evidence but a great deal to do with the social values of the society in which one lives. Invariably, any form of rebellion by women against their status, economic position, and predefined role in a given society has involved, either directly or indirectly, a challenge to the predominant notion of male–female differences and of the 'nature' of the biological sexes. In other words, irrespective of whether the debate has started in the social context of argument for desired change or from within the confines of biology, the question of what is a male and a female has not been one for which a simple answer could be given.

The problem has been, and often still is, that answers which have attempted to deal with differences between the sexes have lumped together the biological and social context and, in so doing, biological explanations for sex differences have subsumed sociological explanations. Social differences have been seen as if they result 'naturally' from biological differences. The confusion of theoretical constructs with the biological facts has led to tautological and circular arguments which have usually worked against any notion of equality between the sexes.

The arguments against women's equality have been illogical and have had little legitimate claim to be based on known biological facts. For instance, in the late nineteenth century, when women began to argue forcefully for entrance rights to universities, a heated counter-debate arose around the Darwinian theory of the evolution of sex differences. One of the issues was whether female brains were smaller, and thus had less intellectual capacity than male brains (Fee 1979). This assumed 'proof' of women's biological inferiority to men eventually had to be discarded when scientific measurements of cranium size showed it to be incorrect (see Salzman 1977). Another argument, promulgated by Spencer, and a much more dangerous myth than that developed by craniologists, was the assumption that women could 'overtax' their brains and thereby 'cause' themselves to have diminished reproductive ability. A reiteration of this view, very persuasively argued at the time, can be found in Clarke's disastrously successful book *Sex in Education*, which haunted at least two generations of girls and was still around after the Second World War (Sayers 1982, p. 9). Yet another argument, now known to have no basis in biology, concerned sexual dimorphism in metabolism. Women were supposed to have a different and inferior form of cell metabolism which caused them to be sluggish, passive, and less able to study. Exactly the same argument was later applied to 'explain' the inferiority of black slaves.

Today, the pseudo-biological debates on women's alleged intellectual inferiority continue to provide reams of 'evidence' for sex differences in ability. Even in the 1980s it was repeatedly and confidently announced that there is now no longer any doubt that boys are superior in mathematical and spatial ability and that this has a biological basis. In one report it was regretted that many women did not seem capable of bringing themselves 'to accept sexual difference in aptitude'. 'The best way to help girls is to accept it and go from there' (quoted in Bleier 1984, p. 103).

Most of these studies have implied that genetic and/or hormonal differences between the sexes have determined the sex differences in behaviour (see later). The social variables have either been totally or largely ignored, and almost always the behaviour in question has been measured in a simple task and extrapolated as if it applied to performance in a far wider social arena. For example, mathematical ability is usually measured in a pen-and-paper performance task applied once only to each subject in the study. Past experience, anxiety about the material being presented in the task, interaction between tester and subject, and many other variables are ignored so that a single numerical score can be given to each subject and this then can be incorporated into statistical analysis for sex differences. The results of such testing are then generalized to a much wider context of so-called mathematical ability spanning simple addition of figures, computer programming, applied mathematics and pure mathematics, plus others. Longitudinal studies of mathematical ability in boys and girls have been rarely conducted, but those which have been done reveal a closing of the gap between performance of girls and boys with increasing age (Bleier 1984, p. 103). Yet, the argument that women are genetically inferior in mathematical ability has been used to keep women out of the sciences and the business world.

In the 1960s, when women began to demand their right to enter the business world at levels of responsibility and leadership, another set of biologically based arguments appeared which were readily usable against the career aspirations of women. The behaviour of women was said to be controlled by the ebb and flow of their hormones, and that during a phase, said to occur 'premenstrually', their behaviour became erratic and unreliable and their intellectual capacity decreased (Dalton 1979). Thus, even if a woman had numerical or mathematical abilities *equivalent* to that of men she could not be employed in a position of responsibility using that ability because her performance would deteriorate for a period of at least four days every month: 'You would not want the president of your bank making a loan under the raging hormonal influence of that particular period' (Edgar Berman, MD, *New York Times*, 26 July 1970). A similar argument was used in the 1970s by commercial airline companies in Australia to prevent women from becoming pilots.

A host of negative behaviours, ranging from mood disturbance to crashing planes and committing crimes and suicide, have been said to occur as 'symptoms' of 'premenstrual tension' (PMT), but, although PMT is claimed to be a medical entity with a hormonal cause, there is no consistency between studies as to the time at which it is said to occur during the menstrual cycle (Parlee 1973). Likewise there is no consistent collection of symptoms which occurs in any one woman. Noticeably, most of these studies have ignored the contribution of social variables. However, two studies have shown that education about menstruation prior to the age of menarche is a significant factor in determining behaviour changes across the cycle (see Rogers 1979). Yet, a rigid belief in hormonal determination of an ill-defined condition, given reality by name only, still persists. Although it may be recognized that not all women suffer from PMT, the believed existence of it has been applied to all women, presumably to raise doubts about women's suitability for certain professions.

It is significant that as the feminist movement gained momentum in the 1960s and 1970s it almost immediately met arguments and theories which countered questions concerning power, status, and freedom with biological answers concerning innateness. The most successful of the movements that developed in the mid-1970s was a branch of biology known as sociobiology and an area which bridged biology and psychology, known as psychobiology.

Sociobiologists such as Wilson (1975), Trivers (1978), Tiger and Fox (1978) and psychobiologists such as Bardwick (1971), Buffery and Gray (1972), Hutt (1972), and Levy and Gurr (1980) have argued that the differences in behaviour between the sexes are determined by biology. The question they all posed was: what was the use of implementing the changes which feminists were demanding in the face of the evidence that the inferior position of women was anchored to their biology?

Some feminists of the 1970s took up the challenge and debated in the media against the issue of biological determinism. These were, for instance, Hubbard *et al.* (1979), Salzman (1977), and the Science for the People group (Ann Arbor Science for the People Editorial Collective 1977) in the USA, Birke and Sayers with the Brighton Women and Science Group (1980) in the UK and Rogers (1975) in Australia. Unfortunately, at that time it was only a small handful of women who entered the arena of debate on biological determinism of sex differences in behaviour. Most feminists either felt that their knowledge of biology was insufficient to tackle the issues head on, or they were unaware of the importance of the biological determinist theories.

Moreover, in the debates on biological determinism versus sex differences, when and wherever they occurred, feminists never arrived at a coherent platform, and even now they are still divided on these issues.

Some feminists adopted a determinist position. They argued that there is a biological basis for a distinct 'feminine' character which is denied existence in a male-dominated society. Their views on biology led them to adopt a standpoint that may best be summed up as a claim for 'equality with difference'. In their political framework, equality of opportunity was not identical with equality and lack of discrimination. Positive discrimination was seen to be needed in order to take into account the special needs of women dictated by their biology. Theirs was a position of aiming for slow changes brought about by educating women to overcome some of the biological limitations which, they had been taught, placed them in inferior positions. For example, Lambert (1978) has argued that the organization of male and female brains is different and biologically determined, thus any change cannot go beyond this fact. Reform rather than revolution is seen as the only acceptable way.

Writers such as Rossi went a step further in these reactionary determinist views of sexual differences, which were dubbed 'biological essentialism' (Sayers 1982, p. 149). This position involved a celebration of women's feminine virtues given to them by their biology. These biological innate talents, such as the ability for child-rearing, needed to be fully recognized, and such recognition would lead to equality (in the sense of difference as being of equal social value). Incidentally, this argument of the late 1970s was not (by any means) very original. Fascist ideologues announced the same principles of 'equality' in the late 1920s even before Hitler came to power (Kaplan and Adams 1989). There still appear to be women who can be persuaded that something as abstract and as dependent on social mores as is 'virtue' can be tied to biology and, worse, that a celebration of feminine virtues could lead to equality. Feminine virtues have been celebrated by men for thousands of years – without much evidence of gaining women any more rights or freedoms.

Another group of feminists who likewise accepted the biological determinist position were far more pessimistic, or radical (depending on your viewpoint). In their view, the so-called 'feminine' character had little chance of developing and blossoming in a male-dominated world and could only be cultivated in isolation. They proposed separatism based on biological difference.

Those feminists who did debate against the biological determinist position drew attention to the fact that there is no scientific evidence for biological determinism of sex differences in behaviour, be it genetic and/or hormonal. While there are certain basic reproductive functions which separate female and male biology into distinct categories, these sex differences do not extend to differences in cognitive function, and therefore cannot explain sex differences in behaviour. Women should not be misled into believing that their inferior place in society is a biological necessity. In their view, equality can be brought about by exposing the fallacies of belief systems which condone social inequalities of women on the basis of pseudo-scientific arguments.

In the following sections we will deal with some aspects of human biology as it impinges on our understanding of female–male distinctions. We will concentrate on the biological variations of the female and male biological sexes and on sexuality and sexual preferences, and we will do so from a feminist, non-determinist perspective. But first, let us look at some of the problems associated with reductionism in science.

SCIENCE AND REDUCTIONISM: SOCIOBIOLOGY

The dominant way of thinking in western science is to reduce explanations to their simplest form. This process of reductionist thinking involves seeing unitary causes for complex sets of events. In sociobiology, human behaviour is explained on the basis of biology or, more specifically, on the basis of genes.

Genes, the hereditary material inside the nucleus of each cell, are known to determine simple physical traits such as eye colour and blood group. The determination of such characteristics is dependent on the production of one protein by one gene. It is the simplicity of these characteristics which has enabled us to understand certain mechanisms of heredity. More complex characteristics, such as the personality traits and motivational patterns of an individual, do not rely on the action of single genes and cannot be explained by referring to hereditary endowment. Yet, this is precisely what sociobiologists do. They claim to explain a wide range of complicated human behaviours by tracing them back to the genes and by making genes the one determinant factor.

Sociobiology postulates that there are genes which determine aggression, territoriality, homosexuality, intelligence, and all the behavioural differences between the sexes (Wilson 1975). In other words, this young discipline radically reduces human behaviour to a simple biological denominator. Ultimately, then, genes can be seen as the sole causal factor for events and behaviours in the social world.

Genetic explanations operate at one level of analysis while behavioural explanations operate at another, very different level (Rose 1984). Clearly, the study of behaviour takes place at many levels. Let us briefly consider the question of 'levels' of analysis more closely in order to make the sociobiologist travesty more obvious. Rose has written the following:

> In dealing with the sciences of complex systems like living organisms, it is generally assumed that there is a hierarchy of orders of analysis, from the physical to the social. Each level in the hierarchy corresponds approximately to the boundaries of one of the traditional scientific disciplines: physics, chemistry, biochemistry, physiology, psychology etc. . . . The hierarchy of levels is not considered symmetrical; it is given an upwards and downwards direction. 'Upwards' is seen as in the direction of increasing complexity; 'downwards' traditionally in the direction of increasingly 'fundamental' or 'basic'. . . . Reductionism, as I have said, claims that in the long run higher order levels will be collapsed into the lower order ones.
>
> (Rose 1982, pp. 11–12)

Any behaviour which involves the interaction of an individual with his or her environment has a place fairly high up in this hierarchy of levels. The organization of genes, on the other hand, is a far less complex set of events and thus belongs to a lower level of the hierarchy. In describing more complex events, we employ a wide variety of terms, descriptions, and concepts. We refer to a biological and to a social world. The language for the description of genes is tied exclusively to biology. To get from a higher level to one lower down, simplifications are necessary: equating of social events with biological events requires gross distortion and non-permissible reduction of many different variables. There are no genes for altruism, for 'dressing up', for empathy. Yet, exponents of sociobiology do not hesitate to attach to these complex behaviours some mysterious 'innate' (i.e. genetic) cause.

The genetic determinist position sees no real potential for change, because men and women are considered to behave in the way biology dictates. According to Wilson (1975), the division between the sexes is rigidly determined by biological differences with little influence of social and cultural values. He believes this to be true for all human societies. He asserts that the genetic differences between the sexes are great enough to cause a substantial division of labour even in the most free and egalitarian of societies.

As we have said, reductionist explanations for genetic determinism of human behaviour increased in popularity as the women's movement became more powerful. The traits which were allegedly determined by the genes, not surprisingly, fitted the stereotypic male in western, capitalist society: aggression, territoriality, IQ, and dominance.

The sociobiological theories were politically very important as they were readily taken up by the media and incorporated into a multitude of disciplines, discussions, and attitudes. A host of social problems were seemingly explained by these pseudo-scientific theories. We still see this happening today. One of the key attractions of these theories is that social ills, injustices, class and power divisions can ultimately be seen as not variable and not socially constructed: if men and women merely act in accordance with their biology, then their respective places in society are 'natural' (i.e. nature-given) and, in some beliefs, even God-given. Any protest by women against their social roles must therefore be unnatural (see Lloyd and Archer 1976).

These sociobiological theories were presented as new scientific ideas, but they were in fact old ideas simply presented in a slightly different way. At other times of social unrest there has been a similar interest in genetic theories of human behaviour. Genetic explanations of the supposedly inferior behaviours of black people were postulated by eugenists such as Francis Galton (1869), Karl Pearson (1901), and Edward Thorndike (1913–14). Rose (1976) examines the racism inherent in what he calls 'the IQ racket'. Biological determinist theories, in their historical context and social ramifications, are part of a wider set of constructs which attempt to give reasons for the oppression of races, classes, and minority groups (Lewontin *et al.* 1984).

Sarah Hoagland, among other feminists, has forcefully argued that rigid social norms for the behaviour of women have persistently functioned as a mechanism to prevent any form of resistance. Any deviation from the norm could be devalued as abnormal and redefined in terms of some undesirable characteristic, but never as resistance, revolt, or protest (Hoagland 1982). The biological determinism of sociobiology, if taken seriously, would be able to achieve the same aims.

More recently a number of sociobiologists have entered into formulating genetic models by which they claim to be able to explain the mating patterns of both human and non-human species (see Austin and Short 1984). On a 'cost–benefit' basis, the female is said to invest a greater biological cost in reproduction than does the male. As she must bear and nurture the offspring, her costs are best benefited by obtaining a male partner and making sure that he stays with her to assist in raising the offspring. On the other hand, for males reproduction has very little biological cost and the best strategy for a male is to impregnate as many females as possible, thus maximizing the passing on of his genes. Hence, sociobiologists deduce that monogamy is a biological imperative for women, and polygamy for men. Therefore, they say, these mating patterns are genetically determined and, by implication, they should not be disturbed by changing social values.

Sociobiological theories for mating strategies have been elaborated into even more bizarre and untestable hypotheses, such as the ideas put forward by Morris (1967), on the one hand, and Gallup (1982), on the other hand, to 'explain' why human females have 'permanently enlarged breasts'. Morris attributed enlarged breasts to the evolution of bipedalism (walking on two feet) and face-to-face mating. He argued that the enlarged breasts are a replica of the buttocks used as a signal for sexual attraction. Gallup has suggested that breast enlargement may serve as advertisement for ovulatory potential, and so compensate for the fact that ovulation is concealed in humans. From this position, he has developed a global explanation for sexual preferences in men, and thus a simple idea based on pseudo-scientific reasoning grows into a broad hypothesis with sociological implications. No account is taken of the relevant psychological or sociological literature, and no attempt is made to test the hypothesis.

As the thinking of sociobiologists has become more and more abstract, it has stepped further into the social and political arena. Sociobiological ideas have been taken up by the media and power interest groups to justify the *status quo*. The basic axiom of thinking which persists in all sociobiological theories is that complex behaviour is tied to genetic causes which have evolved along with the species.

DEFINING MALE AND FEMALE

A child is assigned to either the male or female sex immediately after birth. This decision is made on the basis of whether a penis is present or absent. A penis is usually present when the genetic material is XY (male) and absent when it is XX (female). It is sometimes difficult to decide whether a baby has a penis or an enlarged clitoris at birth. In the past, 'mistakes' in assignment have occurred and have only been uncovered when the growth of the child allowed clearer differentiation. For this reason some larger and more progressive hospitals wait for the results of genetic tests before they announce the sex of the newly born child.

In adolescence, sexual characteristics (both primary, the genitals, and secondary, breasts, beard, voice, etc.) develop in response to hormonal changes. These hormonal changes are governed by the XY or XX genotype, but not exclusively: environmental factors such as nutrition and stress can influence them, particularly during crucial ages.

The genetic possibilities are not exclusively divided into male (XY) and female (XX); a range of other genetic varieties exist (e.g. XO, in which the physical type is that of an underdeveloped female since no sex hormones are produced; XYY, which is male; XXY, which is also male). Added to this, there are considerations such as testicular feminizing syndrome, in which the cells of the body fail to respond to testosterone and do not differentiate into a male pattern even though the genotype is XY and male sex hormones are released. Such individuals are genetically male, and phenotypically (i.e. physically) females. They cannot reproduce. The genotype is the genetic constitution of an individual; the phenotype is the observable characteristics of an individual. How then do we categorize these individuals? To the ordinary individual meeting them in the street there is no question: they are females. To the medical profession they are 'genetic males'.

HORMONES

Sex hormones are also categorized according to the male–female dichotomy. Oestrogen and progesterone are known as the 'female' sex hormones. Testosterone is called the 'male' sex hormone, one of a larger collection of 'male' sex hormones called androgens. In males, testosterone is released from the testes, but it is not exclusive to the male genotype; females release it from the adrenal gland. Females release oestrogen from the ovaries, males from the testes. Thus, while we speak of male and female sex hormones as discrete sex-related entities, this is biologically incorrect (see Bleier 1984, pp. 80–90). There is a wide margin of overlap between the sexes, and both genetic and environmental factors can alter the degree of this overlap.

For example, environmentally induced stress can lower the level of testosterone circulating in the blood of males (Kreuz *et al*. 1972), and stress can block the cyclic pattern of oestrogen and progesterone release in females, thus causing amenorrhoea (cessation of menstruation). Engaging in sexual activity, or even just thinking about it, has been shown to raise testosterone levels in males. In primates, testosterone levels also vary as a consequence of the outcome of social conflict situations (Rose *et al*. 1975). In studies of animals there are numerous examples of environmental stimuli having both short- and long-term effects on the levels of sex hormones circulating in the blood stream. To give just one example, the female dove increases her secretion of oestrogen and progesterone when she hears a male dove cooing. Incidentally, the environmental stimulus of a male cooing has its effect on hormone release in the female via an indirect route: the female vocalizes in response to hearing the male cooing and it is the feedback perception of hearing her own vocalizations which causes the hormone release in the female (Cheng 1983; Cheng and Havens 1986).

Although it used to be thought that testosterone was the hormone which caused differentiation of the male phenotype, it is now known that another androgen, 5α-dihydrotestosterone (5α-DHT) has this function. The androgen 5α-DHT is made from testosterone by the action of an enzyme called 5α-reductase, and if this enzyme is not present in a genetic male the phenotype will be female. There is a family in Dallas, USA, and another in the Dominican Republic carrying a genetic condition which causes a delay in the development of 5α-reductase until puberty (Imperato-McGinley *et al.* 1979). Genetic males with this condition cannot convert testosterone into 5α-DHT and they therefore have a female phenotype. At puberty they acquire the enzyme and, as they can then make 5α-DHT, their genital organs change to male and they develop male secondary sexual characteristics (Wilson *et al.* 1983).

Given the variety of hormonal conditions which occur in individuals who are genetically male or genetically female, and given that these hormones influence physique (voice, fat distribution, breast development, muscular development, facial hair, etc.), it is not surprising that there is a wide amount of overlap between 'male' and 'female' physical types. Male and females do not fit the rigid physical stereotypes portrayed by the media, by medical journals, or biological textbooks. The rigid either/or assignment of the sexes is only a convenient social construct, not a biological reality.

BRAIN FUNCTION

If we delve further into the cellular basis of brain function, we find the division between the sexes becomes even more minimized. There are cells in the brain which take up (have receptors for) the sex hormones, some for oestrogen, some for testosterone, but it is now known that the testosterone must be converted to oestrogen inside the cells before it can have any effect on their function (Hutchison and Steimer 1984). The conversion of testosterone to oestrogen is carried out by an aromatase enzyme, and the level of this enzyme in certain areas of the brain can be altered by social stimuli related to sexual behaviour. Thus, there is no direct, one-way influence of the hormones on the brain; environmental stimuli can influence the power of these hormones to act. There is an intimate interweaving of internal and external input in the complex, whole system.

Though we once thought the brains of males and females were distinctly different in one way or another, we now know this is not so. This means that the claims made by sociobiologists are oversimplified to the point of being incorrect. By reducing explanations of human behaviour to the genes, they ignore the essential and complex role of the brain in controlling behaviour. If the brain is not, at least to any great degree, different in females and males, then how do the genes express themselves to cause behavioural differences between the sexes, if indeed they do?

We are not arguing that there are absolutely no differences between adult male and female brains. After all, environmental events must impinge on brain structure and function in many as yet unrecognized ways, and males and females are raised in different cultural environments. In other words, the brain may change its structure and function in response to learning or experience. Thus sex differences in brain structure and function may result in the adult because females and males have been taught different things, and at different crucial stages of brain development (Zappia and Rogers 1983).

There is recent evidence showing that the sex hormones can influence the growth of neurones. In the presence of sex hormones certain neurones have been shown to send out more branches, which presumably allows them to make more connections to other neurones (Toran-Allerand 1984). Likewise, it has been shown in chickens that testosterone can influence brain organization by reversing the direction of asymmetry for control of certain behaviours (Zappia and Rogers 1987). Despite the fact that it is possible to demonstrate that the sex hormones can influence brain organization, it is not possible to conclude, as Geschwind and Galaburda (1985) have done, that sex hormones cause sex differences in behaviour. Sex hormones appear to be only one contributing factor amongst many equally important and interlocking influences from other sources. Even in chickens, the same brain organization which responds to testosterone treatment can also be influenced by environmental input, *viz.* light exposure of the embryo (Rogers 1982). The final product of brain organization is a complex whole, and no single determining factor can be postulated to be the cause of any one of its functions.

Geschwind and Galaburda (1985) have postulated that sex differences in behaviour are caused by the action of testosterone, which retards the development of the left hemisphere. This, they claim, explains why men have superior mathematical abilities. Although this hypothesis has never been tested in humans, and there would appear to be no way by which it could be tested, the views of Geschwind and Galaburda have been widely accepted and propagated in both the popular and scientific media.

While there have been experiments showing that sex hormones can influence the development of neurones, the same patterns of neuronal growth are also influenced by environmental stimulation, brain injury, nutrition, and the action of other hormones such as thyroxin. A plethora of influences impinge on the development of each neurone and, even at the cellular level, it is impossible to single out a unitary influence of sex hormones as the possible starting point for causing sex differences in behaviour. At higher levels of brain organization, and also at the level of brain function, we find ourselves many steps of reasoning away from any unitary causal hypothesis based on hormone levels.

Added to this, the way in which sex hormones influence brain function can be indirect. It used to be assumed that testosterone could influence brain development by acting directly on the neurones in the brain. In the 1960s Harris (1964) showed that, if a genetically male rat is castrated at birth, it develops a female-type brain with a cyclic control of the output of gonadotropic hormone from the pituitary, as occurs in females, and a preference for adopting the female posture in mating. Injection of testosterone into such an animal at any time during the first five days after its birth leads to a male-type brain with a constant output of pituitary gonadotropic hormones and in mating the adoption of the mounting posture characteristic of males. Thus, Harris concluded that testosterone acts on the developing brain in early life to determine whether it will be 'male' or 'female' in type, and many researchers have extrapolated this hypothesis to humans. In so doing, they have ignored data showing that primates, compared to rats, have less sexual dimorphism of the brain even for such a basic function as controlling the output of pituitary gonadotrophic hormones (see Byrne and Bleier 1987). The data collected from our closest relatives clouds the issue, and so it is ignored. Most noteable amongst the researchers who have extrapolated directly from rats to humans are Money and his co-workers (e.g. Money and Ehrhardt 1972; Money and Matthews 1982) and Dörner (1976), who have suggested not only that testosterone organizes the human brain into 'male' or 'female' but, by extrapolating Harris's data on rats even further, they have postulated that homosexuality, transvestism, and transsexualism are caused by increasing degrees of disturbance of sex hormone levels during the early phases of brain development. This hypothesis has been widely published and accepted both in the medical and popular literature. On a BBC film ('The Fight to be Male') Dörner stated his aim to prevent homosexuality by manipulating the levels of testosterone in the developing foetus. Although Dörner's work has come under increasing amounts of criticism (see Ross 1986), the belief in hormones influencing brain development to cause sex differences in behaviour remains widespread and politically influential.

This has occurred despite the fact that Moore and Morelli (1979) have shown that the results of the original experiment by Harris (i.e. those on which Dörner based his hypothesis) were interpreted incorrectly. Moore and Morelli have found that the adult female rat treats her male and female pups differently. She spends more time licking the anogenital region of the male pups and it has been shown that this licking not only causes their testes to enlarge but also leads to the adoption of male-type behaviour in adulthood. If male pups are castrated they are treated by the mother as females and develop female-type behaviour in adulthood. If female pups are injected with testosterone, they are treated by their mother as males and adopt male-type behaviour in adulthood (Moore 1982).

Thus, the presence of testosterone in early life does not affect brain development directly, as Harris supposed, but indirectly via changing the behaviour of the mother. She, in turn, alters the environment in which, one might say, the brain is raised. As Moore (1985) has said, 'hormones coact and interact with other factors throughout development, . . . brain differences may result from as well as cause functional differences, and . . . hormone-based sources of sex differences may be located throughout the body and in the social surround'. We may expect sex differences in brain organization and function, but these will not simply be biologically determined. They will be the result of a complex interaction of biology and environmental inputs.

We organize our perception of people into socially constructed categories, and frequently operate on simple dichotomous choices such as black-white, rich-poor, young-old, male-female. It is not correct to force biology, and brain function in particular, into these culturally constructed polarities.

THE SANCTIONS OF NORMALITY: THE MYTH OF BIOLOGICAL NORMS

There are a number of important ramifications to rigidly dividing the world into males and females. One problem, to reiterate this point, concerns the biological variation of sex assignment. Within rigid categories, variations from the norm are not easily accommodated. Differences must be either denied, ignored, or, worse, accentuated as deviant.

The questions which feminists have asked have recently gained support from homosexual subcultures. Why is this so? Part of the answer concerns the oppression that can result from biological models. The most obvious link between feminist and homosexual groups can be established by considering the demands associated with biology. Sexual behaviour and reproduction are two criteria upon which an individual may be judged as 'normal', 'mature', 'well-' or 'ill-adjusted'. Sexual behaviour has been seen in the past, and it continues to be seen, as solely determined by biology. A 'normal' male or female is expected to reach sexual maturity, to be attracted to members of the 'opposite' sex, and eventually to seek a spouse and reproduce. We have already established that the notion of the 'opposite' sex is biologically inaccurate. Sexual attraction to the opposite sex is supposed to work 'naturally' to reinforce the male–female dichotomy. Finally, reproduction, a biological event, is purported to be a 'natural' drive that will assert itself for the entire species. The Darwinian idea of the 'survival of the fittest' has once again had new impetus with Dawkins's (1976) model of the 'selfish gene', somehow driven to reproduce the species at all costs.

When we discuss definitions of male and female in the context of biology and social sanctions, we have to deal with groups who do not fit the categories of male and female stereotypes and expectations in order to understand the tremendous pressures on those who cannot or do not wish to conform, and to ascertain the limits of the assumptions of the biological basis for the male–female dichotomy. In other words, we have to examine those cases where the *biological* conceptualization of the male–female dichotomy is obviously contravened or exploded by an individual's biology. In addition, we have to examine those cases where the *behavioural* conceptualizations of the dichotomy are not fulfilled by the individual. Hence, consideration has to be given to phenomena such as transsexuality, transvestism, ambisexuality (possessing secondary and even primary sexual characteristics of both sexes), as well as to an individual's inability or lack of desire to reproduce. The questions of what is normal biology and what is normal behaviour have to be seen in this wider context. The concept of normality is linked to the construct of a male–female dichotomy.

In Latin, the word *normal* means 'square', the carpenter's square. Until the 1830s, the English word 'normal' meant standing at a right angle to the ground. It was only during the 1840s that the term began to designate conformity to a common type. Similarly, in France it took on these connotations only in the 1840s when Auguste Comte spoke of normal states of organisms. This places the modern meaning of 'normal' and 'normality' at the onset of the industrial revolution. Ivan Illich argues that the term has served advanced industrial societies extremely well. The very moment that universal standards are defined, established, and then applied, anything falling outside that standard can be defined as abnormal and, conceivably, can be legitimately attacked (see Illich 1977, pp. 165–75; and Weeks 1981).

Likewise, the concept of disease is tied up with a notion of universal standards. An ailment becomes an entity of abnormality only if standards for the 'normality' of an organism have been found. This occurred only last century, and was the beginning of the greatest advances in medicine. One of the disastrous side-products of the new discovery of disease entities – which could be named, described, and treated as if the rest of the body did not exist – was its application to behaviours for which no physiological basis could be established. Presumably, a person in pain becomes conspicuous, not always because the cause of the pain is obvious, but because his/her behaviour changes.

The new confidence in the belief that one could deduce a physical (internal and biological) event from certain 'abnormal' behaviours quickly led to the application of this 'medical model' to mental phenomena. Over the last century, mental deviance has increasingly been seen as a disease (Sharma 1970).

As said before, although biology and behaviour may interact they are different categories which describe different manifestations. One may be the cause of the other, but it need not be. If it is believed *prima facie* that all behaviour is the result of biology, then there is no need to look for other explanations. But how can such an assumption be made? In psychiatry and psychology, the phenomena to be understood are human social behaviours. The terminology employed for describing such behaviours and clusters of symptoms, however, is couched in physico-biochemical language. The vast agglomeration of disease entities which results from such observations and descriptions of behaviours reflects a medical matrix in the absence of physical symptoms. The process of translation becomes more and more blurred. Psychiatric language speaks about 'mind' as if it were the 'brain', for instance. However, 'mind' is an abstract concept while 'brain' is a biologically concrete concept. The relationship between the two is not clear. To date, many of the so-called 'mental diseases' have not been demonstrably and convincingly anchored to biology. 'Anti-psychiatrists' like Thomas Szasz (1973) and Phyllis Chesler (1972) have spoken at length about the risks of equating variations in human behaviours with disease models.

The history of medicine reveals that the idea of disease entities is a very recent one in human history, not older than two hundred years. Illich (1977) argues that ailments were turned into sickness and sickness into disease.

Once it has been decided to adopt a term for certain manifestations of behaviour and to declare such behaviour a disease, a number of consequences are inevitable. Socially one of the most important ones is the legitimacy given to the medical and other health professions to step in and cure the disease. Expressed differently, the health professions obtain the right to modify, change, and thus control the behaviour of an individual in the absence of physical symptoms, and even in the absence of any discomfort the individual concerned might feel. Many 'patients' voluntarily approach doctors for help and for a cure for their 'deficiencies'. One need not emphasize too strongly that social pressure are often enough incentive for an individual to take such a step. Critics of the medical model have, among other things, argued that medicine functions as an extension of the law, in areas where the arm of the law cannot reach. The treatment of homosexuality, in the view of these critics, then becomes a perverted form of 'correction' of a socially unacceptable behaviour, and thus constitutes a serious infringement of civil liberty and self-expression. The same can be true with respect to the treatment of women in society. Anger, irateness, and aggression by women may be redefined as hysteria, madness, or 'nervous disorder', and therefore may be regarded as behaviour to be corrected, i.e. altered (Hoagland 1982). Such redefinition has the advantage that no one needs to listen to the content of the grievances or complaints. Only very recent writers have been able to maintain and defend the argument that serious infringements of civil liberty and self-expression of women stem from the subjective, normative assessment of female behaviour. It is this medical view of acceptable behaviour for women which may be the reason why women receive twice as many prescriptions for psychoactive drugs as do men (Rogers 1984).

The myth of biological norms is represented in the table below. It shows the great variety in human biological sexual characteristics. This table has a number of serious weaknesses, as only a brief inspection of its categories reveal. Of the seventeen categories only two are regarded as deserving the titles 'normal female' and 'normal male'. In other words, despite the obvious variation of biological phenomena, as variations occurring in nature, most have been declared as aberrations. We have included this table nevertheless because, by analysing it, we can discuss some of the misconceptions and prejudices which may be relatively common in our social world. One of the many misconceptions is the confusion between social and biological phenomena; another is in the problem of defining norms.

At the extremities of the spectrum of the supposed seventeen variations of human sexuality we find the categories of 'normal' male and 'normal' female. All others are marked by various labels. What do these labels represent? Terms such as 'adrenogenital masculinism', 'Turner's syndrome', or 'Klinefelter's syndrome' are clearly medical language. In one instance, the term 'disorder' is used, signalling to the reader that the condition from which the individual 'suffers' is one that can and has been described as a disease.

One of the disastrous consequences of reducing the vast variation of human biology and human behaviour to models of disease and mental and physical ill-health becomes apparent when scanning some of the other categories which the table presents.

You will note that, in the table, the categories male and female homosexuality have deficiencies, which are not found under the categories of normal male and female. To claim that homosexual women may or may not menstruate normally (meaning regularly) while 'normal' women do have regular menstruation is an outright invention. There is absolutely no evidence that such a physical difference exists between homosexual and heterosexual women. Heterosexual women have irregular menstruation as often, or as infrequently, as homosexual women. Hidden in this statement is a further, oppressive, assumption that the normality of a woman can be defined by pointing to the regularity of her menstruation. Be assured that it is common for quite 'normal' women, who may or may not have

Spectrum of human sexual characteristics

	normal female	simple constitutional masculinism	adrenogenital masculinism	female homosexual	female transvestism	female intersex without adrenal disorder	true hermaphrodite	Turner's syndrome	pure gonadal dysgenesis	male intersex testicular feminization syndrome	Klinefelter's syndrome	male transvestism	male homosexual	adrenogenital feminism	simple constitutional feminism	male with hypospadias	normal male
typical sex chromosomes	XX	XX	XX	XX	XX	XX	XX	XO	XY	XY	XXY	XY	XY	XY	XY	XY	XY
gonads (○ female, ● male)	○○	○○	○○	○○	○○	○○	○●	∘ ∘	nil	• •	• •	●●	●●	●●	●●	●●	●●
sex hormones: oestrogens (female)	normal F			normal F	normal F					normal M	normal M	± normal M	normal M	probably subnormal for M		normal M	normal M
sex hormones: androgens (male)	normal F	increased for female	increased for female	normal F	normal F	normal	normal or low	low		normal M	subnormal for M	subnormal for M	normal M	increased	subnormal for M	normal M	normal M
external anatomy																	
phallus: penis / clitoris	normal size	normal size	enlarged	normal or enlarged	normal or enlarged	enlarged	normal penis or enlarged clitoris	normal size	normal or enlarged	normal size	small to moderate	small	normal size	normal size	small	small (may resemble enlarged clitoris)	normal size
urination	F	F	F	F	F	F	F	F	F	F	M	M	M	M	M	F	M
menstruation	normal	irregular or nil	nil	normal or irregular	normal or irregular	normal	usually nil	nil	nil	nil							
fertility	+	+ or −	−	+	+	−	−	−	−	−	−	+ or −	+	−	+	−	+
psychological sex	F	F	F	M or F	neutral or M	F or M	F or M	F	F	F	neutral or M	neutral or F	M, F or both	M	M or rarely F	M	M

Table 1: Spectrum of human sexual characteristics

Source: *Science Journal*, vol. 6 no. 6 (1970), p. 71.

children to go through phases when menstruation is not regular, or even stops.

What has happened here, then, is that medical categories are confused with social ones: that is, some behavioural categories are perceived as if they were diseases. A disease is either curable or, if not, the cause of permanent damage to an organism. The medical model of ascribing the label of 'disease' to any variation from the norm in primary or secondary sexual characteristics, however, must be regarded as an undertaking which has its roots in social attitudes and values.

In table 1, female and male homosexuality as well as transvestism are lumped together with chromosomal and hormonal deficiencies or abnormalities. Clearly, the medical model of human health has also taken hold of categories which are purely social and behavioural. Some researchers today, such as Money and Ehrhardt (1972) and more recently Dörner (1976), would support the medical view of homosexuality as an abnormality induced either by certain oversupplies or undersupplies of relevant hormones at a crucial stage of prenatal development. As we have discussed earlier, this hypothesis is based on erroneous interpretations of data obtained using rats. Apart from their dubiousness, these premises are dangerous when it comes to the treatment of people afflicted with the supposed 'disease'.

There are a number of cases in the last two decades both in Australia and the USA where psychosurgery (frontal lobotomies or leucotomies) or, more recently, cingulotrachotomies (forebrain lesions) and hypothalamic lesions (mid-brain) have been used to 'treat' and/or 'cure' homosexuality. In South Africa and West Germany, for instance, chemical castration by application of anti-androgen therapy is still commonly used. In Australia, a similar effect is achieved by oestrogen therapy. Aversion therapy is used in many western societies now. Among the common punishments used in aversion therapies are the administration of electric shocks or emetic agents (making the 'patient' vomit). In recent times, one Australian doctor has used hot-plate therapy, asking the subject to place his hand on a hot-plate for punishment if he dwelt too long on the 'wrong' picture (Watson 1979). This has more to do with punishing 'deviant' behaviour than modifying hypothesized biological states which have not been shown to exist.

Another look at Table 1 will show that transvestism has also been described in biological terms. Transvestism refers to the behaviour of cross-dressing. Male transvestites prefer to dress up as females, female transvestites prefer to dress up as males. In both male and female transvestism, the sexual orientation is often, if not mostly, heterosexual. Biologically, transvestism has no specific marks. In other words, transvestite individuals are biologically indistinguishable from the general population. In the table, female transvestites are supposed to have either a normal or enlarged clitoris, normal or irregular menstruation, and are allegedly neutral or male in their psychological sex. Male transvestites may apparently 'suffer' from subnormal production of sex hormones, have a small penis, and are neutral or female in their psychological sex. Again, these claims are incorrect. There is no evidence that biological variation in genital construction (size of penis or of clitoris) is intrinsically linked to behaviours such as transvestism. Transvestism has, in fact, been shown to be based on conditioning rather than biology (Walters and Ross 1986).

One last, brief note on the medical model of human sexuality, and also on the table, concerns the issue of reproduction. It is part of our Judaeo-Christian heritage to regard sexual activity as being solely for the purpose of reproduction. The choice of not reproducing was, in the past, considered legitimate for women only if they became nuns. In the nineteenth and early twentieth centuries, the legitimate roles – seen as equivalents of celibacy – were those of governess or school mistress. There were distinctions amongst social classes, of course. An upper-class woman was much more likely to have such an option than a lower-class woman or a peasant.

You will notice that 'fertility' measures are given in Table 1. Of the seventeen categories, eleven are said to be infertile. Among the syndromes which make the individual infertile are androgenital feminism/masculinism, hermaphroditism, pure gonadal dysgenesis, testicular feminization syndrome, Klinefelter's syndrome, and hypospadias.

Clearly, normality and fertility are equated in the table. This is not only medically incorrect but very oppressive. Of course there are 'normal' men and women who do not or cannot reproduce. The reasons are extremely varied and not all are detected and identified. But the diagram implies that persons who cannot reproduce are regarded as somewhat less than 'normal' human beings, and a physical deficit here is taken as a marker of abnormality of sex and gender role.

Variations in reproductive ability are quite common in 'nature' – i.e. amongst all living organisms – and thus quite 'normal'. Normal, in this context, refers to events and patterns that recur with reasonable frequency and are part of the cycle of living organisms. The sanctions of normality function simultaneously as prohibitions concerned with defining deviations from set norms. Social norms have created biological norms of adequacies and inadequacies, meaning that a person who is 'inadequate' in terms of the biological, strictly defined female–male dichotomy and construct is also regarded as inadequate in social terms, and in the extreme, as deviant or 'abnormal'. Although feminists, in concert with environmentalists, are attacking the assumption that biological differences, including reproductive ability, justify the whole scaffolding of constructs which structure women's disadvantage, there is still a great deal of work to be done to eradicate the oppressive assumption that the one way to achieve growth, maturity, and well-adjusted living lies in the 'fulfilment of one's biology': manhood as fathering children, womanhood as bearing and rearing children.

The table contains the theoretical construct of 'disease entities', and this construct is of great importance to any discourse concerning women and biology. It permeates our life so strongly that it is often taken for granted in everyday life.

THE MALE–FEMALE DICHOTOMY AND SEXUAL AROUSAL

We have, so far, discussed biological variations, noted the fluidity between male and female absolutes, and questioned these rigid categorizations which have prevented rational perspectives on both biology and social reality.

Sexual attraction and arousal consists simultaneously of internal psychological events, physiological responses, and other, external, behavioural elements. Biology and environment interact in a very direct way. Sexual arousal, then, is a complex behaviour that cannot be reduced to one or the other variable without serious distortions.

We propose that the male–female dichotomy has a great deal to do with the limited ways in which arousal has so far been studied in the human species. Studies of heterosexuality and homosexuality tend to confine themselves either to descriptions of the sexual act itself or speak about the particular sexual identity of the individual. Whether opposite and/or complementary characteristics are attractive to an individual has been studied; whether the model of father/mother/siblings/other relatives has shaped later sexual responses has been investigated *ad infinitum*. Yet, little is known about why a person seeks a member of the 'opposite' sex or of the same sex for sexual encounters. The malleability and heterogeneity of human sexuality and human sexual responses has been confirmed by Masters and Johnson (1979), who are among the few researchers to recognize and acknowledge this.

We do not usually decide whether a person's sex is male or female on the basis of observation of their genitalia, but deduce this information from their clothing, secondary sexual characteristics, behaviour, etc. Similarly, sexual arousal is usually not initiated by the primary sex organs, but by secondary sexual characteristics and a range of much less sexually specific characteristics (eyes, voice, ears, body size, smile, smell, laughter, personality, etc.). Most individuals can be categorized as male or female on the basis of their genitalia, but each individual's particular set of secondary sexual characteristics and other less sex-specific characteristics is a combination which can lie anywhere along a continuum on which the categories of male and female overlap (Kaplan and Rogers 1985).

CONCLUSION

The fact that the biological differences between the sexes are less than we usually assume is, in itself, enough reason to dispute theories which have anchored sex differences in behaviour to a biological cause. Those who have promoted such theories have used them to argue either that biology prevents social, legal, political, and economic equality between men and women, or that equality can be reached only by a slow process of re-education and reform.

Such reductionist thinking (i.e. emphasis on biological difference) has been used to explain other complex human behaviours, and as a political weapon. Its use in attacking feminism is part of a wider aim to maintain the *status quo* in western capitalist societies.

Once we have constructed our world-view and language around the male–female dichotomy, other concepts are automatically linked to it. The normality–abnormality dichotomy hangs on the male–female dichotomy. If individuals must be fitted into either a male or a female category, then those who do not fit must be abnormal, or disordered, or even diseased. By not recognizing the gradients between male and female, our society assigns a medical label to those who do not fit. These are 'cases' to be 'treated' and, if possible, 'cured'. Thus, we effectively eliminate, and oppress, those who do not fit.

REFERENCES

Ann Arbor Science for the People of Editorial Collective (1977) *Biology as a Social Weapon*, Burgess Publishing, Minneapolis, Minn.

Austin, C. R. and Short, R. V. (1984) *Reproductive Fitness: Reproduction in Mammals*: 4, 2nd edn, Cambridge University Press, Cambridge.

Bardwick, J. M. (1971) *Psychology of Women*, Harper & Row, New York.

Brighton Women and Science Group (1980) *Alice Through the Microscope: The Power of Science Over Women's Lives*, ed. L. Birke, W. Faulkner, S. Best, D. Janson-Smith, and K. Overfield, Virago, London.

Birke, L. and Silverton, J. (eds) (1984) *More than the Parts: Biology and Politics*, Pluto, London.

Bleier, R. (1984) *Science and Gender*, Pergamon Press, New York.

Buffery, A. W. H. and Gray, J. A. (1972) 'Sex differences in the development of spatial and linguistic skills', in C. Ounsted and D. C. Taylor (eds) *Gender Differences: Their Ontogeny and Significance*, Churchill-Livingstone, Edinburgh.

Byrne, W. and Bleier, R. (1987) 'How different are male and female brains', *Trends in Neurosciences*, 10, pp. 198–9.

Cheng, M. F. (1983) 'Behavioural "self-feedback" control of endocrine states', in J. Balthazart, E. Prove, and R. Gilles (eds) *Hormones and Behaviour in Higher Vertebrates*, Springer, Berlin.

Cheng, M. F. and Havens, M. D. (1986) 'Female cooing promotes ovarian development in ring doves', *Abstracts of the First Neuroethology Conference, Tokyo*, p. 63.

Chesler, P. (1972) *Women and Madness*, Avon, New York.
Dalton, K. (1979) *Once a Month*, Harvester Press, Sussex.
Dawkins, R. (1976) *The Selfish Gene*, Oxford University Press.
Dörner, G. (1976) 'Homone-dependent brain development and behaviour', in J. Balthazart, E. Prove, and R. Gilles (eds) *Hormones and Behaviour in Higher Vertebrates*, Springer, Berlin.
Fee, E. (1979) 'Nineteenth century craniology: the study of the female skull', *Bulletin of the History of Medicine*, 53.
Foucault, M. (1978) *A History of Sexuality*, tr. R. Hurley, Pantheon Books, New York.
Gallup, G. G. Jr (1982) 'Permanent breast enlargement in human females: a sociobiological analysis', *Journal of Human Evolution*, 11, pp. 597–601.
Galton, F. (1869) *Hereditary Genius*, Macmillan, London.
Geschwind, N. and Galaburda, A. M. (1985) 'Cerebral lateralisation, biological mechanisms, associations and pathology', *Archives of Neurology*, 42, pp. 428–653.
Harris, G. W. (1964) 'Sex hormones, brain development and brain function', *Endocrinology*, 24, pp. 627–48.
Hoagland, S. L. (1982) 'Femininity, resistance and sabotage', in M. Vettering-Braggin (ed.) *Femininity, Masculinity and Androgyny*, Littlefield, Adams, Totowa, NJ.
Hubbard, R., Henifin, M. S. and Fried, B. (eds) (1979) *Women Look at Biology Looking at Women*, Schenkman, Cambridge, Mass.
Hutchison, J. B. and Steimer, T. L. (1984) 'Androgen metabolism in the brain: behavioural correlates', in De Vries, G. L., de Bruin, J. P. C., Ujlings, H. B. M., and Corner, M. A. (eds) *Sex Differences in the Brain, Progress in Brain Research*, 61, pp. 23–51.
Hutt, C. (1972) *Males and Females*, Penguin, Harmondsworth.
Illich, I. (1977) *Limits to Medicine: Medical Nemesis: the Expropriation of Health*, Penguin, Harmondsworth.
Imperato-McGinley, J., Peterson, R. E., Gautier, T., and Sturla, E. (1979) 'Androgens and the evolution of male gender identity among male pseudohermaphrodites with 5α-reductase deficiency', *Acta Endrocrinologica*, 87, pp. 259–69.
Kaplan, G. T. and Adams, C. (1989) 'Early women supporters of National Socialism: the reaction to feminism and to male-defined sexuality', in *The Attractions of Fascism*, ed. J. Milfull, Berg, Oxford, Hamburg, NY.
Kaplan, G. T. and Rogers, L. J. (1985) 'Breaking out of a dominant paradigm: a new look at sexual attraction', *Journal of Homosexuality*, 10, pp. 71–5.
Kreuz, L. E., Rose, R. M., and Jennings, J. R. (1972) 'Suppression of plasma testosterone levels and psychological stress', *Archives of General Psychiatry*, 26, pp. 479–82.
Lambert, H. H. (1978) 'Biology and equality', *Signs*, 4, pp. 97–117.
Levin, M. (1980) 'The feminist mystique', *Commentary*, December, pp. 25–30.
Levy, J. and Gurr, R. C. (1980) 'Individual differences in psychoneurological organisation', in J. Herran (ed.) *Neuropsychology of Left-Handedness*, Academic Press, New York, pp. 199–210.
Lewontin, R. G., Rose, S., and Kamin, L. J. (1984) *Not in Our Genes*, Pantheon Books, New York.
Lloyd, B. and Archer, J. (eds) (1976) *Exploring Sex Differences*, Academic Press, London.
Masters, W. H. and Johnson, V. E. (1979) *Homosexuality in Perspective*, Little, Brown, Boston.

Money, J. and Ehrhardt, A. A. (1972) *Man and Woman; Boy and Girl: The Differentiation and Dimorphism of Gender Identity from Conception to Maturity*, Johns Hopkins University Press, Baltimore, Md.

Money, J. and Matthews, D. (1982) 'Prenatal exposure to virilising progestins: an adult follow-up of twelve women', *Archives of Sexual Behaviour*, 11, pp. 73–83.

Moore, C. (1982) 'Maternal behaviour of rats is affected by hormonal condition of pups', *Journal of Comparative and Physiological Psychology*, 96, pp. 123–9.

Moore, C. (1985) 'Another psychobiological view of sexual differentiation', *Development Review*, 5, pp. 18–55.

Moore, C. and Morelli, G. A. (1979) 'Mother rats interact differently with male and female offspring', *Journal of Comparative and Physiological Psychology*, 4, pp. 677–84.

Morris, D. (1967) *The Naked Ape*, McGraw-Hill, New York.

Pearson, K. (1901) *National Life from the Standpoint of Science*, A. & C. Black, London.

Parlee, M. R. (1973) 'The premenstrual syndrome', *Psychological Bulletin*, 80, p. 454.

Rogers, L. J. (1975) 'Biology and human behaviour', in J. Mercer (ed.) *The Other Half: Women in Australian Society*, Penguin, Melbourne.

Rogers, L. J. (1979) 'Menstruation', *Australian Family Physician*, 8(8), pp. 923–9.

Rogers, L. J. (1982) 'Light experience and asymmetry of brain function in chickens', *Nature*, 297, pp. 223–5.

Rogers, L. J. (1984) 'Why pharmacological prescription is on the increase', in L. Birke and J. Silvertown (eds) *More than the Parts*, Pluto, London.

Rose, R. M., Bernstein, J. S., and Gordon, T. P. (1975) 'Consequences of social conflict on plasma testosterone levels in rhesus monkeys', *Psychosomatic Medicine*, 37, pp. 50–61.

Rose, S. (1976) 'Scientific racism and ideology: the IQ racket from Galton to Jensen', in H. Rose and S. Rose (eds) *The Political Economy of Science*, Macmillan, London.

Rose, S. (1982) 'From causations to translations: a dialectical solution to a reductionist enigma', in S. Rose (ed.) *Towards a Liberatory Biology*, Allison & Busby, London.

Rose, S. (1984) 'Biological reductionism: its roots and social functions', in L. Birke and J. Silvertown (eds) *More than the Parts*, Pluto, London.

Ross, M. W. (1986) 'Causes of gender dyphoria' in W. A. W. Walters and M. W. Ross (eds) *Transsexualism and Sex Reassignment*, Oxford University Press, Melbourne, pp. 16–25.

Salzman, F. (1977) 'Are sex roles biologically determined?', *Science for the People*, 4, pp. 27–43.

Sayers, J. (1982) *Biological Politics: Feminist and Anti-Feminist Perspectives*, Tavistock, London and New York.

Sharma, S. L. (ed.) (1970) *The Medical Model of Mental Illness*, Magestic, Woodland, Cal.

Szasz, T. S. (1973) *The Manufacture of Madness*, Granada, London.

Thorndike, E. L., (1913–14) *Educational Psychology*, Greenwood, Westport, Conn.

Tiger, L. and Fox, R. (1978) 'The human biogram', in A. L. Caplan (ed.) *The Sociobiology Debate*, Harper & Row, New York.

Toran-Allerand, C. D. (1984) 'On the genesis of sexual differentiation of the central nervous system: morphogenetic consequences of steroid exposure and possible role of α-fetoprotein', in De Vries, G. J., De Bruin, J. P. C., Uylings,

H. B. M., and Corner, M. A. (eds) *Sex Differences in the Brain. Progress in Brain Research*, 61, pp. 63–98.

Trivers, R. L. ([1971] 1978) 'The evolution of reciprocal altruism', in A. L. Caplan (ed.) *The Sociobiology Debate*, Harper & Row, New York.

Walters, W. A. W. and Ross, M. W. (eds) (1986) *Transsexualism and Sex Reassignment*, Oxford University Press, Melbourne.

Watson, L. (1979) 'Homosexuals', in E. M. Bates and P. R. Wilson (eds) *Mental Disorder and Madness*, University of Queensland Press, St Lucia, Queensland.

Weeks, J. (1981) *Sex, Politics and Society: The Regulation of Sexuality Since 1800*, Longman, London and New York.

Wilson, J. D., Griffin, J. E., George, F. W., and Leshin, M. (1983) 'The endocrine control of male phenotypic development', *Australian Journal of Biological Science*, 36, pp. 101–28.

Wilson, E. O. (1975) *Sociobiology: A New Synthesis*, Harvard University Press, Cambridge, Mass.

Zappia, J. V. and Rogers, L. J. (1983) 'Light experience during development affects asymmetry of forebrain function in chickens', *Developmental Brain Research*, 11, pp. 93–106.

Zappia, J. V. and Rogers, L. J. (1987) 'Sex differences and reversal of brain asymmetry by testosterone in chickens', *Behavioural Brain Research*, 23, pp. 261–7.

8

RELIGION

Marie Tulip

> As I left, I looked at the different faces in the pew – and kept on smiling. I saw leaving women I knew, old women, middle-aged women, their children, husbands, young women, all kinds and sorts of people. I knew that we were leaving to do whatever we had to do to become persons.
>
> (Mary Rodda in Daly 1973, p. 144)

Many more women have walked out of the church since this famous exodus from Harvard Memorial Church in 1971. The misogyny of the Judaeo-Christian religious tradition is now widely recognized and attacked by feminists inside and out of church and synagogue. The contradictions between feminism and patriarchal religion are intense and it sometimes seems that the feminist challenge rather than having a liberating effect has made the patriarchal attitudes and structures of western religion more deeply entrenched than ever. The response of many women to this situation is to reject religion altogether. Others, however, have continued to engage in intense dialogue with established religion, or have gone outside it in various ways, to construct new meaning-systems, new forms of religious discourse, which do not do violence to women's experience. Whether Judaeo-Christian religion and feminism are compatible remains an open and controversial question.

This chapter is concerned with feminist responses to the patriarchal construction of women in religious discourse. It is written from an Australian consciousness, dealing largely with American and English texts. It focuses on the Judaeo-Christian tradition as the central expression of religious discourse in western culture, with the emphasis being almost entirely on the Christian aspect of this tradition, and on the more recent feminist construction of women's spirituality. It does not include other contemporary world religions or Aboriginal religion.

Section 1 deals with Mary Daly's comprehensive and radical critique of the patriarchy, and her construction of the women's revolution as an ontological, spiritual revolution. Section 2 focuses on feminist theologians such as Rosemary Radford Ruether and Elisabeth Schüssler Fiorenza, and other feminist groups who attack and seek to transform the Judaeo-Christian tradition while remaining based within it; and section 3 goes outside this tradition to consider women's spirituality as it is being expressed in women's lives and writings, and the movements to organize it in Goddess religion and Witchcraft.

In working to transform the Judaeo-Christian tradition, to appropriate the ancient Goddess religion, or to express in a new language the spiritual dimension of our lives, feminist theology and women's spirituality reject the patriarchal construction of reality and have begun a new naming based in the lives and experience of women.

(1) MARY DALY

I took a deep breath and listened to
the old brag of my heart.
I am, I am, I am.
Sylvia Plath (in Daly 1973, p. 179)

No one has imagined us.
Adrienne Rich (1978, p. 25)

The basis for a feminist theology and spirituality lies in experience as a source of knowledge. But this is not a simple matter. All religious symbols and writings grow out of experience, the experience that individuals and communities have of themselves and of what they receive as revelatory events. This experience is expressed in symbols and structures which are used to interpret and give meaning to new experience and are themselves continually reformed and reinterpreted in the light of the new experience of the community. If the formulations become too rigid and fixed and are not responsive to new experience, they fade and die. Resistance to change is an obvious danger in religions like Christianity which claim their doctrine and scriptures have the objectivity of the Word of God. Nevertheless Christianity has in fact transformed itself in relation to some deep changes in social and cultural patterns, even in such difficult areas as race and class. In relation to women, however, the question still emerges in an acute form.

The difference now is that the basis for change is not just experience, but women's experience. The scriptures and symbols and structures of the Judaeo-Christian tradition have been formed and interpreted by men out of male experience. Women and women's experience as told from their own perspective have been absent from the structures of power and the symbol systems, as well as from the formulating process, and not just absent but deliberately excluded by a theology based on patriarchy.

When women began to articulate their experience to each other and publicly in the late 1960s and early 1970s, what emerged was not simply a rational critique of the tradition requiring that women's experience be added as another aspect, but an explosive rejection of the inherited tradition as partial and unjust. A theology based on male experience was claiming to be universal. Women who had been silenced and objectified in the churches and isolated from each other became newly aware of their alienation and of the unjust structures that caused it. In a culture where men and male experience were the norm, women and women's experience were marginalized and 'other'. The experience that forms the basis for feminist critical consciousness, then, is what Rosemary Ruether describes as 'that experience which arises when women become critically aware of these falsifying and alienating experiences imposed on them as women by a male-dominated culture' (Ruether 1985a, p. 114).[1]

The feminist knowledge that came from the activism and thinking and sharing and sisterhood of the 1970s exploded in a massive critique of the patriarchal church which, while it happened in so many personal and public encounters in so many places, found its most powerful written expression in Mary Daly's *Beyond God the Father*.

What is surprising rereading *Beyond God the Father* fifteen years on, is the energy and optimism of the prose, the passionate momentum of thought and word. Daly begins chapter 1 with the declaration that the women's movement 'can become the greatest single challenge to the major religions of the world, Western and Eastern. Beliefs and values that have held sway for thousands of years will be questioned as never before. This revolution may well be also the greatest single hope for survival of spiritual consciousness on this planet' (Daly 1973, pp. 13–14). By the next page the caricatures of human beings represented by the macho stereotype and the eternal feminine are crumbling, religious symbols have begun to fade and die, and in the becoming of women, 'both activism and creative thought flow from and feed into the evolving woman consciousness' (p. 16). We are carried along on 'a surge of awareness beyond the symbols and doctrines of patriarchal religion' (p. 16). One feels the revolution is almost complete. They were heady days.

In her earlier book, *The Church and the Second Sex* (1968), Daly describes the anti-women teachings and practice of the church from the Bible to the present; she points to the ferment after Vatican II as women began to be aware of the discrimination against them, and calls for 'radical transformation of the negative life-destroying elements of the Church as it exists today' (Daly 1968, p. 179). She situates herself within the church, committed to a 'theology of hope' (p. 181).

By 1973, no longer reformist, Daly has moved out of the church and is living and writing 'on the boundary'. The work of *Beyond God the Father* is, she says, 'not merely on the boundary *between* these (male-created) disciplines [i.e. philosophy and theology], but on the boundary *of* both, because it speaks out of the experience of that half of the human species which has been represented in neither discipline' (Daly 1973, p. 6). Her purpose is 'to study the potential of the women's revolution to transform human consciousness and its externalizations, that is, to generate human becoming' (p. 6). To Daly this is an ontological question, a question of being and nothingness. It has to do with 'the search for ultimate meaning and reality, which some would call God' (p. 6).

Daly's 'transcendence' in some ways resembles Paul Tillich's 'God beyond God'. The problem as she sees it is that the symbol systems and conceptual apparatuses of Judaism and Christianity are a male construct. The reality captured in this sexist 'net of meaning' is partial and therefore false. But it represents itself as universal and is therefore difficult to perceive and even more difficult to break through. Daly's method is to go outside it in order to construct a new interpretation of the universe which is not fixed and oppressive but liberating to both women and men. She finds the capacity and energy to do this in the new 'bonding together of women into a sisterhood for liberation' (p. 1).

To exist humanly, Daly says, is to name the self, the world, and God. Women are reclaiming the right to name, which was stolen from us. The 'method' of the evolving spiritual consciousness of women, for Daly, is 'nothing less than this beginning to speak humanly – a reclaiming of the right to name. The liberation of language is rooted in the liberation of ourselves' (p. 8).

What Daly is attacking is not only the fact that the whole system of theology and ethics was developed by men, but also that it was developed to serve the interests of men. It is based on a system of sexual hierarchy to which patriarchal religion gives its supernatural blessing. The focus of Daly's attack is the symbol system, beginning with God the Father:

> The biblical and popular image of God as a great patriarch in heaven, rewarding and punishing according to his mysterious and seemingly arbitrary will, has dominated the imagination of millions over thousands of years. The symbol of the Father God, spawned in the human imagination and sustained as plausible by patriarchy, has in turn rendered service to this type of society by making its mechanisms for the oppression of women appear right and fitting. If God in 'his' heaven is a father ruling 'his' people, then it is in the 'nature' of things and according to divine plan and the order of the universe that society be male-dominated.
>
> (p. 13)

Daly points out that this God is used oppressively against women in three ways: first, in an overt way when theologians proclaim women's subordination to be God's will, as they have done from the time of Paul and the church Fathers to the present; second, when one-sex symbolism of God and for the human relation to God is used, as, for example, in such statements as, 'Through Jesus as "Lord", "men" become "sons" of the "Father" in "his" "Kingdom"'; and third, when although the basic assumptions appear to be non-sexist, the language used encourages detachment from the reality of the human struggle against oppression in its concrete manifestations. These three categories broadly correspond to what Liz Grosz defines as sexism, patriarchy, and phallocentrism. At this point Daly's criterion for rejecting certain forms of God-talk is whether it hinders human becoming by reinforcing sex-role socialization.

The problem of how to name the divine remains. The God of the Hebrew scriptures, when asked this question, replied 'I am who I am', or in another translation, 'I am becoming who I am becoming'. Perhaps any other name would attempt the impossible by objectifying and thus limiting the infinite, as the name God in effect now does in western culture. Rosemary Ruether suggest God/ess in written but not oral expression. Some feminists use words like 'mother' and 'she', and Carol Christ explores 'the Goddess'. But as Daly says, part of the challenge is to recognize the poverty of all words and symbols and the fact of our past idolatry regarding them, and then to turn to our own resources for bringing about the radically new in our lives. The basic change, she argues, has to take place in women – in our being and self-image. Out of women's surge to self-affirmation and our 'power of presence' to each other, she suggests we perceive transcendence as 'the Verb' (p. 34).

It is not just the image of God as father, however, that Daly sees as oppressive to women, but the whole symbolic pattern constructed by the patriarchal imagination, including the Fall, original sin, the son Jesus as saviour, and Mary the virgin mother.

Daly describes the myth of the Fall as a case of cosmic false naming. Although the story of Adam and Eve is commonly considered a joke, she claims that the myth 'has projected a malignant image of the male–female relationship and of the "nature" of women that is still deeply imbedded in the modern psyche' (p. 45). The projection of guilt upon women is, she says, 'the primordial lie' (p. 47). Having internalized the consciousness of the oppressor, women become divided beings, unable to act or speak. In accepting guilt, women not only see themselves as 'bad' or 'sick' but become so.

The 'original sin' of women, Daly says, is precisely the internalization of guilt and blame. Among its side effects are psychological paralysis, feminine anti-feminism, false humility, and emotional dependence. As victims of the 'scapegoat syndrome', women can never win. Being 'good' or 'bad' within the system is equally destructive. The way out of the imposed 'innocence', or lack of knowledge and choice, of both the good and the bad women is through experiential knowledge, a 'Fall from false innocence into a new kind of adulthood' (p. 67).

Having defined patriarchy as the original sin, Daly sees the choice of a single male as saviour as yet another product of 'supermale arrogance'. Under the conditions of patriarchy, she says, 'the role of liberating the human race from the original sin of sexism would seem to be precisely the role that a male symbol *cannot* perform' (p. 72). She does not deny the evidence that, in Leonard Swidler's words 'Jesus was a Feminist'. But her response is, 'So what?' She does not allow that past history has some prior claim over present experience, or that the past has adequate models for us now. While not denying the 'revelatory power of the personality of Jesus', she believes the church's focus on him as the unique saviour is idolatrous: 'As a uniquely masculine image and language for divinity loses credibility, so also the idea of a single divine incarnation in a human being of the masculine sex may give way in the religious consciousness to an increased awareness of the power of Being in all persons' (p. 71).

The Christ image has been used oppressively against women in various ways: to exclude women from the image of God and from the priesthood because of Jesus's maleness; to intensify the ethic of sacrificial love, humility, meekness, etc. imposed on and often destructive to women; and to give a misleading sense of equality of women and men which may be 'spiritually' true but is not true in any other way.

The image of Mary is also ambiguous for women. On the one hand it is an impossible model, the virgin mother; and on the other it does have some power as a sort of remnant of the ancient image of the Mother Goddess. Daly points out that as doctrine, it reinforces sexual caste, but as a free-wheeling symbol, it 'reflects the power and influence of the Mother Goddess symbol which Christianity was never able to wipe out entirely' (p. 87). Referring to Pope Pius XII's proclamation in 1950 of the doctrine of the Assumption of Mary, Daly says: 'In itself, the image of Mary "rising" says something', though she qualifies this by adding that 'it leaves us, so to speak, up in the air' since at the same time Pius was 'simultaneously pouring forth voluminous utterances on the rightful place of "woman" in society, that is, having an uncontrollable number of babies and serving her male master in dutiful submission' (p. 89). Daly's interpretation of this 'extreme dichotomy between quasi-prophetic symbolic exaltation and social degradation of women by the Roman Catholic Church' (p. 89) is that the church has 'tried to capture female presence and power in a symbol, *using* this to captivate the psyches of women and men, mesmerizing them, binding them in unquestioning loyalty to itself' (p. 90). She sees the survival, however muted, of the Great Goddess, in spite of all the attempts of the patriarchy to obliterate women's history both under patriarchy and in the previous matriarchal period, as a prophetic sign of a new arrival of female presence, the Second Coming not as a return of Christ but as the arrival of women.

The challenge of radical feminism to traditional morality is revolutionary. Daly paints a scathing picture of the hypocrisy of Christian ethics, where obedience, humility, and self-sacrifice are enjoined upon and accepted by women, which only reinforces the abject female situation, while dominant males hold up the values of selflessness and sacrificial love but actually live in quite a different way.[2] This tends to deny responsibility and self-actualization to women, and to stifle honesty in men. Daly calls it a passive ethic, in which sin is basically equated with an offence against those in power, and no attempt is made to develop an understanding of the aggressive and creative virtues. It is women who have actually been the scapegoats and victims of this unrealistic and destructive moral ideal, who are 'in a position to say No to this Christolatrous morality, in which "love" is always privatised and lacking a specific social context, and in which the structures of oppression are left uncriticised' (p. 105).

Against this deceptive and dehumanizing ethic, Daly sets an ethic of revelatory courage: 'The driving revelatory force that is making it possible for women to speak – and to *hear* each other speak – more authentically about God is courage, . . . existential courage to confront the experience of nothingness' (p. 23). This means leaving the security of sex-roles which lead to self-reduction, confronting the shock of non-being with the courage to be. It means facing the anxieties of loss (of jobs, friends, social approval), guilt over refusing to do what society demands, and meaninglessness when one emerges into a world without models. This confrontation with the anxiety of non-being is revelatory, making possible the relativization of structures that are seen as human products, and therefore not absolute or ultimate. Courage to be is the key to the revelatory power of the feminist revolution.

When she considers particular moral questions such as abortion, Daly points out that ethical positions put forward as 'reasonable solutions' are often belied by the realities of sexual politics in the society in which we actually live. The morality of abortion cannot be considered without taking into account the powerlessness of women in sexually hierarchical society. Daly says that 'a community really expressive of authentic religious consciousness would coincide with the women's movement in pointing beyond abortion to more fundamental solutions, working toward the development of a social context in which the problem of abortion would be unlikely to arise' (p. 113). She contrasts this with patriarchal power structures, which do not operate in this humanizing way. Rather, they are structures of alienation, and the logical expression of their power is in 'the Most Unholy Trinity of Rape, Genocide, and War' (p. 114).

In *Beyond God the Father* the power of Daly's critique of the patriarchal nature of Judaeo-Christian religion comes from her brilliant analysis of the way power is structured in terms of male reality and then maintained by a symbol system which keeps that structure in place. The system is demonic. It is partial and fixed, it absolutizes itself, and it is cut off from its living roots, the power of being, and the capacity for transcendence. The chief victims are women, but it is women who can go outside the system and through facing nothingness can rediscover true Be-ing and hope and creative life. It is through women's new ways of living that new structures will grow as women rename the world.

Daly's next book, *Gyn/Ecology: The Metaethics of Radical Feminism* (1978), is much more widely known to feminists than *Beyond God the Father*, because in it she has moved right away from more traditional Christian language and any kind of God-talk into a much more clearly woman-centred consciousness. Instead of 'God' she talks of 'the Goddess' or 'the Verb', 'transcendence' has become 'the Otherworld', and women are Hags, Spinsters, Crones, and Furies. The style explodes into a pyrotechnic display of verbal invention and playfulness, and the language has a rich accumulation of connotations, sexual and bodily as well as spiritual and cultural. Gynocentric writing, says Daly, 'means risking. Since the language and style of patriarchal writing simply cannot contain or carry the energy of women's exorcism and ecstasy, in this book I invent, dis-cover, re-member' (Daly 1978, p. 24). Nevertheless, the critique is basically the same as in *Beyond God the Father* except that it is raised to a much greater intensity, while the vision for the future has taken off into its own orbit of abstraction Daly says it is 'about the journey of women becoming, that is, radical feminism' (p. 1).

Daly is again writing from the particular point in time of the breakthrough moment. She says, 'Breaking through the Male Maze is both exorcism and ecstasy', and she never moves further into woman-consciousness than this explosive point which energizes her to spin visions of the future and pour fury on the past. The exorcism here takes two forms: the First Passage of the book and the journey gives a detailed analysis of the myths and language of patriarchy, and particularly of Christian patriarchy, dis-covering their destructiveness to women and their 'deadly deceptions', as, for example, that they replace the Tree of Life by 'the necrophilic symbol of a dead body hanging on dead wood' (p. 18). The Second Passage analyses five forms of the planetary phenomenon of oppression of women, which Daly calls the murder/dismemberment of the Goddess – that is, the Self-affirming being of women: Indian suttee, Chinese footbinding, African female genital mutilation, European witch-burning, American gynecology. In her description of these five forms of atrocity, the accumulation of concrete historical detail gives body and weight to her religious understanding of them and parallels the mythological murder analysed in the First Passage. Ecstasy, the focus of the Third Passage, comes from Sparking, that is, 'building the fires of gynergetic communication and confidence', and Spinning, which is 'the creating of a new, woman-identified environment'. But ecstasy is also a continuing aspect of Daly's style, which she names 'ludic cerebration' (p. 23).

In a world without models Daly did begin to imagine a world other than patriarchy, but for several reasons it does not carry due weight. First, the energy of the naming is ahead of what it names. However much Daly would like to be Spinning and Sparking in a women's Otherworld, it remains a world of abstraction which she is not able to adequately support with embodied experience, and she is in fact feeling the pain of being a feminist in this world. Speaking as a brave Voyager in *Gyn/Ecology*, Daly says that when we experience depression, brokenness, the fragmentation of our minds/bodies, 'Our resilient response is Spinning/Weaving the pattern behind the fragmentation. Crones compose cosmic tapestries, expressing/reflecting/creating the integrity of our be-ing' (p. 412). But in fact, as Mary Daly, her response to her own and other women's pain is the huge authentic howl of rage that is the Second Passage of this book.

Second, Daly's Gyn/ecological Journeying is not for the weak and allows no compromise. She attacks women who work within patriarchal structures as 'fembots' or 'painted birds'. She sees women's refuges, health centres, and affirmative action programmes as compromising and subverting, as are 'linguistic reforms which do not imply radical analysis'. In contrast to 'such timid constructs', Daly says, 'the new physical spaces – like the new semantic/cognitive/symbolic spaces – will be dis-covered/created further out/in the Otherworld Journey'. This is cold comfort for women who need such services now. The response of one of my friends to *Gyn/Ecology* was 'What about childcare?' Indeed Daly does ignore or belittle practical reforms and reformist political action, and appears to take no account of poverty, unemployment, sickness, the need for childcare, etc. But it must also be said that those involved in social reform often misread Daly.[3] Hester Eisenstein comments: 'Her call for a more radical form of feminism . . . seemed to point toward a "Journey" that was psychic and inward-looking, rather than toward more fundamental social change' (Eisenstein 1984, p. 115). And further, 'Daly's journey turned away from a confrontation with patriarchy'. Who is to say whether the social or the symbolic is the more 'fundamental'? Surely for women the struggle is important on both fronts. Daly's willingness to engage in all-out battle with the demonic forces of patriarchy on the level of language, image, myth, symbol, ritual, and concept is hugely confrontational. The Otherworld to which Daly invites us to journey with her involves claiming our own power and reality and saying no to the power of patriarchy, which exists outside us in institutions as well as in our heads, 'even feminist heads'. Her great anger is commensurate with the great destructiveness of patriarchy to women as she invites us to affirm our own autonomy and subjectivity, and to live creatively in a world we ourselves name.

(2) FEMINISTS WITHIN THE JUDAEO-CHRISTIAN TRADITION

> God didn't mean anything to me – except as a coping device – until I began to realize that justice-making and love-making and making-the-connections are where God lives and moves and has God's being.
>
> (Carter Heyward, in *God's Fierce Whimsy*, The Mudflower Collective, 1985, p. 119)

The huge energy of Daly's no to the 'edifice of patriarchy' with 'all its religious infrastructures and their secular derivatives' (Daly 1978, p. 39), performed a valuable service for all feminists in naming the full extent of the destructive power of misogynism. Daly of course came to reject the church as unredeemable, but other feminists continue the struggle to transform it. I want in this section to consider the work of Rosemary Radford Ruether, Elisabeth Schüssler Fiorenza, and certain other groupings of feminists working from within a Christian or Jewish framework.

Rosemary Ruether and dualism

Rosemary Ruether and Mary Daly were a kind of duo for Christian feminists during the 1970s, two powerful thinkers and writers both coming out of a Roman Catholic tradition and both challenging the powers of the patriarchy in a fierce struggle. The focus of Ruether's attack in her analysis not only of feminist theology but of other liberation theologies as well, is the dualistic and hierarchical world-view that she sees as underlying the oppressor–oppressed relationships that liberation theologies are addressing. Ruether sets her critique in broad sweeps of history. Going back into early agricultural societies, she says that 'for the first two millennia of recorded history, religious culture continued to reflect the more holistic view of society of the neolithic village, where the individual and the community, nature and society, male and female, earth goddess and sky god were seen in a total perspective of world renewal' (Ruether 1972, pp. 118–19). But then in the first millennium BC this communal world-view of humanity and nature, male and female, started to break down. For the Hebrew desert people, the pattern of death and resurrection was cut loose from organic harmonies and became instead the historical pattern of wrath and redemption. Later still, as the hopes for renewal projected into a historical future came to be seen as unrealizable within history, the prophetic drive to be free from nature ended in a vision of an apocalyptic negation of history: a cataclysmic world destruction and angelic new creation (p. 120).

Ruether sees Christianity as the heir of this apocalyptic Judaism and also of classical Neo-Platonism, combining the image of a male warrior God with the exaltation of the intellect over the body. All the basic dualities, she claims, have their roots in this apocalyptic–Platonic religious heritage of Christianity – 'the alienation of the mind from the body; the alienation of the subjective self from the objective world; the subjective retreat of the individual, alienated from the social community; the domination or rejection of nature by spirit' (Ruether 1972, p. 115). But 'the alienation of the masculine from the feminine is the primary sexual symbolism that sums up all these alienations. The psychic traits of intellectuality, transcendent spirit and autonomous will that were identified with the male left the woman with the contrary traits of bodiliness, sensuality and subjugation' (pp. 115–16).

Ruether sees this antithesis as the basis for the profound conditioning of men and women into social roles, and for the splits between public and private, reason and passion, work and home, which trap women in a social reality that makes liberated personhood impossible. Ruether sees the struggle of the transcendent ego to free itself from bondage to nature reflected in the 'exclusively male God who creates out of nothing, transcending nature and dominating history'. This theology has its counterpart in 'a world-destroying spirituality that projects upon the female of the race all its abhorrence, hostility and fear of the bodily powers from which it has arisen and from which it wishes to be independent' (1972, p. 122).

Theologically, Ruether analyses the Fall, the alienation between humanity and God, in terms of sexism, which she sees as beginning in self-alienation, experienced as estrangement between the self and the body. Biological differences are translated into a power relationship which is projected onto and totalized in social structures and cultural modes that eliminate woman's autonomous personhood to define her solely in terms of male needs and negations. 'Women become the victims of the very process by which the male seeks to triumph over the conflict represented by these dualities; are limited and repressed into that same sphere of immanence and materiality which the male sought to escape, transcend and dominate' (Ruether 1973, pp. 1224–5). The primary way of experiencing the alienation of mind from body is fear of sexuality. Through this alienation woman is depersonalized and turned into a sex-object, to be used 'rightly' for procreation or abused 'wrongly' for 'carnal pleasure' (p. 1225), but not really encountered as a person through sexuality. Ruether calls this the 'Puritan–Prurient' syndrome.

Ruether discusses the issue of the ordination of women in the context of the alienation within the church between male and female, clergy and people, theological education and ministry, as well as the alienation between the 'real world' and the 'encapsulation of the Church in the sphere of privatized sentimentality' (Ruether 1975, p. 82). The ordination of women 'threatens the entire psychodynamics by which the God–human, the soul–body, the clergy–laity, and finally the Church–world relationships have been imaged in terms of sexual hierarchicalism' (1975, pp. 78–9). Ruether sees the conservatives as correct in recognizing that the revolution represented by the ordination of women in significant numbers threatens the foundations of the whole symbolic structure which sacralizes not only these sexist dualisms but also dualisms of racism, the subjugation of lower classes and colonized people, and even anti-Semitism, which operate out of much the same language of sexist dualism, i.e. the elevation of the 'head' people over the 'body' people. But this is precisely why the ordination of women is necessary, so that the church can recover its role as the representative of liberated humanity. 'The gospel of the Church', Ruether maintains, 'must again come to be recognised as the social mandate of history, not the means of setting up a new regime of domination or, on the other hand, of withdrawing into a private world of individual salvation' (1975, pp. 82–3).

Ruether analyses many other aspects of the dominations and hierarchies of race, social class, and nature as well as sex, and explores the relations between them. She uses many different typologies in wide-ranging and detailed historical and social contexts, constantly interweaving aspects of different yet parallel oppressions in a context which includes the religious, economic, historical, sociological, and the psychological. Starting from a situation of oppression, she moves through a complex unravelling of the historical and social threads, analyses them in terms of a severe critique of structures of domination and subjugation, and works towards a holistic vision in which the dualities are reconciled in a new society of justice and peace. Where Daly's discourse tends towards a world of symbol, myth, and abstraction, Ruether's is oriented to the political struggle to transform the unjust structures of domination within history. Her style is both prophetic and political as she constantly exposes the structures of oppression and exploitation. She is not calling people to enter an Otherworld but to transform this one. Ultimate redemption, she says, cannot be divorced from historical redemption, and 'it is wrong not to interrelate the final or ultimate horizon of redemption, which is beyond all imagining, with that available horizon of social justice, peace and love toward which we can begin to struggle here and now' (Ruether 1973, p. 1228).

Ruether sees four 'levels of problematic' which the analysis of women's liberation must reckon with. The first stage is subjective and psychological, involving the process of raising consciousness and exorcizing debasing self-images projected upon and internalized by the oppressed. 'It involves the exploration of the history of sexism and the reconstruction of its ideology in order to loosen its hold on the self and to permit the gradual growth of self-definition over against a world defined in male terms' (Ruether 1975, p. 29). The second stage is 'one of social praxis, where we must begin to see the way women as a group are entrapped by the systemic structuring of male–female roles, and envision a radically restructured society'. Third, 'women must become self-critical about their own class and racial contexts'. And fourth, 'our vision of a new society of social justice must reckon with the ecological crisis' (1975 pp. 29–31).

Ruether defines anger and pride as theological virtues. 'Anger corresponds to the power to transcend false consciousness and break its chains . . . Self-esteem resurrects in the oppressed . . . the image of human nature as originally created – as good' (1973, p. 1226). And she fully acknowledges the healing quality of women coming together in sisterhood. Yet there is some driving energy for change in Daly's prose that is not present in Ruether's. Although she is radical and revolutionary in many ways, Ruether's vision of the process of reconciliation is, I believe, not yet deep enough. She describes the need and the process for achieving women's autonomy, but the responsibilities of men and the church in the process of change are left a little vague. Ruether names and analyses the sin of sexism very powerfully and envisions a richly reconciled community, but she does not engage directly or deeply enough in the actual power struggle between women and men and between women and the patriarchal church. She assumes that as women free themselves as oppressed, they will also free the oppressors. She had not at this stage seen ways for women to claim collective power against the power of men and the patriarchal church. Her analysis moves too quickly from alienation to reconciliation.

Ruether's later work

Ruether's major work is *Sexism and God-Talk: Toward a Feminist Theology* (1983), a culmination of her wide-ranging earlier work. Claiming that classical theology has been based on the experience of a male elite, she uses women's experience to transform the traditional theological doctrines of God, creation, sin, Christology, the church, and eschatology. Ruether says the present crisis of religion is so radical that the very nature of religious knowledge is seen as promoting alienation rather than integration of the human person. Against this she constructs a new theology based on the critical principle of the promotion of the full humanity of women, and situated in what she constructs as an alternative historical community and tradition more deeply rooted than those that have become corrupted. She builds this from aspects of five traditional areas – the prophetic–liberating principle of the Bible, which denounces oppressive ideologies and systems of domination, and which Ruether extends beyond its biblical applications to apply also to sexism; the countercultural movements of early Christianity and church history such as Gnostics, Montanists, some Puritans, the Quakers, and Shakers, all of whom promoted an egalitarian vision in some ways; the basic categories of Christian theology; some pagan Goddess religions; and the modern post-Christian movements, liberalism, Marxism, and romanticism. All of these are treated in a dialectic relationship, allowed to critique each other so that the transformed Christianity that emerges denounces all systems of domination and calls for mutuality of all people regardless of sex, race, or social group, and including nature and the earth.

Christianity is problematic for women in having a male 'saviour'. Ruether sees the problem, but claims Jesus's maleness is irrelevant. She argues that once the mythology about Jesus as Messiah or divine Logos, with its traditional masculine imagery, is stripped off, the central importance of Jesus is his renewal of the prophetic vision. He did not validate the existing social and religious hierarchy, but spoke on behalf of the marginalized and despised groups of society. He identified with poor and outcast women, those at the bottom of the pile. He revised God-language by using the familiar Abba for God, by speaking of the Messiah as servant rather than king, and by not just turning hierarchy upside down but aiming at a new reality in which hierarchy and dominance are overcome as principles of social relations.

In *Sexism and God-Talk* Ruether has constructed a new radically transformed non-sexist Christian theology. It is a brilliant achievement. But it is inadequate in two respects. The first is in the area of symbols. However clearly and correctly Ruether interprets Jesus as non-sexist, the fact remains that for many women it is impossible to accept him as a liberating religious symbol today. Maleness clings to him, and his maleness is specifically used by the Roman Catholic Church to exclude women from the priesthood. For the present he remains a tool of the patriarchy. The word 'God' is also not part of the living spirituality of many feminists. Ruether suggests God/ess as a written form, but also uses God. These symbols are too laden with patriarchal freight to be anything but obstacles for many women. The second limitation is that there is a gap in Ruether's analysis and I think what is missing is the energy and dynamic power associated with the consciousness-raising groups in the early 1970s. Ruether has not yet situated herself within the consciousness of groups of self-identified women, which I believe is where women's real power for change comes from. She points to some few congregations where non-sexist Christianity is taking form (a clergy-led revolutionizing of the local church), and to some feminist base communities through which, if they remain in a creative dialectic with the institutional church, the church will be regenerated. But as Ruether herself points out,

> the alternative nonsexist, nonclassist and nonexploitative world eludes us as a global system. This is not so much because of our inability to imagine it correctly as because of the insufficient collective power of those already converted to an alternative vision. The powers and principalities are still very much in control of most of the world. The nucleus of the alternative world remains, like the church (theologically,

as the church), harbingers and experimenters with new human possibilities within the womb of the old.

(1983, pp. 233–4).

In this reference to 'the church' does Ruether mean those few small congregations and feminist groups? The large capacity of her mind and imagination to construct a new feminist theology is somehow at odds with its miniscule appearance. Even the remnant was surely not as minute as this? To explain this gap it is necessary to leap to the other side of a chasm between two kinds of religious feminist knowledge – that represented by rational discourse like Ruether's own, and the knowledge of small groups of women living out a new construction of reality in relation to their own encounter with the divine in their lives.

To some extent Ruether made this leap herself after *Sexism and God-Talk*, as evidenced by her book *Women-Church* (1985c). *Womanguides*, also published in 1985, is more like the old Ruether, focused on building a new feminist-centred tradition by gathering historical texts that correct the patriarchal bias and begin the process from which a new canon might emerge. Is a feminist canon a contradiction in terms, one wonders, even an emerging one? What appears as a new departure for Ruether is that she includes some contemporary texts in a new openness to stories and parables being written by women in the present, expressing a new feminist consciousness. This finds fuller expression in her book *Women-Church*, which will be discussed later in this section in relation to Christian feminist groups. First I want to turn to another major feminist theologian who also writes from within the Roman Catholic Church.

Elisabeth Schussler Fiorenza

As we have seen, Ruether uses the discourse of rational historical and theological analysis to critique the sexist dualisms she sees as underlying the structures of domination of church and society, and uses the critical principle of the full humanity of women as the basis for transforming them into a reconciled holistic world based on mutuality. Fiorenza's work is centred not in rational analysis or particular critical principles but in communities of women. For her, the goal of feminist theology is not 'full humanity' since humanity as we know it is male-defined. 'The central spiritual and religious feminist quest', she maintains, is 'the quest for women's self-affirmation, survival, power, and self-determination' (Fiorenza 1985, p. 126). Feminist spirituality for her is communal, and revelation takes place not in texts or the tradition but in gatherings of women, both past and present. As Fiorenza points out, women understand very well the ways in which the Bible is used against us, particularly in these days of the Moral Majority and the New Right, but it is also true that the 'Bible has inspired and continues to inspire countless women to speak out and to struggle against injustice, exploitation and stereotyping' (Fiorenza 1984, p. xiii). Far from wanting to defend the Bible against its feminist critics, Fiorenza sees the task of feminist interpretation as bringing out as clearly as possible both its oppressive and its liberating power. The only way this can happen is through a critical process of feminist assessment and evaluation, based in the contemporary experience of self-identified women, in women-church (1984, pp. xvi–xvii).

For Fiorenza the recovery of early Christian women's history is an essential part of the quest for our heritage and our power. Speaking of cultures in which biblical religion is still influential, she says 'a cultural and social feminist transformation of Western society must take into account the biblical story and the historical impact of the biblical tradition, . . . We will either transform it into a new liberating future or continue to be subject to its tyranny whether we recognize its power or not' (1983, p. xix).[4]

Fiorenza claims early Christian history as women's own past. It is because androcentric western language and religion have erased women from history that biblical religion as we receive it is so sexist. Her major work, *In Memory of Her: A Feminist Theological Reconstruction of Christian Origins* (1983), is an attempt to reconstruct early Christian history as women's history, first, in order to restore women's stories to early Christian history, and second, to reclaim this history as the history of women and men. Otherwise the biblical texts and traditions formulated and codified by men will remain oppressive to women, culturally as well as religiously.

Fiorenza argues that biblical texts are not verbally inspired revelation but historical formulations within the context of a religious community. In setting the texts in this context, she is seeking to construct a model in which women are not hidden and invisible, a model that allows us to perceive the human reality which has been represented in a distorted form in androcentric texts and research. Her aim is both to undermine the legitimization of patriarchal religious structures, and also to empower women in their struggle against such structures. This recovery of women's history in early Christianity is claiming the Christian past as women's own past, not just as a male past in which women participated only on the fringes or were not active at all. In fact Fiorenza says that 'in the second and third centuries Christianity was still defending itself against the accusation that it was a religion of women and uncultured people. The task, therefore, involves not so much rediscovering new sources as rereading the available sources in a different key' (1983, p. xx).

Fiorenza uses Thomas Kuhn's notion of scientific paradigms to explain this 'different key': it is a revolutionary paradigm shift from an androcentric to a feminist interpretation of the world. The debate between androcentric scholarship and feminist scholarship reveals a competition between rival paradigms; the transition from one to the other depends on the emerging paradigm producing its own institutional structures and support groups, as the feminist paradigm is doing with women's centres and study programmes – small beer as yet, one might think, compared with the pervasive and entrenched patriarchy! Nevertheless, what is at issue for Fiorenza in her work is not just a 'feminist reconstruction of history and a renaming of the world, but a fundamental change of both scholarship and the academy'. Feminist studies, then, and her own work, are 'primarily accountable to the women's movement for societal–ecclesial change rather than to the academy' (1983, p. xxii).

Although the androcentric texts present women either as absent or silent or in their traditional roles in patriarchy, Fiorenza claims this 'must not be allowed to cancel out the history and theology of the struggle, life and leadership of Christian women who spoke and acted in the power of the Spirit' (1983, p. 36). She puts women at the centre of her reconstructed history, remembering both their sufferings in religious patriarchy and their integral part in the struggle for an egalitarion vision against patriarchal domination.

With a wealth of detail and meticulous scholarship Fiorenza reconstructs two distinct forms of early Christianity: the Jesus movement in Palestine and the Christian missionary movement in the Graeco-Roman cities. Both were inspired by Jesus but they saw him in quite different lights.

The Jesus movement was a discipleship of equals whose central symbol was the festive table of a royal banquet or wedding feast, celebrating the '*basileia*' (kingdom) of God already present in their midst. Unlike the Pharisees, they did not observe the ritual purity of the 'holy table' but shared their meal with all. And unlike John the Baptist, who lived as an ascetic, preparing for the judgement and restoration to come, Jesus enjoyed the festive meal so much that he was seen as a 'glutton and a drunkard, a friend of the tax-collectors and sinners' (Luke 7:34), an indication that for him 'salvation and wholeness' was already experientially available. Already the blind see, the deaf hear. Jesus stresses the everyday possibility of Israel's wholeness, inclusive of every person, and engendering the wholeness of every human being. In his ministry, 'God is experienced as all-inclusive love, . . . a God of graciousness and goodness who accepts everyone without exception' (1983, p. 130). Fiorenza associates this God with the female divine wisdom, Sophia, and says Jesus probably understood himself as the prophet and child of Sophia. She is 'a people-loving spirit who shares the throne of God', and Fiorenza says it is as her messenger that Jesus calls 'all who labour and are heavy laden' and promises them rest and shalom (1983, p. 134).

Fiorenza claims the Jesus movement was egalitarian, included women's leadership, and challenged and opposed the patriarchal ethos through the praxis of equal discipleship. In place of the patriarchal family it put a neo-familial community, one that does not include fathers, i.e. those who claim the authority of the father, because that is reserved for God alone. In so far as the new 'family' of Jesus has no room for 'fathers', it implicitly rejects their power and status and thus claims that in the messianic community all patriarchal structures are abolished. What Fiorenza shows through this reconstruction is that 'in the discipleship of equals the "role" of women is not peripheral or trivial, but at the center, and thus of utmost importance to the praxis of "solidarity from below" ' (p. 152). As a feminist vision, she says, 'the basileia vision of Jesus calls all women without exception to wholeness and selfhood, as well as to solidarity with those women who are impoverished, the maimed, the outcasts of our society and church' (p. 153). In the face of the violence such a vision and commitment will encounter, it enables us not to despair or give up the struggle. It empowers us to walk upright, freed from the double oppression of societal and religious sexism and prejudice (1983, pp. 153–4).

The second movement, the early Christian missionary movement, spread Christianity throughout the Graeco-Roman world and extended it to gentiles as well as Jews. Paul, the great apostle and missionary to the gentiles, whom we know about because his activity is the focus of the book of Acts, was only one of many missionaries, women as well as men, and he was not the most prominent or influential at the time. Although women only appear in Acts in auxiliary roles or as opponents, Fiorenza shows that they acted not only as rich patronesses of the movement but also as prominent leaders and missionaries. They were engaged in this work both before Paul and independently of him: 'Without question they were equal and sometimes even superior to Paul in their work for the gospel' (p. 161). Women were leaders both as missionaries and in the house churches which were central to the early Christian missionary movement. The house church association offered an equal share in its life to all its members, and these associations of equals were therefore in tension with the traditional patriarchal household structures.

The Christian missionary movement based itself on the experience of the power of the Spirit. Jesus has been raised 'in power' to become the Spirit, Sophia, Lord, and Liberator. Those who are 'in Christ' are filled with the Spirit, women and men equally. They become 'a new creation'. According to Paul, the Spirit has entered history in a new way in Jesus Christ and the Christians, but has not yet transformed history completely. Paul sees the new creation as transforming the 'mind' but does not stress that it should also change the social–political relationship of Christians.

The famous quotation from Galatians 3:28, that 'in Christ there is neither male nor female', is 'a key expression not of Pauline theology but of the theological self-understanding of the Christian missionary movement which had far-reaching historical impact' (1983, p. 199). These words are widely used by twentieth-century women challenging the patriarchal structures of the contemporary church. Paul is, however, a doubtful ally. Although as part of the early missionary movement he affirmed women's equality and independence and encouraged them 'to remain free of the bondage of marriage', at the same time he subordinated 'women's behaviour in marriage and in the worship assembly to the interests of Christian mission', whereas he did not put such restrictions on men (1983, p. 236).

After Paul's time the Christian community became even more compromised by its concessions to the patriarchal structures of the Graeco-Roman household and society. 'In historical retrospective', Fiorenza concludes, 'the New Testament's sociological and theological stress on submission and patriarchal superordination has won out over its sociological and theological stress on altruistic love and ministerial service. Yet this "success" cannot be justified theologically, since it cannot claim the authority of Jesus for its own Christian praxis (1983, p. 334). Wherever the gospel is read, 'what the women have done is not totally forgotten because the gospel story remembers that the discipleship and apostolic leadership of women are integral parts of Jesus' alternative praxis of agape and service' (1983, p. 334).

The significance of Fiorenza's work is not that early Christianity was pure in some way, but that its actual forms were communal, egalitarian, opposed to the patriarchal family, with women in leadership roles and women's experience central to the life of the community, 'God' was imaged as Sophia, the divine female wisdom. These early Christian communities and households were always in tension with the patriarchal household and societal structures, and this patriarchal oppression grew stronger in the last half of the first century and its effects are already apparent in the New Testament itself, both in the androcentric bias of the texts and in the choice of which texts are included in the canon compared with what is left out. It is this oppressive patriarchal aspect of the Bible that is now used as authoritative by the twentieth-century patriarchal church to maintain its power by, for example, excluding women from leadership roles and from ordination.

By constructing an alternative history, Fiorenza has undermined the traditional historical power base of the patriarchal church and given feminists access to a crucial part of history in which their role was, and was seen to be, central. To individual feminists this may seem unimportant; but in terms of transforming the actual tradition of biblical interpretation and its use in the interests of patriarchy, so that it can now be clearly seen as a tradition which has always had both a liberating and an oppressive side, the importance of Fiorenza's work is profound.

Fiorenza situates herself very strongly and clearly in the community of women. Women are her people, 'all the women in the world' (1983,

p. 343), and it is to women that she sees herself as accountable. Her vision for the future is of a community of equals, including all women, bonded in sisterhood for empowerment and living in solidarity with the oppressed and the impoverished, the majority of whom are women and children dependent on women. These women (and Fiorenza does not exclude men so long as they are women-identified) would gather in *ekklesia*, i.e. free assemblies, to decide their own spiritual–political affairs, in a way they cannot do in a patriarchal church.

Women acting together

At this point Ruether's work and Fiorenza's work come together, joining also the many groupings of Christian women in the United States who are in the process of forming Women-Church. It is an energizing coming-together of women similar to that of the consciousness-raising groups in the early 1970s. Church women, mainly Catholic, are collecting their power and beginning both a profound affirmation of themselves as church, and a corresponding public challenge to the sinful assumption of power by the patriarchal authority figures and male-dominated councils, the Pope included. In mid-1987 a Women-Church group in Sydney read a feminist protest creed in the Domain as John Paul II paraded past in the popemobile. In the United States huge gatherings of women, lay and religious, are theologizing and acting together.

There is a difference between this movement and the earlier (1970s) women's liberation movement in the churches. In the 1970s, consciousness-raising and feminist theologizing changed a lot of women's lives and made an impact particularly in Protestant churches in many countries round the world. The Commission on the Status of Women of the Australian Council of Churches is just one of many such groups. Women were reflecting on our newly expressed experience in the light of the tradition of faith. Our theologizing was communal. We took our own and each other's experience seriously, 'hearing one another to speech', to use Nelle Morton's words, and the shared action/reflection that grew out of it became itself the experience which led to more shared reflection and action, and so on. The 'faith' became totally new in this praxis. We lived it, and articulated it in our social and religious communities, in politics and protests and publications. And we called for and worked for transformation of all the sexist structures, language, and forms of the patriarchal church and society.

What has changed is that where we saw ourselves, and were seen to be, 'on the boundary', in some way marginalized, in Exodus *from* the church (although we also claimed we *were* the church), the present groupings of women, particularly the Women-church movement, claim in Ruether's words that 'the Church is in Exodus with us'. Women have moved from the margins to the centre. As Fiorenza puts it, Christian feminists 'do not relinquish their biblical roots and heritage. As the *ekklesia* of women, we claim the center of Christian faith and community in a feminist process of transformation' (1985, p. 126).

The energy and power for change in our individual lives as well as in communities and in the church itself, come, I believe, from women acting together, acting for ourselves, for liberation. The women's movement has always known this, and Fiorenza is now putting it into religious terms when she says 'the place of divine revelation and grace is . . . not the Bible or the tradition of a patriarchal church but the *ekklesia* of women and the lives of women who live the "option for our women selves" ' (1985, p. 128). It is not *only* for our selves that we act, but it is necessary to make this claim to distinguish proper moral action for oneself and others from the destructive altruism and self-sacrifice expected of women which required putting the welfare and interests of others, especially men, first, and devaluing the welfare and interests of women. Women acting for liberation in fact identify themselves in solidarity with all oppressed groups, believing that no one is free till all are free.

With her book *Women-Church* it seems to me that Rosemary Ruether has changed her stance. In *Sexism and God-Talk* she stood somewhere outside the process, envisioning a point of reconciliation of all the dualisms, and called us to move towards it. Although her feminist theology is a great work of analysis and visioning, it has a detachment from the power that motivates and sustains change. But in *Women-Church* it is as though she were describing her own style when she says 'It is not enough to hold an ideology of criticism and social analysis . . . or to engage in rational theoretical discourse . . . One needs communities of nurture . . . and deep symbols and symbolic actions to guide and interpret the actual experience of the journey from sexism to liberated humanity' (Ruether 1985c, p. 3). Ruether says women are suffering from 'linguistic deprivation' in contemporary churches, where 'their words for women are so ambivalent, their power so negative, that attendance at their fonts poisons our souls' (1985c, p. 5). Women 'cannot wait for the institutional churches to reform themselves enough to provide the vehicles of faith and worship that women need in this time' (1985c, p. 4). The first hundred pages give a historical and theological rationale for Women-Church as a community of liberation from patriarchy, and the next two hundred give liturgical forms and rituals written by many women for events in women's lives – the onset of menstruation, marriage, divorce, coming out as a lesbian, embarking on new stages of life, menopause, sickness, and death. There are also special liturgies for moments of crisis and healing, times when women cry out for 'words of understanding, for hands laid on in healing, but find nothing but silence and closed doors in most churches' (1985c, p. 6). Each ritual needs to be adapted for the particular person, time, and place it is intended for.

It remains to be seen what will happen to this new movement which is beginning not only to form 'communities of nurture', but also to institutionalize itself with symbols, rituals, its own theology and emerging pluralistic practice. Is it replicating too closely some of the constricting forms of the old? Ruether believes it should avoid schism and remain in creative dialectic relationship with the existing institutional churches, eventually forming a renewed community with them, but not so quickly as to short-circuit the dismantling of clericalism and the formation of Women-Church as an autonomous community.

Women-Church is only one of the many groups, communities, and networks, some taking institutional form and some not, where feminist theology is taking place in the actual lives of women in many places round the world. This theologizing shares much of the same ground as feminist praxis in the wider women's movement – telling our stories, discovering ourselves as subject, affirming our bodies and our sexuality as good, renaming and reconstructing the world in solidarity with other women in the struggle against all oppressions. Crucially, for feminists, 'reality' or 'life' or 'spirituality' is relational. The focal point, Fiorenza says, is 'not a holy book or a cultic rite, not mystic experience and magic incantation, but a set of relationships' (1983, p. 345). Carter Heyward talks of it in terms of 'our strength', which she says is 'the power that we touch together, not alone' (Heyward 1984, p. 127).

As well as being relational, feminist knowledge respects particularity, in contrast to the universalizing and idealizing of 'classical malestream theology' (Mudflower 1985, p. 26), which overrides diversity. *God's Fierce Whimsy* (The Mudflower Collective 1985), written by a collective of seven Black, Hispanic and White Christian women, brilliantly reveals the deep risking of difference and conflict and confrontation that is unavoidable if theology is going to be truly inclusive and alive, as the women assert and confront each other with the particularities of their own experience of race, class, sexuality, and heterosexism.

These seven women agree that in this project sexuality was the hardest subject to talk about, and that lesbianism, in particular, is 'shaking the foundations of the Christian theological enterprise' (p. 180). The lesbian 'bears the image of the woman who rejects fundamentals upon which the church is built' (p. 181), and reveals the depth and extent of the homophobia, heterosexism, and sexism in the Christian tradition: 'the root of the discrimination is the lack of acceptance of the importance, and intrinsic goodness, of sexuality in all human beings' (p. 185). They present their discussion on sexuality in a reconstructed form to reflect 'a prism of the passionate theological possibility we so earnestly desire' (p. 181):

> Sister Yellow: Sexual pleasure, or orgasm, is really about ecstasy – at least that's what it is for me. And ecstasy is a central religious theme,

even a mark of revelation. It's led me to suspect that controlling women's sexuality is also about controlling alternative sources of religious knowledge.
Sister Lavender: Well, the reason I teach in the area of sexuality is that I know of no more profound theological issue. I am convinced that, to the extent that we are afraid of our sexual being, we're afraid of God, because what is God if not the wellspring of our creativity, our relationality, our ecstasy, our capacity to touch and be touched at the core of our being?
Sister Gold: You're right there. These men, and a lot of women too, demonstrate by the ways they live their lives, and certainly by the ways they write theology, that they are terrified of God . . . But you know, some of them don't mean any of these real-life dynamics when they use the word God.
Sister Lavender: Nope, all they mean is something to speculate about. Something to keep themselves busy wondering about.
(pp. 194–5)

It is a far cry from the transcendent Father-God of traditional theology to this divine spirit, energy, power, passion of women's theology, which is more focused on immanence and arises from our body selves and daily lived reality in the context of love and justice.

There is a sort of implicit as well as explicit religious feminist knowledge in a recent book by Quaker feminists in Britain, *Bringing the Invisible into the Light* (Quaker Women's Group 1986). Although very different in mood to *God's Fierce Whimsy*, it is similar in its sense of immanence and its political–ethical focus. The women speak of their experience in simple direct stories, very moving in their vulnerability and courage, stories praising Eve's adventurous, even dangerous, act of seeking wisdom, rediscovering the Gnostics' perception of the divine as female and male, stories of incest and wife-battering, of grieving for a still-born baby, of a woman finding she is lesbian and her surprise at being glad, of a lone mother, of sexist language, peace and war, of Greenham Common. They show the power of women's active love and presence as what Beverly Harrison calls 'radical moral creativity' (Harrison 1985, p. 10). Harrison claims that, contrary to what we have been taught, women have historically been active rather than passive: 'Though our culture has come to disvalue women's role, and with it to disvalue nurturance, genuine nurturance is a formidable power' (p. 10).

The action of women at Greenham Common is, I believe, a clear and visible expression of the power of feminist spirituality in our time, in confrontation with oppressive power. The women put their bodies on the line, as they put their 'ribbon and wool, flowers and photos' (Quaker Women's Group 1986, p. 95) on the fence, to confront the US military [illegible]en's action is not always so dramatic or so visible, but it [illegible]erful. As Harrison says, 'Because we do not understand love [illegible]r to act-each-other-into-well-being we also do not understand [illegible]f our power to thwart life and to maim each other. The fateful [illegible]rs' (1985, p. 11). At Greenham the risks of an ethic of radical love [illegible]rturance are evident in its clear challenge to those in power and its threat to the status quo. Radical love, as Harrison says, 'is a dangerous and serious business' (p. 19).

At Greenham, of course, many of the women are not Christian, but it is perhaps the most powerful expression of the energy and passion of feminist spirituality in Britain. Writing about Christian feminism in Britain in *A Map of the New Country: Women and Christianity* (1983), Sara Maitland suggests that Christian women are drawing their inspiration from the secular women's movement. Speaking of the church, she says that 'feminist theology and perspectives have not really got off the ground yet' (p. 104). Women are, however, beginning to form 'small, unstructured, totally autonomous groups' which, with their warmth, caring, and sisterhood, are presenting a challenge and a model for change to the institutional church. A deep struggle is taking place for ordination of women, but even there Maitland sees 'an apparent willingness to court co-option and eliminate a more radical and feminist critique of the church' (p. 109). Maitland herself develops a sustained critique of many aspects of the church, and she and other writers, such as Monica Furlong and Rosemary Haughton, explore spirituality, ethics, and theology in relation to women, but the old forms have a deep strength in Britain and change is difficult without a deeper and more widely accepted feminist analysis of church sexism.

Telling stories has always been the main way in which religious knowledge is presented and passed on, and this process is quite powerfully 'blowing in the wind' now in such immediate real-life stories as those in the Quaker anthology just mentioned, as well as in novels such as Alice Walker's *The Color Purple* (1982), appearing simultaneously on newsstands and in theological schools, and New Zealander Keri Hulme's *The Bone People* (1983). The classic analysis and creation of both a story and storytelling in relation to feminist theology is Judith Plaskow's 'The Coming of Lilith' in *Womanspirit Rising* (1979). 'We took Lilith for our heroine', says Plaskow, 'and yet, most important, not Lilith alone. We try to express through our myth the process of our coming to do theology together. Lilith by herself is in exile and can do nothing. The real heroine of our story is sisterhood, and sisterhood is powerful' (pp. 205–6). Lilith, of course, is Adam's first wife. She doesn't like being ordered around so leaves Adam and the Garden. Eve is created and eventually finds out about Lilith and climbs over the wall to see her. 'They taught each other many things, and told each other stories, and laughed together, and cried, over and over, till the bond of sisterhood grew between them.' And later,

'God and Adam were expectant and afraid the day Eve and Lilith returned to the garden, bursting with possibilities, ready to rebuild it together' (p. 207). Storytelling and sisterhood, telling our own stories to each other, remain the basis for feminist theologizing, oral, written, and academic.

(3) WOMEN'S SPIRITUALITY

> The ascending archetypal symbols of the feminine unfold today in the psyche of modern Every woman. They encompass the multiple forms of the Great Goddess. Reaching across the centuries we take the hands of our Ancient Sisters. The Great Goddess alive and well is rising to announce to the patriarchs that their 5,000 years are up – Hallelujah! Here we come
>
> Mary Beth Edelson (1976)

> Our destiny is rather to generate the divine in us and between us.
>
> Luce Irigaray (1986, p. 3)

> I notice that I cannot believe what I know.
>
> Christa Wolf (1984, p. 78)

> I think it pisses God off if you walk by the color purple in a field somewhere and don't notice it.
>
> Alice Walker (1982, p. 167)

Spirituality is concerned with who we are – in our body selves, in relation to others, to nature, the earth, and the cosmos, and to the energy or spirit that is in and among us in those relationships. It is not a disembodied or spiritualized affair, somewhere out of this world, but very much in and of this world, our daily living and our personal, social, and political relationships. It is about power. It comes from the Latin word for breath – it is as close as our breathing, and like the wind it 'bloweth where it listeth'. It links us all in the cosmic dance.

In the Judaeo-Christian tradition, as we have seen, this complex of relationships is organized in a patriarchal way, and Jewish and Christian feminists are involved in a deep political/spiritual struggle to transform that tradition into one that empowers women and brings people of all races, classes, and social groupings into a relation of justice and mutuality with each other and the earth. Since it is in terms of this Judaeo-Christian tradition that western cultures for the most part find their religious expression, it is crucial for women (and not only women) that it be transformed and its destructive power ended. Some women are in that struggle and there tends to be something heroic about it – about Daly and Ruether and some of the women in *God's Fierce Whimsy*.

There is another kind of women's spirituality which is not heroic in any grand sense, although it is still political and courageous. It involves finding the divine in ourselves, in our body truth, in the 'small places' of our lives, our daily pleasure and work, our relationships, away from inflated egos and ambitions. It involves being centred in your own body, perhaps through meditation or yoga, being aware of and affirming yourself as part of the living, breathing universe. Transcendence in this spirituality comes through immanence, the body, the here and now, being in touch with the spirit within nature and history, not rising above them to some other realm. For women to assume their own autonomy in this way is possible, of course within Christianity, but only in an oppositional way, in which we constantly reinterpret the male symbols (Father, Son, etc.), the devaluing and silencing of women, the ethic of masochistic self-sacrifice and putting others before self. Women need, and are claiming, a more direct connection with the divine.

Women's spirituality casts a very wide net and links up with other religions such as Buddhism, Hinduism, and Sufism (although these too have their patriarchal forms), and also with other disciplines such as healing, psychology, drama, poetry, art. It finds expression in a multitude of different ways and is often not named as spiritual. The phenomenon of women's spirituality is however becoming so widespread that it is increasingly recognized. In New York in 1973 I saw Ntosake Shange's Broadway play *For Colored Girls Who Have Considered Suicide When the Rainbow Is Enuf*. At the end the group of women on stage move to touch the one in the centre who has told her horrific story. The action moves from horror to silence, touch, nurture, and a gradual sense of communal power. As the song 'i found god in myself & i loved her/i loved her fiercely' gathered momentum, the whole audience joined in and got up and danced in an incredible release of energy and ecstatic power. In Sydney in 1978 *The Awful Truth Show* created with a comic buoyancy a similar sense of women's presence to each other, an example, I believe, of the 'arrival of female presence' which Mary Daly describes as the 'Second Coming', and there was the same eruption of ecstatic energy and song. It comes from the release of a truth which, though long silenced, is still deeply known.

Because of the way women are defined in traditional religion, our spiritual consciousness tends to go underground and women rarely admit it publicly or even to themselves. In the women's movement in Australia in particular, because the church has been so inimical to women's autonomy women have seen all religion as destructive and it was only in the late 1970s that women's spiritual consciousness began to find tentative public expression. In 1985 Ryl Currey spoke to about 500 women in Victoria 'to find out if spirituality is a normal part of human functioning' (Currey 1985, p. 3). In a wide variety of groups she asked one question, 'what are you living for?', and that was followed by general discussion. Currey found that the churches are not, on the whole, offering women any valid means of

expressing their spirituality. Women are not regarded as
contributing in a theological or spiritual way, even those wit
theology. Women's work and values, 'nurturing, loving, a
laterally and juggle 17 different thoughts and actions at once
either ignored or actively ridiculed. Currey says that 'what wo
to do is to follow through the consequences for themselves of attempting to genuinely care for people. If you do that openly and honestly for a number of years you have to eventually face the "black hole" and eventually your spirituality and God' (p. 5). Although they 'do not talk easily' (p. 10) about it, the women reveal a very varied and detailed awareness of their spirituality and its importance for them. Most of them said they couldn't talk to men about it and argued that with a few exceptions men couldn't cope with this sort of discussion.

Currey says, 'I had always doubted my own spiritual experiences, I realized, because so few spiritual writers (male) described what I feel as an *ordinary occurrence*. Many give it names and positions which make it seem rare and given only to saintly people . . . What to men seems mystical and totally out of the ordinary, is for women totally ordinary, totally normal' (p. 9).

It is interesting that the daily experience of the 'ordinary women' Currey interviewed leads them to a 'black hole' experience, similar to Daly's encounter with 'nothingness', and on to their own discovery of spirituality and the shy expression of it in their own words, information which Currey says was given 'carefully, thoughtfully, sensitively, emotionally, often painfully and passionately . . . Its truth is that it records what's happening' (p. 9). The pattern is the same as the one Carol Christ (Professor of Women's Studies and Religious Studies at San Jose State University) develops further in *Diving Deep and Surfacing* (1980), where she explores women's spiritual quest in the work of contemporary writers: Chopin, Atwood, Lessing, Rich, and Shange. Christ sees this quest as beginning in an *experience of nothingness* related to women's alienation from conventional religious solutions. This is often followed by an *awakening* in which the 'powers of being' are revealed, grounding women in a new sense of self and empowerment and a new orientation to the world. This may occur through *mystical identification* in nature or in community with other women, and is followed up by a *new naming* of self and reality which often reflects a new wholeness, overcoming dualisms and anticipating the integration of spiritual and social quests (pp.13–14).

By mysticism Carol Christ means 'a woman's direct experience of her grounding in the powers of being that sometimes, but not always, takes the form of identification between the self and the powers of being' (p. 19). Alice Walker gives a wonderful example of it in *The Color Purple*, where Shug says to Celie, 'My first step away from the old white man was trees. Then air. Then birds. Then other people. But one day when I was sitting quiet and feeling like a motherless child, which I was, it come to me: that feeling of being part of everything, not separate at all' (1982, p. 167). Christ points out that women's mystical experiences in some ways resemble and in some ways differ from those discussed by classical theorists. They are similar in being, to use William James's characteristics, ineffable (words can point to but not fully express them), noetic (they have a sense of illumination, revelation, or awakening), transient, and passive, which is interpreted by Christ as a male way of experiencing surrender of ego, which women see rather as a union or integration with the power or powers of being ('that feeling of being part of everything'). For women, mystical experience also involves and transforms the whole self, as Evelyn Underhill understood, but where Underhill separated the spiritual and the mundane, women's spirituality seeks now to overcome that split (Christ 1980, pp. 20–1).

For many women this direct experience of and union with or grounding in the powers of being occurs in nature. In Australia it is the bush, the land, the desert which provide not only the transient empowering mystical experiences but also a more long-term sense of our authentic selves grounded in our own power and the power of the universe. *Tracks* (1980) is Robyn Davidson's story of her 1,700 mile journey across the desert from Alice Springs west to the coast with four camels. After two years' preparation and all her goodbyes, she sets out:

> Around me was magnificence. Light, power, space and sun. And I was walking into it. I was going to let it make or break me . . . I felt like dancing and calling to the great spirit . . . I was seeing it all as if for the first time, all fresh and bathed in an effulgence of light and joy, as if a smoke had cleared, or my eyes been peeled, so that I wanted to shout to the vastness, 'I love you. I love you, sky, bird, wind, precipice, space sun desert desert desert'
>
> (p. 111)

Davidson also experiences the absence of the spirit, which is a big part of any religious life. Two weeks out she writes, 'It was all nice of course and even fun sometimes, but hey, where was the great clap of the thunder of awareness that, as everyone knows, knocks people sideways in deserts' (p. 136). And later,

> as I walked through that country, I was becoming involved with it in a most intense and yet not fully conscious way. The motions and patterns and connections of things became apparent on a gut level . . . When this way of thinking became ordinary for me, I too became lost in the net and the boundaries of myself stretched out for ever . . . It is not a mystical experience, or rather, it is dangerous to attach these

> sorts of words to it. They are too hackneyed and prone to misinterpretation . . . It is something that happens, that's all.
>
> (pp. 195–6)

For many Australian women the strongest experience of this kind has been in relation to communal political activity such as the protest actions against US bases at Pine Gap, against uranium mining at Roxby Downs, and the Anzac Day marches mourning all women raped in all wars everywhere. There are many such occasions, big or small, risky or celebratory, when women take a stand for our commitments. These actions involve participation in a confrontation of values where women put their bodies on the line for a just, peaceful, nurturing, life-affirming world, against war-making, injustice, rape of women and the earth. Even in moments of risk and danger women say 'I feel right, and at peace. It is good to be doing this.' There is often an overwhelming sense of union with the powers of being and justice and love. It is undoubtedly a spiritual experience, in Carol Christ's terms a mystical experience, although many women would be very uncomfortable with those words and I have no wish to impose them on women who reject them. As at Greenham Common, the power transforms lives and spreads round the world.

Janice Raymond refers to this difference between those who see something as spiritual and those who don't as 'not a disagreement of fact but an incommensurate way of experiencing' (1986, p. 213; the words are from Mary Catherine Bateson). Raymond says the 'transcendent possibilities of female friendship may be viewed as illusion or as "really real" ', but she is clear that her own vision of female friendship is 'spiritual and religious'. Her book is a passionate and critical analysis of Gyn/affection and female friendship, which for her include but are not equated with lesbianism. Raymond does not essentialize or sentimentalize female friendship, but she sees it as providing women with 'a culture that has a vitality, elan, and power of its own'; she argues that 'Female friendship gives depth and spirit to a political vision of feminism and is itself a profoundly political act. Without Gyn/affection, our politics and political struggles remain superficial and more easily short-circuited' (p. 29). Raymond goes on to say, 'My vision of Gyn/affection sees female friendship as having revelatory power and as a realization of transcendence which creates for women ever-new possibilities of this-worldly existence. The "Other-worldly" power of female friendship revitalizes the power of women together in the real material world of female life and living' (p. 213).

The most powerful and clear-sighted expression of the spiritual dimension of women together is in the poetry of Adrienne Rich. The experience she points to as the basis for our 'new naming' is the deep meeting between two women: 'eye to eye / measuring each other's spirit, each other's / limitless desire, / a whole new poetry beginning here' (1978, p. 76). As well as lesbian love, she celebrates the joy, pain and power of many other relationships between women – mother/daughter, sisters, friends, and women working or exploring together – as well as the possible choice of solitude. Her 'Dream of a Common Language' has already begun to be realized in the 'Yes' of the women mountain-climbers to each other as they experience their strength, and in the reverence for life and beauty of women who walk away from 'the argument and jargon in a room' and find value in the small treasures of daily life and nature and creativity.

In a different way Judith Plaskow affirms the 'yeah, yeah experience' of sisterhood, when a woman hears and affirms her own experience put into words by someone else. It is 'the process through which we come to be sisters . . . all the many individual moments of recognition and illumination through which I come to a new awareness of my situation and myself' (Christ and Plaskow 1979, p. 200). Plaskow sees the stages as analogous to the stages in a religious journey, but like Raymond sees that some women who share the experiences would not share the religious words (pp. 202–3).

Charlene Spretnak in *The Politics of Women's Spirituality: Essays on the Rise of Spiritual Power within the Feminist Movement* (1982) talks of 'women's elemental power' (p. xvii), which she connects with 'our power to form people from our very flesh and blood and then to nourish them from our breasts', 'the fact that we run on cosmic time, i.e. share the cycles of the moon'; and with 'many moments in a woman's life wherein she gains experiential knowledge, in a powerful body/mind union, of the holistic truths of spirituality' (p. xvii). Spretnak emphasizes that women perceive *connectedness* in life, and also the consciousness of oneness. Referring to 'reclaimed' menstruation, to the 'peaceful, expansive mindstate after orgasm, and to pregnancy, natural childbirth, and motherhood', Spretnak says 'the experiences inherent in women's sexuality are expressions of the essential, holistic nature of life on Earth; they are "body parables" of the profound oneness and interconnectedness of all matter/energy, which physicists have discovered in recent decades at the subatomic level . . . In a culture that honored, rather than denigrated such "body truth," the holistic realities would be guiding principles of ethics and structure' (p. xviii). Spretnak does not exclude men from such knowledge, since 'All minds contain all possibilities', but she concedes that 'women seem to have an elemental advantage' (p. xix). The magazine *WomanSpirit* presents celebrations and explorations and rituals of an amazing variety by women writers and artists about their bodies and their connectedness with nature and each other. Judy Chicago, in her art and writing, uses female imagery related to our bodies and sexuality to explore and express the reality of women's lives with a dimension of spiritual power.

The ancient religion of the Goddess

There is a great multiplicity of ways in which women's spiritual experience is being expressed and named. Some women have begun to organize these areas of experience into religious systems, the most developed of which are Goddess religion and Witchcraft. In some ways Merlin Stone laid the groundwork for the contemporary rediscovery of Goddess religion in *Paradise Papers* (1976), although Elizabeth Gould Davis, in her myth-making book *The First Sex*, had already put together a wealth of material from history, archaeology and myth showing that 'women's contribution to civilization has been greater than man's, and man has overlooked her long enough' (1972, p. 18). Stone writes about the Great Goddess, collecting fragments of information from many sources to reveal a 'vast and major religion, one that had affected the lives of multitudes of people over thousands of years' (Stone 1976, p. 14). The Goddess had different names in different areas – Ashtoreth in the Bible, Astarte in Canaan, the Queen of Heaven, Inanna, Nut, Amet, Istar, Isis, Asherah, Attar, Hathor, and many more. The earliest of the small female figurines, made of stone and bone and clay, sometimes called Venus figures, have been found from Spain to Russia and go back to Upper Palaeolithic times around 25,000 BC. Archaeologists connect these earliest finds with the later Goddess-worshipping societies in the Neolithic periods of the Near and Middle East (9,000–7,000 BC) when agriculture developed, and Goddess worship can be traced from then to historical times (3,000–2,000 BC) and then in written accounts up to AD 500 when Christian emperors of Rome and Byzantium closed down the last Goddess temples (Stone 1976, pp. 26–35). Goddess worship was practised from 25,000 BC to AD 500, whereas Noah only appeared in 2,400 BC, and Abraham, the first of the biblical prophets, in 1,800–1,550 BC. The changeover from Goddess worship to worship of a male god began with the Indo-European invasions about 4,000 BC (Gimbutas 1982, p. 23), so the period of Goddess worship in Europe is about five times longer than the timespan of biblical religion.

Much of the evidence for this knowledge has been obliterated and there continues to be huge resistance to it, partly because of the self-absolutizing nature of patriarchy. Also, much of the evidence has only recently been discovered, and the interpretations and hypotheses about it take varying lines. Nevertheless, the antagonism of patriarchal religion to Goddess religion is clear. It is still referred to as a 'cult' (the cult of Diana, but not the cult of Jesus), the religious practices are called 'fertility rites' and the revered priestesses are called 'temple prostitutes'. The Bible itself does not mention that the very widespread and deeply held religion it was challenging had a female deity. Ashtoreth is mentioned, though not as female, and the focus of enmity is her consort, Baal. The incredible battles between the Hebrews and the Goddess-worshipping people are described in the book of Joshua, with the fierce destruction by the Hebrews of the towns and temples and people and almost all the records of the Goddess worshippers. In breaking the huge silence about this long period of Goddess worship and its violent suppression, Stone and others are revealing the Judaeo-Christian tradition as constructed within history and their work is thus having a profoundly relativizing effect. The 'In the beginning' of Genesis is seen to be fairly recent compared with the much longer period of Goddess worship. Jahweh and the idea of male monotheism are de-absolutized, and alternatives become imaginable and possible.

Marija Gimbutas, Professor of Archaeology at UCLA, characterizes the Goddess-oriented societies of Old Europe (i.e. Europe before about 4,000 BC) as egalitarian, probably based in small theocratic kingdoms or city-states, with a queen-priestess as ruler. 'There was no ranking along a patriarchal masculine–feminine value scale as there was in Europe after the infiltration of steppe pastoralists, who introduced the patriarchal and the patrilinear system' (1982, p. 23). In Old Europe, 'the Goddess ruled absolutely over human, animal and plant life. The Goddess, not Gods, spontaneously generated the life-force and created the universe . . . The male god was an adjunct of the female Goddess, as consort or son' (p. 24). Females supervised the preparation and performance of rituals, baked the bread and wove the sacred garments, and made and decorated pots for different rites. The Goddess cannot be simplistically reduced to an Earth or Mother Goddess: 'the images of deities portray far more than the single maternal metaphor' (p. 27). Gimbutas says the shapes and symbols show they 'were intended to project a multiplicity of divine aspects and a variety of divine functions' (p. 27). She believes the two primary aspects of the Goddess presented are, first, as 'She Who Is the Giver of All and Taker of All', and second, 'Her association with the periodic awakening of nature: She is springtime, the new moon, rebirth, regeneration, and metamorphosis. Both go back to the Upper Palaeolithic (i.e. 25,000 BC)' (p. 28). Gimbutas lists many images associated with these aspects – snakes, fish, frogs, zigzags, meanders, spirals, eggs, phalluses, whirls, bees, butterflies, owls, crescents, horns, to name a few. Stone mentions as widespread such symbols as the serpent, the dove, and the double axe; the focus on the triple aspect of the Goddess, as a young woman, a woman giving birth, and an old woman; and also the relationship with the son/lover who dies and is mourned annually, the sacred sexual union, and the sexual customs of the temple.

In contrast, the invading steppe people, as Gimbutas describes them, were pastoralists. The chief tasks were done by men, the new ideology was an apotheosis of the horseman and warrior, and they made weapons rather than pottery or sculpture. Instead of sacred myths about the moon, water, and the female, the religion of the pastoralists had sky and sun gods and focused on sky phenomena such as thunder and lightning (pp. 30–1).

Some women believe that after its almost total suppression by AD 500, the Goddess religion went underground, appearing in the witchcraft or 'old religion' of the Middle Ages, and also in a drastically weakened form in the veneration of Mary, mother of Jesus. A similar weakening happened to words like virgin, which had previously meant a woman-for-herself, and now became defined in terms of sexual intercourse with men. Where pre-patriarchal sculpture and painting showed images of women expressing 'an attitude toward the female charged with awareness of her intrinsic importance, her depth of meaning, her existence at the very center of what is necessary and sacred' (Rich 1976, p. 93), later images of Mary in art often show her as sad, submissive, usually looking at her son rather than out at the world as the women in earlier images do.

Goddess religion today

Women who are interested in Goddess religion today do not wish to go back nostalgically to a bygone matriarchal fantasy world or an ancient authority pattern. Rather they are finding in the Goddess tradition a rich and usable symbol system which functions in many ways to give them access to their own power and identity. As Carol Christ points out in her essay 'Why Women Need the Goddess' (Christ and Plaskow 1979), 'Religious symbol systems focused around exclusively male images of divinity create the impression that female power can never be fully legitimate or wholly beneficent' (p. 275). But since symbols function at deep non-rational levels of the psyche, 'they cannot simply be rejected, they must be replaced' (p. 275). Otherwise the mind reverts to them at times of crisis. Many women who reject patriarchal religion find the Goddess symbols emerge, sometimes spontaneously, to fulfil a positive and important role. Christ shows how Goddess symbolism 'undergirds and legitimates the concerns of the women's movement, much as God symbolism in Christianity undergirded the interests of men in patriarchy' (p. 276). Recognizing that women have different views of the 'meaning' of this symbol, Christ suggests a new way of doing 'thealogy' (Naomi Goldenberg's word; 1979), where people's relation to a common symbol could be made primary, and varying interpretations acknowledged.

Of the many meanings of the Goddess, Christ chooses four to discuss: first, as a symbol of the 'legitimacy of female power as a beneficent and independent power' (p. 277), in stark contrast with the view of patriarchy that women are dependent beings and that women's power is inferior and dangerous; second, the affirmation of the female body and the life cycle expressed in it, its connections with cycles of nature, and acceptance of ageing and death as well as life; third, the positive valuation of will in a

Goddess-centred ritual, encouraging the assertion of individual will not in the arbitrary ego-centric way of patriarchy but in co-operation with natural energies and the energies created by the wills of others; and fourth, the celebration of women's bonds to each other, particularly the mother–daughter bond which is missing or distorted in Christianity and other patriarchal religions and culture because the mother must socialize her daughter to become subordinate to men. In the four areas, Christ says the 'mood' created by the symbol of the Goddess is one of positive joyful celebration and affirmation of female freedom and independence, of the female body and will, and of women's bonds to each other, as mothers and daughters, as colleagues and co-workers, as sisters, friends, and lovers. (pp. 277–86)

Witchcraft today

Starhawk approaches Goddess religion through Witchcraft, which, she says, takes its teachings from nature, not a set of beliefs or a sacred book, and is 'perhaps the oldest religion extant in the West' (1979, p. 2). She traces its history from the ice age 35,000 years ago, through the time of the witchburnings when nine million witches were executed, to its modern revival. Like Carol Christ she sees it as empowering for women: 'Through the Goddess we can discover our strength, enlighten our minds, own our bodies, and celebrate our emotions. We can move beyond narrow, constricting roles and become whole' (Starhawk 1979, p. 9). The symbolism of the Goddess is not a parallel structure to the symbolism of God the Father:

> The Goddess does not rule the world; She *is* the world. Manifest in each of us, She can be known internally by every individual, in all her magnificent diversity. She does not legitimize the rule of either sex by the other and lends no authority to rulers of temporal hierarchies. In Witchcraft, each of us must reveal our own truth. Deity is seen in our own forms, whether female or male, because the Goddess has her male aspect. Sexuality is a sacrament. Religion is a matter of relinking with the divine within and with her outer manifestations in all of the human and natural world.
>
> (p. 9)

Starhawk says the rise of Goddess religion makes some politically oriented feminists uneasy, but she claims it 'conveys the spiritual power both to challenge systems of oppression and to create new, life-oriented cultures' (p. 10). The ethic of Witchcraft is love for life in all its forms and respect for all living things. It does not foster guilt but demands responsibility: 'What you send, returns three times over' (p. 12). It seeks to overcome the dualisms of patriarchy by seeing them not as opposites but as polarities which are in balance, not at war. No one is damned or viewed as evil or scapegoated. The organization of Witchcraft is based on covens, autonomous groups of up to thirteen members, usually all women but sometimes including men, with total authority over what happens in the group. In *The Spiral Dance* Starhawk describes many rituals, spiritual exercises, spells, invocations, chants, and blessings which embody and impart their own knowledge in a way that cannot be experienced except through their actual enactment.

In a time when all religious language has become suspect to feminists, the language and symbols and rituals of Goddess religion and Witchcraft have been revived and appropriated by some contemporary feminists as a way of going outside patriarchal forms and language. Certainly, some women find through them a way towards empowerment, autonomy, and joy. Others believe there is something contrived and artificial about taking the language of these old religions and using it as a basis on which to construct a religious language and ritual for today. No doubt this is true, and although the wisdom embodied in these religions can still be enlightening and enriching, the language of spells and covens comes as a strange imposition on twentieth-century sensibilities and does not function directly as an organic religion growing out of our own culture. The symbol of the Goddess, too, remains a personification of the divine and in that sense is felt by some women to be limiting, a reversal of the objectifying male god symbol. Perhaps such outside triggers are needed if we are to break the patriarchal pattern. Many women find words like spirit, energy, divine power, acceptable ways of referring to the powers of being, life, death, regeneration, transformation that we experience in ourselves and our relations with others and with nature. As Carol Christ says, speaking of the forces of life and of death and destruction, 'It is not individuals, but the process of life transforming into death into life that is eternal – or seems so from a human perspective. The individual can gain a sense of transcendence from recognising participation in these larger life and death forces' (1980, p. 10).

CONCLUSION

In that participation, women need a language which is not patriarchal in order to express, and even to experience, our own experience. We do not yet have that new language, but as women struggle to transform the languages of traditional religions such as Judaism and Christianity, or to appropriate old religions such as Goddess religion and Witchcraft, or to find new ways of resolving this dialectic relation between language and our experience as women, there is emerging a detailed reflection on women's culture and experience in conversation and stories and theological writing from which knowledge of our religious selves is being glimpsed and shared.

Women are still strangers in a strange land, but that allows us a freedom to recognize the spirit among us.

A sign of women's freedom which breaks out in many stories and in groups of women together is laughter. Hélène Cixous (1981, pp. 42–3) tells the wonderful Chinese story of the king who commanded his general to train the king's wives, all 180 of them, to be soldiers. When the general taught them the language of the drum-beats, instead of learning the code the women started laughing. The more the general spoke, the more they fell about laughing. The code said that falling about laughing instead of becoming soldiers ought to be deemed mutinous and incur the death penalty. Because the king could not go back on an order, the two leading women had to be put to death. The general beheaded them. The other women learnt to be soldiers in silence and with no mistakes. So, under patriarchy, women lose their heads to the sword or to silence. Feminine disorder, its laughter, is submitted to the threat of decapitation. Cixous maintains, however, that women 'have it in them to affirm the difference, *their* difference' (p. 50). But for a woman to do this, 'first she would have to *speak*' (p. 50). The moribund religious patriarchy of today is beginning to be unsettled by what Cixous calls 'feminine disorder'. As she says, it is still risky for women to speak, to write, to set out into the unknown to look for ourselves. We may get our heads cut off. Many women are on the journey.

NOTES

1 See Ruether (1985a, pp. 111–16) for an elaboration of this view.

2 See Valerie Saiving's elaboration of this in her pioneering 1960 essay, where she argued that the ethical system of Christian obedience and self-giving love was constructed on the basis of male experience and could be destructive to women (Saiving 1979).

3 The danger of feminists adopting too narrow a focus has its parallel in the American woman's movement of the nineteenth century, when the focus on the vote was made at the expense of other issues. The work of Matilda Joslyn Gage, for example, was pushed aside, including her scholarly *Woman, Church and State: The Original Exposé of Male Collaboration against the Female Sex*, a work remarkable for its comprehensive and devastating attack on the church's oppression of women, and for the way it raises the whole range of issues of contemporary feminism. Sally Roesch Wagner claims that if Gage's broad view had won the day, 'We might not have had to start our movement over again from scratch' (Gage 1980. p. xxxix).

4 See Letty Russell (1985) for an indication of recent feminist hermeneutics. Feminist theologians and biblical scholars no longer try to make excuses for the Bible's sexism. Rather, they agree that is conceived and written by men from an androcentric perspective in a strongly patriarchal time and culture. They advise 'a stance of radical suspicion' (Sakenfeld 1985). As well as Ruether and Fiorenza, such scholars as Trible (1984) and Russell (1985) are doing fascinating and crucial work in hermeneutical method, and important biblical interpretation is being done from particular contexts, such as Cannon (1985) on the emergence of

black feminist consciousness, and Thistlethwaite (1985) on the relation of feminist interpretation to battered women. On the issue of authority, Farley (1985) and Tolbert (1983) demonstrate that interpretation is always finally a subjective activity. But although the canon is now de-absolutized, the paradoxical nature of the Bible for feminists, as a book of both liberation and oppression, remains.

REFERENCES

Cannon, K. G. (1985) 'The emergence of Black feminist consciousness', in L. M. Russell (ed.) *Feminist Interpretation of the Bible*, Blackwell, Oxford and New York.

Christ, C. P. and Plaskow, J. (eds) (1979) *Womanspirit Rising: A Feminist Reader in Religion*, Harper & Row, New York.

Christ, C. P. (1980) *Diving Deep and Surfacing: Women Writers on Spiritual Quest*, Beacon Press, Boston.

Cixous, H. (1981) 'Castration or decapitation?', *Signs* 7:11, pp. 41–55.

Currey, R. (1985) 'Report of a study of women's spirituality in Victoria, 1985' (draft copy).

Daly, M.(1968) *The Church and the Second Sex*, Harper & Row, New York.

Daly, M.(1973) *Beyond God the Father: Toward a Philosophy of Women's Liberation*, Beacon Press, Boston.

Daly, M. (1978) *Gyn/Ecology: The Metaethics of Radical Feminism*, Beacon Press, Boston.

Davidson, R. (1980) *Tracks*, Jonathan Cape, London.

Davis, E. G. (1972) *The First Sex*, Penguin, Baltimore, Md.

Edelson, M. B. (1976) 'Speaking for myself', *Lady Unique*, 1:56. Quoted in C. P. Christ and J. Plaskow (eds) (1979) *Womanspirit Rising: A Feminist Reader in Religion*, Harper & Row, New York, pp. 277–8.

Eisenstein, H. (1984) *Contemporary Feminist Thought*, Allen & Unwin, Sydney and London.

Farley, M. (1985) 'Feminist consciousness and the interpretation of scripture', in L. M. Russell (ed.) *Feminist Interpretation of the Bible*, Blackwell, Oxford and New York.

Fiorenza, E. S. (1983) *In Memory of Her: A Feminist Theological Reconstruction of Christian Origins*, Crossroad, New York.

Fiorenza, E. S. (1984) *Bread Not Stone: The Challenge of Feminist Biblical Interpretation*, Beacon Press, Boston.

Fiorenza, E. S. (1985) 'The will to choose or to reject: continuing our critical work', in L. M. Russell (ed.) *Feminist Interpretation of the Bible*, Blackwell, Oxford and New York.

Gage, M. J. (1980) *Woman, Church, and State: The Original Exposé of Male Collaboration Against the Female Sex*, Persephone Press, Watertown, Mass.

Gimbutas, M. (1982) 'Women and culture in Goddess-oriented Old Europe', in C. Spretnak (ed.) *The Politics of Women's Spirituality: Essays on the Rise of Spiritual Power within the Feminist Movement*, Anchor Books, New York.

Goldenberg, N. (1979) *The Changing of the Gods*, Beacon Press, Boston.

Harrison, B. W.(1985) *Making the Connections: Essays in Feminist Social Ethics*, Beacon Press, Boston.

Heyward, C. (1984) *Our Passion for Justice: Images of Power, Sexuality, and Liberation*, Pilgrim Press, New York.

Hulme, K. (1983) *The Bone People*, Spiral/Hodder & Stoughton, Auckland.
Irigaray, L. (1986) *Divine Women*, Local Consumption, Sydney.
Maitland, S. (1983) *A Map of the New Country: Women and Christianity*, Routledge & Kegan Paul, London.
Morton, N. (1985) *The Journey is Home*, Beacon Press, Boston.
The Mudflower Collective (1985) *God's Fierce Whimsy*, Pilgrim Press, New York.
Plaskow, J. (1979) 'The coming of Lilith: toward a feminist theology,' in C. P. Christ and J. Plaskow (eds) *Womanspirit Rising: A Feminist Reader in Religion*, Harper & Row, New York.
Quaker Women's Group (1986) *Bringing the Invisible into the Light: Some Quaker Feminists Speak of their Experience*, Quaker Home Service, London.
Raymond, J. (1986) *A Passion for Friends: Toward a Philosophy of Female Affection*, Women's Press, London.
Rich, A. (1976) *Of Woman Born: Motherhood as Experience and Institution*, W. W. Norton, New York.
Rich, A. (1978) *The Dream of a Common Language: Poems 1974–1977*, W. W. Norton, New York.
Ruether, R. R. (1972) *Liberation Theology: Human Hope Confronts Christian History and American Power*, Paulist Press, New York.
Ruether, R. R. (1973) 'Sexism and the theology of liberation: nature, fall and salvation as seen from the experience of women', in *The Christian Century*.
Ruether, R. R. (ed.) (1974) *Religion and Sexism: Images of Woman in the Jewish and Christian Traditions*, Simon & Schuster, New York.
Ruether, R. R. (1975) *New Woman, New Earth, Sexist Ideologies and Human Liberation*, Dove, East Malvern, and Seabury Press, New York.
Ruether, R. R. (1983) *Sexism and God-Talk: Toward a Feminist Theology*, Beacon Press, Boston.
Ruether, R. R. (1985a) 'Feminist interpretation: a method of correlation', in L. M. Russell (ed.) *Feminist Interpretation of the Bible*, Blackwell, Oxford and New York.
Ruether, R. R. (ed.) (1985b) *Womanguides: Readings Toward a Feminist Theology*, Beacon Press, Boston.
Ruether, R. R. (1985c) *Women-Church: Theology and Practice of Feminist Liturgical Communities*, Harper & Row, San Francisco.
Russell, L. M. (ed.) (1985) *Feminist Interpretation of the Bible*, Blackwell, Oxford and New York.
Saiving, V. (1979) 'The human situation: a feminine view', in C. P. Christ and J. Plaskow (eds) *Womanspirit Rising: A Feminist Reader in Religion*, Harper & Row, New York.
Sakenfeld, K. D. (1985) 'Feminist uses of biblical materials', in L. M. Russell (ed.) *Feminist Interpretation of the Bible*, Blackwell, Oxford and New York.
Shange, N. (1977) *For Colored Girls Who Have Considered Suicide When the Rainbow Is Enuf*, Macmillan, New York.
Spretnak, C. (ed.) (1982) *The Politics of Women's Spirituality: Essays on the Rise of Spiritual Power within the Feminist Movement*, Anchor Books, New York.
Starhawk (1979) *The Spiral Dance: A Rebirth of the Ancient Religion of the Great Goddess*, Harper & Row, New York.
Stone, M. (1976) *Paradise Papers: The Suppression of Women's Rites*, Virago and Quartet Books, London.
Thistlethwaite, S. B. (1985) 'Every two minutes: battered women and feminist interpretation', in L. M. Russell (ed.) *Feminist Interpretation of the Bible*, Blackwell, Oxford and New York.

Tolbert, M. A. (1983) 'Defining the problem: the Bible and feminist hermeneutics', *Semeia*: 28, pp. 113–26.
Trible, P. (1984) *Texts of Terror: Literary-Feminist Readings of Biblical Narratives*, Fortress Press, Philadelphia.
Tulip, M. (1978) 'The awful truth', *Magdalene*, 1978: 4, pp. 13–16.
Walker, A. (1982) *The Color Purple*, Women's Press, London.
Wolf, C. (1984) *Cassandra*, Virago Press, London.
Zikmund, B. B. (1985) 'Feminist consciousness in historical perspective', in L. M. Russell (ed.) *Feminist Interpretation of the Bible*, Blackwell, Oxford and New York.

FURTHER READING

Budapest, Z. (1976) *The Feminist Book of Lights and Shadows*, Luna Publications, Venice, Cal.
Chicago, J. (1975/1982) *Through the Flower*, Women's Press, London.
Collins, S. D. (1974) *A Different Heaven and Earth*, Judson Press, Valley Forge.
Daly, M. (1984) *Pure Lust: Elemental Feminist Philosophy*, Beacon Press, Boston.
Franklin, M. (ed.) (1986) *The Force of the Feminine*, Allen & Unwin, Sydney.
Franklin, M. and Jones, R. S. (eds) (1987) *Opening the Cage*, Allen & Unwin, Sydney.
Frye, M. (1983) *The Politics of Reality: Essays in Feminist Theory*, Crossing Press, New York.
Furlong, M. (1971/1984) *Travelling In*, Cowley Publications, Cambridge.
Furlong, M. (1975/1982) *Christian Uncertainties*, Cowley Publications, Cambridge.
Garcia, J. and Maitland, S. (eds) (1983) *Walking on Water: Women Talk about Spirituality*, Virago, London.
Gimbutas, M. (1974/1982) *The Goddesses and Gods of Old Europe*, Thames & Hudson, London.
Hall, N. (1980) *The Moon and the Virgin: Reflections on the Archetypal Feminine*, Women's Press, London.
Heresies (1978) 'The Great Goddess issue'.
Journal of Feminist Studies in Religion.
Kramer, H. and Sprenger, J. (1971) *The Malleus Maleficarum*, Dover, New York.
Lorde, A. (1984) *Sister Outsider*, Crossing Press, New York.
Magdalene (1973–87).
Mariechild, D. (1981) *Mother Wit: A Feminist Guide to Psychic Development*, Crossing Press, New York.
Morris, M. (1982/3) 'A-mazing grace: notes on Mary Daly's poetics', *Lip*, 7, pp. 30–41.
Neumann, E. (1955/1972) *The Great Mother: An Analysis of the Archetype*, Princeton University Press, Princeton, NJ.
Pagels, E. (1979) *The Gnostic Gospels*, Random House, New York.
Plaskow, J. (1980) *Sex, Sin, and Grace: Women's Experience and the Theologies of Reinhold Neibuhr and Paul Tillich*, University Press of America, Washington DC.
Quest (1975) 1:4, 'Women and spirituality'.
The Rippling Web, Womanspirit Connective, Adelaide.
Roe, J. (1986) *Beyond Belief*, New South Wales University Press, Kensington.
Signs (1976) 2:2; (1983) 9:1.
Skuse, J. (1985) *Feminism and Religion*, N.S.W. Women's Advisory Council, Sydney.

Stanton, E. C. (1895/1974) *The Woman's Bible*, Arno Reprint, New York.
Starhawk (1982) *Dreaming the Dark: Magic, Sex and Politics*, Beacon Press, Boston.
Stone, M. (1979) *Ancient Mirrors of Womanhood: Our Goddess and Heroine Heritage*, vols 1 and 2, New Sibylline Books, New York.
Thiering, B. (1973) *Created Second? Aspects of Women's Liberation in Australia*, Family Life Movement of Australia, Sydney.
Thiering, B. (ed.) (1977) *Deliver us from Eve*, Australian Council of Churches (N.S.W.) Commission on the Status of Women, Sydney.
Trible, P. (1978) *God and the Rhetoric of Sexuality*, Fortress Press, Philadelphia.
Trinity Occasional Papers (1984) 3:1, Issue on women in the Australian church.
Warner, M. (1976) *Alone of All Her Sex: The Myth and the Cult of the Virgin Mary*, Alfred A. Knopf, New York.
Womanspirit Magazine (1974–84).

Part IV

FEMINIST INTERVENTIONS

9

RADICAL FEMINISM: CRITIQUE AND CONSTRUCT

Robyn Rowland and Renate D. Klein

INTRODUCTION

This chapter is both a construction of Radical Feminism, and an implied critique. In writing it, we became acutely aware that because of its very nature, Radical Feminism has concentrated on creating its theory in the writing of women's lives and the political analysis of women's oppression. Little time has been devoted to defining and redefining our 'theory'. Where socialist, liberal, and semiotic feminism have convenient existing theoretical structures to manipulate and re-manipulate, stretching them like a skin across the drum of women's experiences, Radical Feminism creates a new political and social theory of women's oppression, and strategies for the end of that oppression, which comes from women's lived experiences.

So Janice Raymond writes her theory of women's friendships, their passion and the obstacles involved in befriending women. In doing so she critiques hetero-reality: the value system of women as being 'for' men, upon which patriarchy rests. Kathleen Barry, Catharine MacKinnon, Susan Griffin, and Andrea Dworkin explore the international sexual slavery trade, pornography, and woman-hating, thus creating their theories of the social control of women, women's bodies, our sexuality, and our lives.

Radical Feminists frequently combine creative writing and theory, such as in the poetry and prose of Adrienne Rich, Audre Lorde, Robin Morgan, Susan Griffin, and Judy Grahn. Here the passion of Radical Feminism can be fully expressed, because it is a theory of the emotional as well as the rational intellect.

Theory and practice are interdependently intertwined. Anne Koedt, Judith Levine, and Anita Rapone touched on this in their introduction to *Radical Feminism* in 1973 when they wrote: 'the purpose in selecting and organising this anthology was to present primary source material not so much *about* as *from* the Radical Feminist Movement' (our italics, p. viii). Radical means 'pertaining to the root'; Radical Feminism looks at the roots of women's oppression. As Robin Morgan says (1978, p. 9):

> I call myself a Radical Feminist, and that means specific things to me. The etymology of the word 'radical' refers to 'one who goes to the root'. I believe that sexism is the root oppression, the one which, until and unless we *up*root it will continue to put forth the branches of racism, class hatred, ageism, competition, ecological disaster, and economic exploitation. This means, to me, that the so-called revolutions to date have been coups-d'états between men, in a half-hearted attempt to prune the branches but leave the root embedded – for the sake of preserving their own male privileges.

Radical Feminism's revolutionary intent is expressed first and foremost in its woman-centredness: women's experiences and interests are at the centre of our theory and practice. It is the only theory *by* and *for* women. Radical Feminism names *all* women as part of an oppressed group, stressing that no woman can walk down the street or even live in her home safely without fear of violation by men. But French feminist Christine Delphy points out that like all oppressed people, many women do not like to accept that they are part of an oppressed group, developing various forms of denial in order to avoid identification.

Feminism itself has marginalized Radical Feminism, moving into a comfortable and easy libertarianism, stressing individualism rather than collective responsibility; or into socialism with its ready made structures to attack, withdrawing the heat from the main actors of patriarchy: men themselves.

More than ten years after the publication of *Feminist Practice: Notes From the Tenth Year* (1979) – a self-published pamphlet by a group of English Radical Feminists – many of the comments about the place of Radical Feminism still ring true (p. 1)

> We are all agreed that we would call ourselves Radical Feminists and that we want to do something about the fact that we feel our politics have been lost, have become invisible, in the present state of the WLM [Women's Liberation Movement]. We feel that this was partly Radical Feminism's own fault, for in England we have not written much for ourselves – concentrating on action – and so being defined (maligned?) by others by default.
>
> We feel that Radical Feminism has been *a*, if not *the*, major force in the WLM since the start, but as factions started to emerge it has rarely been women who called themselves radical feminists who have defined radical feminism. For a long time it was used as a term of abuse to corral those aspects of WL which frightened those concerned with male acceptability, those aspects which most threatened their image of respectability. Radical Feminists became a corporate object of derision which these women and men could then dissociate themselves from.

We do not intend here a history of Radical Feminism as space does not permit it. But our generation was not the first to see where the enemy of women worked and slept and how they upheld their dominance over women. For example, Hedwig Dohm in Germany, Susan B. Anthony, Matilda Joslyn Gage, and Charlotte Perkins Gilman in the US, Christabel Pankhurst (before her socialism) and Virginia Woolf in England, and Vida Goldstein in Australia are but a few of our predecessors.[1] And in November 1911, a Radical Feminist review, *The Free Woman*, began publishing weekly as a forum for revolutionary ideas about women, marriage, politics, prostitution, sexual relations, and issues concerning women's oppression and strategies for ending it. It was banned by booksellers, and many suffragists objected to it because of its critical position on their obsession – 'feminism is the whole issue, political enfranchisement a branch issue' they wrote (in Tuttle 1986, p. 117).

Radical Feminism embraces a variety of positions, and is constantly developing, changing and expanding, thus defying attempts to label and neatly categorize it. We cannot make the definitive statement, but we will outline its essence, influenced no doubt by our own values and political positions as Radical Feminists.[2]

DEFINITIONAL STATEMENTS FROM RADICAL FEMINISM

As space is limited, we choose to concentrate on the general principles shared by the various streams within Radical Feminism rather than on the differences between them. The first and fundamental theme is that women as a social group are oppressed by men as a social group and that this oppression is the *primary* oppression for women. Patriarchy is the oppressing *structure* of male domination. Radical Feminism makes visible male control as it is exercised in every sphere of women's lives, both public and private. So reproduction, marriage, compulsory heterosexuality, and motherhood are primary sites of attack and envisaged positive change.

Robin Morgan catches the excitement of Radical Feminism in her definition in *Going Too Far* (1978, p. 13).

> it wasn't . . . a wing or arm or toe of the Left – or Right – or any other male-defined, male-controlled group. It was something quite Else, something in itself, a whole new politics, an entirely different and astoundingly radical way of perceiving society, sentient matter, life itself, the universe. It was a philosophy. It was immense. It was also most decidedly a real, autonomous Movement, this feminism, with all the strengths that that implied. And with all the evils too – the familiar internecine squabbles.

A second central element characteristic of Radical Feminism is that it is created by women for women. Christine Delphy points out that people from the Left for example, are fighting on behalf of someone else, but that (1984, p. 146)

> the contradictions which result from this situation are foreign to feminism. We are not fighting for others, but for ourselves. We and no other people are the victims of the oppression which we denounce and fight against. And when we speak, it is not in the name or in the place of others, but in our own name and in our own place.

Radical Feminism stresses that 'emancipation' or 'equality' on male terms is not enough. A total revolution of the social structures and the elimination of the processes of patriarchy are essential. In her paper published originally in 1979 titled 'I Call Myself a Radical Feminist' British writer Gail Chester outlined her position, clearly defining herself as 'active in and believing in the need for, a strong, autonomous, revolutionary movement for the liberalisation of women' (p. 12). To her Radical Feminism is both socialist in its intent and revolutionary.

Mary Daly defines Radical Feminism in terms of the selfhood of women. Reclaiming and remaking language she exhorts women to take their true Selves back, and become self-acting, self-respecting. In *Gyn/Ecology* (1978), she calls Radical Feminism a 'journey of women becoming' (p. 1). Mary Daly has a unique style in which she reworks language for Radical Feminist purposes. Her work is impassioned, poetic and deals with spiritual dimensions. She sees the Radical Feminist task as changing consciousness, rediscovering the past and creating the future through women's radical 'otherness'. In her own words (p. 39): 'Radical Feminism is not reconciliation with the father. Rather it is affirming our original birth, our original source, movement, surge of living. This finding of our original integrity is re-membering our Selves.'

In the introduction to the first issue of the French feminist journal *Questions Feministes* (1977) – a journal of Radical Feminist theory – the editors identify their political perspective as Radical Feminist, recognizing that the political struggle they are involved in is that against 'the oppression of women by the patriarchal social system' (p. 5). They outline some of the underlying principles of Radical Feminism: the refusal to accept the projection of 'woman' as existing outside of society; the notion that the social existence of men and women was created rather than being part of their 'nature'; women claim the right not to be 'different' but to be 'autonomous'; a definition of a materialist approach to analysing women's oppression based on the fact that 'all women belong to the same social class' (p. 7).

That women form a social class is an inherent part of Radical Feminism. Ti-Grace Atkinson wrote in 1974 that: 'The analysis begins with the feminist *raison d'être* that women are a class, that this class is political in nature, and that this political class is oppressed. From this point on, Radical Feminism separates from traditional feminism' (p. 41). She saw the 'male/female system' as 'the first and most fundamental instance of human oppression', adding that 'all other class systems are built on top of it'. She writes (p. 73):

> Women will not be free until all oppressed classes are free. I am not suggesting that women work to free other classes. However in the case of women oppressing other women, the exercise of class privilege by identification in effect locks the sex class into place. In identifying one's interests with those of any power class, one thereby maintains the position of that class. As long as any class system is left standing, it stands on the backs of women.

In the Introduction to *Feminist Practice: Notes from the Tenth Year* (1979), the principles of women's liberation were clearly delineated. From this manifesto we can pull together some common threads: Radical Feminism insists that women as a social class or a social group are oppressed by men as a social group as well as individually by men who continue to benefit from that oppression and do nothing to change it; the system through which men do this has been termed patriarchy; Radical Feminism is women-centred and stresses both the personal as political and the need for collective action and responsibility; it is 'power' rather than 'difference' which determines the relationship between women and men. And finally, that 'whatever we do we mean to enjoy ourselves while we do it'.

THEORY AND PRACTICE

Because the theory is based in the experience of women's lives, it is part of the value system of Radical Feminism that 'the personal is political'. In Gail Chester's words (1979, p. 13): 'Radical Feminist theory is that theory follows from practice and is impossible to develop in the absence of practice, because our theory is that practising our practice is our theory'.

Misunderstandings have occurred because critics claim that Radical Feminism has rejected theory. But it has always maintained that we *do* need theory for understanding women's experiences, for evaluating the causes of women's oppression, and for devising strategies for action. But we *have* rejected theory which is too esoteric, too divorced from the reality of women's experiences, too inaccessible to the majority of women whom feminism is supposed to serve.

Chester argues that Radical Feminist theory has not been recognized as 'a theory' because it hasn't always been written down (p. 14): 'If your theory is embodied in your practice, then the way you act politically has as much right to be taken as a serious statement of your theoretical position as writing it down in a book which hardly anybody will read anyhow'.

Charlotte Bunch has written that theory is not 'simply intellectually interesting', but that it is 'crucial to the survival of feminism'. It is not an academic exercise but 'a process based on understanding and advancing the activist movement' (1983, p. 248). To this end, Radical Feminist theory is not an objective exercise, disengaged from women themselves. A theory which begins with women, places women and women's experiences at the centre, and names the oppression of women, involves a holistic view of the world, an analysis which probes every facet of existence for women. It is not, as Bunch indicates, a 'laundry list of "women's issues" ', but 'provides a basis for understanding every area of our lives . . . politically, culturally, economically, and spiritually' (1983, p. 250).

Bunch cautions Radical Feminists against becoming tired and feeling that feminist theory is too slow in bringing about change. At these times 'feminists are tempted to submerge our insights into one of the century's two dominant progressive theories of reality and change: democratic liberalism or Marxist socialism' (p. 250). Bunch argues that while feminism can learn from both of these streams of theory, it must not become embedded within them or too tied to them because our view of the world is an alternative view which is autonomous and women-centred.

For her, theory 'both grows out of and guides activism in a continuing, spiralling process' (p. 251). It can be divided into four interrelated parts: a description of what exists and the naming of reality; an analysis of why the reality exists and the origin of that oppression; determining what should exist in a vision for the future; and strategies on how to change that reality (pp. 251–3).

An example of the coalescence between theory and practice is the development of collective action. Through collectives Radical Feminists strive to eliminate the concepts of hierarchy which place power in the hands of a few over the many. They are attempts to work in a collaborative fashion towards a common goal, giving value to each woman, allowing her a voice, yet making all members collectively responsible for action.

A theory which grounds itself in the understanding of the basic violence of men towards women also energizes activism at the point where women need most help, for example within the Rape Crisis Centre Movement and the Women's Refuge Movement. Grassroots organizing at the level of women's daily existence and survival stresses the ongoing struggle against patriarchal violence. It also stresses the belief that in every day of our lives women can make an inroad into the destruction of negative self-image and negative life experience which male-dominated society hands to us. So the revolution takes place every day not in an unimagined future. In Gail Chester's words (1979, pp. 14–15):

> Because Radical Feminists do not recognise a split between our theory and practice, we are able to say that the revolution can begin now, by us taking positive actions to change our lives . . . it is a much more optimistic and humane vision of change than the male-defined

notion of the building towards a revolution at some point in the distant future, once all the preparations have been made.

PATRIARCHY

Radical Feminists have been wrongly accused of developing a 'conspiracy theory' with its intimations of paranoia. This political strategy is intended to reduce and oversimplify the Radical Feminist analysis of male power. Ironically however, patriarchy as a concept is now used by all forms of feminism, and socialist feminists in particular struggle to make it 'marry' with socialism. (See, for example, Sargent 1981.)

Patriarchy is the domination of men over women. Kate Millett's early work (1971) is a good example of the approach that 'sex is a status category with political implications'. Male power, that is patriarchy, dominates over class, religion, race, and culture, though it appears in varied forms at different historical periods. Millett explored this enforcement of male power through ideology, biology, myth, the family, economic and educational opportunities, and through the use of force by men. Shulamith Firestone's analysis (1970), on the other hand, placed more power on biology and the entrapment of women through their reproductive ability. If that trap was removed, she argued, women would have greater opportunities for equality.

Patriarchy is a universal value system, though it exhibits itself in different forms culturally and historically.[3] Ruth Bleier defines it thus (1984, p. 162):

> By patriarchy I mean the historic system of male dominance, a system committed to the maintenance and reinforcement of male hegemony in all aspects of life – personal and private privilege and power as well as public privilege and power. Its institutions direct and protect the distribution of power and privilege to those who are male, apportioned, however, according to social and economic class and race. Patriarchy takes different forms and develops specific supporting institutions and ideologies during different historical periods and political economies.

Patriarchy is a system of structures and institutions created by men in order to sustain and recreate male power and female subordination. Such structures include: institutional structures such as the law, religion, and the family; ideologies which perpetuate the 'naturally' inferior position of women; socialization processes to ensure that women and men develop behaviour and belief systems appropriate to the powerful or powerless group to which they belong.

The *structures* of patriarchy which have been established in order to maintain male power have been clearly analysed by Radical Feminists. *Economic* structures have been dealt with in books by, for example, Lisa

Leghorn and Katherine Parker (1981). Hilda Scott (1984) clearly demonstrates the increasing feminization of poverty. *Political, legal*, and *religious* structures are dominated by men who ensure that they maintain those positions. Women's right to vote is only a recent event historically. Within the legal profession, few women sit on the higher benches in the court system. Within the private domain of the *family*, marriage, and reproduction, men have structured a system whereby woman's reproductive capacity leaves her vulnerable and powerless, domestically exploited, and entrapped in economic dependence.

Patriarchal *ideology* maintains these structures. The family is maintained through the concept of romantic love between men and women, when in fact marriage contracts have traditionally had an economic base. Women's labour within the family, which has been unpaid and unacknowledged, and which includes the emotional servicing of members of the family as well as their physical servicing, continues to be defined as a 'labour of love'. Men have managed to create an ideology which defines men as the 'natural' owners of intellect, rationality, and the power to rule. Women 'by nature' are submissive, passive, and willing to be led. Processes such as the socialization of children encourage this situation to continue. So, for example, in playground games, boys soon learn that they are to act and girls to create an 'audience' for male performance.

The construction of the *family* and of the economic dependence of women on men also interrelates with the ideology of hetero-reality and the structures of heterosexuality. Adrienne Rich (1980) has analysed the compulsory nature of heterosexuality and its function as a political institution. She argues that men fear that women could be indifferent to them and that 'men could be allowed emotional – therefore economic – access to women *only* on women's terms' (p. 643). The compulsory nature of heterosexuality defines men's access to women as natural and their right.

In a broader analysis Janice Raymond (1986) has created the term hetero-*reality*, that is the belief that in our world woman is created *for* man. Hetero-reality determines that the single woman is defined as 'loose' in the promiscuous sense. So the state of being free and unattached with respect to men is translated into the negative state of being available to any man.

The patriarchal system operates to maintain the unequal power balance between women and men by using language and knowledge to construct definitions of masculine and feminine behaviour which support the established power imbalance. Dale Spender has addressed these issues through her analysis of language, showing how men have constructed and controlled language in order to reinforce women's subordinate position. She is also reclaiming 'women of ideas' historically and the knowledge that they have created. Spender shows the continuity of women's resistance to patriarchy and the constancy of the men's elimination of them from the record of knowledge. In *Women of Ideas and What Men Have Done to Them* she writes (1982, p. 5):

> I have come to accept that a patriarchal society depends in large measure on the experience and values of males being perceived as the *only* valid frame of reference for society, and that it is therefore in patriarchal interests to prevent women from sharing, establishing and asserting their equally real, valid and *different* frame of reference, which is the outcome of different experience.

Spender stresess that men have controlled knowledge and therefore made women invisible in the world of ideas. Structures within patriarchy are established in order to maintain the view that there is no problem with the fact that men are more powerful than women. As she says (1982, p. 7): 'Patriarchy requires that any conceptualisation of the world in which men and their power are a central problem should become invisible and unreal. How could patriarchy afford to accept that men were a serious problem?'

Patriarchy also has a material base in two senses. First, the economic systems are structured so that women have difficulty getting paid labour in a society which values only paid labour and in which money is the currency of power. Women without economic independence cannot sustain themselves without a breadwinner. They cannot leave a brutal husband, they cannot withdraw sexual, emotional, and physical servicing from men, they cannot have an equal say in decisions affecting their own lives, such as where they might live. Radical Feminism has therefore stressed the necessity for women to exercise economic power in their own lives.

Women's oppression through unpaid domestic service in the home is primary in the patriarchal system of support. Christine Delphy, whose Radical Feminism stems from a Marxist base, argues that 'patriarchy is the system of subordination of women to men in contemporary industrial societies, that this system has an economic base, and that this base is the domestic mode of production' (1984, p. 18). This domestic mode of production is also a mode of consumption and circulation of goods. It differs from the capitalist mode of production because 'those exploited by the domestic mode of production are not *paid* but rather *maintained*. In this mode, therefore, consumption is not separate from production, and the unequal sharing of goods is not mediated by money' (1984, p. 18). Delphy argues that the analysis of women's oppression which places women in a traditional class analysis, is not adequate because it cannot account for the particular exploitation of unwaged women. Men are the class which oppresses and exploits women, which benefits from their exploitation.

The second material base which Radical Feminism names as crucial to the liberated existence of women is that of woman's body herself. Internationally, it is a woman's body which is the currency of patriarchy.

Kathleen Barry has shown in *Female Sexual Slavery* (1979) that the international traffic in women operates extensively in the social control of women. Women in marriage are seen to be 'owned' by their husbands and cannot bring a civil case of rape in most countries. Women's bodies are used in advertising and pornography alike, objectified and defined as 'other' and available for male use.

Men control the laws of reproduction, for example male parliaments and male-run pharmaceutical companies determine the forms of contraception available and the extent of their use.[4] Male-controlled governments determine women's access to safe abortion. Male law determines the civil powerlessness of women in bringing rape or incest charges against men. As Delphy notes (1984, p. 217) 'feminism, by imprinting the word oppression on the domain of sexuality, has annexed it to materialism'.

Men as a group enjoy the privileges of power. It is in their best interests to maintain the existing patriarchal system, and they have structured the world in order to maintain this unequal power imbalance, for example, in their structuring of pay inequality, and the sex-segregated work world. They need to maintain the unpaid labour of women; the emotional and physical servicing of women; the sense of being in control which they feel individually and collectively. A man exerts power over *all* women, and over *some* men. Men continue to do it because they need to live their emotional lives vicariously through women. And they control reproduction because they need to control procreation to ensure their genetic continuity – hence their recent attempts to develop new reproductive technologies and genetic engineering. They experience both a fear and an envy of women (O'Brien 1981; Rowland 1987).

Thus male power is maintained and defined through a variety of methods: through institutions within society, through ideology, through coercion or force, through the control of resources and rewards, through the politics of intimacy, and through personal power. The simplistic labelling of an analysis of patriarchy as 'conspiracy theory' conveniently allows critics of Radical Feminism to dismiss this analysis of women's oppression.

UNIVERSALITY: CLASS AND RACE ISSUES

Radical Feminism has been accused of a 'false universalism'; an unjustified assumption of female commonality (Eisenstein 1984). Indeed, Radical Feminism does see the oppression of women as universal, crossing race and culture boundaries, as well as those of class and other delineating structures such as age and physical ability. Radical Feminists make no apologies for that. Sexual slavery within marriage was an accusation of Christabel Pankhurst's in the nineteenth century in Anglo-Saxon England, and sexual slavery as a trade has been documented and traced by Kathleen

Barry (1979) in many countries in the twentieth century. We have been accused of ignoring difference – of being indifferent to difference. But Radical Feminism welcomes and *acknowledges* the diversity of women, while stressing our similarities and the differences between women and men.

The concept of sisterhood has been important within Radical Feminism, underlining a belief that to undermine male power women need to form a cohesive revolutionary group. Sisterhood is a moving and potentially radicalizing concept of united women. Sonia Johnson ran a historical campaign for the US Presidency in 1984 on a Radical Feminist platform. She writes (1986, p. 14): 'One of the basic tenets of Radical Feminism is that any woman in the world has more in common with any other woman – regardless of class, race, age, ethnic group, nationality – than any woman has with any man'.

In *Sisterhood is Global* (1984) Robin Morgan draws together contributions from feminists in seventy countries, the majority of which are Third World countries. She begins with a quote about the global position of women in the Report to the UN Commission on the Status of Women (p. 1): 'While women represent half the global population and one-third of the labour force, they receive one-tenth of the world income and own less than one per cent of world property. They also are responsible for two-thirds of all working hours'. Morgan then proceeds to draw together the commonality of women through the various feminist representations in the book. These include among many the following aspects which we will briefly summarize.

Two out of three of the world's illiterates are women, and while the general literacy rate is increasing, female illiteracy is rising. Only a third of the world's women have access to contraceptive information or devices. In the developing world women are responsible for more than 50 per cent of all food production. In industrialized countries women still are paid only one-half to three-quarters of men's wages. Most of the world's starving are women and children. Twenty million people die annually of hunger-related causes and one billion endure chronic undernourishment and poverty. The majority of these are women and children. Women and children constitute more than 90 per cent of all refugee populations. Women in all countries bear the double burden of unpaid housework in association with any paid work they do.

Many countries have stories of the invisibility of women's history. Everywhere women fight to control their own bodies. Organized patriarchal religion operates world-wide in order to maintain women in subservient positions. The right to safe abortion is under constant attack in most countries. Laws concerning marriage continue to militate against women's independence and freedom. The basic right to divorce has still to be won in many countries. Female sexual slavery is a constant issue, and this is particularly true in Asia and the Pacific. Violence against women through rape, pornography, and battery is a continuing global issue.

And the connections continue. Robin Morgan comments that the contributions in *Sisterhood is Global* cross cultures, age, occupations, race, sexual preference, and ideological barriers, and so does the Women's Liberation Movement itself. She speaks of the resistance shown in all countries to patriarchy, and the sense of solidarity and unity that the women express (1984, p. 19):

> Contributor after Contributor in this book contests a class analysis as at best incomplete and at worst deliberately divisive of women. Article after article attempts valiantly to not minimise the differences but to identify the similarities between and among women . . .
>
> Rape, after all, is an omnipresent terror to all women of any class, race, or caste. Battery is a nightmare of emotional and physical pain no matter who the victim. Labour and childbirth feel the same to any woman. A human life in constraint – such suffering is not to be computed, judged or brought into shameful competition.

Radical Feminism thus holds that women are oppressed primarily and in the first instance as *women*. But because of differences in our lives created by, for example culture and class, women experience that oppression differentially, and it expresses itself differentially. Radical Feminism has from the beginning striven to deal with such differences. As Susan Griffin remembers (1982, p. 11):

> And of course, we carried the conflicts and differences of society into our world. Within us there were working-class women, middle-class women, white women, women of colour, Jewish women, Catholic women, heterosexual and lesbian women, women with and without children. We had to learn to speak among ourselves not only about our shared oppression but about the different conditions of our lives, and like any movement, we have at times faltered over these differences, and quarrelled over the definition of who we are.

As early as 1969 there was a 'Congress to Unite Women' in which many of these issues were raised. In workshops women addressed the question 'how women are divided: class, racial, sexual, and religious differences'. Conclusions included the following (Koedt *et al.* 1973, p. 309):

> We will work with all women recognising that the uniqueness of our revolution transcends economic, racial, generational, and political differences, and that these differences must be transcended in action, the common interest of our liberation, self-determination and development of our political movement.
>
> All women are oppressed as women and can unite on that basis; however, we acknowledge that there are differences among women,

> male-created – of economic and social privilege, race, education, etc. – and that these differences are real, not in our heads. Such divisions must be eliminated. They can only be eliminated by hard work and concrete action, not by rhetoric.

In the late spring of 1971 there was a Radical Feminist conference in Detroit, USA. The many issues discussed there are outlined by Robin Morgan (1978). Among them were the difficulties of relationships with men, the difficulties about decisions concerning children and lesbianism. 'What about our ageism and older women? How can white feminists concretely support the growing feminism among minority women?' (p. 156).

In 1978, the problems of racial differences were discussed by Adrienne Rich in her prose piece 'Disloyal to civilization: feminism, racism, gynephobia' in which she writes about the separation of black and white women from each other and points out the difficulty and the pain and anger involved in these delineations. Rich acknowledges 'the passive or active instrumentality of white women in the practice of inhumanity against black people' (1979a p. 284). But she argues against what she calls the ludicrous and fruitless game of 'hierarchies of oppression' including the liberal guilt reflex on the part of women whenever racism is mentioned. There is danger, she argues, that guilt feelings provoked in white women can become a form of social control, paralysing rather than leading women to relate honestly to the nature of racism itself. She warns white women against the possibilities of colluding with white male power to the disadvantage of black women.

But as Bell Hooks (1984) points out, there are also cultural differences. She stresses the importance of learning cultural codes. She quotes an Asian American student of Japanese heritage who was reluctant to participate in feminist organizations because she felt feminists spoke rapidly without pause. She had been raised to pause and think before speaking and therefore felt inadequate in feminist groups.

This example raises the varieties of categorization which delineate different groups of women. Robin Morgan (1984) points out in her global analysis of the Women's Liberation Movement the many forms of division that can operate, including clanism, tribalism, the caste system, religious bigotry, and rural versus urban living. Looking at the various possible categories reminds us that racism itself is an ideology. As Rosario Morales, of Puerto Rican background, comments (1981, p. 91):

> everyone is capable of being racist whatever their colour and condition. Only some of us are liable to racist attack . . . *guilt* is a fact for us all, white and coloured: and identification with the oppressor and oppressive ideology. Let us, instead, identify, understand, and feel with the oppressed as a way out of the morass of racism and guilt.

The criticism that Radical Feminism has not dealt with class is mean to imply that we do not consider economics to be of importance, and that we do not understand the battle against capitalism. This is patently not true in the work for example, of Lisa Leghorn and Katherine Parker, and of French theorist Christine Delphy. But, as Delphy comments (1984, p. 147):

> but we materialist feminists, who affirm the existence of several – at least two – class systems, and hence the possibility of an individual having several class memberships (which can in addition be contradictory); we do think that male workers are not, as victims of capitalism, thereby absolved of the sin of being the beneficiaries of patriarchy.

The delineation of women as a class itself implies that men benefit in concrete and material ways from their oppression and exploitation of women. Whatever the political regime, it is women who do the unpaid domestic labour and men who gain from it. It is women who service sexually and emotionally.

Radical Feminism acknowledges that women experience their oppression differentially depending upon class. In the early 1970s, two members of the US collective The Furies published an anthology on *Class and Feminism* (Bunch and Myron 1974) in which Radical Feminist authors grappled with the problems engendered by class differences among feminists. Consistently since that time Charlotte Bunch has stressed a class analysis within Radical Feminism. In her words (1981a, p. 194):

> Women's oppression is rooted both in the structures of our society, which are patriarchal, and in the sons of patriarchy: capitalism and white supremacy. patriarchy includes not only male rule but also heterosexual imperialism and sexism; patriarchy led to the development of white supremacy and capitalism. For me, the term patriarchy refers to all these forms of oppression and domination, all of which must be ended before all women will be free.

In her discussion of sexuality she points out that there can be a breaking of class barriers among lesbians where 'cross-class intimacy' occurs. This is particularly true for middle-class women because

> lesbianism means discovering that we have to support ourselves for the rest of our lives, something that lower- and working-class women have always known. This discovery makes us begin to understand what lower- and working-class women have been trying to tell us all along: 'what do you know about survival?'
>
> (p. 71)

Again, the personal is *political*. Radical Feminists will not devote women's energy to the traditional socialist revolution, though we share some values in common, such as the oppressive nature of capitalism. We do not have faith that such man-made revolutions will ensure women's autonomy. Bonnie Mann analyses socialism in action in Nicaragua, pointing out the positive values inherent in the work of the Sandinista government and in the fact of such a revolution, but noting also that there are no known lesbians in Nicaragua and no safe abortion. She writes (1986, p. 54):

> But there is a lesson here that history teaches her radical feminist students who have long since rejected the ideological reduction of patriarchy to capitalism by the left, for those of us who know a socialist or communist revolution is not the answer to the global slave-status of women. The lesson is this: anything that strikes a blow to such a large root of suffering, of evil in this world, sends reverberations through the very foundations of patriarchal power. And these reverberations ring with the possibility of radical, lasting change.

WOMEN'S BODIES

Radical Feminism has stressed women's control of our bodies as essential to liberation. The issue has been dealt with in three primary ways; through the Women's Health Movement; through an analysis of the body as a primary site of women's oppression; and through a discussion of sexuality.

The women's health movement

As part of its analysis of the structures of patriarchy, Radical Feminism has argued that medicine is male-controlled, operating to control women socially to the detriment of our health. In the late 1960s the Women's Health Movement gathered momentum, developing since then in international scope with diverse approaches to women's health. It has revised the way women's health has been viewed, stressing self-help and prevention rather than a reliance on hi-tech, expensive, and dangerous technologies and drugs.

Radical Feminists argued for safe and freely available abortion and contraception. 'The right to choose' in the issue of abortion was a slogan which encapsulated the right of a woman to decide whether or not she wished to maintain a pregnancy and rear a child. Women of colour made us aware of the limitations of the concept of choice within this slogan by stressing that while white women were being controlled by their lack of access to abortion, black women were being controlled by constant sterilization without consent. The British anthology *No Turning Back* documents this (Feminist Anthology Collective 1981, p.145).

> Obviously, the fact that the black women are sterilised against their will while white women are finding it harder and harder to get abortions, is related to the attempts to limit the black population on the one hand, and to force white women out of paid employment on the other. A campaign around 'a woman's right to choose' must relate to the different needs and demands of all women and in so doing recognise that the problems of black women do not mirror those of white women.

The recognition that 'choice' has to be redefined has also led to the analysis of the way women in the Third World have dangerous contraceptive drugs dumped upon them, such as the increasing use of Depo-Provera, and the analysis of the way international aid is tied to such things as sterilization programmes for women (see Akhter 1987).

One of the landmarks of the Women's Health Movement was the initial revolutionary action of self-help gynaecology. In April 1971 in Los Angeles, Carol Downer showed women for the first time how to use a speculum to examine their own vagina and cervix and the bodies of other women. In these actions, women came to see for the first time inside themselves. They were no longer solely for the male medical gaze. These actions demystified women's bodies and made the gynaecological ritual more obvious in its humiliation of women. Ellen Frankfort remembers (1973, p. ix):

> I hate to use the word 'revolutionary', but no other word seems accurate to describe the effects of the first part of the evening. It was a little like having a blind person see for the first time – for what woman is not blind to her own insides? The simplicity with which Carol examined herself brought forth in a flash the whole gynaecological ritual; the receptionist, the magazines, the waiting room, and then the examination itself – being told to undress, lying on your back with your feet in stirrups . . . no–one thinking that 'meeting' doctor for the first time in this position is slightly odd.

The development of women's health centres was an essential part of this form of activism. The intention was to develop alternative health measures for dealing with some of the most common ailments that women suffer from, such as monilia and cystitis, with a focus on developing preventative procedures. And these were to be women-centred: services run *for* women, *by* women.

In 1969, when little information was available on women's health, the Boston Women's Health Collective put out the first edition of *Our Bodies,*

Ourselves which became a basic reference text for women all over the world. The second and third editions published in 1984 and 1985 have continued this tradition with an expanded view of women's health and the medical system which attempts to control it. Stressing preventative measures, and the need for women to understand how our bodies work, this book is an act of resistance against misogynist health care throughout the world.

Women's bodies as a primary site of women's oppression

More than any other theory of women's oppression, Radical Feminism has been unafraid to look at the violence done to women by men. It has shown that this violence to women's bodies and women's selves has been so intrinsic to patriarchal culture as to appear 'normal' and therefore justifiable. So rape, pornography, and sexual slavery affects one particular group of 'bad' women (see Barry 1979) and not other 'good' women. The message is that if women 'behave' they will be spared. This procedure not only ensures the intimidation of women in their daily behaviour, but splits women from each other, classifying one group of women as justifiably abused.

A large amount of empirical work has been done by Radical Feminists on sexual violence, documenting the evidence on rape (for example Susan Brownmiller 1975); incest (for example Elizabeth Ward 1984); pornography (for example Andrea Dworkin 1981; Susan Griffin 1981) and sexual slavery (Kathleen Barry 1979). There is no space here to deal with such an extensive body of work, but Kathleen Barry's work on female sexual slavery is an example of the development of Radical Feminist theory and practice.

Barry has documented sexual slavery on an international level (1979). She begins by tracing the original work carried out by Josephine Butler in the first wave of women's protest against sexual slavery in the nineteenth century. She then goes on to detail current practices of sexual slavery. For example, since 1979, agencies promoting sex tourism and mail-order brides have been operating in the US and many European countries. This amounts to the buying of women from Latin America and Asian countries: 'This practice, built upon the most racist and misogynist stereotypes of Asian and Latin American women, is a growing part of the traffic in women which is a violation of the United Nations conventions and covenance' (p. xiii).

Female sexual slavery is used to refer to the international traffic in women and forced street prostitution, which, as Barry amply shows, is carried out with the same methods of sadism, torture, beating, and so on which are used to enslave women internationally into prostitution. She looks behind the façade that intimates to us that the white slave trade ended in the nineteenth century. She points out that although there is a white slave trade in eastern countries, there is an Asian slave trade in western societies.

Barry resists the argument that prostitution is purely an economic exploitation of women. When economic power becomes the cause of women's oppression 'the sex dimensions of power usually remain unidentified and unchallenged' (p. 9). Touching again on the resistance even of feminists to deal with the sexual oppression of women in its raw form she writes (p. 10):

> Feminist analysis of sexual power is often modified to make it fit into an economic analysis which defines economic exploitation as the primary instrument of female oppression. Under that system of thought, institutionalised sexual slavery, such as is found in prostitution, is understood in terms of economic exploitation which results in the lack of economic opportunities for women, the result of an unjust economic order. Undoubtedly economic exploitation is an important factor in the oppression of women, but here we must be concerned with whether or not economic analysis reveals the more fundamental sexual domination of women.

She goes on to point out that people are justifiably horrified at the enslavement of children, but this has become separated from the enslavement of women. This process distorts the reality of the situation, implying that it is tolerable to enslave women but not tolerable to enslave children. She writes (p. 9): 'As I studied the attitudes that accept female enslavement, I realised that a powerful ideology stems from it and permeates the social order. I have named that ideology cultural sadism'.

Barry explores the economic reasons for the cover-up of the international trade of women and the basis of male power which is involved in it. She instances, for example, the INTERPOL analysis of sexual slavery which is conveniently hidden from public scrutiny. INTERPOL has prepared two comprehensive reports based on their own international surveys 'which they have suppressed' (p. 58). So in their 1974 report, contained in Barry's appendix, one of the conclusions is that 'the disguised traffic in women still exists all over the world' (p. 296).

Initially Barry herself had flinched from the task of unveiling the traffic in women. She talks about the difficulties of coming face to face with this raw brutality towards women, which includes the seduction of women into slavery by promises of love and affection, or the brutal kidnapping and forcible entry of women into prostitution and sexual slavery. But much as Radical Feminism has dealt with the horror of pornography, rape, and incest, Barry believes that for women it is important to know the truth about the sexual violence to women. Women have been bullied into denying that it exists. We have been forced into colluding in the secrecy of sexual violence to women. We are unable to bear the feeling of vulnerability which that gives to all women (p. 13):

> Hiding has helped keep female sexual slavery from being exposed. But worse than that, it has kept us from understanding the full extent of women's victimisation, thereby denying us the opportunity to find our way out of it through political confrontation as well as through vision and hope . . . knowing the worst frees us to hope and strive for the best.

As theory and practice are intertwined in Radical Feminism, Barry has been involved since 1980 with the establishment of the International Feminist Network Against Female Sexual Slavery which launched its first meeting in Rotterdam in 1983. From twenty-four countries women came to expose the traffic in women, forced prostitution, sex tourism, military brothels, torture of female prisoners, and the sexual mutilation of women. In each country the network operates collectively to deal with their specific culturally based problem areas. For example, the most effective work against sex tourism and the mail-order bride industry (which operates quite effectively between Australia and Thailand among other countries) has been done by Asian feminists, particularly the Asian Women's Association in Japan and the Third World Movement Against the Exploitation of Women in The Philippines. Again, this demonstrates the global perspective of Radical Feminism.

From the empirical work of women in the area of sexual violence has come the development of theories of what Barry calls 'sexual terrorism'. This terrorism she explains 'is a way of life for women even if we are not its direct victims. It has resulted in many women living with it while trying not to see or acknowledge it. This denial of reality creates a form of hiding' (p. 12). Radical Feminism will not collaborate in this blindness, but names and addresses the basic and primary violence done to women as a social group and to individual women at the level of their daily lives.[5]

Similar work is occurring within the area of the new reproductive technologies. Here, Radical Feminists are analysing the way patriarchal medicine again is sadistically brutalizing women's bodies in the name of 'curing' infertility. No preventative measures are offered. Little attempt is made to understand the causes of infertility. No analysis takes place of the structures which create the desperate desire to have children.

Radical Feminism names the alliance between commercial interests and reproductive technologists or 'techno-patriarchs' within the structures which currently wrench power from women in the procreative area. We refuse the naive political analysis which posits that it is possible for women to gain some control over these technologies, and that then it will be acceptable to use them. Our analysis shows that the technology is not value-free and is in itself sadistic in its abuse of women and their bodies. (See for example

Arditti *et al.* 1984; Corea 1985; Corea *et al.* 1985; Spallone and Steinberg 1987.)

Again, from this theoretical and empirical work has come the development of an international network, the Feminist International Network of Resistance to Reproductive and Genetic Engineering (FINRRAGE). Based on national regional groups working in a collective fashion, Radical Feminists are educating women at the grassroots level as well as working on political strategies in order to stop the control and abuse of women's bodies.

Sexuality

Because of the Radical Feminist analysis of the oppression of women through male sexuality and power, and because of the demand to take back our bodies, Radical Feminism has defined sexuality as political. The interrelationship between heterosexuality and power was named.

In 1982 Catharine MacKinnon argued that heterosexuality is the 'primary social sphere of male power' (p. 529) and that this power is the basis of gender inequality. It is to feminism what work is to Marxism – 'that which is most one's own yet most taken away' (p. 515). Heterosexuality is the structure which imposes this appropriation of woman's self, 'gender and family its congealed forms, sex roles its qualities generalised to social persona, reproduction a consequence, and control its issue' (p. 516).

It was within Radical Feminism that lesbian women began to demand their right to choose a lesbian existence. In a summary article first published in the *Revolutionary and Radical Feminist Newsletter*, no. 10, 1982, the London Lesbian Offensive Group expressed their anger at anti-lesbian attitudes within the movement and at heterosexual feminists because they:

> do not take responsibility for being members of an oppressive power group, do not appear to recognise or challenge the privileges which go with that, nor do they bother to examine how all this undermines not only our lesbian politics, but our very existence.
>
> (1984, p. 255).

When heterosexual feminists do not acknowledge their privileged position, lesbian women feel silenced and made invisible. The article outlines clearly the privileges which heterosexual feminists experience over lesbian feminists in spite of the real fact of the oppression of heterosexual women. For example, many have access to male money, they have the privilege of the assumptions of being considered 'normal' instead of 'deviant'. In short, they have automatic benefits by virtue of the fact that they are attached to a man.

Lesbian feminists suffer under the law in a variety of ways. Often they are not free to claim their lesbian lifestyle for fear of retaliation in the workplace, in terms of housing rights, in terms of being ostracized. In issues over custody of children, the battles for lesbian women are bloodier and more likely to fail (see, for example, Chesler 1986).

In retaliation for the oppression of lesbian women by heterofeminists, in 1979 the Leeds Revolutionary Feminist Group published a stinging attack. They accused women in heterosexual couples of shoring up male supremacy (p. 65): 'Men are the enemy. Heterosexual women are collaborators with the enemy . . . every woman who lives with or fucks a man helps to maintain the oppression of her sisters and hinders our struggle.' Part of the basic argument against heterofeminism is the argument that heterosexual women service male power and privilege. By directing their energy towards a specific man within the social group men, women's energy is once more taken from women and given to men.

Although there are substantial difficulties and dangers in being lesbian in a heterosexual world, the pleasures of living a lesbian existence were also clearly outlined in the Leeds article (p. 66):

> The pleasures of knowing that you are not directly servicing men, living without the strain of the glaring contradiction in your personal life, uniting the personal and the political, loving and putting your energies into those you are fighting alongside rather than those you are fighting against.

In an afterword which was added before republication in 1981, the Leeds group commented that this paper had been written for a workshop at a Radical Feminist conference in 1979. Some of their comments they later found to be offensive and inconsistent. For example, 'we now think that "collaborators" is the wrong word to describe women who sleep with men, since this implies a conscious act of betrayal' (p. 69).

For some women within the Women's Liberation Movement the issues of lesbianism and heterosexuality caused an irreparable split. For others, the debate increased their awareness, as did discussions around class and culture, about their own positions of privilege or oppression within the social group woman, and within feminism itself. Some lesbian feminists moved to develop an analysis of the position of lesbian feminism within the Women's Movement. An analysis of the choice of Radical Feminist heterosexuality is yet to be written.

Charlotte Bunch named lesbian feminism as the political perspective on 'the ideological and institutional domination of heterosexuality' (1976, p. 553). As she put it, lesbian feminism means putting women first in an act of resistance in a world in which life is structured around the male. Discussing the first paper issued by radical lesbians, 'The Woman-Identified Woman', she takes up the expanded definition of lesbianism as the idea of woman-identification and a love for all women. Behind this is the belief in the development of self-respect and a self-identity in relation to women, rather than in relation to men.

In 1975 Bunch had already said that 'heterosexuality means men first. That's what it's all about. It assumes that every woman is heterosexual; that every woman is identified by and is the property of men' (1981a, p. 69). Bunch thus stated what Adrienne rich later theorized in her influential paper on compulsory heterosexuality (1980) and Janice Raymond developed in her work on female friendship (1986). Bunch argued that heterosexism supports male supremacy in the workplace and is supported through the oppressive structure of the nuclear family. It is being fed by the actual or more often supposed benefits to women who continue life within the accepted norm of heterosexuality: the privileges of legitimacy, economic security, social acceptance, legal and physical protection – most of which do not hold true anyway for the majority of women in heterosexual relationships.

Adrienne Rich (1980) analysed the way in which heterosexuality had been forced upon women as an *institution*, and the way women had been seduced into it (in the same way as she had previously analysed motherhood as an institution; see Rich 1976). Lesbian existence represents a direct assault on the male's right of access to women.

Most importantly, though, was the term she coined: the 'lesbian continuum'. It was to have a major effect in reuniting lesbian and heterosexual feminists in their attempts to both validate the differences between their lives *and* strive towards developing a common political platform. Her lesbian continuum includes

> a range – through each woman's life and throughout history – of woman-identified experience; not simply the fact that a woman has had or consciously desired genital sexual experience with another woman. If we expand it to embrace many more forms of primary identity between and among women, including the sharing of a rich inner life, the bonding against male tyranny, the giving and receiving of practical and political support; . . . we begin to grasp bits of female history and psychology which have lain out of reach as a consequence of limited, mostly clinical, definitions of 'lesbianism'. (p. 649)

Extending this analysis of heterosexuality and the way it has controlled women's energy, women's sexuality and women's culture, Janice Raymond created the term 'hetero-reality'. She writes (1986, p. 11):

> While I agree that we are living in a heterosexist society, I think the wider problem is that we live in a hetero-relational society, where most of women's personal, social, political, professional, and economic relations are defined by the ideology that woman is for man.

Smashing the myth that women do not bond together and that hetero-reality has always been the norm, Raymond traces the history of women's friendship, of women as friends, lovers, economic and emotional supporters, and of companions. She attacks the dismembering of female friendships arguing that this represents a 'dismembering of the woman-identified Self' (p. 4). She emphasizes the intimacy in women's relationships, stressing that passionate friendships need not be of a genital-sexual nature.

Raymond coins the term *Gyn/affection* in order to be inclusive of all women who put each other first, whether lesbian or not. At the basis of her discussions of sexuality is the Radical Feminist belief in the political necessity of woman-identified feminism. It means that a woman's *primary* relationships are with other women. It is to women that we give our economic, emotional, political, and social support. In the words of Rita Mae Brown (1975, p. 66):

> A woman-identified woman is one who defines herself in relationship to other women and most importantly as a self apart and distinct from other selves, not with function as the centre of self, but being . . . a woman can best find out who she is with other women, not with just one other woman but with other women, who are also struggling to free themselves from an alien and destructive culture. It is this new concept, that of woman-identified woman, that sounds the death knell for the male culture and calls for a new culture where cooperation, life and love are the guiding forces of organization rather than competition, power and bloodshed. This concept will change the way we live and who we live with.

Implicit in many of these statements is an assumption of separatism, which has been seen as a political strategy, a space in which to create women-identification and the regeneration of women's energy and women's Selves. Charlotte Bunch writes of her time living in a totally separatist community of women as one in which personal growth and political analysis could be more readily developed. Despite the fact that she ultimately rejected total separatism because of the isolation it involved, as a political strategy it still has its uses. In Bunch's words (1976, p. 556): 'Separatism is a dynamic strategy to be moved in and out of whenever a minority feels that its interests are being overlooked by the majority, or that its insights need more space to be developed.'

In her paper 'In Defence of Separatism' (1976), Australian Susan Hawthorne has outlined the degrees of separatism which operate within Radical Feminism. She points out that it is impossible to be a feminist and not believe in separatism in one of its degrees. She includes among acts of separatism: valuing dialogue with other women and engaging in women-only groups; engaging in political and social action with other women;

attending women-only events – including events where women can have a good time!; working in an environment which is run by and for women; giving emotional support to women; engaging in sexual relationships with women; participating in groups which are concerned with women's creativity and the creation of women's culture; living in an all-women environment without contact with men.

It is this last degree of separatism which is predominantly understood as its definition. This is perceived as the most threatening form of separatism because it suggests that women can successfully live in the world independent of men. Indeed, this conception of separatism within the Radical Feminist framework is an empowering one. As Marilyn Frye writes (1983, p. 105):

> When our feminist acts or practices have an aspect of separatism, we are assuming power by controlling access and simultaneously by undertaking definition. The slave who excludes the master from her hut thereby declares herself *not a slave.* And *definition* is another face of power.

MOTHERHOOD AND THE FAMILY

The institution of the family is a primary institution of patriarchy. Chained to the theory and practice of hetero-reality and compulsory heterosexuality, the father-dominated family, with its dependent motherhood for women, has enslaved women into sexual and emotional service. For most women this includes unpaid domestic labour. In the bastion of the family, the private oppression of women is experienced on a daily level. It may be expressed through its physical manifestation in assault, its economic manifestation in male control of resources and decision-making, its ideological control through the socialization of women and children, and/or its control of women's energy in emotional and physical servicing of men and children. In addition, as Andrea Dworkin says (1974, p. 190): 'The nuclear family is the school of values in a sexist, sexually repressed society. One learns what one must know: the rules, rituals, and behaviours appropriate to male–female polarity and the internalised mechanisms of sexual oppression.'

Marriage itself has been seen as prostitution, where a woman trades sexual servicing for shelter and food. Sex is compulsory in marriage for women, ensuring heterosexuality within the economic bargain. As Sheila Cronan wrote (1973, p. 214):

> It became increasingly clear to us that the institution of marriage 'protects' women in the same way that the institution of slavery was said to 'protect' blacks – that is, that the word 'protection' in this case is simply a euphemism for oppression.

The patriarchal ideology of motherhood has also been scrutinized. During the early years of this most recent wave of the Women's Liberation Movement, many women rejected motherhood as an enslaving role within patriarchal culture. Since that time, feminists have tried to rewrite the definitions of motherhood, leading us to a more positive vision of what the experience might be like if women could determine the conditions. Adrienne Rich has written (1979b, p. 196):

> This institution – which affects each woman's personal experience – is visible in the male dispensation of birth control and abortion; the guardianship of men over children in the courts and the educational system; the subservience, through most of history, of women and children to the patriarchal father; the economic dominance of the father over the family; the usurpation of the birth process by male medical establishments.

Although motherhood is supposedly revered, its daily reality in patriarchy is tantamount to a degraded position. Motherhood is also only admirable when the mother is attached to a legal father. The pressure on women to undertake the mothering role is intense, as men are fearful that women will choose to discontinue mothering or have children without a man.

In *Of Woman Born* (1976) Rich delineated two meanings of motherhood: the *potential* relationship of a woman to her powers of reproduction and to children, and the patriarchal *institution* of motherhood which is concerned with male control of women and children. One of the most bewildering contradictions in the institutionalization of motherhood is that 'it has alienated women from our bodies by incarcerating us in them' (p. 13).

Just as heterosexuality is compulsory, so too is motherhood. Women who choose not to mother are outside the 'caring and rearing' bond and attract strong social disapproval. Women who are infertile, on the other hand, are subjects of pity and even derision. The institutionalization of motherhood by patriarchy has ensured that women are divided into breeders and non-breeders. Motherhood is therefore used to define woman and her usefulness.

WOMEN'S CULTURE

Emerging out of the concept of separatism as an empowering base and a belief in establishing and transmitting traditions, histories, and ideologies which are woman-centred, Radical Feminism strives to generate a women's culture through which women can artistically recreate both their selves and their way of being in the world outside of patriarchal definition. So, for example, Judy Chicago creates 'The Dinner Party' with two hundred places set for women of history who have made important contributions to women's culture as well as society at large. So Radical Feminist artists, painters, and writers resist the male-stream definitions of art and culture, redefining both stylistically and in their content what culture and art are and might be for women.

Many Radical Feminists are involved in writing (prose and poetry), film-making, sculpture, theatre, dance, and so on in their daily practice of Radical Feminism. For Radical Feminist poets and novelists, language becomes an essential code in redefining and restructuring the world with women as its centre. As Bonnie Zimmerman put it 'language is action' (1984, p. 672).

Within the creation of a woman's culture, the arts are not the sole areas of work. Feminist scientists for example are trying to generate visions of a new science and technology which would not be exploitative of people and the environment. Having critiqued masculine science, Radical Feminists are developing new ways of conceptualizing science (Bleier 1986).

Mary Daly attempts to reconceptualize the world as it might look from a perspective in which women's different needs and interests form the core of cultural practices and their theoretical underpinnings (1978, 1984). In her unique analysis of the oppression of women (1978, 1984), including her stress upon the daily physical and mental violence done to women, she recreates language, a sense of the spiritual, and a sense of physical being. She emphasizes the importance of naming, in that to name is to create the world. She also stresses the need to recreate and refind our original selves, before we were mutilated by patriarchy and subjugated to patriarchal definitions of the feminine self. She refuses to accept the woman-hatred within existing language, redefining for example 'spinster' and 'hag' in a positive way.

As Radical Feminism struggles to refind our cultural history and recreate culture around women, it is constantly misunderstood, labelled 'cultural feminism', and defined as 'non-political'. This is a false representation as the redefining of culture is interrelated with the development of a liberating ideology in tune with the autonomous being of people. It attacks male control of the concept of culture and patriarchal use of culture for the purposes of indoctrination of both women and men into patriarchal ideology. It is essentially *political*.

BIOLOGICAL ESSENTIALISM

A frequent criticism of Radical Feminism is that it supports a biologically based 'essential' division of the world into male and female. In particular this accusation is charged against Radical Feminists working in the area of violence against women who name men as members of the social group 'man', as well as individual men where relevant, as oppressors of women.

The facts are that men brutally oppress women as Radical Feminists have empirically shown. But why do men do this? Can it be changed? Kathleen Barry has addressed these issues in her analysis of sexual slavery which we discussed earlier. She states the truism that men do these things to women because 'there is nothing to stop them' (1979, p. 254). Her analysis of the *values of patriarchy* and theories which supposedly account for male violence is too detailed to discuss here. The important point to stress is that Radical Feminism cannot be reduced to a simplistic biological determinist argument. That its critics often *do* thus reduce it is a political ploy which takes place in order to limit the effectiveness of its analysis. We know that women have good reasons for being frightened to name men as the enemy, particularly when they live in hetero-relationships. Women are not fools. We know the kind of punishment which may be meted out for exposing patriarchy and its mechanisms (see Cline and Spender 1987).

Christine Delphy argues that the concept of gender – that is the respective social positions of women and men – is a construction of patriarchal ideology and that 'sex has become a pertinent fact, hence a perceived category, because of the existence of gender' (1984, p. 144). Therefore, she argues, the oppression creates gender, and in the end, gender creates anatomical sex (p. 144): 'in a sense that the hierarchical division of humanity into two transforms an anatomical difference (which is in itself devoid of social implications) into a relevant distinction for social practice'.

Radical Feminists are well aware of the dangers of rooting analysis in biology. If men and women are represented as having 'aggressive' and 'nurturing' charcteristics because of their biology, the situation will remain immutable and the continuation of male violence against women can be justified. But this is not to say that there are not differences between the sexes. This is patently so. These differences, however, do not need to be rooted in biology nor do they need to be equated with determinism. As the editors of *Questions Feministes* put it (1980, p. 14): 'we acknowledge a biological difference between men and women, but it does not in itself imply a relationship of oppression between the sexes. The struggle between the sexes is not the result of biology'.

Men are the powerful group. But men need women, for sexual and emotional servicing, for unpaid labour, for admiration, for love, and for a justification of the existing power imbalance (see Cline and Spender 1987). In order to maintain the more powerful position and so feed on their need of women without being consumed by it, men as a powerful group institutionalize their position of power. This involves the need to structure institutions to maintain that power, the development of an ideology to justify it, and the use of force and violence to impose it when resistance emerges (see also Rowland 1988).

It is possible that differences between women and men arise out of a biological base but in a different way to that proposed by a reductivist determinism. The fact that women belong to the social group which has the capacity for procreation and mothering, and the fact that men belong to the social group which has the capacity to carry out, and does, acts of rape and violence against women, must intrude into the consciousness of being female and male. This analysis still allows for change in the sense that men themselves could change that consciousness and therefore their actions. It also allows women to recognize that we can and must develop our own theories and practices and need not accept male domination as unchangeable.

Existing differences between women and men may have been generated out of the different worlds we inhabit as social groups, including our experience of power and powerlessness. But this is not to say that these differences are immutable. The history of women's resistance is evidence of resistance to deterministic thinking, as is the history of the betrayal by some men who support feminism, of patriarchy.

WOMEN'S RESISTANCE, WOMEN'S POWER

In our relation to men as the more powerful group, women do have some crucial bargaining areas: withdrawing reproductive services, emotional and physical labour, domestic labour, sexual labour, and refusing consent to being defined as the powerless, thereby verifying man's right to power. The withdrawal of services from men is an act of resistance; in Dale Spender's words (1983, p. 373): 'making men feel good is *work*, which women are required to undertake in a patriarchal society; refusing to engage in such work is a form of resistance.'

In *Powers of the Weak* (1980) Elizabeth Janeway lists the power of *disbelief* as a form of resistance. The powerful need those ruled to believe in them and believe in the justice of their position. But, as Janeway points out, if women refuse to endorse men's domination it signifies a lack of sanction of the authority of the ruler by the ruled, and destabilizes their sense of security.

Importantly, women can also exercise the power of disbelief with respect to the self of woman as defined by man. Janeway explores it thus (1980, p. 167):

> Ordered use of the power to disbelieve, the first power of the weak, begins here, with the refusal to accept the definition of one's self that is put forward by the powerful. It is true that one may not have a coherent self-definition to set against the status assigned by the established social mythology, but that is not necessary for dissent. By disbelieving, one would be led toward doubting prescribed codes of behaviour, and as one begins to act in ways that deviate from the norm in any degree, it becomes clear that in fact there is just not one way to handle or understand events.

A further 'power of the weak' lies in the collective understanding of a shared situation. Through collective political action and through consciousness-raising techniques, women have developed a sense of female identity and solidarity. The collective action and networking of the International Network of Female Sexual Slavery, and the International Network of Resistance to Reproductive and Genetic Engineering are examples of women educating for activism against violence against women. Women's health centres and the development of refuges and rape crisis centre are other examples of collective actions of resistance.

Radical Feminists are also developing women-centred approaches to changing the law. Catharine MacKinnon and Andrea Dworkin attempted to introduce a law in the United States to ensure that the victims of pornography had a right to take civil action against their abusers (MacKinnon 1987).

The creation of Radical Feminist knowledge itself, such as that contained within the works described above, represents an act of women's resistance. Radical Feminism has often been described as a state of rage. People – men and women – who have comfortable, safe lives fear that rage. It implicates them in the oppression of women, either as members of the oppressing group or of the oppressed group. Radical Feminism reminds women of their own moments of exploitation or abuse, and these memories are not welcome. Such down-to-earth knowledge intimates the possibility of a lack of control. As Susan Griffin remembers (1982, pp. 6–7):

> As I became more conscious of my oppression as a woman, I found myself entering a state of rage. Everywhere I turned I found more evidence of male domination, of a social hatred of, and derogation of women, of increasingly insufferable limitations imposed upon my life. Social blindness is lived out in each separate life. Like many women, I had been used to lying to myself. To tell myself that I wanted what I did not want, or felt what I did not feel, was a habit so deeply ingrained in me, I was never aware of having lied. I had shaped my life to fit the traditional idea of a woman, and thus, through countless decisions large and small, had sacrificed myself. Each sacrifice had made me angry. But I could not allow myself this anger. For my anger would have told me that I was lying. Now, when I ceased to lie, the anger I had accumulated for years was revealed to me.

Radical Feminists are angry because patriarchy oppresses women, but we are also filled with a sense of empowering well-being through bonding with other women and a joy in the liberation from accepting patriarchy and hetero-reality as immutable ingredients of human existence. Radical Feminist writings are sometimes rejected because of their openly voiced anger and passionate call to end women's oppression.[6] But Radical

Feminism *is* passionate. We are passionately committed to women's liberation and through our work we hope to empassion others. Nothing less will do if we are to break the brutal tyranny of man and develop theories and practices for a future in which women can live self-determined as well as socially responsible lives.

ACKNOWLEDGEMENTS

We would like to acknowledge Christine Zmroczek's invaluable contribution in unearthing early Radical Feminist writings and facilitating the interchange between us from one continent to another. We would also like to note that this chapter was written in 1987.

NOTES

1 See Dale Spender (1983), for a collection of historical writings on feminist theorists.
2 There is a great need for books on Radical Feminist theory. To date the gap still exists for works about Radical Feminism by radical feminists.
3 For examples of its universality see Morgan (1984) and Seager and Olson (1986).
4 Radical Feminists also stress the importance of applying a women-centred analysis to the various forms of population control as they oppress women in so-called Third World countries. See for example Vimal Balasubrahmanyan (1984) and Viola Roggenkamp (1984) on India, and Farida Akhter (1987) and Sultana Kamal (1987) on Bangladesh.
5 Pornography is another crucial site for Radical Feminist theory and practice. A discussion of the recent developments (1986) in the USA and strategies developed by Andrea Dworkin and Catharine MacKinnon would deserve a chapter of its own. Due to limitations of space, however, we have to refer the reader to the following references: Dworkin (1981); Griffin (1981); Lederer (1980); Linden *et al.* (1982); Marciano (1980); Rhodes and McNeill (1985).
6 See Frye (1983), 'A Note on Anger', for an excellent discussion of the meaning of this anger.

REFERENCES

Akhter, Farida (1987) 'Statistics for wheat: a case study of relief wheat for attaining sterilization target in Bangladesh', in Patricia Spallone and Deborah L. Steinberg (eds) *Made to Order*, Pergamon Press, Oxford and New York.
Arditti, Rita, Duelli Klein, Renate, and Minden, Shelley (1984) (eds) *Test-Tube Women: What Future for Motherhood?*, Pandora Press, London.
Atkinson, Ti-Grace (1974) *Amazon Odyssey*, Links Books, New York.
Balasubrahmanyan, Vimal (1984) 'Women as targets in India's family planning policy', in Rita Arditti, Renate Duelli Klein, and Shelley Minden (eds) *Test-Tube Women*, Pandora Press, London and Boston.
Barry, Kathleen (1979) *Female Sexual Slavery*, New York University Press, New York and London.
Bart, Pauline and O'Brien, Patricia (1985) *Stopping Rape: Successful Survival Strategies*, Pergamon Press, Oxford and New York.

Bleier, Ruth (1984) *Science and Gender: A Critique of Biology and its Theories on Women*, Pergamon Press, Oxford and New York.

Bleier, Ruth (ed.) (1986) *Feminist Approaches to Science*, Pergamon Press, Oxford and New York.

Boston Women's Health Collective (1969) *Our Bodies, Ourselves*, Simon and Schuster, New York.

Brown, Rita Mae (1975) 'Living with other women', in Charlotte Bunch and Nancy Myron (eds) *Lesbianism and the Women's Movement*, Diana Press, Baltimore, Md, pp. 63–7.

Brownmiller, Susan (1975) *Against Our Will: Men, Women and Rape*, Simon & Schuster, New York.

Bunch, Charlotte (1976) 'Learning from lesbian separatism', in *Ms. Magazine*; reprinted 1980 in Ruth Sheila (ed.) *Issues in Feminism: A First Course in Women's Studies*, Houghton Mifflin, Boston, pp. 551–6.

Bunch, Charlotte (1981a) 'Not for lesbians only', in *Building Feminist Theory: Essays from Quest, A Feminist Quarterly*, Longman, New York and London.

Bunch, Charlotte (1981b) 'The reform tool-kit', in *Building Feminist Theory: Essays from Quest, A Feminist Quarterly*, Longman, New York and London.

Bunch, Charlotte (1983) 'Not by degrees: feminist theory and education', in Charlotte Bunch and Sandra Pollack (eds) *Learning Our Way: Essays in Feminist Education*, Crossing Press, New York.

Bunch, Charlotte (1987) *Passionate Politics: Feminist Theory in Action*, St Martin's Press, New York.

Bunch, Charlotte and Myron, Nancy (eds) (1974) *Class and Feminism*, Diana Press, Baltimore, Md.

Chesler, Phyllis (1986) *Mothers on Trial*, Seal Press, Seattle, Wash.

Chester, Gail (1979) 'I call myself a Radical Feminist', in *Feminist Practice: Notes from the Tenth Year*, In Theory Press, London.

Cline, Sally and Spender, Dale (1987) *Reflecting Men at Twice Their Natural Size*, André Deutsch, London.

Corea, Gena (1985) *The Mother Machine: Reproductive Technologies from Artificial Insemination to Artificial Wombs*, Harper & Row, New York.

Corea, Gena *et al.* (1985) *Man-Made Women: How New Reproductive Technologies Affect Women*, Hutchinson, London.

Cronan, Sheila (1973) 'Marriage', in Anne Koedt *et al.* (eds) *Radical Feminism*, Quadrangle Press, New York, pp. 213–21.

Daly, Mary (1978) *Gyn/Ecology: The Metaethics of Radical Feminism*, Beacon Press, Boston.

Daly, Mary (1984) *Pure Lust: Elemental Feminist Philosophy*, Beacon Press, Boston.

Delphy, Christine (1984) *Close to Home*, Hutchinson, London.

Dworkin, Andrea (1974) *Woman-Hating*, E. P. Dutton, New York.

Dworkin, Andrea (1981) *Pornography: Men Possessing Women*, Women's Press, London.

Eisenstein, Hester (1984) *Contemporary Feminist Thought*, Unwin Paperbacks, London and Sydney.

Feminist Anthology Collective (1982) *No Turning Back: Writings from the Women's Liberation Movement, 1975–1980*, Women's Press, London.

Feminist Practice: Notes From the Tenth Year (1979) In Theory Press, London.

Firestone, Shulamith (1970) *The Dialectic of Sex: The Case for Feminist Revolution*, Bantam, New York.

Frankfort, Ellen (1973) *Vaginal Politics*, Bantam, New York.

Frye, Marilyn (1983) *The Politics of Reality: Essays in Feminist Theory*, Crossing Press, New York.
Griffin, Susan (1981) *Pornography and Silence: Culture's Revenge Against Nature*, Women's Press, London.
Griffin, Susan (1982) *Made From This Earth: Selections from her Writing, 1967–1982*, Women's Press, London.
Hawthorne, Susan (1976) 'In defence of separatism', unpublished honours thesis, La Trobe University, Melbourne, Australia.
Hooks, Bell (1984) *Feminist Theory, From Margin to Center*, South End Press, Boston.
Janeway, Elizabeth (1980) *Powers of the Weak*, Alfred A. Knopf, New York.
Johnson, Sonia (1986) 'Telling the truth', *Trivia*, 9, pp. 9–33.
Kamal, Sultana (1987) 'Seizure of reproductive rights? A discussion on population control in the Third World and in the emergence of new reproductive technologies in the west', in Patricia Spallone and Deborah L. Steinberg (eds) *Made to Order*, Pergamon Press, Oxford and New York.
Koedt, Anne, Levine, Ellen and Rapone, Anita (1973) *Radical Feminism*, Quadrangle, New York.
Leeds Revolutionary Feminist Group (1979) *Love Your Enemy? The Debate Between Heterosexual Feminism and Political Lesbianism*; republished 1981 by Only Women Press, London.
Lederer, Laura (ed.) (1980) *Take Back the Night: Women on Pornography*, William Morrow, New York.
Leghorn, Lisa and Parker, Katherine (1981) *Woman's Worth: Sexual Economics and the World of Women*, Routledge & Kegan Paul, London.
Linden, Robin R., Pagano, Darlene R., Russel, Diana E. H., and Star, Susan Leigh (eds) (1982) *Against Sadomasochism: A Radical Feminist Analysis*, Frog in the Well, California.
London Lesbian Offensive Group (1984) 'Anti-lesbianism in the Women's Liberation Movement', in Hannah Kanter, Sarah Lefanu, Sheila Shah, and Carole Spedding (eds) *Sweeping Statements. Writings from the Women's Liberation Movement 1981–83*, Women's Press, London.
MacKinnon, Catharine (1982) 'Feminism, Marxism, method and the state: an agenda for theory', *Signs*, 7:3, pp. 515–44.
MacKinnon, Catharine (1987) *Feminism Unmodified: Discourses on Life and Law*, Harvard University Press, Cambridge, Mass.
Mann, Bonnie (1986) 'The Radical Feminist task of history: gathering intelligence in Nicaragua', *Trivia*, 9, pp. 46–60.
Marchiano, Linda ('Linda Lovelace') (1980) *Ordeal: An Autobiography*, US Citadel Press, New Jersey.
Millett, Kate (1971) *Sexual Politics*, Avon Books, New York.
Morales, Rosario (1981) 'We're all in the same boat', in *This Bridge Called My Back: Writings by Radical Women of Color*, Persephone Press, Massachusetts, pp. 91–6.
Morgan, Robin (1978) *Going Too Far*, Vintage Books, New York.
Morgan, Robin (1984) *Sisterhood is Global*, Anchor Press/Doubleday, New York.
O'Brien, Mary (1981) *The Politics of Reproduction*, Routledge & Kegan Paul, London and Boston.
Questions Feministes (1980) 'Editorial: variations on some common themes', I:1, pp. 1–19.
Raymond, Janice (1986) *A Passion for Friends: Toward a Philosophy of Female Friendship*, Beacon Press, Boston.

Rhodes, Dusty and McNeill, Sandra (eds) (1985) *Women Against Violence Against Women*, Only Women Press, London.
Rich, Adrienne (1976) *Of Woman Born: Motherhood as Experience and Institution*, W. W. Norton, New York.
Rich, Adrienne (1979a) 'Disloyal to civilization: feminism, racism, gynophobia', in *On Lies, Secrets and Silence*, W. W. Norton, New York, pp. 275–310.
Rich, Adrienne (1979b) 'Motherhood in bondage', in *On Lies, Secrets and Silence*, W. W. Norton, New York, pp. 195–7.
Rich, Adrienne (1980) 'Compulsory heterosexuality and lesbian existence', *Signs*, 5:4, pp. 631–60.
Roggenkamp, Viola (1984) 'Abortion of a special kind: male sex selection in India', in Rita Arditti, Renate Duelli Klein, and Shelley Minden (eds) *Test-Tube Women*, Pandora Press, London and Boston.
Rowland, Robyn (1987) 'Technology and motherhood: reproductive choice reconsidered', *Signs*, 12:3, pp. 512–28.
Rowland, Robyn (1988) *Woman Herself: A Women's Studies Transdisciplinary Perspective on Self-Identity*, Oxford University Press, Melbourne.
Sargent, Lydia (ed.) (1981) *Women and Revolution: A Discussion of the Unhappy Marriage of Marxism and Feminism*, South End Press, Boston.
Scott, Hilda (1984) *Working Your Way to the Bottom: The Feminisation of Poverty*, Pandora Press, London.
Seager, Joni and Olsen, Ann (1986) *Women in the World: An International Atlas*, Pan, London and Sydney.
Spallone, Patricia and Steinberg, Deborah L. (eds) (1987) *Made to Order: The Myth of Reproductive and Genetic Progress*, Pergamon Press, Oxford and New York.
Spender, Dale (1982) *Women of Ideas and What Men Have Done to Them*, Routledge & Kegan Paul, London.
Spender, Dale (1983) 'Modern feminist theorists: reinventing rebellion', in Dale Spender (ed.) *Feminist Theorists: Three Centuries of Women's Intellectual Traditions*, Women's Press, London, pp. 366–80.
Tuttle, Lisa (1986) *Encyclopedia of Feminism*, Longman, London.
Ward, Elizabeth (1984) *Father–Daughter Rape*, Women's Press, London.
Zimmerman, Bonnie (1984) 'The politics of transliberation: lesbian personal narratives', *Signs*, 9:4, pp. 668–82.

10

SOCIALIST FEMINISMS

Louise C. Johnson

INTRODUCTION

Socialist Feminism comprises a set of interventions by feminists into socialist and especially Marxist theory, which aims to analyse and end the oppression of women in capitalist societies. As such Socialist Feminism is built upon key texts, writers, political events, and organizations which comprise the Marxist tradition. It is these which have helped shape the agenda for Socialist Feminist debates and reformulations of Marxism.

This chapter will chart a selective course through Socialist Feminist writings drawn from nineteenth- and twentieth-century Britain, North America, and Australia. Isolating key theorists in the Socialist Feminist Tradition is not an easy task, but when the mentors of contemporary Socialist Feminists are sought, it is not in the work of Utopian Socialists or later theorists such as Lenin or Kollontai, but usually in the writings of Karl Marx and Friedrich Engels. The theoretical hegemony of Marx and Engels has set a problematic agenda for Socialist Feminists. For exactly what terms such as 'value', 'class', 'social reproduction', 'historical materialism', and 'alienation' meant for Marx and Engels is itself debatable. How exactly they relate to and construct the position of women is even more contentious, though such concepts have both limited and inspired much subsequent analysis. After a critical examination of these key notions in the work of Marx and Engels, this chapter will consider Socialist Feminist theorizations of women in the realms of *production* and *social reproduction* and the relations between Marxism and Feminism.[1] This discussion will include an analysis of how these theorizations have been informed by a materialist conception of *patriarchy*.

In the course of this discussion it will be argued that theorizations by Marx and Engels marginalized gender relations and made any specific consideration of women within their problematic extremely difficult, if not impossible. Those Socialist Feminists who have attempted to situate women in Marxism have had to move from *applying* the concepts to women, to *redefining* those same concepts. The result is a series of reformulations which owe much to other feminist priorities and theorizations, a major debt to historical materialism but little to the many other ideas developed by Marx and Engels. What constitutes this new materialist foundation of contemporary Socialist Feminism will be questioned in the final section, as 'minority' women begin to articulate *their* Socialist Feminisms. Their critique highlights excluded positions in Socialist Feminist theorizing – exclusions based on race or colour, and the origin of much Socialist Feminism in the material experience of white, privileged women. New directions for Socialist Feminism therefore involve further reformulations of Marxist theory, up to the point of its abandonment, and a new multiplicity of historically grounded, theoretical interventions.

KARL MARX AND FRIEDRICH ENGELS: CLASS, FAMILY RELATIONS, AND THE POSITION OF WOMEN

The socialist tradition long predates the work of Marx and Engels. In the theorizations and practices of nineteenth-century Utopian Socialists there was extensive consideration of gender oppression within capitalism (Taylor 1980, 1983). From being integral to a conceptualization of capitalism, women's position is increasingly marginalized in socialist work by a focus on paid labour and class relations. This occurs with the rise in importance of Marxism and a male-dominated organized Left (Hartmann 1981; Mitchell 1971).

While any straightforward account of the writing of Marx and Engels rides over enormous debate as to what they *really* said, it is a necessary starting point (Jaggar 1983). Longtime friend and co-author Friedrich Engels described Marx's ideas as a synthesis of the German idealist philosophy of Hegel, French political theory, and English political economy – especially the work of Adam Smith and David Ricardo (McLellan 1983, p. 24). Many of Marx's writings were both critiques and radical reformulations of these lions of nineteenth-century philosophy, political theory, and economics. In this exercise, Marx began by situating their thought materially and historically and in so doing revealed that analyses generated by bourgeois philosophers and economists expressed their privileged class interests (Marx and Engels 1976, p. 59).

In contrast, Marx saw his own work as moving beyond the appearance of bourgeois society, constructed as it was by these dominant class interests, both to uncover the true workings of capitalism and to speak from the position of those most oppressed by it – the working class. In such a way Scientific Socialism would replace bourgeois/Utopian Socialism and the ideas of the ruling class would be revealed as mere obfuscatory ideologies.

The method to achieve such an analysis of capitalism for Marx was dialectical historical materialism. Marx and Engels describe the reasoning as follows:

> As individuals express their life, so they are. What they are, therefore, coincides with their production, both with *what* they produce and with *how* they produce. Hence what individuals are depends on the material conditions of their production.
>
> (1976, pp. 31–2)

Beginning with *material conditions* and at a high level of *abstraction* it is not always clear to subsequent interpreters where an abstract analysis of a mode of production ends and a more concrete analysis of a social formation begins – in particular, at what point gendered beings can enter the analysis. Nor is it clear just how non-sexed any notion of an abstract individual can or should be. Does the use here by Marx of 'the individual' imply not abstraction but a grounding of his theory on the experience of men? The fact that men and women can and usually do have quite different relations to 'nature', to the means of production and to biological reproduction, may thereby be situated *outside* the Marxist problematic from the beginning. For me this is indeed the case, but Marx's abstract schematization of capitalism has also proved a vital starting point for Socialist Feminists, especially as they apply to women the principles of historical materialism and extend Marx's consideration of production to include reproduction.

The material foundation of Marxism is a fundamental element incorporated into subsequent Socialist Feminist discussions. Such a foundation, primarily in the realm of *economic production* however, is a key part of Marx's analysis which has been questioned by feminists. For there is no *logical* reason why social action on nature to create the means of subsistence is any more a fundamental necessity than action between people for the purpose of biological reproduction. As Mary O'Brien has argued, Hegelian dialectics could just as easily have been materially grounded upon the social *relations of reproduction* (O'Brien 1981, 1982). Such a focus is not possible within Marx's theory. But a dual focus on production and reproduction *was* possible and it is one taken up later by Engels.

Central to later debates has been Marx's conception of *labour*. Much of Marx's theoretical edifice rests on this concept and it remains an issue for Socialist Feminists whether its conceptualization may be readily applied or whether it excludes a specific consideration of women's as well as men's labour. For Marx, in the transition from feudal to the capitalist mode of production, the means to produce wealth – tools, expertise, land – were centralized into the hands of one class; the bourgeoisie. Deprived of the means of production, the proletariat retains only its ability to labour. Such a class embodies the ability to create *value* by the application of *labour power* to nature and the transformation of nature into commodities. As commodities with some utility they contain a *use value*. This value and the labour power contained within this product can be realized only if others want the commodity – if it has an *exchange value* in the marketplace. In return for such *productive labour* the worker receives a wage, which has within it two components – one a measure of profit or the *surplus value* appropriated by the capitalist; and the other, the product of *necessary labour*, is used by the workers to sustain themselves, their family, and the next generation (Marx 1974).

It is questionable whether these abstract notions of 'labour' and 'value' preclude or open the possibility of a specific consideration of women. How exactly women's unpaid domestic labour fits into this schema becomes an urgent question for Socialist Feminists. I would argue that such a formulation of labour, while admittedly a theorization of *capitalist class relations*, assumes and is built upon the sexual division of labour. For labour has value only in relation to the wage; while the necessary wage has integral to it a component for domestic life and worker 'reproduction'. Women's work becomes theoretically relevant only when it becomes like men's – paid – while domestic labour is a vital but untheorized component of 'social reproduction'.

There is a third class within Marx's schematization of capitalism – a group which is only tenuously linked to the production process at any one time – the underemployed, the unemployed, and the immigrant worker. This group comprises various parts of the *reserve army of labour*, ready to be mobilized when production needs to be expanded rapidly and then demobilized during times of recession. Whether women form a sepecific subgroup of this reserve army of labour is an issue taken up by Socialist Feminists in their dual efforts to apply Marxist theory to the position of women and to explain the particular place of women in contemporary capitalism.

For Marx it is these class relationships which provide the motor for history. For there exists an antagonism of interests between the two basic classes – of worker and bourgeoisie – which generates continuous conflicts. The capitalist strives to increase the amount of surplus value extracted from the worker while the workers seek to raise their share of what they produce.

Separated from nature, deprived of the means to produce subsistence, and subject to increasing discipline and regulation as wage labourers, Marx argued that workers lost touch with their own selves. As a result of the wage–labour relation, workers were not only exploited but they were also *alienated* from their labour, each other, nature, and their species being (McLellan 1983; Ollman 1976).

It is in this conception of *wage labour*, especially its value, and its daily and generational reproduction that Marx leaves the place of women under capitalism specifically untheorized, though simultaneously building in their presence as dependent *others* within this concept. It is the contradictions and silences within this conception of wage labour which prove enormously problematical for those Socialist Feminists attempting to apply Marxism to analyses of women's labour – in the home and as wage labourers.

If the primary focus of Marx was on production relations, Friedrich Engels embarks on an extended analysis of social reproduction and the family.

Engels constructs in *The Origin of the Family, Private Property and the State* (1975), an argument which both ties women to the family and class relations and sets the agenda for much Socialist Party and state activity to liberate women. As Michèle Barrett writes: 'This work, whatever its failings, has been highly influential in Marxist thinking on the family and women's oppression and has provided the starting point of a materialist analysis of gender relations' (1980, p. 48).

Engels's essay focuses on pre-modern, pre-capitalist families whose male–female relations are very different from those under capitalism. His argument rests on ethnomethodological studies which document the existence of familial arrangements in which women have power. Thus, Engels maintains, in the eras of Savagery and Barbarism, in various forms of group marriages, women had power within the household; over the management of their productive and reproductive labour and over descent and inheritance (Engels 1975, pp. 106, 113–14). The transition from such an era to the present class-based 'civilization' – from group tomonogamous marriage – involves the 'world historic defeat of the female sex' by men (p. 120). It is this transition which is of most interest in that it reveals the logic of Engels's analysis and the implicit contradictions within it which have been the focus of much Socialist Feminist debate.

If the communalistic household 'is the material foundation of that supremacy of . . . women' (p. 113), why women come to occupy this realm is not made clear by Engels. He writes: 'The division of labour between the sexes is determined by quite other causes than by the position of women in society' (p. 113). Rosalind Delmar isolates in Engels's and Marx's work these 'quite other causes' in the 'spontaneous sexual division of labour arising out of physiological difference' – of women as child breeders (1979, p. 284). She goes on to castigate this implicit biological origin of the sexual division of labour as a major flaw in Engels's analysis (1979, p. 285).

A fundamental problem in Engels's analysis for Socialist Feminists then, is the assumption of a 'natural'/physiological foundation for the division between women and men. Though this division is *later* to enter particular social relations and to be theorized by Engels within these, the question of *origins* is consigned to the realm of the non-historical. As Moira Maconachie writes in a recent collection (Sayers *et al*. 1987) which reconfirms the importance of Engels's work to contemporary Socialist Feminism: 'Engels makes the family an object of historical enquiry but regards the relationship between men and women as already constituted'

(p. 108). How relations between kinship and production interact to move a family from one stage to another is explained for Engels by property and labour relations. He argues that it was an alteration in property relations which comprised the 'new, social forces' (1975, p. 117) that gave men ascendant power over women. With their initial command over outdoor food collection and labour, the domestication of animals and the ownership of slaves in this realm gave men more material power. Engels continues:

> Thus on the one hand, in proportion as wealth increased it made the man's position in the family more important than the woman's, and on the other hand created an impulse to exploit this strengthened position in order to overthrow, in favor of his children, the traditional order of inheritance.
>
> (p. 119)

The conversion of men's greater wealth into power over women thus derives from a recognition of the male role in the creation of children and an 'impulse' to control the disposal of that wealth amongst *his* children. Once this power is asserted, it takes on even more oppressive dimensions. The monogamous family thus becomes *patriarchal* as women's power to control her labour in the household and as a reproducer is not only destroyed, but reoriented to the service of men.

From what does this oppression of one sex by another derive? In Engels's work there is a dual answer to this question – one which is extensively theorized, and the other consigned to the feminine and to nature. Engels argues explicitly that male power over women derives from their command over material resources and a wish to control the disposal of those resources. It is this focus which is extensively developed by theorists discussing The Woman Question[2] and by some contemporary Socialist Feminists working within the organized Left (Waters 1972).

But there are other impulses moving this historical motor: desire, sexuality, and anxieties over paternity. These forces also cause changes in social and familial relations to occur. So, for example, men *needed* to have control over inheritance and be assured of their paternity. It was this desire which produced the imperative to defeat 'mother right' (Engels 1975, pp. 119, 120). For Engels too the sole sexual drive is to heterosexual monogamous coupling and not 'the abominable practice of sodomy' (p. 128). These desires and drives are not closely examined or theorized by Engels and do not become part of the Socialist Feminist theoretical field until questions of ideology, desire, and subjectivity enter Marxism and feminism (Coward 1984; Mitchell 1979; Sayers 1987). It is from this perspective, for example, that Mary Evans questions the assumptions of heterosexuality and 'natural' sexual urges in Engels's account (1987, pp. 84 and 85).

What does take analytic priority in Engels's examination of the family is the material world of property and production. This focus is most clear when he describes the 'modern' marriages amongst the different classes. The bourgeois marriage is a marriage 'of convenience' (a property exchange) negotiated by 'the' parents (or rather arranged by the fathers). In this the class position of the women is that of her father and he in turn guarantees the like class of the husband. In the proletarian marriage, the wife assumes the class position of her husband – and so it is as a proletarian wife that she enters the labour market. *Class* positions are therefore something men occupy. A woman assumes the class position of the man whose 'family' she inhabits – be it her father or husband.

From being a primary division, therefore, sexual differentiation is obliterated by the primacy within Marxist analysis of class antagonism. The agency for thus rendering women's particular position invisible is the family, divided only by class and not sex. A major contradiction within Engels's account, therefore, is the simultaneous rendering of male–female relations as crucial, but then subsuming them within the theoretically and politically more important class relations.

This linking of women to the family has both limited and opened up theoretical possibilities for later Socialist Feminists as they grapple with the class position of women and the importance of the family in structuring women's oppression.

For Socialist Feminists, the problems of subsuming women within a male-headed family differentiated primarily by class relations, become even more acute when the socialist future is projected.

To achieve the end of women's oppression, Engels proposes the extension of legal equality to them (1975, p. 137) and then their mass entry into public industry (p. 138). Such moves would be a prelude to the alliance of *all* women with the working class to socialize the means of production, abolish private property, and usher in an age of monogamous sex love.

If the oppression of women is built upon the economic and legal power of men over them and if that power is class-based, then indeed it follows that abolishing private property and socializing production destroys the economic foundation of women's position. However, the experience of socialist countries has been used to question this logic (Bengelsdorf and Hageman 1979; Cliff 1984; Coward 1983; Davin 1987; Einhorn 1981; Eisen 1984; Mitchell 1971; Porter 1980; Randall 1979; Rowbotham 1972; Scott 1976; Stacey 1979) and the logic itself has been questioned and reformulated. Some Socialist Feminists have accepted, with qualifications, the priority to theorize social reproduction and production as separated but related sites of oppression (for example Beechey 1977 and Vogel 1983). Others have seen in the dual emphasis on production and social reproduction a valuable way to reconsider Engels's work (see the essays in Sayers *et al.* 1987 by Humphries, Gimeniz, and Redclift) and to direct

Socialist Feminist theorizing (Eisenstein 1979b; Hartman 1981; Kuhn and Wolpe 1978). The debt to Marx and Engels remains central in all of these departures. But others see the specific absence of women in that analysis as crippling and question the analytical priority given to Marxism (Delphy 1984; Campioni and Gross 1983; Matthews 1984a).

Campioni and Gross (1983), for example, see in the triumph of Marxism a systematic process whereby this political theory is absorbed into various institutions and comes to dominate the field of oppositional discourse. They argue that this occurs because of the phallocentrism of Marxism and its sharing with bourgeois liberal theory of many common assumptions about truth, reason, reality, and causality. As a result, they conclude, Marxism is not radically 'other' to capitalism except as a method and is *unable* to incorporate feminist demands.

In much subsequent Socialist Feminist work, Marx's and Engels's historical materialism does provide a foundation on which Marxist categories can be modified and a base from which to build new theorizations of women's materiality. These various reinterpretations though, must be situated within both the history of western Marxism and the women's liberation movement.

THE WOMAN QUESTION, THE NEW LEFT, AND WOMEN'S LIBERATION

It was with great optimism that Socialist Feminists looked to the Bolshevik Revolution in 1917 to realize their dual goals of socialism and female emancipation in Russia. For the theory promised that a working-class revolution would automatically liberate women. Even though the revolution had contravened much of Marxist orthodoxy; especially in the vital leadership role played by a disciplined, centralized party; women were an active force in the events of 1917 and in reforms which followed (Cliff 1984; Lenin 1982; Porter 1980; Rowbotham 1972).

Under the stresses of war and counter-revolution during the 1920s and 1930s many of the pro-woman reforms were abandoned, as women's liberation was put off to a more distant future. Nevertheless the inspiration of the early years of the Soviet revolution remains. So too do the positions held by Left parties derived from the thought of Marx, Engels, Lenin, Kollontai, and Trotsky. These can be summarized (though are not necessarily uniformly held by derivative Left parties) as:

(i) the primacy of a historical materialist analysis;
(ii) the primacy of the class struggle over all other forms of struggle;
(iii) the importance of a party organized along hierarchical lines, with a centrally determined position on issues and a brief to lead revolutionary activities;

(iv) a consideration of women (or any other subgroup) *within* a historical-materialist, class-based analysis;
(v) the origin of women's oppression as a physiological weakness related to childbearing which was transformed in the distant past to male control of women's labour and private property, and the monogamous patriarchal family;
(vi) women's liberation will follow from their alliance with the working class to seize the means of production and property and then to socialize production, domestic labour, and child-rearing.

These positions, in general, which were borne by the organized Left through the Second World War and Cold War, were then re-evaluated by the New Left in the 1950s and 1960s and confronted Radical Feminism in the 1970s.[3]

By the 1960s a new generation – confronted in the United States, Britain, and Australia with the Vietnam war and other Third World revolts, Black Power movements, and an upsurge of student radicalism around these issues – produced a revival of critical interest in the thought of Karl Marx. The earlier identification of revolutionary socialism with the horrors of Stalinism and a Marxism which looked more and more mechanical and economistic now came under review (O'Brien 1970).

THE RE-EMERGENCE OF SOCIALIST FEMINISM

It was in the pages of the *New Left Review*, a major arena for the critical revaluation of Marxism, that one of the earliest statements on contemporary Socialist Feminism appeared. In the December 1966 issue, Juliet Mitchell published 'Women: the longest revolution' (1966). The essay was given even wider circulation in the often reprinted book *Woman's Estate* (1971). Mitchell wrote of previous socialist work on The Woman Question: 'To this point, the liberation of women remains a normative ideal, an adjunct to socialist theory, not structurally integrated into it' (1971, p. 81). She described the related experiences of many women in both radical groups and socialist parties – a phenomenon similarly encountered in France, England, Holland, the United States, and Australia – where women were generally treated with contempt, rarely as political equals and useful only as whores or wives. She wrote:

> Not one single left-wing movement: working-class, Black or student can offer anything to contradict this experience. . . . Radical feminism – the belief in the *primary* and paramount oppression of women was born as a phoenix from the ashes of this type of socialism. If socialism is to regain its status as *the* revolutionary politics (in addition to the scientific analysis it offers of capitalist society) it has to make good its practical sins of commission against women and its

> huge sin of omission – the absence of an adequate place for them in its theory.
>
> (1971, p. 86)

Radical Feminism dominated the early years of the women's liberation movement's second wave. Most energy was concentrated on the articulation of women's oppression and organized movements for its amelioration. Socialist women too were caught up in this activity, and it was some years before Mitchell's call for a feminist reconsideration of Marxism occurred, a process greatly aided by the foundation Mitchell set down in 1966. Much of her essay was concerned with welding Marxist method to feminist priorities around what she argued were the four key structures of women's situation: production, reproduction, sexuality, and the socialization of children (Mitchell 1971, p. 101).

In the essay and her subsequent work (1979; Mitchell and Rose 1982), Mitchell drew heavily on the reinterpretation of Marxism given by Louis Althusser. As a result ideology, as a material and cultural force, became paramount. Her analysis of women's oppression in turn looked to the exchange theory of Lévi-Strauss and the psychoanalysis of Sigmund Freud and Jacques Lacan to construct a view of patriarchy which placed sexuality to the fore in feminist debate.

For Mitchell patriarchy is the symbolic law of the father. Under capitalism this law is primarily expressed as ideology. Patriarchal law, she argued, can be overturned by a *cultural* revolution. This revolution is necessary at the same time as the socialist revolution destroys capitalist relations if women are to be liberated from patriarchal as well as class oppression. The linking of psychoanalysis and Marxism by Mitchell, while a crucial re-intervention for feminists, has been critically assessed by a number of Socialist Feminists for its inadequate *material* grounding of psychoanalytic theory (Beechey 1979; Eisenstein 1979a). Her work though has inspired other Socialist Feminists in their pursuit of material foundations for ideology, sexuality, and subjectivity (Barrett 1980; Coward 1983), though the distance from Marxism attained in such quests raises the question of whether such work can still be seen as part of the Socialist Feminist tradition.

Mitchell's 1966 essay moved the socialist discussion of The Woman Question on to the feminist agenda. It owes much to theorizations within the New Left and to Radical Feminism. Major additions heralded by Mitchell were a focusing of interest on women as a specific group; a legitimation of concerns for 'personal life'; and a focus on biological and social reproduction. Her essay also situates Socialist Feminism squarely within the various theoretical debates which were occurring at the time, especially the reformulation of Marxism by Louis Althusser and a subsequent interest in ideology; and the reclaiming of Sigmund Freud's work on the acquisition of gender identities.

But at the time Socialist Feminists did not go on to further theorize Mitchell's four structures of women's oppression. It was rather her more general quest to apply Marxist theory to feminist questions which was taken up.

The eminence accorded the work of Marx and Engels, especially by women whose political education had occurred within the New Left, led theorists in two main directions: to a focus on *production* and *social reproduction*. Until 1979 these areas assumed analytic priority for Socialist Feminists with sexuality and the socialization of children re-entering consideration only more recently.

SOCIAL REPRODUCTION AND DOMESTIC LABOUR

In an early influential text, Betty Friedan opened her study of *The Feminine Mystique* (1963) in North America with a summary of a key tension bedevilling middle-class women at the time, that between an image of the ideal woman, dedicated to husband, home and children, and the question which flowed from the daily grind of this experience: 'Is this all?' (p. 13). The analysis which followed joined another study of the captive, housebound woman in Britain by Hannah Gavron (1966) to make the work of women in the home not only visible, but an object of theorization (Bland *et al.* 1978, p. 36).

The first Socialist Feminist attempt at such a theorization was by the Canadian Margaret Benston. Explicitly building on Juliet Mitchell's earlier discussion of women's 'marginal' work, she also criticizes her emphasis on 'superstructural' rather than 'basic economic factors' (1969, p. 202). From there Benston draws her analytical direction from Engels and the political economist Ernest Mandel rather than from Mitchell or Althusser, to argue:

> that the roots of the secondary status of women are in fact economic . . . women as a group do indeed have a definite relation to the means of production and . . . this is different from that of men. . . . If this special relation of women to production is accepted, the analysis of (their) situation fits naturally into a class analysis of society.
>
> (p. 199)

This specific relation to production is the unpaid domestic labour of women. The home was seen by Benston as a pre-capitalist site of production where a woman's labour produced use values rather than exchange values and was paid for by the male wage. While women could enter the labour force, they had no structural responsibility in this area and such participation was ordinarily regarded as transient (p. 201). Legitimately performing work only in the home, Benston saw women as a vast 'reserve of labour' (p. 206) who entered a secondary labour market because of this identification. Benston's paper joined those by Peggy Morton (1970) and Mariarosa Dalla

Costa and Selma Jones (1972) to set the terms of a protracted debate in Socialist Feminist theory as to the meaning, status, revolutionary potential, and value of domestic labour. The debate became even more intense as an international campaign demanding wages for housework built upon it.

Mary McIntosh (1982) summarizes the various *theoretical* dimensions of the Domestic Labour Debate:

> whether housework was 'productive' or 'unproductive' in the technical Marxist sense of producing surplus value, whether housework was an integral part of the capitalist mode of production or had only an indirect relation to it, whether unpaid housework served to raise or lower the value of the husband's labour power, whether or not housewives were part of the working class, whether what is now done as housework could ever be socialized under capitalism.
>
> (pp. 110–11)

In short, the debate quickly assumed the character of a battle over the efficacy of Marxism to explain (women's) domestic labour.

A look at some specific statements within this vast debate will illustrate this general observation and chart a course in the debate from a primary focus on Marxist theory to a greater concern with the oppression of women.[4] As a result, there occurs in Socialist Feminist theorizing on domestic labour, a regrounding upon a more broadly conceptualized *experience* of domestic labour rather than upon the relevance of Marxist categories to it.

In Britain, though the issue had been extensively canvassed in magazines, pamphlets, and discussions within the women's movement (Seccombe 1973, p. 4), domestic labour entered mainstream New Left politics as Juliet Mitchell's ideas had done seven years before – through the pages of the *New Left Review*. In 1973 Wally Seccombe sought to situate 'The housewife and her labour under capitalism' more explicitly and 'rigorously' then Benston, Dalla Costa and James had done within the Marxist problematic. Seccombe argued that in *Capital*, Marx laid out a framework within which domestic labour clearly fitted. He proceeds to describe capitalism in a similar vein to that of Benston, as comprising an 'industrial unit' and a more backward 'domestic unit'. Akin more to petty commodity production than commodity capitalism, the domestic unit is linked to capital in a key way – by producing the commodity labour power in a daily and generational cycle. Such domestic labour while vital is not 'productive' in the Marxist sense of generating surplus value and therefore, within this problematic, it has no 'value'. It does, though, have to be sustained and it is this cost which is met by the labourer's wage. It is this which is paid for by the necessary labour component of the working day.

The intense argument which followed over the next seven years in the pages of the *New Left Review* and elsewhere was primarily concerned with the accuracy or otherwise of Seccombe's reading of Marx, with adding further theoretical rigour to Benston, James, and Dalla Costa, and with assessing the usefulness of Marxist concepts to an analysis of women's labour in the home (Coulson *et al.* 1975; Edholm *et al.* 1977; Fox 1986; Gardiner 1975, 1976; Molyneux 1979).

Paul Smith (1978) takes the concern with Seccombe's (mis?)reading of Marx to its logical concusion when he writes:

> Domestic labour is, then, not problematic for Marx's theory of value because it is not part of its object, the production and exchange of commodities. Consequently, it does not form part of the capitalist mode of production of commodities, but rather one of its external conditions of existence which it continually reproduces.
>
> (p. 211)

Not only did Seccombe misread Marx, but so too by implication did the bulk of those engaged in the Domestic Labour Debate as the participants misguidedly grappled with the relevance of Marxist categories to housework. Smith therefore prioritizes Marxist theory over the issue of women's oppression or domestic labour. In concluding that domestic labour doesn't fit, Smith continues to conduct the debate within a Marxist rather than a feminist problematic. Marxism is never seen to be inadequate, just feminist applications of it!

Bonnie Fox points out that a focus on domestic work, the family, and the relevance of Marxist theory to women's labour has provided some key theoretical insights from which to build a materialist analysis of women's position both in the home and more generally (1986, pp. 181–9). Many Socialist Feminists, while acknowledging the problems of the debate, also accept many of its assumptions in their analyses. There remains a commitment to *apply* Marxism in some way. Increasingly though, this desire has been focused on specific concepts – such as labour, production, and reproduction – and on the method of historical materialism (Burton 1985; Delphy 1976, 1984; Vogel 1983). More recently *feminist* concerns have moved Socialist Feminists beyond a preoccupation with Marxism to questions of sexuality and power.

In 1983 for example, Lise Vogel reasserted 'the power of Marxism to analyse the issues that face women today in "their" struggle for liberation' (p. 2) by developing 'a theoretical approach that puts child bearing and the oppression of women at the very heart of every class mode of production' (p. 8). She argues that the need by the ruling class for the daily and generational replacement of labour power heightens the significance of women's biological power to bear children and creates the material conditions for a sexual *and* a patriarchal division of labour between home and work and in the home. What form this takes is a historical rather than a theoretical question (pp. 136–50). In such a way Vogel argues that

Marxism can be extended to provide a materialist theorization of women in class societies. Her analysis builds on the Domestic Labour Debate and Marxist categories, but to these adds explicit consideration of biological reproduction, and women's experience of gender oppression as well as class relations. In this she prioritizes the analysis of women's oppression and women's materiality over Marxist theory.

A similar priority leads Christine Delphy in a different direction. First published in France in 1970, but not in English until 1976 and again in 1984, Delphy's pamphlet on 'The main enemy' argues for the separateness and primacy of the domestic world for women. It is this world which she proposes as a separate mode of production in which women are exploited.

Yet unlike others in the Domestic Labour Debate, Delphy does not analyse this domestic or family mode of production using Marxist categories, but rather examines the labour performed by married women in France with concepts only loosely derived from Marx. From this she concludes that women's labour is not controlled by or of primary benefit to capital but is performed *for* men. Not only does this relationship constitute the material foundation of oppression for all women, but it gives them a common class or caste status from which to challenge it (pp. 67–72). Delphy thereby *prioritizes* women's oppression within a *'materialist' analysis.*

Maxine Molyneux, when evaluating Delphy's essay, criticizes her careless use of Marxist categories. Concepts such as 'mode of production' and 'labour power', Molyneux argues, have been transformed 'into empiricist, common sense, constructs . . . quite at variance with conventional definitions' (1979, p. 7).

Such criticisms may indeed stem from a concern with conceptual accuracy and rigour, but they also confirm an observation made by Campioni and Gross on the unquestioned status of Marxism. For, they argue, Marxism is a theory which acts as a standard to which all else is compared and found wanting (1983, pp. 116–17). Nevertheless Delphy's work brings to the fore in Socialist Feminist debate male oppression of women, and suggests that such a focus may ultimately be impossible within a Marxist problematic. This re-prioritizing of women's oppression has been vitally important in post-1980 Socialist Feminist theorizations – impelled in part by the Women's Movement's new concerns with male power and violence (Segal 1987) but also, I would suggest, by the status of theoreticians such as Delphy and by the inadequacies revealed in Marxism by feminists attempting to *apply* it to women working at home and elsewhere.

Such a shift is also evident in another area of Socialist Feminist concern: production and class relations.

PRODUCTION AND CLASS RELATIONS

Juliet Mitchell writes of *production*, one of her four key 'structures of women's situation': 'far from women's *physical* weakness removing her from productive work, her *social* weakness has . . . made her the major slave of it . . . women have been *forced* to do "women's work"' (1971, pp. 103–4). The causes, nature, and possibilities of ending the low status of 'women's work' have been of great interest to Socialist Feminists – delimiting the site not only for theoretical interventions but also direct actions (Cockburn 1984; Coote and Campbell 1982; Hague and Carruthers 1981; Segal 1987). A focus on paid work was impelled by its analytic priority in Marxism, but it can also be seen as a response to the concrete changes occurring from the 1960s of women entering the labour market and experiencing particular forms of oppression and ghettoization within it (Anthias 1980, p. 50). As with domestic labour, theorizations of women's place in production began with attempts to situate them within existing Marxist categories. These categories were subsequently re-formulated first by adding new gender-specific categories – such as the sexual division of labour – and then by grounding conceptualizations more explicitly on gender-sensitive, historical materialist analyses. The result of these later studies has been to transform the Marxist foundations of Socialist Feminism. Such shifts will be detailed by considering how women have been theorized as a reserve army of labour within the framework of a sexual division of labour and how, in turn, this relates to class.

Veronica Beechey begins her 'Notes on female wage labour in capitalist production' (1977) with the work of Marx and Engels, though she quickly points to the need to go beyond them (p. 48). It is women's specific place within the family – as a childbearer and rearer, and as a domestic labourer paid by the male wage to reproduce labour power – that for Beechey shapes their utility for capital and forms the basis of their specific place within the reserve army of labour.

It is therefore *married* women 'who do not, by virtue of the existence of the family, have to bear the total costs of production and reproduction out of their own wages' (p. 54) and thereby it is they who are of particular value to capitalists and whose entry into the labour force is usually resisted by white, male, skilled workers. It is the cheapness and family orientation of married women workers which positions them in a particular way in the class structure, for it allows them to become a subgroup of the reserve army of labour and the working class. The constitution and mobilization of women as this reserve army is related by Beechey to the role of the state, to the historical conditions of labour recruitment and to the existence of working-class resistance in Britain.

Evaluation of Beechey's conceptualization of women's wage labour has been both theoretically and empirically based. Floya Anthias (1980) and

Lucy Bland *et al.* (1978) question Beechey's use of Marx's reserve army of labour idea and the theoretical place of women within it. For example, Lucy Bland and others argue for the need to consider more than production relations when the reserve army of labour is theorized. They write:

> it is this role in the family which limits the extent to which we can *understand* women's subordination *only* through the economic relations of capital. We are, therefore, directed 'outside' the relations of capital to the patriarchal relations between women and men which capital 'takes over', and to the particular ideological constitution of femininity that those relations construct.
>
> (Bland *et al.* 1978, p. 35)

It is from this position that they introduce sexuality and patriarchy into the constitution of wage work, 'women's work', and the reserve army of labour. Even labour power, they argue, is charged with sexuality so that, for example, the secretary or the boutique assistant is valued very much because of her sexuality.

The importance of sexuality to the constitution of production relations has become more apparent as Social Feminists have engaged in detailed studies of particular workplaces and new international divisions of labour (Cavendish 1982; Cockburn 1981; Elson and Pearson 1981; Game and Pringle 1983; Milkman 1982; Phillips and Taylor 1980; Pollert 1981; Westwood 1984). These studies are also further challenging the applicability of the reserve army thesis. In particular historical and contemporary studies in Britian (Bruegel 1979), Australia (Currey *et al.* 1978; Power 1983), and the United States (Milkman 1982) have re-emphasized the importance of the sexual division of labour in shaping the experience of women workers in times of capitalist crisis.

As a result of changing material conditions affecting the employment of women and new theoretical priorities in the areas of sexuality, power, and the family, the previous attempts by Socialist Feminists to *apply* Marxism to analyses of women's waged work have been transformed into the recasting of Marxist categories. The move is towards a historical materialist conception in which women are variously constructed and oppressed by sexuality, the family, and by work (paid and unpaid). Such a move is also evident in theorizations of class.

Women's relations to the class system delimited by Marx have perennially foundered on the formulation of class as a concept only relevant to *waged* workers. The argument over women's place in the 'reserve army of labour' is about their availability, utility, and dispensability in the paid labour force. Other discussions of class also concentrate on where women fit in a hierarchy of occupations – though they are always seen as occupying a particular, lesser, or secondary position within a sexually differentiated workforce (Baron and Norris 1976; West 1978; CSE Group 1982).

It is therefore hard to disagree with Kuhn and Wolpe's introduction to Jackie West's attempt to theorize women's class position:

> while the conclusion here is that the only basis for analysing the class position of women is through capitalist labour relations and the specificity of women's position within them, the problem of how to deal with married women who are not paid workers . . . is left unresolved.
> (1978, p. 221)

The move from this conclusion to an abandoning of 'class' as a concept inapplicable to women has rarely occurred amongst Socialist Feminists (an exception being Matthews 1984c). Rather, the theoretical question remains but is sidestepped by those who *believe*, from experience, political training, and theoretical grounding in Marxism, that class remains a fundamental determinant of social relations in capitalist societies.

Class as something lived through the family unit and through paid work, experienced differently by women and men at particular junctures, becomes for Anne Phillips the means to write about *Divided Loyalties* (1987). For Phillips, gender and class provide the basis of unity but also division in nineteenth- and twentieth-century Britain. Class remains an abstract, objective, but never clarified category for Phillips. In her description women adopt the classes of their fathers or husbands and of their paid workplace at various times, but her main concern is with class as a dynamic, lived and gendered reality. She writes: 'Class has undoubtedly defined the experience of women; the female experience has in turn defined the meaning of class. But the way this has happened has altered through time' (1987, p. 29). Her concern then is not with the relevance of Marxist notions of class to women, but with how a loosely apprehended division between the working class and the middle class assumes a complex set of meanings and realities over time. The objective is not a broadened Marxist orthodoxy but a theoretically informed, historically grounded account which will offer some clues to answer a vital contemporary question: how can a women's movement, built on a notion of gender unity, also acknowledge and respect our divided loyalties: our class, racial, and ethnic differences?

In this Phillips is responding to the critique of Socialist Feminism by women of colour as much as to the bluntness of Marxist theorizations on class. It is a move also impelled by the inadequacy of general theorizations on the relationship of Marxism and feminism, capitalism and patriarchy (pp. 20–1).

MARXISM AND FEMINISM OR MARXIST FEMINISM?

After a period in Socialist Feminist theorizing dominated by efforts to relate Marxism to women's paid and unpaid labour, concern shifted in the late 1970s to specifying the theoretical links between a concept widely used by Radical Feminists and Women's Liberationists – patriarchy – and Marx's theory of capitalism. While for many women who maintained their links with the organized Left this question was already answered – so that women's oppression was coterminous with their family and class position and would end as a result of a party-led socialist revolution (Ehrenreich 1975; Smith 1977; Waters 1972) – to many others it was of vital theoretical concern.

In both the United States and Britain, between 1978 and 1981, there emerged concerted attempts to link Marxism and feminism. The problem was no longer defined as fitting women into Marxist categories, but rather as *uniting* and *transforming* two quite separate theoretical traditions. Reviewing some of this work Diana Adlam (1979) described two approaches to this problem: one prioritized patriarchy and saw capitalism as but one particular modification of patriarchal relations (Eisenstein 1979b; McDonough and Harrison 1978); and the other constructed capitalist relations as essences conditioned in the form of their appearance by the *needs* of patriarchy (Beechey 1978; Hartmann 1981).

The attempts to fuse Engel's concern with *both* production and reproduction, to theoretically unite Marxism and feminism, thus prove ultimately unsatisfactory. The efforts by, for example, Zillah Eisenstein (1979b) and Heidi Hartmann (1981) to generate a grand theory of capitalist patriarchy collapse under their own dualistic assumptions; and also, I would argue, from the ultimate incompatibility of the two political and theoretical projects. These attempts though do push the debates boldly ahead in a number of different directions and create an important legacy in their *materialist* definition of patriarchy.

Through such theorizations by Eisenstein, Hartmann, and others *patriarchy* enters Socialist Feminist discourse. While use of the concept has generated a heated debate (Alexander and Taylor 1980; Beechey 1979; Court 1983; Kuhn 1978; Magarey 1984; Rowbotham 1979; Women's Publishing Collective 1976) its incorporation into Socialist Feminism moves to centre stage the issue of male power. For, once male power is seriously prioritized, as Christine Delphy had earlier argued, Marxist theory is revealed as increasingly inadequate. The attempts to weld Marxist to feminist theory stumble on this point. The problem has led to the increasingly *non-Marxist* theorizations in the name of Socialist Feminism already suggested in discussions of domestic and paid labour, and to more historically grounded studies of particular situations (Phillips 1981, 1987; Matthews 1984b). For some, with whom I must agree, it has led to the conclusion that theories of Marxism and patriarchy are ultimately incompatible (Adlam 1979); and that Marxism itself may be thoroughly sexist and unable to incorporate feminist concerns (Campioni and Gross 1983; Delphy 1984; Matthews 1984a), though its method and historical materialist base can still be of use.

FEMINIST HISTORICAL MATERIALISMS?

Theorizations which detach themselves from the Marxist tradition and prioritize female materiality and oppression have occurred in all three countries considered in this chapter.

In 1983 Mia Campioni and Elizabeth Gross writing in a Sydney-based journal portrayed Marxism as a 'Master-knowledge of the left' which relegated 'other forms of knowledge and struggle to a secondary or auxiliary position' (1983, p. 117). These 'others' included the feminist struggle for women's liberation. As a result of the institutional position of Marxism within the academy, trade unions, and the organized Left, the definition of itself as radically other to capitalism and its theoretical assumptions, they argue that Marxism is phallocentric. Further, they suggest that the concepts and values of Marxism and its dominance of the Left political field 'are in fact effects of the suppression of the problem of sexual difference' (p. 133). They elaborate:

> One of the most striking elisions of marxist theory is its neglect and ignorance of the role of the body in constituting consciousness and in characterising exploitation and oppression . . . marxism has seriously arrested work done by feminists and others on specifying that particular forms of bodies and bodily processes mark out differences between subjectivities, that subjectivity is sexed. By simply dismissing all of this as biologism and essentialism, the necessary analysis of biological existence and its representation in psychical life is neatly pre-empted, and the role of men in women's oppression is conveniently ignored.
>
> (p. 132).

From this point they urge a historical materialist feminism grounded upon women's bodies. This is not a Radical Feminist call based on a unified female biology, but derives from a multifaceted conception of the body. They write:

> This implies that there cannot be one or even two kinds of subject, but many different kinds, bounded not simply by the biological body but by its necessary social and individual signification. The body is

> not simply the 'seat' of subjectivity; it is also the target of technologies of power and forms of social control in all cultures.
>
> (pp. 132–3).

Further detail as to what form this analysis could take is merely suggested in such a passage. But in another country, a sensitivity to the sexed body and to the technologies and ideologies which define it has led the American Donna Haraway (1985) to outline a transformed Socialist Feminism.

Haraway bases her reformulation within a Socialist Feminism concerned not only with production relations but also culture, post-modernism, and utopianism, as well as women's diversity and contradictory interests. She also grounds her theorization on the new high-tech world of information technology – a world in which the interface between human and machine, home and work, idealism and materialism is breached. It is a world where a 'cyborg myth' transgressing these and other boundaries can form the basis for seizing control of the processes engendering our domination. She writes:

> The actual situation of women is their integration/exploitation into a world system of production/reproduction and communication called the informatics of domination. The home, workplace, market, public arena, the body itself – all can be dispersed and interfaced in nearly infinite, polymorphous ways, with large consequences for women and others. . . . One important route for reconstructing socialist–feminist politics is through theory and practice addressed to the social relations of science and technology, including crucially the systems of myth and meanings structuring our imaginations. The cyborg is a kind of disassembled and reassembled, post-modern collective and personal self. This is the self feminists must code.
>
> (1985, p. 82).

For Haraway such coding is not to be attained by the generation of grand theories but by the 'subtle understanding of emerging pleasures, experiences, and powers with serious potential for changing the rules of the game' (p. 91). Such understandings create cyborg myths, oppositional discourses, potent subjectivities which challenge and rewrite the material and cultural grids of our oppressions. One such myth Haraway describes as *Sister Outsider*, or 'women of color':

> In my political myth, Sister Outsider is the offshore woman, whom U.S. workers, female and feminized, are supposed to regard as the enemy preventing their solidarity, threatening their security. Onshore . . . Sister Outsider is a potential amidst the races and ethnic identities of women manipulated for division, competition, and exploitation in the same industries.
>
> (p. 93)

With subjectivities defined by 'fusions of outsider identities', 'women of color' have contested these definitions and done so by writing themselves. As Haraway concludes: 'Cyborg writing is about the power to survive, not on the basis of original innocence, but on the basis of seizing the tools to mark the world that marked them as other' (p. 94).

In Britain too, a new direction and one of the most profound questionings of the material foundations of Socialist Feminism itself, has emerged from 'women of colour'. Building on a broader political movement for the recognition of institutionalized racism and drawing on American Black Feminism, a number of challenges were made in the mid-1980s to 'Imperial feminism' (Amos and Parmar 1984). Quickly exposed by such challenges were some of the power relations occupied by those who were defining Socialist Feminist theory. As Michèle Barrett and Mary McIntosh wrote in their effort to reconsider their book *The Anti-Social Family* (1982) from an awareness of race and ethnicity:

> Most . . . white feminist writers are middle-class intellectual women who are immersed in specifically British traditions of education and political thought, largely left and libertarian. Most of them, however disadvantaged they may feel as women, have immense privileges in terms of race and class, which give them access to publishing, the media, teaching, public meetings of various kinds. These privileged white feminists, such as ourselves, have been able to make their voices heard, and to some extent at least, respected.
>
> (1985, p. 25)

The exchange surrounding this attempt contained in the pages of the (Socialist) *Feminist Review* reveal the discursive foundations of much contemporary Socialist Feminism and suggest a new materialist base from which different theoretical interventions will come. For not only do Barrett and McIntosh acknowledge their own class and racial privileges, but they *begin* a process of questioning Socialist Feminist theory in these terms – as something produced by mainly white, middle-class women, using a Leftist tradition largely unconcerned with racism. It is from these positions that they look again at their own work on the division of labour, the family, and patriarchy. All of these concepts are found to 'negate the existence and experience of black women' (1985, p. 35), but not all are thereby in need of a radical reconceptualization, for Barrett and McIntosh remain bound to a particular branch of the Socialist Feminist tradition. So, for example, 'patriarchy' as an 'unambiguous male dominance' (p. 38) is rejected for a definition which is specific to social relations, one which 'combine(s) a public dimension of power, exploitation or status with a dimension of personal servility' (p. 39). As a non-general, all-embracing formulation, Barrett and McIntosh see this redefined notion of patriarchy as able to incorporate the diverse experiences of women, blacks under slavery, and black women's 'personal service' work in contemporary Britain (p. 39). However, as Hazel Carby observed:

> we find that even this refined use of the concept cannot adequately account for the fact that both slaves and manumitted males did not have this type of patriarchal power. . . . There are very obvious power structures in both colonial and slave formations and they are predominantly patriarchal . . . the historically specific forms of racism force us to modify or alter the application of the term 'patriarchy' to black men. Black women have been dominated 'patriarchally' in different ways by men of different 'colours'.
>
> (1984, p. 218)

Barrett and McIntosh's evaluations of other concepts are similarly criticized as being too blunt to encompass the diversity of experiences structured by class, race, and sex. More seriously, their reformulations are seen as unable to include the particular case of black women. So, for example, they reject the point made by Hazel Carby that black families have 'functioned as a prime source of resistance to (racial) oppression' (1984, p. 214) as one from which they should re-evaluate their position on the 'Anti-social family' (Barrett and McIntosh 1985, p. 423). In this they follow the analytic imperatives of Socialist Feminism which prioritize class and social reproduction as the major sites of oppression for women. As Althusserians they also transform racism into ethnic difference operating primarily in the realm of the ideological. Not only is the horror of racism rendered outside the 'academic' discourse, but ultimately so is its theoretical importance. What is sidestepped is the necessary transformation of that theory in the light of black women's experience, an experience not of ethnicity but of racism (Kazi 1986; Mirza 1986; Ramazanoglu 1986). As Hamidi Kazi concludes her assessment of Barrett and McIntosh's reflection: 'They have thus hidden the real issues of racism, sexism and the capitalist exploitation of black women behind ethnic characteristics' (1986, p. 90). Barrett and McIntosh do not *theorize* the question of race – though they point to the urgency of such a task (1985, p. 41). Heidi Safia Mirza responds:

> The fact that we can articulate our own and others' economic, political and social realities within the confines of a black feminist analysis can seem very threatening to socialist-feminists, who have hitherto conducted themselves as the vanguard of our oppression from their intellectual ivory towers.
>
> (1986, p. 104)

While none of the women engaged in this exchange reject the importance of theoretically articulating class, sex, ethnicity, and race, it is primarily at the level of political practice that their analyses are conducted – not in the realm of debating Marxist theory. The implications are that such theory and those who champion it derive from a white Socialist Feminist tradition and they have to recognize their own powerful and particular positions (Bhavnani and Coulson 1986). By implication Socialist Feminists must acknowledge the different materialist positions occupied by women who define themselves as racially or ethnically different as a source of new transformations of the Socialist Feminist intervention.

CONCLUSION

Building on a particular set of texts in the Marxist tradition, Socialist Feminist interventions have occurred first to include women into and then progressively to transform and ultimately to abandon, much of the Marxist problematic. Shifts have occurred in the light of different feminist theorizations impacting upon Socialist Feminism – especially from psychoanalysis and cultural criticism – and as a result of different political priorities, which have moved women's oppression by men, and finally racial oppression, on to the theoretical agenda. The present point then is a multiplicity of possible directions all loosely embracing *historical materialism* as the place from which new Socialist Feminist interventions will be made.

NOTES

1 In an earlier version of this chapter other areas of interest to Socialist Feminists – in particular the family, the state, sexuality, and ideology – were included. Space prevents a detailed inclusion here of this work.

2 From the time of Marx and Engels until the re-emergence of a self-conscious Socialist Feminism in the 1970s Socialists have considered the position of women in their theory, in their parties, and in their states under the rubric 'The Woman Question'. In such considerations the priorities accorded class over gender in analyses and action is rarely questioned, and the theoretical place of women is, by implication, located outside mainstream considerations. This is unlike the approach taken in the 1970s and 1980s by those seeing themselves as Socialist Feminists.

3 The question of the alignment or non-alignment of Socialist Feminist women with organized Left parties ranging from the far Left to Labour parties has been a vital issue for many women especially in Britain and Australia (Ballantyne 1979; Campbell 1984; Rowbotham *et al.* 1979; Segal 1987). Space does not permit a detailed examination of this issue here.

4 Such a shift is not only being urged by those theorists critical of the Domestic Labour Debate and by those informed by other theoretical developments, but also by theorizations embedded in careful empirical studies of women's domestic worlds. Thus Meg Luxton's (1986) study of three generations of working-class households draws out the class and patriarchal relations of the small, remote, single-industry Canadian town of Flin Flon. The result for Roberta Hamilton confirms the importance of such studies in reorienting the Domestic Labour debate to the 'experience of women's oppression' (1986).

REFERENCES

Adlam, D. (1979) 'The case against capitalist patriarchy', *m/f*, 3, pp. 83–102.

Alexander, S. and Taylor, B. (1980) 'In defence of "patriarchy" ', *New Statesman*, 1 February, p. 161.

Amos, V. and Parmar, P. (1984) 'Challenging imperial feminism', *Feminist Review*, 17, pp. 3–19.

Anthias, F. (1980) 'Women and the reserve army of labour: a critique of Veronica Beechey', *Capital and Class*, 10, pp. 50–63.

Ballantyne, G. (1979) 'Who decides? Perspectives on the abortion campaign', *Scarlet Woman*, 8, pp. 23–30.

Barrett, M. (1980) *Women's Oppression Today: Problems in Marxist Feminist Analysis*, Verso, London.

Barrett, M. and McIntosh, M. (1982) *The Anti-Social Family*, Verso, London.

Barrett, M. and McIntosh, M. (1985) 'Ethnocentrism and socialist-feminist theory', *Feminist Review*, 20, pp. 25–47.

Barron, R. D. and Norris, G. M. (1976) 'Sexual divisions and the dual labour market', in D. L. Barker and S. Allen (eds) *Dependence and Exploitation in Work and Marriage*, Longman, London, pp. 47–69.

Beechey, V. (1977) 'Some notes on female wage labour in capitalist production', *Capital and Class*, 3, pp. 45–66.

Beechey, V. (1978) 'Women and production: a critical analysis of some sociological theories of women's work', in A. Kuhn and A. M. Wolpe (eds) *Feminism and Materialism: Women and Modes of Production*, Routledge & Kegan Paul, London, pp. 155–97.

Beechey, V. (1979) 'On patriarchy', *Feminist Review*, 3, pp. 66–82.

Bengelsdorf, C. and Hageman, A. (1979) 'Emerging from underdevelopment: women and work in Cuba', in Z. Eisenstein (ed.) *Capitalist Patriarchy and the Case for Socialist Feminism*, Monthly Review Press, New York, pp. 279–95.

Benston, M. (1969) 'The political economy of women's liberation', in E. H. Altbach (ed.) *From Feminism to Liberation*, Shenkman, Cambridge, Mass., pp. 199–210.

Bhavnani, K. K. and Coulson, M. (1986) 'Transforming socialist feminism: the challenge of racism', *Feminist Review*, 23, pp. 81–92.

Bland, L., Brunsdon, C., Hobson, D., and Winship, J. (1978) 'Women inside and outside the relations of production', in Women's Studies Group (eds) *Women Take Issue: Aspects of Women's Subordination*, Centre for Contemporary Cultural Studies, Hutchinson, London, pp. 35–77.

Bruegel, I. (1979) 'Women as a reserve army of labour: a note on recent British experience', *Feminist Review*, 3, pp. 12–23.

Burton, C. (1985) *Subordination: Feminism and Social Theory*, Allen & Unwin, Sydney.

Campbell, B. (1984) 'Transforming the socialist movement', *Australian Left Review*, 83, pp. 10–15.

Campioni, M. and Gross, E. (1983) 'Love's labours lost: Marxism and feminism', in J. Allan and P. Patton (eds) *Beyond Marxism?: Interventions After Marx*, Intervention Publications, Sydney, pp. 113–41.

Carby, H. V. (1984 'White woman listen! Black feminism and the boundaries of sisterhood', in *The Empire Strikes Back: Race and Racism in 70s Britain*, Centre for Contemporary Cultural Studies, Hutchinson, London, pp.212–35.

Cavendish, R. (1982) *Women on the Line*, Routledge & Kegan Paul, London.

Cliff, T. (1984) *Class Struggle and Women's Liberation*, Bookmarks, London.

Cockburn, C. (1981) 'The material of male power', *Feminist Review*, 9, pp. 41–58.
Cockburn, C. (1984) 'Trade unions and the radicalizing of socialist feminism', *Feminist Review*, 16, pp. 43–6.
Coote, A. and Campbell, B. (1982) *Sweet Freedom: The Struggle for Women's Liberation*, Picador, London.
Coulson, M., Magas, B., and Wainwright, H. (1975) 'The housewife and her labour under capitalism – a critique', *New Left Review*, 89, pp. 59–72.
Court, D. (1983) 'The centrality of patriarchy', *Arena*, 65, pp. 162–71.
Coward, R. (1983) *Patriarchal Precedents: Sexuality and Social Relations*, Routledge & Kegan Paul, London.
Coward, R. (1984) *Female Desire: Women's Sexuality Today*, Paladin, London.
CSE Sex and Class Group (1982) 'Sex and class', *Capital and Class*, 16, pp. 78–93.
Currey, C., Moore, M., and O'Sullivan, G.(1978) 'The reserve army under seige', *Scarlet Woman*, 7, pp. 11–13.
Dalla Costa, M. and James, S. (1972) *The Power of Women and the Subversion of the Community*, Falling Wall Press, London.
Davin, D. (1987) 'Engels and the making of Chinese family policy', in J. Sayers, M. Evans, and N. Redclift (eds) *Engels Revisited: New Feminist Essays*, Tavistock, London, pp. 145–63.
Delmar, R. (1979) 'Looking again at Engels's "Origin of the family, private property and the state"', in J. Mitchell and A. Oakley (eds) *The Rights and Wrongs of Women*, Penguin, Harmondsworth, pp. 271–87.
Delphy, C. (1976) *The Main Enemy*, Women's Research and Resources Centre, London.
Delphy, C. (1984) *Close to Home: A Materialist Analysis of Women's Oppression*, Hutchinson in association with The Explorations in Feminism Collective, London.
Edholm, F., Harris, O., and Young, K. (1977) 'Conceptualising women', *Critique of Anthropology*, 3:9 and 10, pp. 101–30.
Ehrenreich, B. (1975) 'Speech to the National Conference on Socialist Feminism', *Socialist Revolution*, 26:5(4), pp. 85–93.
Einhorn, B. (1981) 'Socialist emancipation: the women's movement in the German Democratic Republic', *Women's Studies International Quarterly*, 4:4, pp. 435–52.
Eisen, A. (1984) *Women and Revolution in Vietnam*, Zed, London.
Eisenstein, Z. H. (1979a) *Capitalist Patriarchy and the Case for Socialist Feminism*, Monthly Review Press, New York.
Eisenstein, Z. H. (1979b) 'Developing a theory of capitalist patriarchy and socialist feminism', in Z. Eisenstein (ed.) *Capitalist Patriarchy and the Case for Socialist Feminism*, Monthly Review Press, New York, pp. 5–40.
Elson, D. and Pearson, R. (1981) 'The subordination of women and the internationalisation of factory production', in K. Young, C. Wolkowitz, and R. McCullough (eds) *Of Marriage and the Market: Women's Subordination in International Perspective*, CSE Books, London, pp. 144–66.
Engels, F. (1975) *The Origin of the Family, Private Property and the State*, International Publishers, New York.
Evans, M. (1987) 'Engels: materialism and morality', in J. Sayers, M. Evans, and N. Redlift (eds) *Engels Revisited: New Feminist Essays*, Tavistock, London, pp. 81–97.
Fox, B. (1986) 'Never done: the struggle to understand domestic labour and women's oppression', in R. Hamilton and M. Barrett (eds) *The Politics of Diversity*, Verso, London, pp. 180–9.
Friedan, B. (1963) *The Feminine Mystique*, Penguin, Harmondsworth.

Game, A. and Pringle, R. (1983) *Gender at Work*, Allen & Unwin, Sydney.
Gardiner, J. (1975) 'Women's domestic labour', *New Left Review*, 89, pp. 47–58.
Gardiner, J. (1976) 'Political economy of domestic labour in capitalist society', in D. L. Barker and S. Allen (eds) *Dependence and Exploitation in Work and Marriage*, Longman, London, pp. 109–20.
Gavron, H. (1966) *The Captive Wife: Conflicts of Housebound Mothers*, Penguin, Harmondsworth.
Hague, D. and Carruthers, L. (1981) 'Socialist-feminism and trade unions: work in the P.S.A.', *Scarlet Woman*, 13, pp. 2–5.
Hamilton, R. and Barrett, M. (eds) (1986) *The Politics of Diversity*, Verso, London.
Haraway, D. (1985) 'A manifesto for cyborgs: science, technology and socialist feminism in the 1980s', *Socialist Review*, 15:2, pp. 65–107.
Hartmann, H. (1981) 'The unhappy marriage of marxism and feminism: towards a more progressive union', in L. Sargent (ed.) *Women and Revolution*, South End Press, Boston, pp. 1–41.
Jaggar, A. M. (1983) *Feminist Politics and Human Nature*, Harvester Press, Sussex.
Kazi, H. (1986) 'The beginning of a debate long due: some observations on ethnocentrism and socialist-feminist theory', *Feminist Review*, 22, pp. 87–91.
Kuhn, A. (1978) 'Feminism and materialism', in A. Kuhn and A. M. Wolpe (eds) *Feminism and Materialism: Women and Modes of Production*, Routledge & Kegan Paul, London, pp. 1–10.
Kuhn, A. and Wolpe, A. M. (eds) (1978) *Feminism and Materialism: Women and Modes of Production*, Routledge & Kegan Paul, London.
Lenin, V. I. (1982) 'Women and society', in K. Marx, V. I. Lenin, F. Engels, and J. V. Stalin (eds) *The Woman Question: Selections*, International Publishers, New York, pp. 49–55.
Luxton, M. (1986) 'Two hands for the clock: changing patterns in the gendered division of labour in the home', in R. Hamilton and M. Barrett (eds) *The Politics of Diversity*, Verso, London, pp. 35–52.
McDonough, R. and Harrison, R. (1978) 'Patriarchy and relations of production', in A. Kuhn and A. H. Wolpe (eds) *Feminism and Materialism: Women and Modes of Production*, Routledge & Kegan Paul, London, pp. 11–41.
McIntosh, M. (1982) 'The family in socialist-feminist politics', in R. Brunt and C. Rowan (eds) *Feminism, Culture and Politics*, Lawrence & Wishart, London, pp. 109–29.
McLellan, D. (1983) *Marx*, Fontana/Collins, Glasgow.
Magarey, S. (1984) 'Can there be justice for women under capitalism? Two views. Questions about "Patriarchy"', in D. Broom (ed.) *Unfinished Business: Social Justice for Women in Australia*, Allen & Unwin, Sydney, pp. 181–7.
Marx, K. (1974) *Capital: A Critical Analysis of Capitalist Production*, vol. 1, Progress Publishers, Moscow.
Marx, K. and Engels, F. (1976) *Karl Marx, Friedrich Engels: Collected Works*, vol. 5, Lawrence & Wishart, London.
Matthews, J. J. (1984a) 'Putting women first', *Australian Left Review*, 83, pp. 16–19.
Matthews, J. J. (1984b) *Good and Mad Women*, Allen & Unwin, Sydney.
Matthews, J. J. (1984c) 'Deconstructing the masculine universe: the case of women's work', in *All Her Labours: Working It Out*, ed. Women and Labour Publications Collective, Hale & Ironmonger, Sydney, pp. 11–23.
Milkman, R. (1982) 'Redefining "women's work": the sexual division of labour in the auto industry during World War II', *Feminist Studies*, 8:2, pp. 336–72.
Mitchell, J. (1966) 'Women: the longest revolution', *New Left Review*, 40. pp. 11–37.
Mitchell, J. (1971) *Woman's Estate*, Vintage Books, New York.

Mitchell, J. (1979) *Psychoanalysis and Feminism*, Penguin, Harmondsworth.
Mitchell, J. and Rose, J. (eds) (1982) *Feminine Sexuality: Jacques Lacan and the Ecole Freudienne*, Macmillan, London.
Mirza, H. S. (1986) 'The dilemma of socialist-feminism: a case for black feminism', *Feminist Review*, 22, pp. 103–5.
Molyneux, M. (1979) 'Beyond the domestic labour debate', *New Left Review*, 116, pp. 3–27.
Morton, P. (1971) 'Women's work is never done', in H. Altbach (ed.) *From Feminism to Liberation*, Schenkman, Cambridge, Mass., pp. 211–27.
O'Brien, P. (1970) 'Some overseas comparisons', in R. Gordon (ed.) *The Australian New Left: Critical Essays and Strategy*, Heinemann, Melbourne.
O'Brien, M. (1981) *The Politics of Reproduction*, Routledge & Kegan Paul, London.
O'Brien, M. (1982) 'Feminist theory and dialectical logic', *Signs*, 7:1, pp. 144–57.
Ollman, B. (1976) *Alienation: Marx's Conception of Man in Capitalist Society*, Cambridge University Press.
Phillips, A. (1981) 'Marxism and feminism', in Feminist Anthology Collective (eds) *No Turning Back: Writings from the Women's Liberation Movement 1975–80*, Women's Press, London, pp. 90–108.
Phillips, A. (1987) *Divided Loyalties: Dilemmas of Sex and Class*, Virago, London.
Phillips, A. and Taylor, B. (1980) 'Sex and skill: notes towards a feminist economics', *Feminist Review*, 6, pp. 79–88.
Pollert, A. (1981) *Girls, Wives and Factory Lives*, Macmillan, London.
Porter, C. (1980) *Alexandra Kollontai: A Biography*, Virago, London.
Power, M.(1983) 'Women as a reserve army: the experience of Australian women in the 1974–82 crisis', paper presented to Conference on 'Australia and Canada: Differing consequences for women of a common culture', Vancouver.
Ramazanoglu, C. (1986) 'Ethnocentrism and socialist-feminist theory: a response to Barret and McIntosh', *Feminist Review*, 22, pp. 83–6.
Randall, M. (1979) 'Introducing the family code', in Z. Eisenstein (ed.) *Capitalist Patriarchy and the Case for Socialist Feminism*, Monthly Review Press, New York, pp. 296–8.
Rowbotham, S. (1972) *Women, Resistance and Revolution*, Penguin, Harmondsworth.
Rowbotham, S. (1979) 'The trouble with patriarchy', *New Statesman*, 21/28 December, pp. 970–1.
Rowbotham, S., Segal, L., and Wainwright, H. (1979) *Beyond the Fragments: Feminism and the Making of Socialism*, Merlin Press, London.
Sayers, J. (1987) 'For Engels: psychoanalytic perspectives', in J. Sayers, M. Evans, and N. Redclift (eds) *Engels Revisited: New Feminist Essays*, Tavistock, London, pp. 57–80.
Sayers, J., Evans, M., and Redclift, N. (eds) (1987) *Engels Revisited: New Feminist Essays*, Tavistock, London.
Scott, H. (1976) *Women and Socialism: Experiences from Eastern Europe*, Allison & Busby, London.
Seccombe, W. (1973) 'The housewife and her labour under capitalism', *New Left Review*, 83, pp. 3–24.
Segal, L. (1987) *Is the Future Female?* Virago, London.
Smith, D. E. (1977) *Feminism and Marxism: A Place to Begin, A Way to Go*, New Star Books, Vancouver.
Smith, P. (1978) 'Domestic labour and Marx's theory of value', in A. Kuhn and A. M. Wolpe (eds) *Feminism and Materialism: Women and Modes of Production*, Routledge & Kegan Paul, London, pp. 198–219.

Stacey, J. (1979) 'When patriarchy kowtows: the significance of the Chinese family revolution for feminist theory', in Z. Eisenstein (ed.) *Capitalist Patriarchy and the Case for Socialist Feminism*, Monthly Review Press, New York, pp. 299–348.
Taylor, B. (1980) 'Lords of creation: Marxism; feminism and "Utopian" socialism', *Radical America*, 14:4, pp. 41–6.
Taylor, B. (1983) *Eve and the New Jerusalem*, Virago, London.
Vogel, L. (1983) *Marxism and the Oppression of Women: Towards a Unitary Theory*, Pluto, London.
Waters, M. A. (1972) 'Feminism and the marxist movement', *International Socialist Review*, October, pp. 8–23.
West, J. (1978) 'Women, sex and class', in A. Kuhn and A. M. Wolpe (eds) *Feminism and Materialism: Women and Modes of Production*, Routledge & Kegan Paul, London, pp. 220–53.
Westwood, S. (1984) *All Day Every Day: Factory and Family in the Making of Women's Lives*, Pluto, London.
Women's Publishing Collective (Cooper, S., Crowley, S., and Holtam, C.) (1976) *Papers on Patriarchy*, Patriarchy Conference, London.

11

CONCLUSION
A note on essentialism and difference

Elizabeth Grosz

Feminist theory is necessarily implicated in a series of complex negotiations between a number of tense and antagonistic forces which are often unrecognized and unelaborated. It is a self-conscious reaction on the one hand to the overwhelming masculinity of privileged and historically dominant knowledges, acting as a kind of counterweight to the imbalances resulting from the male monopoly of the production and reception of knowledges: on the other hand, it is also a response to the broad political aims and objectives of feminist struggles. Feminist theory is thus bound to two kinds of goals, two commitments or undertakings, which exist only in an uneasy and problematic relationship. This tension means feminists have had to tread a fine line between intellectual rigour (as it has been defined in male terms) and political commitment (as feminists see it), that is, between the risks posed by patriarchal recuperation and those of a conceptual sloppiness inadequate to the long-term needs of feminist struggles or between acceptance in male terms, and commitment to women's terms.

The ways in which feminists have engaged in the various projects of constructing or fabricating a knowledge appropriate to women – while keeping an eye on male academic traditions as well as on feminist politics – have left many open to criticism from both directions. From the point of view of masculine conceptions of theory-evaluation, including notions of objectivity, disinterested scholarship, and intellectual rigour, feminist theory is accused of a motivated, self-interested, 'biased' approach, in which pre-given commitments are simply confirmed rather than objectively demonstrated;[1] and from the point of view of (some) feminist 'activists', feminist theory is accused of playing male power games, of participating in and contributing to the very forms of male dominance that feminism should be trying to combat. It is not altogether surprising that underlying both criticisms is a common demand for a *purity* of position – an intellectual purity in the one case (untainted by social and political factors which militate against or interfere with the goals of scholarly research) and a political purity in the other (free from influence of patriarchal and masculinist values). Male-dominated theories require the disavowal of the socio-political values implicit in the production of all knowledges and the creation of a supposedly value-free knowledge; while feminist political purists require the disavowal of the pervasive masculinity of privileged knowledges and social practices, including feminist forms.

In spite of the sometimes puerile and often naive extremism of both types of objection, they do nevertheless articulate a real concern for feminist theory, highlighting an untheorized locus in its self-formation: by what criteria are feminists to judge not only male theory but also feminist theory? If the criteria by which theory has been judged up to now are masculine, how can new criteria be formulated? What would they look like? Can such criteria adequately satisfy the dual requirements of intellectual or conceptual rigour as well as political engagement? Is it possible to produce theory that comprises neither its political nor its intellectual credibility? In what ways is feminist theory to legitimize itself in theoretical and political terms? These questions are not idle or frivolous. They are of direct relevance to the ways in which feminist theory is assessed, and may help to clarify a number of issues which have polarized feminist theorists in unproductive ways.

In this brief note, I would like to use a major dispute between feminist theorists – the debate between so-called feminisms of equality and feminisms of difference – to raise the question of the dual commitments of feminist theory and the need to devise appropriate criteria for its assessment. Is the concept of sexual difference a breakthrough term in contesting patriarchal conceptions of women and feminity? Or is it a reassertion of the patriarchal containment of women? Is the concept essentialist or is it an upheaval of patriarchal knowledges?

ESSENTIALISM AND ITS COGNATES

Feminists have developed a range of terms and criteria of intellectual assessment over the last twenty or so years which aim to affirm, consolidate, and explain the political goals and ambitions of feminist struggles. These terms have tended to act as unquestioned values and as intellectual guidelines in assessing both male-dominated and feminist-oriented theories. Among the most frequent and powerful of these terms are those centred around the question of the *nature* of women (and men) – essentialism, biologism, naturalism, and universalism. While these terms are closely related to each other, sharing a common concern for the fixity and limits definitionally imposed on women, it is important to be aware of the sometimes subtle differences between them in order to appreciate the ways in which they have been used by and against feminists. These terms are commonly used in patriarchal discourses to justify women's social subordination and their secondary positions relative to men in patriarchal society.

Essentialism, a term which is rarely defined or explained explicitly in feminist contexts, refers to the attribution of a fixed essence to women. Women's essence is assumed to be given, universal, and is usually, though not necessarily, identified with women's biology and 'natural' characteristics. The term usually entails biologism and naturalism, but there are cases in which women's essence is seen to reside, not in nature or biology, but in certain given psychological charcteristics – nurturance, empathy, supportiveness, non-competitiveness, and so on. Or women's essence may be attributed to certain activities and procedures (which may or may not be dictated by biology) observable in social practices, intuitiveness, emotional responses, concern, and commitment to helping others, etc. Essentialism entails that those characteristics defined as women's essence are shared in common by all women at all times: it implies a limit on the variations and possibilities of change. It is not possible for a subject to act in a manner contrary to her nature. Essentialism thus refers to the existence of fixed characteristics, given attributes, and ahistorical functions which limit the possibilities of change and thus of social reorganization.

Biologism is a particular form of essentialism in which women's essence is defined in terms of their biological capacities. Biologism is usually based on some form of reductionism: social and cultural factors are regarded as the effects of biologically given causes. In particular, biologism usually ties women closely to the functions of reproduction and nurturance, although it may also limit women's social possibilities through the use of evidence from neurology, neurophysiology, and endocrinology. Biologism is thus an attempt to limit women's social and psychological capacities according to biologically established limits: it asserts, for example, that women are weaker in physical strength than men, that women are, by their biological natures, more emotional than men, and so on. In so far as biology is assumed to constitute an unalterable bedrock of identity, the attribution of biologistic characteristics amounts to a permanent form of social containment for women.

Naturalism is also a form of essentialism in which a fixed nature is postulated for women. Once again, this nature is usually given biological form, but this is by no means an invariant. Naturalism may be asserted on theological or on ontological rather than on biological grounds: for example, it may be claimed that women's nature is derived from God-given attributes which are not explicable or observable simply in biological terms; or, following Sartrean existentialism or Freudian psychoanalysis, there are as it were ontological invariants which distinguish the two sexes in, for example, the claim that the human subject is somehow naturally free or that the subject's social position is a function of his or her genital morphology. More commonly however, naturalism presumes the equivalence of biological and natural properties.

While also closely related to essentialism, biologism, and naturalism, universalism need not be based on the innate or fixed characteristics. It is usually justifed in terms of some essential or biological characteristics, but universalism may be conceived in purely social terms. It refers to the attributions of invariant social categories, functions, and activities to which all women in all cultures are assigned. This may be the result of biology or ontology, but just as frequently it may reflect universal social or cultural requirements, such as the sexual division of labour or the prohibition of incest. Unlike essentialism, biologism, or naturalism, in which not only the similarities but also the differences between women may be accounted for (race and class characteristics can also be explained in naturalistic, biologistic, or essentialist terms), universalism tends to suggest only the commonness of all women at all times and in all social contexts. By definition, it can only assert similarities, what is shared in common by all women, and what homogenizes women as a category.

These four terms are frequently elided: each has commonly served as a shorthand formula for the others. In charging theories with these conceptual commitments, feminists assert that they are necessarily complicit in reproducing patriarchal values: in claiming that women's current social roles and positions are the effects of their essence, nature, biology, or universal social position, these theories are guilty of rendering such roles and positions unalterable, necessary, and thus of providing them with a powerful political justification. They rationalize and neutralize the prevailing sexual division of social roles by assuming these are the only, or the best, possibilities, given the confines of the nature, essence, or biology of the two sexes. These commitments entail a range of other serious problems: they are necessarily ahistorical; they confuse social relations with fixed attributes; they see these fixed attributes as inherent limitations to social change; and they refuse to take seriously the historical and geographical differences between women across different cultures as well as within a single culture.

It is not surprising that these terms have become labels for danger zones or theoretical pitfalls in feminist assessments of patriarchal theory. One could be sure that the theories one analysed were tinged with patriarchal values whenever a trace of them could be discerned. They are the critical touchstones of assessment, self-evident guidelines for evaluating patriarchal theories and the patriarchal residues or adherences of feminist theories. These terms seem unquestionably problematic; they indicate, at least at first glance, a rare harmony between the principles of feminist politics and those of intellectual rigour, for they are problematic in both political and theoretical terms. Yet their value as criteria of critical evaluation for feminist as well as patriarchal theory is not as clear as it might seem.

SEXUAL IDENTITY/SEXUAL DIFFERENCE

Among the most central and contested issues in contemporary feminist theory are the terms in which women's social, sexual, and cultural positions are to be understood. This kind of question is, moreover, crucially positioned at the heart of the conflict between feminist politics and the requirements of patriarchal knowledges. Is woman to be assigned an identity and socio-cultural position in terms that make it possible for women to be conceived as men's equals, or is woman's identity to be conceived in terms entirely different from those associated with and provided by men? This question implies two other related questions: are the frameworks of prevailing patriarchal knowledges capable of bestowing on women the same basic capacities, skills, and attributes they have posited for men? And if so, are these frameworks adequate for characterizing not only what women share in common with men (what makes both sexes human) but also what particularizes women and distinguishes them from men?

The positions of a number of pioneer feminists in the history of second-wave feminism, including Simone de Beauvoir, Betty Friedan, Eva Figes, Kate Millett, Shulamith Firestone, Germaine Greer, and others could be described as egalitarian. This broad position assumes that the liberation of women from patriarchal constraints entailed opening up social, economic, political, and sexual positions previously occupied only by men. These theorists in different ways believed that women have been unfairly excluded from positions of social value and status normally occupied by men. Women in patriarchy were regarded as socially, intellectually, and physically inferior to men, a consequence of various discriminatory, sexist practices, practices which illegitimately presumed that women were unsuited for or incapable of assuming certain positions. This belief was fostered not only by oppressive external constraints but also by women's own compliance with and internalization of patriarchal sexual stereotypes.

Egalitarian feminists – among whom we should include, in spite of their differences, liberal and socialist feminists – were reacting to the largely naturalist and biologistic presumptions on which much of social and political theory is based. If it is in women's *nature* to be passive, compliant, nurturing, this is a 'natural' index, guide or limit to the organization of society. Defenders of patriarchal social order assume that social and cultural relations should conform and be conducive to '(human) nature'. Its goal is not the augmentation and reorganization of 'nature' but simply its confirmation. The divisions and inequalities between the sexes were seen as the effects of a nature that should not be tampered with. This provides a ready-made justification for the most conservative and misogynist of social relations: they are treated as if they were the effects of nature alone.

Egalitarian feminists claim that women are as able as men to do what men do. The fact that women were not regarded as men's equals was, they claimed, not result of nature, but of patriarchal ideologies, discriminatory socialization practices, social stereotyping, and role-playing. They were, in other words, the results of culture not nature, of social organization rather than biological determinants, and were thus capable of being changed. Indeed, if women's social roles are dictated by nature, feminism itself becomes impossible for resistance to nature is, in one sense at least, impossible. Feminism is founded on the belief that women are capable of achievements other than those recognized and rewarded by patriarchy, other than those to which women's 'nature' has hitherto confined them.

As a category, women were consistently underrepresented in positions of social authority and status, and overrepresented in socially subordinate positions. Girls systematically underachieve and are inadequately prepared for social success; while boys' social roles maximize their social potential. Feminism began largely as a struggle for a greater share of the patriarchal pie, an equal access to social, economic, sexual, and intellectual opportunities. These early feminists of equality were bound up in what Kristeva has called 'the logic of identification', an identification with the values, norms, goals, and methods devised and validated by men:

> In its beginnings, the women's movement, as the struggle of suffragists and of existential feminists, aspired to gain a place in linear time as the time of project and history. In this sense, the movement, while immediately universalist, is also deeply rooted in the socio-political life of nations. The political demands of women; the struggles for equal pay for equal work, for taking power in social institutions on an equal footing with men; the rejection, when necessary, of the attributes traditionally considered feminine or maternal insofar as they are deemed incompatible with insertion in that history – all are part of the *logic of identification* with certain values: not with the ideological (these are combatted, and rightly so, as reactionary) but, rather, with the logical and ontological values of a rationality dominant in the nation-state.
>
> (Kristeva, 1981, pp. 18–19)

In place of the essentialist and naturalist containment of women, feminists of equality affirm women's potential for equal intelligence, ability, and social value. Underlying the belief in the need to eliminate or restructure the social constraints imposed on women is a belief that the 'raw materials' of socialization are fundamentally the same for both sexes: each has analogous biological or natural potential, which is unequally developed because the social roles imposed on the two sexes are unequal. If social roles could be readjusted or radically restructured, if the two sexes could be re-socialized, they could be rendered equal. The differences between the sexes would be no more significant than the differences between individuals. These feminist arguments for an egalitarian treatment of the two sexes was no doubt threatening to patriarchs in so far as the sex-roles the latter presumed were natural could be blurred through social means, women could become 'unfeminine', men 'unmasculine' and the sovereignty of the nuclear family, marriage, monogamy, and the sexual division of labour could be undermined. Where it was necessary to recognize the changeable nature of sex roles and social stereotypes, as feminists of equality advocated, this was not, however, suficient to ensure women's freedom from sexual oppression. The more successful egalitarian programmes become, the more apparent it was that there were a number of serious drawbacks in its political agenda. These include:

1 The project of sexual equality takes male achievements, values, and standards as the norms to which women should also aspire. At most, then, women can achieve an equality with men only within a system whose overall value is unquestioned and whose power remains unrecognized. Women strive to become the *same* as men, in a sense, 'masculinized'.
2 In order to achieve an equality between the sexes, women's specific needs and interests – what *distinguishes* them from men – must be minimized and their commonness or humanity stressed. (This may, for example, explain the strong antipathy to maternity amongst a number of egalitarian feminists,[2] a resistance to the idea that women's corporeality and sexuality makes a difference to the kinds of consciousness or subjects they could become.)
3 Policies and laws codifying women's legal rights to equality – anti-discriminatory and equal opportunity legislation – have tended to operate as much against women as in their interests: men, for example, have been able to use anti-discrimination or equal opportunity regulations to secure their own positions as much as women have.
4 In this sense, equality becomes a vacuous concept, in so far as it reduces all specificities, including those that serve to distinguish the positions of the oppressed from those of the oppressor. One can be considered equal only in so far as the history of the oppression of specific groups is effaced.[3]
5 Struggles for equality between the sexes are easily reduced to struggles around a more generalized and neutralized social justice. This has enabled a number of men to claim that they too are oppressed by patriarchal social roles, and are unable to express their more 'feminine' side. The struggles of women against patriarchy are too easily identified with a movement of reaction against a general 'dehumanization', in which men may unproblematically represent women in struggles for greater or more authentic forms of humanity.

6 The project of creating equality between the sexes can only be socially guaranteed in the realm of public and civic life. And, even if *some kind* of domestic equality is possible, an equality at the level of sexual and particularly reproductive relations seems impossible in so far as they are untouched by egalitarianism.
7 Most significantly, even if the two sexes behave in the same ways, perform the same duties and play the same roles, the social *meanings* of their activities remains unchallenged. Until this structure of shared meanings is problematized, equality in anything but a formal sense remains impossible.

Try as it may, a feminism of equality is unable to theorize sexual and reproductive equality adequately. And this, in turn, results in its inability to adequately theorize women's specific positions within the social and symbolic order. Kristeva makes clear the link between sexual and symbolic functioning:

> Sexual difference – which is at once biological, physiological, and relative to reproduction – is translated by and translates a difference in the relation of subjects to the symbolic contract.which *is* the social contract: a difference, then, in the relationship to power, language and meaning. The sharpest and most subtle point of feminist subversion brought about by the new generation will henceforth be situated on the terrain of the inseparable conjunction of the sexual and the symbolic, in order to try to discover, first, the specificity of the female, and then, in the end, that of each individual.
>
> (1981, p. 21)

In opposition to egalitarian feminism, a feminism based on the acknowledgement of women's specificities and orientated to the attainment of autonomy for women has emerged over the lat ten years or more. From the point of view of a feminism of equality, feminisms of difference seem strangely reminiscent of the position of defenders of patriarchy: both stress women's differences from men. However, before too readily identifying them, it is vital to ask how this difference is conceived, and, perhaps more importantly, who it is that defines this difference and for whom. For patriarchs, difference is understood in terms of inequality, distinction, or opposition, a sexual difference modelled on negative, binary, or oppositional structures within which only one of the two terms has any autonomy; the other is defined only by the negation of the first. Only sameness or identity can ensure equality. In the case of feminists of difference, however, difference is not seen as difference *from* a pre-given norm, but as *pure difference*, difference in itself, difference with no identity.[4] This kind of difference implies the autonomy of the terms between which the difference may be drawn and thus their radical incommensurability.

Difference viewed as distinction implies the pre-evaluation of one of the terms, from which the difference of the other is drawn; pure difference refuses to privilege either term. For feminists, to claim women's difference from men is to reject existing definitions and categories, redefining oneself and the world according to women's own perspectives.

The right to equality entails the right to be the same as men; while struggles around the autonomy imply the right to either consider oneself equal to another or the right to reject the terms by which equality is measured and to define oneself in different terms. It entails the right to be and to act differently. The concept of difference, as it is used by a number of contemporary feminist theorists, including Luce Irigaray, Jane Gallop, Hélène Cixous, and others. It implies, among other things:

1 A major transformation of the social and symbolic order, which, in patriarchy, is founded by a movement of universalization of the singular (male) identity. Difference cannot be readily accommodated in a system which reduces all difference to distinction, and all identity to sameness.
2 Difference resists the homogenization of separate political struggles, in so far as it implies not only women's differences from men, and from each other, but also women's differences from other oppressed groups. It is not at all clear that, for example, struggles against racism will necessarily be politically allied with women's struggles, or conversely, that feminism will overcome forms of racist domination. This of course does not preclude the existence of common interests shared by various oppressed groups, and thus the possibility of alliances over specific issues; it simply means that these alliances have no *a priori* necessity.
3 Struggles around the attainment of women's autonomy imply that men's struggles against patriarchy, while possibly allied with women's in some circumstances, cannot be identified with them. In acknowledging their sexual specificity, men's challenge to patriarchy is necessarily different from women's, which entails producing an identity and sexual specificity for themselves.
4 The notion of difference affects not only women's definitions of themselves, but also of the world. This implies that not only must social practices be subjected to feminist critique and reorganization, but also that the very structures of representation, meaning, and knowledge must be subjected to a thoroughgoing transformation of their patriarchal alignments. A politics of difference implies the right to define oneself, others, and the world according to one's own interests.

THE DIFFERENCE THAT MAKES A DIFFERENCE

Feminists involved in the project of distinguishing women's sexual differences from those of men have been subjected to wide-ranging criticisms, coming from both feminist and non-feminist directions. They face the same general dilemma confronting any feminist position which remains critical of the frameworks of patriarchal knowledges yet must rely on their resources: from the point of view of traditional, male-governed scholarly norms, their work appears utopian, idealistic, romantic, polemical, fictional, but above all, without substantial content or solid evidence and justification; and from the point of view of other forms of feminism – particularly from Marxist or socialist feminism – it appears essentialist and universalist. On the one hand, they are accused of straying too far from biological and scientifically validated information; and on the other, of sticking too closely to biological evidence. It seems that both these criticisms misunderstand the status of claims made by many feminists of difference, judging them in terms inappropriate to their approach.

Charges of essentialism, universalism, and naturalism are predictable responses on the part of feminists concerned with the idea of women's social construction: thus *any* attempt to define or designate woman or femininity is in danger of these commitments, in so far as it generalizes on the basis of the particular, and reduces social construction to biological preformation. Any theory of femininity, any definition of woman in general, any description that abstracts from the particular, historical, cultural, ethnic, and class positions of particular women verges perilously close to essentialism. Toril Moi provides a typical response to a feminism of difference in her critique of Irigaray's notion of woman or the feminine:

> any attempt to formulate a general theory of femininity will be metaphysical. This is precisely Irigaray's dilemma: having shown that so far femininity has been produced exclusively in relation to the logic of the same, she falls for the temptation to produce her own positive theory of femininity. But, as we have seen, to define 'woman' is necessarily to essentialize her.
>
> (1985, p. 139)

This, however leads to a paradox: if women cannot be characterized in any general way, if all there is to femininity is socially produced, then how can feminism be taken seriously? What justifies the assumption that women are oppressed as a sex? If we are not justified in taking women as a category, then what political grounding does feminism have? Feminism is placed in an unenviable position: either it clings to feminist principles, which entail its avoidance of essentialist and universalist categories, in which case its rationale as a political struggle centred around women is problematized; or else it accepts the limitations patriarchy imposes on its conceptual schemas and models, and abandons the attempt to provide autonomous, self-defined terms in which to describe women and femininity. Are these the only choices available to feminist theory – an adherence to essentialist doctrines, or the dissolution of feminist struggles into localized, regional, specific struggles, representing the interest of particular women or groups of women?

Posed in this way, the dilemma facing feminists involves a conflict between the goals of intellectual rigour (avoidance of the conceptual errors of essentialism and universalism) and feminist political struggles (struggles that are directed towards the liberation of women as women). But is this really a choice feminists must face? Is it a matter of preference for one goal over the other? Or can the linkages between theory and political practice be understood differently so that the criteria of intellectual evaluation are more 'politicized' and the goals of political struggle are more 'theoretized'?

Gayatri Spivak sums up this dilemma well in her understanding of concepts and theoretical principles, not as guidelines, rules, principles, or blueprints for struggle, but as tools and weapons of struggle. It is no longer a matter of maintaining a theoretical purity at the cost of political principles; nor is it simply a matter of the *ad hoc* adoption of theoretical principles according to momentary needs or whims: it is a question of negotiating a path between always impure positions, seeing that politics is always already bound up with what it contests (including theories), and theories are always implicated in various political struggles (whether this is acknowledged or not):

> You pick up the universal that will give you the power to fight against the other side and what you are throwing away by doing that is your theoretical purity. Whereas the great custodians of the anti-universal are obliged therefore simply to act in the interest of a great narrative, the narrative of exploitation while they keep themselves clean by not committing themselves to anything. . . . [T]hey are . . . run by a great narrative even as they are busy protecting their theoretical purity by repudiating essentialism.
>
> (Spivak 1984, p. 184)

The choice, in other words, is not between maintaining a politically pure theoretical position (and leaving the murkier questions of political involvement unasked); or espousing a politically tenuous one which may be more pragmatically effective in securing social change. The alternatives faced by feminist theorists are all in some sense 'impure' and 'implicated' in patriarchy. There can be no feminist position that is not in some way or other involved in patriarchal power relations; it is hard to see how this is either possible or desirable, for a freedom from patriarchal 'contamination' entails feminism's incommensurability with patriarchy, and thus the inability to criticize it. Feminists are not faced with pure and impure options. All options are in their various ways bound by the constraints of patriarchal power. The crucial political question is which commitments remain, in spite of their patriarchal alignments, of use to feminists in their political struggles? What kinds of feminist strategy do they make possible or hinder? What are the costs of holding these commitments? And the benefits? In other words, the decision about whether to 'use' essentialism, or to somehow remain beyond it (even if these extremes were possible) is a question of calculation, not a self-evident certainty.

In challenging the domination of patriarchal models which rely on essentialism, naturalism, biologism, or universalism, egalitarian feminists have pointed to the crucial role these assumptions play in making change difficult to conceive or undertake: as such, they support, rationalize, and underpin existing power relations between the sexes. But in assuming that feminists take on essentialist or universalist assumptions (if they do, which is not always clear) in the same way as patriarchs, instead of attempting to understand the ways in which essentialism and its cognates can function as strategic terms, this silences and neutralizes the most powerful of feminist theoretical weapons – feminism's ability to use patriarchy and phallocratism against themselves, its ability to take up positions ostensibly opposed to feminism and to use them for feminist goals.

> I think it is absolutely on target to take a stand against the discourses of essentialism, universalism as it comes to terms with the universal – of classical German philosophy or the universal as the white upper class male . . . etc. But *strategically* we cannot. Even as we talk about *feminist* practice, or privileging practice over theory, we are universalising. Since the moment of essentialising, universalising, saying yes to the onto-phenomenological question, is irreducible, let us at least situate it at the moment; let us become vigilant about our own practice and use it as much as we can rather than make the totally counter-productive gesture of repudiating it.
>
> (Spivak 1984, p. 184)

In other words, if feminism cannot maintain its political freedom from patriarchal frameworks, methods, and presumptions, its implication in them needs to be acknowledged instead of being disavowed. Moreover, this (historically) necessary use of patriarchal terms is the very condition of feminism's effectivity in countering and displacing the effects of patriarchy: its immersion in patriarchal practices (including those surrounding the production of theory) is the condition of its effective critique of and movement beyond them. This immersion provides not only the conditions under which feminism can become familiar with what it criticizes: it also provides the very means by which patriarchal dominance can be challenged.

NOTES

1 For an account of the challenges feminist theory has posed to male conceptions of objectivity, particularly in science, see Grosz and de Lepervanche (1988).

2 Kristeva makes this point forcefully in her analysis of the 'two generations of

feminists' outlined in her paper 'Women's Time' (1981). She refers there to de Beauvoir's anti-maternal position, a position also analysed in Mackenzie (1986).

3 This is Kristeva's understanding of the effects of a fundamental egalitarianism, which produces, among other things, the oppressive structure of anti-Semitism: assimilationism entails the repression of the specific history of oppression directed towards the Jew. This is why Sartre's position in *Anti-Semite and Jew*, in spite of his intentions, is anti-Semitic. As Kristeva suggests: 'the specific character of women could only appear as nonessential or even nonexistent to the totalizing and even totalitarian spirit of this ideology. We begin to see that this same egalitarian and in fact censuring treatment has been imposed, from Enlightenment Humanism through socialism, on religious specificities and, in particular, on Jews' (1981), p. 21.

4 This difference between difference and distinction is suggested by Derrida in his conception of *différance*, which is in part based on his reading of Saussure's notion of *pure difference* in language. Although Derrida does not use this terminology himself, Anthony Wilden's careful gloss on these terms helps to clarify many of the issues at stake in Derrida's as well as in feminist conceptions of diffence (see Wilden 1972, ch. 8).

REFERENCES

Grosz, E. A., and Lepervanche M. de (1988) 'Feminism and science', in B. Caine, E. A. Grosz, and M. de Lepervanche (eds) *Crossing Boundaries: Feminisms and the Critique of Knowledges*, Allen & Unwin, Sydney.

Kristeva, J. (1981) 'Women's time', *Signs*, 7:1.

Mackenzie, C. (1986) 'Simone de Beauvoir: philosophy and/or the female body', in C. Pateman and E. Gross (eds) *Feminist Challenges: Social and Political Theory*, Allen & Unwin, Sydney.

Moi, T. (1985) *Sexual/Textual Politics: Feminist Literary Theory*, Methuen, London.

Spivak, G. (1984) 'Criticism, feminism and the institution', *Thesis Eleven*, 10/11.

Wilden, A. (1972) *System and Structure: Essays in Communication and Exchange*, Tavistock, London.

NOTES ON CONTRIBUTORS

ELIZABETH GROSZ teaches in the General Philosophy Department at the University of Sydney. She is the author of *Sexual Subversions: Three French Feminists* (1989) and *Jacques Lacan: A Feminist Introduction* (1990), and has co-edited a number of anthologies on feminist theory.

SNEJA GUNEW has studied in Australia, Canada, and England. She currently teaches in literary studies at Deakin University, Victoria. She has published widely in the area of feminist theory. Her most recent research has concentrated on questions of cultural, in relation to gender, differences through an examination of non-Anglo/Celtic writings in Australia. She has edited two anthologies of such writings – *Displacements: Migrant Storytellers* (1981) and *Displacements 2: Multicultural Storytellers* (1987) – and co-edited *Beyond the Echo: Multicultural Women's Writing* (1988); *Telling Ways: Australian Women's Experimental Writing* (1988); and *Striking Chords: Multicultural Literary Criticism* (forthcoming). She is completing a monograph, 'Framing marginality: non Anglo-Celtic writing in Australia' which redefines ways of theorizing Australian literature and culture.

LOUISE C. JOHNSON was trained primarily as a geographer but left Sydney and that discipline in 1979 as a Marxist geographer to teach Australian studies and then women's studies at Deakin University. She became involved in Socialist Feminist politics in Melbourne and this guided her research into sexual and spatial divisions of labour in the Australian textile industry. The problems of seriously using Marxist theory to answer feminist questions on women's work began a process of questioning, most recently informed by a criticial reappraisal of Radical and Socialist Feminist writing. This is still occurring in her new capacity as a 'feminist geographer' trying to define feminist geography in her teaching and published work.

GISELA T. KAPLAN studied in Berlin, Munich and Melbourne and gained her Ph.D. from Monash University (Melbourne). Major publications include: a jointly-edited book, *Hannah Arendt: Thinking, Judgement,*

Freedom (1989) and chapters in the following: *Feminine/Masculine and Representation*, edited by A. Cranny-Francis and T. Threadgold (1989); *Women's Movement of the World*, v.4 (1989); *Australian Welfare: Historical Sociology*, ed. R. Kennedy (1988). She is joint editor of *The Australian and New Zealand Journal of Sociology* and is currently completing a book on contemporary Western European Feminism. Her research interests include: political sociology, sociology of culture, gender and ethnic issues. She is currently based in the Department of Economic History, University of New England, Armidale, NSW.

RENATE D. KLEIN holds degrees from Zurich University in biology (MSc), the University of California at Berkeley (BA) and London University (Ph.D.), both in women's studies. With Gloria Bowles she co-edited *Theories of Women's Studies* (1983) and since 1981 she has been the European editor of *Women's Studies International Forum*. She also co-edits (with Gloria Bowles and Janice Raymond) the ATHENE series, an international collection of feminist books. Her current work is on reproductive and genetic engineering and its impact on women. She is co-editor with Rita Arditti and Shelley Minden of *Test-Tube Women: What Future for Motherhood?* (1984), co-author with Gena Corea *et al.* of *Man-Made Women* (1985) and editor of *Infertility: Women Speak Out About Their Experiences of Reproductive Medicine* (1989). In 1986 she was awarded the Georgina Sweet Fellowship to do research on the experiences of women who drop out of test-tube baby programmes in Australia which she continued as post-doctoral research fellow at Deakin University, Australia till 1989. In 1990 she will be a Distinguished Visiting Professor in Women's Studies at San Diego State University, USA. She is a founding member of the Feminist International Network of Resistance to Reproductive and Genetic Engineering (FINNRAGE) and acted as its International Co-ordinator from 1985 to 1987.

LESLEY J. ROGERS obtained her first degree from Adelaide University. She then lived in the USA for four years, some of which time was spent in postgraduate studies at Harvard University and the rest working in research at New England Center Hospital in Boston. She completed her Doctorate of Philosophy degree in ethology at Sussex University before returning to Australia in 1972. For the next thirteen years she taught medical and science students at Monash University, apart from one year at the Australian National University, and conducted research into brain development and behaviour. In 1987 she was honoured by being awarded the degree of Doctor of Science from Sussex University for this research. Throughout the 1970s until now she has been an active feminist, lecturing and writing widely in the area of gender and biology. She is now an Associate Professor of the Physiology Department at the University of New England.

PHILIPA ROTHFIELD has a Ph.D. in Philosophy, from Monash University, which was written on textual analysis in relation to phenomenology, structuralism and Marxist theories of ideology. Since then, she has written on French feminism, semiotics and cultural/media analysis. More recently, she has published on the body, in relation to both French feminism and dance. This latter work is influence by her experience as a performer in contemporary dance and in women's theatre. Her current research project is on feminist theory, politics, and postmodernism. This project involves developing a de-centred theory of knowledge, which allows for a politics of difference at a number of levels.

ROBYN ROWLAND's doctorate is in social psychology. She is senior lecturer in women's studies at Deakin University, Deputy Dean of the School of Humanities, and has taught women's studies for over fifteen years. She is author of *Woman Herself: A Transdisciplinary Perspective on Women's Identity* (1988) and editor of *Women Who Do, and Women Who Don't, Join the Women's Movement* (1984). Her most recent publications are a feminist analysis of the new reproductive technologies, in, for example, *Made to Order: The Myth of Reproductive and Genetic Progress* (1987). She is Australian and Asian editor of *Women's Studies International Forum* and Australian editor of *Issues in Reproductive and Genetic Engineering: Journal of International Feminist Analysis*. She is author of *Living Laboratories. Women and the new Reproductive Technologies* (1991). She has two books of poetry published: *Filigree in Blood* (1982) and *Perverse Serenity* (1990).

HAZEL ROWLEY studied French and German at Adelaide University and wrote her Ph.D. on French women's autobiographical writing – in particular Simone de Beauvoir and Violette Leduc. Since 1984 she has been teaching literature at Deakin University. She is currently writing a biography of Christina Stead. Her research interests are feminist theory, Australian literature, and contemporary European and Australian autobiographical writing.

SUSAN SHERIDAN lectures in women's studies at the Flinders University of South Australia and has been involved in women's studies since 1973. She is a graduate of the universities of Sydney and Adelaide and has taught literary studies at the South Australian College of Advanced Education and Deakin University. An editor of *Australian Feminist Studies*, she has published widely in feminist and literary journals. Her book on the fiction of Christina Stead has appeared in the Harvester Key Women Writers series and she has edited *Grafts: Feminist Cultural Criticism* (1988).

MARIE TULIP graduated from the University of Queensland and spent four years in the United States, doing an MA in French and teaching

French and Latin in Chicago. Since 1970 she has been active in the women's movement in Sydney, especially in the area of religion, working on the Commission on the Status of Women of the Australian Council of Churches and on the *Magdalene* collective. She teaches continuing education courses in feminism and religion and contemporary women's poetry. Recent publications include *Women in a Man's Church* (ACC 1983), and chapters in *Force of the Feminine* (Allen & Unwin 1986) and *Opening the Cage* (Allen & Unwin 1987).

INDEX

Abel, Elizabeth 199
Aboriginal women 1, 31, 43
abortion 235, 281, 285
activism as knowledge 40
Adam and Eve 233
Adlam, Diana 321
'agit-prop' 40
Alexander technique 138
Althusser, Louis 104, 110, 182–3, 313; and feminism 69–71; and theory of ideology 63–9, 134–6
Andreas-Salome, Lou 151
androcentric scholarship 245
androgyny, ideals of 131
Anthias, Floya 318
Anthony, Susan B. 273
anthropos 124
Anti-Social Family, The (Barrett & MacIntosh) 324
archaeological method 80–2, 85
Aristotle 128, 155, 156–7
art, and feminism 137
Ashtoreth 259
Asian Women's Association (Japan) 289
Athens 128
Atkinson, Ti-Grace 274–5
Australia, as clearing house 1
Australian National University 47
avant-garde writers 193, 194–5
Awful Truth Show, The 254

Baal 259
Barrett, Michèle 126 , 190, 308, 324, 325
Barry, Kathleen 280–1, 287–9, 297
Bataille, Georges 139
Bateson, Mary Catherine 257
Beauvoir, Simone de 17, 42, 61, 157, 158, 180–1, 336
Beechey, Veronica 318
behaviour, (ab)normal 218–19; complex 210; negative 207; differences in 215–16; social norm 211
Being and Nothingness (Sartre) 62, 158
Bell, Diane 31
Belsey, C. 27
Benjamin, Walter 141
Benston, Margaret 314
Beyond God the Father (Daly) 231, 235 236
binary logic 100
binary oppositions 93
biologism 334
biology, determinist position in 208–9; importance of 205; norms 217–24, 221; and radical feminism 296–8
Bland, Lucy *et al.* 319
Bleier, Ruth 277
body/ies, categorization of 107–8; control over 137–9; emphasis on 92; and experience 140; and mind 136–7; as mindful 139; women's, how treated 285–90
Bone People, The (Hulme) 252
Boston Women's Health Collective 286
Boxer, Marilyn 44, 46, 47, 48
Braidotti, Rosi 200
brains, function of 214–17; overtaxing 206
breasts, size of 212
Brennan, Teresa 131
Bringing the Invisible into the Light (Quaker Women's Group) 251
Brown, Rita Mae 293

Bunch, Charlotte 275–6, 284, 291–2, 293
Burke, Carolyn 193

Caddick, Allison 139
Campbell, Beatrix 41
Campioni, Mia and Elizabeth Gross 311, 317, 322
Capitalism 62, 122
Carby, Hazel 31, 325
Care of the Self, The (Foucault) 90
Carter, Angela 139
Cartesian dualism 136
castration 99, 105–6; chemical 222; complex 178, 179, 189
celibacy 223
Centuries of Childhood (Aries) 42
Charcot, J. M. 175
Chesler, Phyllis 219
Chester, Gail 274, 275, 276–7
Chicago, Judy 258, 295–6
Chinese story 264
Chodorow, Nancy, on Freud 189–92
Christ, Carol 255, 257, 260, 261–2, 263
Christian ethics, hypocrisy of 234–5
Christianity, early history 244; missionary movement 246–7; as problematic 242; reconstructed 243–8
Church and the Second Sex, The (Daly) 231
Cixous, Hélène 111, 197–8, 264
class 309–10; and socialist feminism 320; universality of oppression 280–3, 284
Cohen, Bonnie Bainbridge 138
Color Purple, The (Walker) 252, 255–6
'Compulsory heterosexuality and lesbian existence' (Rich) 29
concepts, dichotomous structuring of 93
Congress to Unite Women (1969) 282–3
consciousness raising 38, 129–32, 240
cosmos 153
Coward, Rosalind 28
Coyner, Sandra 49
CR *see* consciousness raising
Critique of Dialectical Reason, The (Sartre) 62
Critique of Pure Reason (Kant) 164
Cronan, Sheila 294
Culler, J. 124–5
culture, theory of 123; women's 295–6
Currey, Ryl 254–5

Dalla Costa, Mariarosa 314
Daly, Mary 41, 162, 240, 274, 296; discussed 230–7
Damned Whores and God's Police (Summers) 42
Darwinian theory 206, 217–18
Daughters of the Dreaming (Bell) 31
Davidson, Robyn 256
Dawkins, R. 218
deconstruction 92–103
Deleuze, Gilles 27; and F. Guattari 84
Delphy, Christine 20, 23, 26, 41, 272, 273, 279, 284, 297, 317, 321
Derrida, Jacques 108, 110, 125, 197; and deconstruction 92–103; and feminism 100–3
Descartes, René 64, 72, 136, 164
desire 77
determinism 63
Dialectic of Sex, The (Firestone) 181
difference 101–2, 333, 340–3; sexuality and textuality 97–100
difference/differance 95–6
Differences 51
Diotima 151
Discipline and Punish (Foucault) 85–6
discourse 18–20, 111, 122, 157, 321; learned 23
'Discourse on Language, The' (Foucault) 19, 80
discrimination 149; structural 40
disease, concept of 218–20, 222
displacement 77
Dohm, Hedwig 273
Domestic Labour Debate 315–17
Dorner, G. 222
Downer, Carol 286
Dworkin, Andrea 299

ecstasy 236
education 16; expansion of 38–9; formal 13; power of 45–6
ego 74
'ego instincts' 184
'ego psychology' 71–2, 185
Eisenstein, Hester 24, 237
Eisenstein, Zilla 128

Elizabeth, Princess 151
Engels, Friedrich 304, 305–11
Enlightenment 17, 121, 125
equality 274, 333, 339; arguments against 206; aspiration to 157–9
Erikson, Erik 181–2
essentialism 333–5, 341; biological 208, 296–8
'Eternal Feminine', notion of 187
Evans, Mary 45, 309
Existentialism 17, 62, 181
exogamy, law of 73
experience 13, 24, 27, 140–1, 231, 258; past and present 40–1; politics of 41
explanation,decentred 124

Fall, the 239
family 305–11; construction of 278
fantasies, masculine 107
Feldenkreis, Moshe 138
female, concept of essential 24
female imaginary 111, 196
female principle 16
Female Sexual Slavery (Barry) 280
feminine,according to Cixous 197–8
Feminine Mystique, The (Friedan) 181, 314
'Femininity' (Freud) 177, 178, 179–80; (Lacan) 187–8
feminism 13; in caricatured form 103–4; conservative 159–61; as construct 25–7; as critique 23–5; debate 179–80; dilemma facing 342; egalitarian 157–9, 336–9; exclusions 29–31; goals 343; masculinity and power 103–11; materialist 20; as political 160; questioned 160–1; second-wave 21, 24; strategy 342–3; textual 20; *see also* Radical Feminism and Socialist Feminism
Feminist International Network of Resistance to Reproductive and Genetic Engineering (FINRRAGE) 290
Feminist Practice; Notes from the Tenth Year 272, 275
'Feminist readings: French texts/ American contexts' 199
Feminist Review 324
feminist spirituality 243–4
Figes, Eva 336
'Fight to be male, The' 216
film theory 136
FINRRAGE 290
Fiorenza, Elisabeth Schussler, discussed 243–8
Firestone, Shulamith 42, 182, 277, 336
Flinders University 46
For Colored Girls Who Have Considered Suicide (Ntozake Shange) 254
Foucault, Michel 16, 17, 19, 22, 43, 108, 110, 122, 136, 139; and feminism 90–2; on power 22, 80–92
Fowler, Roger 18
Fox, Bonnie 316
Frankfort, Ellen 286
Frankfurt School 42
Free Woman, The 273
French Communist Party (PCF) 62
Freud, Sigmund 17, 41, 70, 72, 74, 76, 125, 175, 177–9, 313; feminist hostility toward 180–3
'Freud and Lacan' (Althusser) 182–3
Friedan, Betty 181, 314, 336
Frye, Marilyn 294
Furlong, Monica 252
Furman, Nelly 20

Gage, Matilda Joslyn 273
Gallop, Jane 131, 162, 194
Gallup, G. G. 213
Galton, Francis 211
Gatens, Moira 111, 131–2, 138–9, 162
Gavron, Hannah 314
gender 13, 126, 131, 163, 313; concept of 51, 297; relations 304; roles 190; and sex distinction 131–2; studies 52; and subjectivity 123
Gender and History 51
Genders 51
genealogical method 85–6
genes 209–10, 212, 218
genetic determinism 211
Geschwind, N. and A. M. Galaburda 215
Gilbert, Sandra 199
Gilman, Charlotte Perkins 273
Gimbutas, Marija 260

God, how to name 233; maleness of 242; popular image of 232; as Sophia 247
Goddess, religion of 259–63, 263
God's Fierce Whimsy (Mudflower collective) 250–1, 253
Golden Notebook, The (Lessing) 127
Goldstein, Vida 273
Gordon, Linda 51, 52
Grand Coolie Dam, The (Piercy) 128
Greenham Common 1, 251–2, 257
Greer, Germaine 336
Griffin, Susan 282, 299
Gross, Elizabeth (*see also* Groz, E.) 48
Grosz, Elizabeth 3, 5, 6, 9–10, 42, 233
group/s, processes 39–40; socially disadvantaged 40
Gubar, Susan 199
Gyn/affection 257, 293
Gyn/Ecology (Daly) 236–7, 274

Hall, Stuart 123, 135
Haraway, Donna 323–4
Harris, G. W. 216, 217
Harrison, B. W. 252
Harrison, Jane 44
Hartsock, Nancy 24
Harvard Memorial Church 229
Houghton, Rosemary 252
Hawthorne, Susan 293
health 138, 285–7
Hegel, G. W. F. 305
Heloise 151
Henriques *et al.* 126, 130, 131
Hernton, Calvin 42
hetero-reality 278, 292–3
heterosexuality 290–4, 295
Hindu beliefs 137
'hinge words' 97
History of Sexuality, The (Foucault) 82, 84, 85, 86, 108, 139
Hoagland, Sarah 210
Homer 153
homophobia 40
homosexuality 210, 216, 222
Hooks, Bell 283
hormones 207, 213–14, 215, 216, 217, 223
Horney, Karen 179–180, 181
hot-plate therapy 222
Hulme, Keri 252
humanism 63, 123, 124–5; dichotomy of 132
Hypatia 151

'I' 75, 185–6
'I Call Myself a Radical Feminist' (Chester) 274
'I think therefore I am' 136
Idea of a Social Science, The (Winch) 161
identity 132; sense of 14, 134–5
'Ideological State Apparatuses' (ISAs) 67–70, 104
ideology 104–5; according to Althusser 63–9; defined 83; as eternal 68; as omnipresent and transhistorical 67; and power 69; and repression of women 126; theory of 134–6
'Ideology and ideological state apparatuses' (Althusser) 66
Illich, I. 219
imaginary relations, notion of 185
'In Defence of Separatism' (Hawthorne) 293–4
incest 40, 73
individual 183–4
infertility 289
Interim (Kelly) 134
International Feminist Network Against Female Sexual Slavery 289
INTERPOL 188
IQ 211
Irigaray, Luce 101, 162, 195–7, 341
ISAs *see* Ideological State Apparatuses

Jacobus, Mary 199
Jakobson, Roman 77
Janet, Paul 175
Janeway, Elizabeth 298
Jardine, Alice 122–3
Jesus, image of 234; as non-sexist 242
Jesus movement 245–6
Jones, Ann Rosalind 195
Jones, Ernest 179–180
Jones, Selma 315
jouissance 188
Joyce, James 193
Judaeo-Christian tradition 229, 230, 235, 253, 263; and feminists 238–53

Kant, Immanuel 164
Kantian concept 17
Kazi, Hamidi 325
Kelly, Mary 133–4
Kelly-Gadol, Joan 49
Klein, Melanie 179–180
Klinefelter's syndrome 220, 223
knowing, defined 14
Knowing Body, The (Steinman) 140
knowledge,described 14–16; institutional 14, 23–4; logocentric 78; naive 43; paradoxes of 31; phallocentric 78; political cost of 20–1; and power 22–3; subjugated 43–4; truth-effects of 88
Koedt, Anne 271
Kristeva, Julia 23, 101, 139, 193–5, 337, 339
Kristeva Reader, The (Moi) 195
Kruger, Barbara 133
Kuhn, Thomas 244

labour, domestic 314–17
Lacan, Jacques 70, 105, 107, 195, 313; and feminism 78–80; on Freud 183–8; and sexuality 79; on symbolic and imaginary 73–5; on the unconscious 751–8; view of Woman 187–8
Laing and Cooper 41
Lambert, H. H. 208
language 14, 17–18, 124; feminine use of 197; gender biased 25–6; liberation of 232; and philosophy 94; and signification 73
'Laugh of the Medusa, The' (Cixous) 198
Lauretis, Teresa de 27–8, 31
Laws, The (Plato) 154
Le Doeuff, Michele 162, 163–5
Learning Liberation (Thompson) 45
Leeds Revolutionary Feminist Group 291
Leghorn, Lisa 277–8
lesbian/s 284, 290–2; critiques 29–30
Lessing, Doris 127
Lévi-Strauss 313
Levine, Judith 271
liberal paradigm 132
Lippard, Lucy 133, 139
Lloyd, Genevieve 16, 17, 162–3
logic 155–6
logocentrism 94, 100, 101
London Lesbian Offensive Group 290

McIntosh, Mary 315, 324, 325
MacKinnon, Catharine 290, 299
MacMillan, C. 160–1
McRobbie, Angela 133
Madness and Civilization (Foucault) 80, 81
Magarey, Susan 48, 50
'mainstreaming debate' 49
male theorists and feminism 103–11
male/female definition 212–13
male/female dichotomy 217, 218, 224, 225
Man of Reason, The (Lloyd) 162–3
Mandel, Ernest 314
Marcuse 182
marginalized groups 20–1
marriage 281, 294, 310
Marx, Karl 17, 64–5, 70, 71, 122, 125, 304, 305–11, 311, 312
Marxism 13, 26, 27, 41, 66, 81, 84–5, 104, 110, 241, 305, 313, 315, 316–17, 319, 321–2; economistic 62, 63; and feminist challenge 126; influence of 28–9
Mary, image of 234, 260
Masters, W. H. and V. E. Johnson 224
materialism, historical 65–6
materialisms 322–6
mathematical ability 207
meaning 18, 135
menstruation 220, 222, 258
meta-language 195
metaphor/s 77, 78; concrete, analysed 164–5; of women 97–100, 102, 108–9
metonymy 77, 78
Mies, Maria 28
Mill, J. S. 148
Millett, Kate 42, 182, 277, 336
'mirror-stage' 74
misogyny 163
Mitchell, Juliet 37, 42, 71–2, 131, 176, 177, 180, 182, 312, 314, 315, 318; on Freud 188–92
modernity 121
Moi, Toril 132, 195, 341
Molyneux, Maxine 317

Money, J. 216; and A. A. Ehrhardt 222
Moore, C. and G. A. Morelli 216–17
Moraga, C. and G. Anzaldua 30
Morales, Rosario 283
More, Sir Thomas 164
Morgan, Robin 271–2, 273, 281–2, 283
Morris, Desmond 213
Morton, Nellie 248
Morton, Peggy 314
mother-child dyad 75, 190–1
motherhood, and the family 294–5
myths 323

Name-of-the-Father 184, 185, 193
narcissism 74, 106, 128
National Women's Studies Association (NWSA) 45, 46
naturalism 334
New Left 41, 311–12, 314
New Left Review 189, 312, 315
Nietzsche, I. 80, 92, 99, 110, 125
No Turning Back 286

object–relations theory 190
O'Brien, Mary 162
Oedipus complex 73, 74, 76, 84, 105, 178, 179, 184, 185, 186, 189, 191
Of Woman Born (Rich) 295
'On narcissism: an introduction' (Freud) 74
oppression 279, 299, 310; in philosophy 151–3; primary 273; three types of 149–51; universality of 280–5
Origin of the Family, The (Engels) 306
original sin 233
Other 73
Otherworld 237
Our Bodies Ourselves (Boston) 286–7

Pankhurst, Christabel 280
Parker, Katherine 278
Parvati, Jeanne 137
patriarchy 87, 92, 125, 324, 332, 335; concepts 25–7; defined 149–50; as eternal 192; ideology 278; ideology as political 296; knowledge 60; material base 279–80; as oppressing structure 273; as original sin 233–4; paradigms 25, 109; in philosophy 152, 165–6, 169–70; and radical feminism 277–80; and religious discourse 229; symbolic law of the father 313; values of 297
Paul, the apostle 246–7
Pearson, Karl 211
penis 105, 184, 189
personal is political, the 21, 127–8, 285
perspectivism 167
phallic symbolic 196
Phallocentrism 60, 91, 100–1, 110, 126, 150, 152
phallogocentrism 193, 197
phallus 73, 75, 105, 110, 184, 185
Phenomenology 17, 62, 95
Phillips, Anne 320
philosophical oppositions 153–4
philosophy 16; birth of 153; feminist, outline for 166–70; French 61–3; history of 147–9; and language 94; patriarchal beliefs 165–6, 169–70; sexism in 149–57; and treatment of women 149–57
Piercy, Marge 128
Pisan, Christine de 151
Pius XII, Pope 234
Plaskow, Judith 252, 258
Plato 128, 136, 153, 154, 155
pleasure principle 76
PMT *see* premenstrual tension
politics, cultural 40; feminist 43
Politics of Women's spirituality (Plaskow) 258
Post-Partum Document (Kelly) 133–4
postmodernism 133–4
postructuralism 13, 125
power 107; according to Foucault 80–92; analytics of 88; defined 22–3; and heterosexuality 290; male exerted 280; in patriarchal religion 235–6; and social structure 89; what it is not 87–90; of women 257, 298–300, 309
power structures 39
Powers of Horror (Kristeva) 139
Powers of the Weak (Janeway) 298
premenstrual tension (PMT) 207
production, and socialist feminism 318–20; of subjects 66–9
'Proper Names' 93, 98, 110
prostitution 287–8
protest action 251–2, 257
'Psychanalyse et Politique' (Cixous) 197

psychiatry 80, 219
psychoanalysis 13, 66, 72, 78, 79, 95; Chodorow's view of 190–2; explained 175–7; Foucault on 84; and French feminism 192–8; Freudian, how regarded 180–3; as source of inspiration 106
Psychoanalysis and Feminism (Mitchell) 42, 71, 188–9
psychobiology 208
psychology 219
psychosurgery 222
public/private distinction 128–9, 160
Puritan-Prurient syndrome 239
Pythagoras 153

Quakers 251, 252
Questions Feministes 274, 297

race, universality of oppression 283–5
racism 30, 42, 324–6
Radical Feminism 24, 29, 159, 161, 162–7, 234, 313, 322; and biology 296–8; definitional statements 273–5; intent 272; and patriarchy 277–80; resistance and power 298–300; and sexuality 290–4; theory and practice 275–7 *see also* feminism and Socialist Feminism
Radical Feminism (Koedt *et al.*) 271
Rainer, Yvonne 133
rape 40, 137, 257, 287
Rape Crisis Centre Movement 276
Rapone, Anita 271
Rawls, John 161
Raymond, Janice 257, 278, 292, 293
reason 16, 154–5
Recherches sur l'imaginaire philosophique (Le Doeuff) 163
redemption 240
reductionism 210–11
Reich 182
relativism 167
religion 16; and female discrimination 231
repression 77, 186–7
'Repressive State Apparatuses' (RSAs) 67
reproduction 223, 277, 280; technologies concerning 289–90
Republic, The (Plato) 154
resistance, to men 298–300
Revolutionary and Radical Feminist Newsletter 290
'revolutionary reforms' 48
Ricardo, David 305
Rich, Adrienne 21, 29–30, 44, 257–8, 278, 283, 292, 295; on lesbianism 29–30
Richards, J. R. 160–1
Roman Catholics 238, 242
Rose, S. 210, 211
Rossi 208,
Rothfield, Philipa 4, 17
Rowbotham, Sheila 26, 27
RSAs *see* Repressive State Apparatuses
Ruether, Rosemary 231; discussed 238–43, 249–50

Sadeian Woman, The (Carter) 139–40
Safouan, Moustafa 105–6
Sartre, Jean-Paul 17, 62, 158
Saussure, Ferdinand de 75, 95, 101, 124
scapegoat syndrome 233
science 20; and ideology 64–6
Science for the People Group 208
scientific paradigms 244
Scott, Joan 51
Search for a Method, The (Sartre) 62
Seccombe, Wally 315, 316
Second Sex, The (de Beauvoir) 42, 60, 157, 181
semiology 14, 17, 20
semiotics 135, 193
Sex in Education (Clarke) 206
sex/gender distinction 131–2
sexism, in philosophy 149–57
Sexism and God-Talk: Towards a Feminist Theology (Ruether) 241, 242, 243, 249
sexual, differences 206–7, 208, 215, 217; dualism, in theology 238–43; harassment 40; instincts 184; interaction 140; and sensual 139–40; slavery 281–2, 287–8; specificity 109; violence 287, 288–9
Sexual Politics (Millett) 42, 182
sexuality 183, 309, 319; development of 176; explored 131; identity and

sexuality (*cont.*):
difference 336–40; and radical feminism 290–4
Sheridan, Susan 15–16
sign systems 14
signifier/s 73, 95, 105, 184
Sister Outsider 323
sisterhood, concept of 281
Sisterhood is Global (Morgan) 281–2
Smith, Adam 305
Smith, Paul 316
Snow, C. P. 42
social variables 206
Socialist Feminism 29; and production 318–20; re-emergence of 312–14; as set of interventions 305–26 *see also* feminism and Radical Feminism
sociobiology 207–8, 209–12
sodomy 309
Sophia, divine female wisdom 247
Speculum of the Other Woman (Irigaray) 195, 196
Spencer, Herbert 206
Spender, Dale 278–9
spirituality, women's 253–63
Spivak, Gayatri 29, 102, 103, 342, 343
Spretnak, Charlotte 258
Stalin 311, 312
Starhawk 262
Steinman, Louise 138, 140
sterilization 286
Stimpson, Catherine 23, 49, 51
storytelling 252–3, 264
strategy/ies, feminist 59–60, 342–3; of marginality 47
Strathern, Marilyn 49
stress 213
structures, dominated by men 278
subject, anti-humanist critique of notions 104; individual 17–18, 21–2; production of 66–9; as split 186; universal 133
subject-in-process, the 136
subjectivity 135–6; fracturing of 133; materialistic theory of 107; notion of 121–2
Suleiman, Susan Rubin 199–200
Summers, Anne 42
super-ego 178
Swidler, Leonard 234
symbolic 193; and imaginary 73–5
Symbolic Father 73, 75
syndromes, various 220, 223, 233
Szasz, Thomas 219

Taylor, Charles 121, 124
techno-patriarchs 289
texts, classical 128; of modernity 129
Thatcher, Margaret 23
theology 16; construction of new 241–2
theory, background 61–3; concept of 17–18; as critique and construct 59; feminist 26–31, 41–3, 43, 110; humanist forms of 123; influence of Althusser 69–71; male dominated 13, 103–9, 332; neutrality of 20; not neutral 26; objective 21; and patriarchal knowledge 60–1; social 124–5; unity of 16–17; woman-centred 122
Theory of Justice, The (Rawls) 161
Third World Movement Against the Exploitation of Women in the Philippines 289
This Sex Which Is Not One (Irigaray) 196
Thompson, Jane 45
Thorndike, Edward 211
Tillich, Paul 232
Tracks (Davidson) 256
trade unions 40, 127
transcendence 254
transvestism 222–3
truth 88, 91, 93; absolute 13; as legitimate 21; women and 99 truth effects 13
'Truth and power' (Foucault) 82
Turner, Bryan 137
Turner's syndrome 220

unconscious 75–8, 125, 183, 186; described 176–7; notions of 130
'Unconscious, The' (Freud) 76
Underhill, Evelyn 256
universalism 335, 341
Use of Pleasure, The (Foucault) 90, 108
Utopia (More) 164
Utopian Socialists 304, 305

Vincennes, University of 195, 197
Vogel, Lise 316–17

Walker, Alice 252, 255–6
West, Jackie 320
'Why Women Need the Goddess' (Crist) 260
Williams, Raymond 42
Winch, Peter 161
witchcraft 262–3, 263
WLM *see* Women's Liberation Movement
Wolff, Janet 128–9
Wollstonecraft, Mary 15, 43
Woman, notion of 99, 187
Woman Question, The 309, 313
'Womanhood and the inner space' (Erikson) 181–2
Woman's Estate (Mitchell) 42, 189, 312
WomanSpirit 258
Womanspirit Rising (Plaskow) 252
'Women: the Longest Revolution' (Mitchell) 189
women, exclusion of in philosophy 156–7; material reality of 25; and metaphor 97–100, 102; nature of 333; ordination of 239–40; political action of 251–2, 257; as secondary 148; as sex objects 137; Third World 29, 30–1; treatment of 219–20
Women of Ideas and What Men Have Done to Them (Spender) 279
Women-Church 248–50
Women-Church (Ruether) 243, 249
Women's Health Movement 285, 296
Women's Liberation Movement 36, 37, 126–32, 130, 272, 282,
283, 291; four stages of 240–1
Women's Refuge Movement 276
women's studies 36–7; and feminist scholarship 48–52; growth and change 44–8; nature and scope 49–50; object of 51
'women's work' 319
Woolf, Virginia 14, 193, 273
writing, feminine/masculine 197–8

Yale French Studies 199

Zimmerman, Bonnie 296